P9-DME-359

Sheltie Talk

You can't buy loyalty, they say
I bought it though, the other day;
You can't buy friendship, tried and true,
Well just the same, I bought that too.

I made my bid, and on the spot
Bought love and faith and a whole job lot
Of happiness, so all in all
The purchase price was pretty small.

I bought a single trusting heart,
That gave devotion from the start.
If you think these things are not for sale,
Buy a brown-eyed puppy with a wagging tail.

(author unknown, From the
Interlocking Shetland Sheepdog
Club newsletter)

Sheltie Talk

BY BETTY JO MCKINNEY AND BARBARA HAGEN RIESEBERG

REVISED BY BETTY JO MCKINNEY

Alpine Publications Inc.
P.O. Box 7027 • Loveland, CO 80537 • (303) 667-2017

Credits:

Book Design - Joan M. Harris
Cover Photos - Front: upper left, Lloyd Price;
lower left, Dear Photos; right, Dick Carter;
Back Cover: Dick Carter.
Typesetting and Layout - Artline, Loveland, Colorado

ISBN 0-931866-17-0
Library of Congress Card No. 75-45831

Copyright © 1976 by Betty Jo McKinney and Barbara Hagen Rieseberg.
Copyright © 1985 by Betty Jo McKinney

All rights reserved. No part of this book may be used or reproduced in any manner whatsoever without written permission from the publisher, except in the case of brief quotations embodied in critical reviews. For permission, write to Alpine Publications, Inc., P. O. Box 7027, Loveland, CO 80537.

This book is available at special quantity discounts for breeders and for club promotions, premiums, or educational use. Write for details.

Printed in the United States of America.

Revised Edition
Dedicated to

Barbara Hagen Rieseberg
1947 - 1980

"A book is the only immortality."
Choate

ACKNOWLEDGEMENTS TO ORIGINAL EDITION

Our very special thanks to:

Jo Parker, Parcana Shelties, Phyllis Holst, Sarabande Shelties, Kathleen Holdren, Malachi Shelties, and trainer Lewis V. Cross for contributing acticles, photographs, and research information.

Dr. Glenn Severin, D.V.M., and other faculty members in the Colorado State University College of Veterinary Medicine and Biomedical Sciences, and to Dr. Melissa Culver, D.V.M., Valley Veterinary Clinic, Longmont, Colorado, for reviewing some of the more technical chapters and contributing information.

The Sheltie owners, breeders, and exhibitors who supplied photographs.

And to the many others without whose help this book would have been impossible.

ACKNOWLEDGEMENTS TO SECOND EDITION

No book is a "one person show," and this edition of Sheltie Talk is certainly no exception. It would not have been possible without the help of many, many Sheltie folk. I especially want to thank those persons who sent photographs, contributed information, or made suggestions on the revision, and to the photographers who have captured our breed so beautifully on film.

A special thank you is due Barbara Ross, Happy Glen, for assisting at photography sessions, grooming for most of the photos in the grooming chapter, and for, with infinite patience, being my "sounding board" during the writing process.

Special thanks are also due Paula Crosby for taking over the office while I was "on leave" to write, and to Joan Harris and Hope Hicks for their excellent production work.

Acknowledgements would not be complete without saying thank you from the heart to those many friends and breeders whose support have made it all possible.

Betty McKinney
1984

Contents

Introduction

When we first started in Shelties, each of us was lucky enough to find a few dedicated breeders to guide us in our endeavors. We are thankful for their help and for the solid foundation they gave us when we were just beginning to fix our ideals. Since then we have met many novices in the breed who have had to do without such guidance.

One day in 1974 we were remembering the hours and months we spent painstakingly searching for information during those early days. Barbara had embarked enthusiastically on her new hobby in 1961 in the thriving metropolis of Sheridan, Wyoming (population 13,000). The nearest dog show was 150 miles away, and she soon discovered to her chagrin that she was the only person in town who showed dogs. With no classes or breeders nearby, Barbara learned grooming, structure, bloodlines, and training through long-distance calls, letters, an ever increasing library, and much experimentation. She credits Beverly Baird, Apple Acres Shelties, from whom she purchased her first show dogs, for hours of patient guidance and constructive advice, and for instilling the wisdom to recognize virtue in more than one type of Sheltie.

Betty Jo was more fortunate, living near a metropolitan area with several shows and training classes. She owes her special thanks to Dick and Beverly Muhlenhaupt, Traceville Shelties, for sparking her interest and encouraging her in both obedience and conformation, To Tom Coen, Macdega, for helping her obtain foundation breeding stock, to Luella Thompson, Cinder Glo, for helping her form sound basic ideals on which to found a breeding program, to the Centennial Shetland Sheepdog Club of Greater Denver, and most of all to Barbara, whose guidance has been invaluable.

Even with the help of other breeders, there was much to be learned on our own. We remembered searching the libraries and bookshelves for written material. The most complete work on Shelties available then was by an English author and, while excellent, not entirely applicable. In order to learn the basics we combed separate books on genetics, breeding theory, training, nutrition, gait, and so on, only to discover later that some of the material was not pertinent to Shelties. Some subjects weren't to be found at all.

We also recalled, that winter day, how many novices still come to us with really basic questions to which they have been unable to find answers. Many complain about the unwillingness of experienced breeders to help the beginner. We felt we could improve the situation; thus, the idea for SHELTIE TALK was born.

Undoubtedly there are many more qualified than we to compile a comprehensive book about the Shetland Sheepdog; we only wish they had. However, by pooling our varied resources we hope to provide a convenient source of basic information on the breed and to share with you our concern that the very unique Sheltie character not be lost in the quest for the ultimate show dog.

Barbara, under the banner of "Silverleaf," has bred and exhibited Shelties and other breeds including German Shepherds, Norweigan Elkhounds, Keeshonden, and Bearded Collies. Among these are several champions, many group winners, three nationally ranked top ten show winners, several top winning and producing Beardies, and the second top producing Elkhound bitch in the nation. Shelties were her first love, and she credits her appreciation of true Sheltie character to her first champion, Apple Acres True Blue, C.D.

Betty Jo has contributed many years of background in the publications field, as well as 10 years experience gained in maintaining a small group of Shelties at "Kinni Kennels." She has bred or exhibited several champions and numerous point winners. She claims a number of obedience title holders, including high-scoring Sheltie at the 1968 national specialty.

We hope that our combined experience and knowledge presented in SHELTIE TALK will be helpful to those starting a few years behind us. Perhaps, too, we can add a new dimension to some established ideas. We believe it takes serious breeders to preserve any breed, and we encourage you, our reader, to become one of the thoughtful few concerned with preserving true Sheltie type and character.

Betty Jo McKinney
and
Barbara Hagen Rieseberg
1976

Ch. Halstor's Peter Pumpkin, the breed's top sire, at twelve years of age. Owner, Tom Coen, Macdega. (Photo by Krook)

Toonie Dog to Champion 1

The Sheltie—a special dog. Loyal. Above average in canine intelligence. A near-human capacity for understanding and compassion.

The Shetland Sheepdog is a small, alert, rough-coated working dog resembling the *ideal* Collie in miniature. He appears as a sable (brown), tricolor (black with tan points and white markings), blue merle (merle with tan points and white collar markings), and a black or blue bicolor (without the tan points on face and legs).

The breed standard requires the Sheltie to be sound, sturdy, and agile, and therefore he is one of the hardiest of the registered breeds. His thick, double coat protects him from the elements and enables him to withstand exposure and extremes of temperature. Although originally bred as an outdoor dog, he is also happy to be at his master's side as a house pet and adapts readily to apartment style living.

He has grace, beauty of expression and balance; he is also a practical, useful canine. It is his nature to please and obey, willingly and naturally. He seems to have an innate sense of politeness and cleanliness, for instance often housebreaking himself. He excells in obedience, from novice to utility, and even in tracking. The instinct to guard and protect, another trait as old as the breed itself, makes the Sheltie an excellent farm or stock dog. Some exhibit natural herding ability, while others pick it up readily with training.

His most striking features are his uncanny ability to sense when something is wrong and his extremely strong awareness of property boundaries. He likes to work; lacking the opportunity to herd animals he may take over the children, keeping them where they should be or at least letting others know if something is wrong.

His working dog instinct lends the Sheltie to inventive ways of pleasing his master—bringing in slippers or the evening paper, or leash as a hint for an evening walk. Kept as a house pet, the dog becomes so much a part of the family that he soon knows the habits, desires and idiosyncracies of his owner. He is a pleasure to live with; a delight to own.

A BRIEF HISTORY

There is little doubt that the small working Collie, from which the modern show Collie derives, was likewise the progenitor of the Shetland Sheepdog. The actual origin, however, is lost in the mists of the Shetland Islands and cannot be traced completely by records, but tradition makes the Sheltie as old as the islands themselves.

A group of about 100 small islands, the Shetland Islands lie about 50 miles off the northern coast of Scotland, and as far north as most of Norway. Only about one fourth of them are inhabited; the remainder are used solely to pasture the ponies, cattle, and sheep. The largest island, Mainland, is about 60 miles long and no part of it is over three miles from the seashore.

"One cannot comprehend either the physical characteristics or the mental qualifications of any breed...without an adequate knowledge of the native land whence it came...."

Catherine E. Coleman
The Shetland Sheepdog, 1943

It is a land of rugged, rocky coasts, with coastal storms sweeping over the entire islands at frequent intervals. The climate is harsh and damp, with only a few protected inlets sheltered well enough to grow crops. Winter days are short and cold; summers are brief with the sun visible 24 hours a day.

The Island's first inhabitants were a small, dark race of people, the Picts, who gave the land its reputation for being inhabited by "pixies" or fairies. Later the Norsemen overran the islands, and then the Scots as well, so that today the inhabitants are a mixture of the three races, just

fields, it was the toonie dog's responsibility to drive them away from the crops and back to the pasture. This he did with no help from the crofter.

During the summer the herds were ferried to outlying islands and left, often in sole charge of the dogs, with occasional checks being made by the crofter. In the fall, the dogs rounded up the stock and helped bring them back to the mainland. Thus, you can see that the early Shelties were used more for driving and protecting than for actual herding.

Thule Norna, an example of an early Sheltie. (Photo courtesy of Sea Isle Kennels)

Ch. Victory of Pocono C.D.X., grandson of Ch. Peabody Pan, shows improved Collie type. Victory was ASSA Best of Breed in 1942. (Photo from ASSA Bulletin Board)

as their dogs are a combination of the native breeds of each of these peoples.

Due to sparseness of vegetation and ruggedness of climate, the islands over the centuries have produced every living thing in diminutive size. Shetland ponies, sheep, and cattle grow much smaller when bred on the islands than do their counterparts on the mainlands. Likewise, the "toonie" (town) or "peerie" (fairy) dogs were reduced replicas of their ancestor, the Collie.

For years the islanders' chief occupations were fishing and raising the Shetland sheep, whose long, soft wool made Shetland wool products in demand the world over. A few of the inlets, however, were fertile enough to grow crops, and here the crofters had small farms, generally unfenced. If sheep and cattle wandered to the cultivated

It is thought that the dogs were originally brought to the islands on fishing fleets of the Norse and Scots. Influence of the Greenland Yakki dogs, the King Charles Spaniel, and both the Welsh and Scotch working Collie was evident in the *early* Sheltie. He had a thick coat slightly shorter than that of the Collie; semi-erect ears like the Collie, prick ears of the Yakki dog, or drooping ears of the Spaniel. Wavy coats, an influence of the Spaniel, and tails that curled over the back, a trait of the Yakki, appeared frequently.

Most of the original Shelties were somewhat Collie-like in appearance. The crofters selected a small animal, because they could see no reason to feed a larger one. The dogs were the crofter's working partners—sharing his life during the lonely hours, sleeping with him, caring for his sheep, guarding his property. This close association with humans, plus the instinct of generations of herding dogs in his genetic makeup, gave the Sheltie uncanny understanding of people and an intense sense of responsibility. The crofters selected for these qualities, as well as for ability to work, stamina, courage, and intelligence, and they succeeded in fixing these traits quite dependably in the breed. They cared little about the dog's physical appearance, however, so the physical type remained varied.

was organized in Scotland. The breed was on its way to international recognition!

Because of the differences in physical type, there was disagreement from the beginning about a show standard. The first Shelties were exhibited in the toy group, and ranged in size from eight to twelve inches. The Shetland Collie Club stated that the Sheltie should be "similar to the rough (show) Collie, but in miniature, with the height not to exceed 15 inches at the shoulder." The Scotch Club described the Sheltie as "an ordinary collie in miniature, height about 12 inches."

Ch. Peabody Pan, imported by Betty Whelen, became one of our most influential sires.

Ch. Mowgli, by Ch. Wee Laird ex Jean of Anahassitt (by Laird and out of his sister, Ch. Downfield Grethe).

Chestnut Lassie, dam of Chestnut Rainbow, the beginning of the Chestnut Line.

THE SHOW SHELTIE

In the late 1800's many of the crofts were assumed by large commercial sheep operations that brought in larger sheep from the mainland and larger Scotch Collies with which to work them.

Since he could not handle a herd of 500 or more large sheep, the Sheltie became primarily a lap dog. Pomeranians and other small types were introduced into the breed, bringing with them a tendency to domed skulls and large, round eyes. This further diversified type and the true toonie dog was in danger of extinction.

In 1908 in Lerwick the Shetland Collie Club was founded in an effort to safeguard the breed. A year later a club

The Sheltie was first benched at Crufts in 1908, and by 1912 they were beginning to make an impression in the show ring, but type and size differences continued to abound. Show Collie type was well established at this time, so Collie crosses were introduced in an effort to improve type. With them came a considerable increase in size. Some breeders chose to maintain the ideal of twelve inches, but generally sacrificed Collie type to achieve it. In practice, the desired type and the ideal size did not inherit together.

In 1913 the Scotch Club finally altered its 12-inch height limit to an "ideal" of 12 inches. This was also the approach of the English Shetland Collie Club when it was formed in 1914. The English standard described the breed as "having the general appearance of the show Collie in

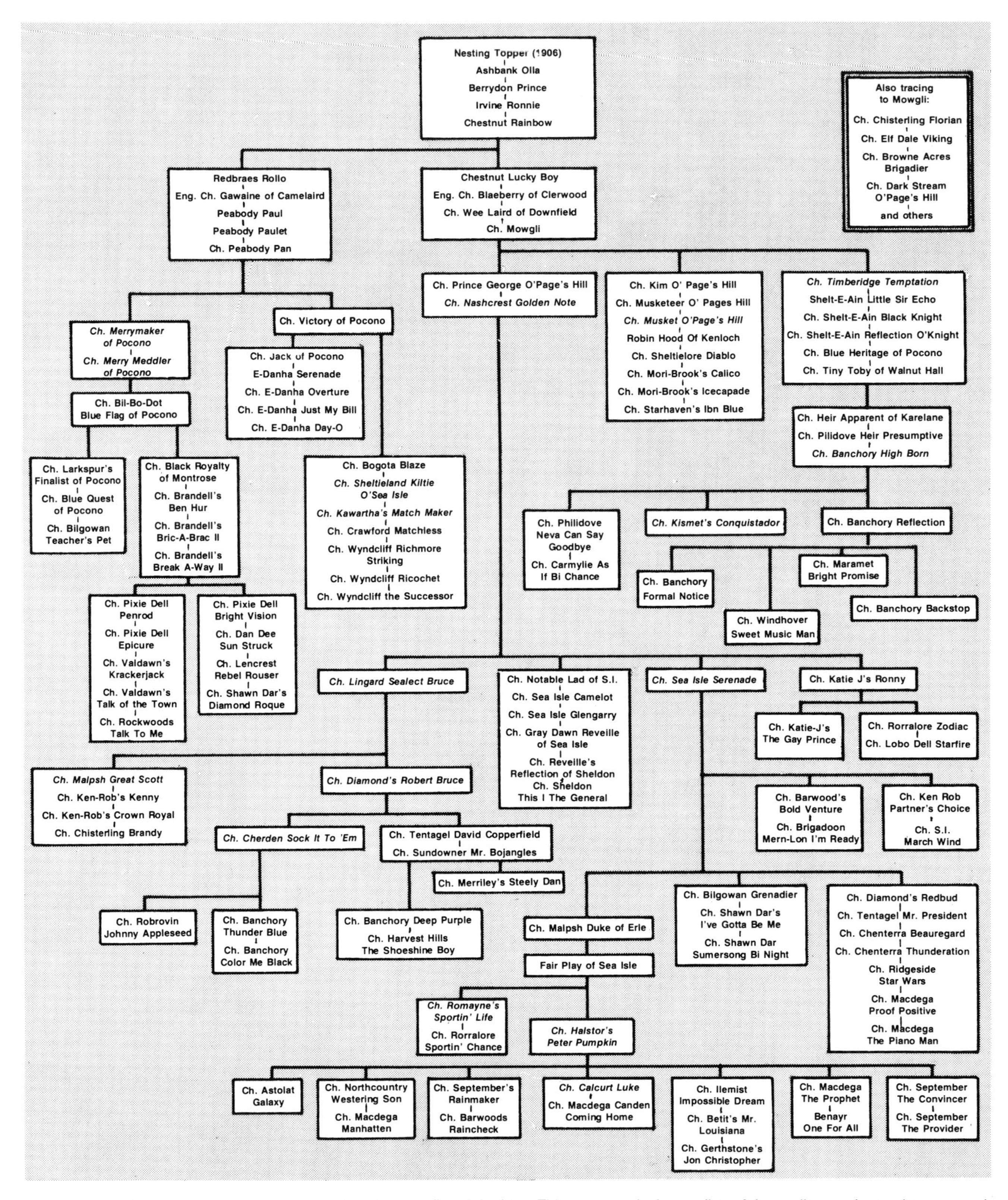

One way to trace the geneology of a dog is by a "tail male" chart. This traces only the top line of the pedigree, sire to sire, to grandsire, etc., and ignores the rest of the pedigree. We found the following chart interesting in that most of the top producing sires (in italics) trace directly to one of two dogs, either Ch. Peabody Pan, imported by Betty Whelen in 1935, or Ch. Wee Laird of Downfield, imported by Mrs. Dreer. Both are descendents of Chestnut Rainbow, for whom the Chestnut or Che line is named. The other major line, BB, named for its founding sire, Butcher Boy, has carried down through sons and daughters, but we were unable to locate a tail male line tracing directly to this dog.

miniature." This appearance seemed to be preferred, and the Scottish Club soon revised its standard accordingly. For the first time, the clubs were in agreement.

Another problem was encountered when Collie breeders voiced such opposition to the use of the name "Shetland Collie" that the breed was renamed Shetland Sheepdog. Even with all the Collie crosses being done, especially by Mountfort and Elfin Park, these early Shelties bore little resemblance to the show Collie of that day.

Diversity of type continued to be a problem, however, and as breeding increased in England more small Collie lines were introduced. It was largely the descendants from these crosses that were brought to the United States as foundation stock for American kennels. Chestnut Lady, prominent in American lines, was from a Collie cross.

THE SHELTIE COMES TO AMERICA

The first Shelties were imported to the U.S. around 1910, but breeding was sharply curtailed during World War I and did not pick up sharply again until the mid 1920's. Early kennels who had tremendous influence on American bloodlines included Catherine Coleman Moore's "Sheltieland," Miss Fredericka Fry's "Far Sea Kennels," the Dreer's "Anahassitt Kennels," and Mrs. Katherine Edward's "Walnut Hall."

Fredericka Fry was elected first president of the American Shetland Sheepdog Club when it was founded in 1929, and Catherine Coleman was responsible for writing the first breed Standard. It stood until 1952. The ASSA barred all Collie crosses from the registry, and the Standard called for an "ideal Collie in miniature, height 12 to 15 inches." In 1936 this was revised to ask for an ideal height of 14½ inches and the club adopted a "gentleman's agreement" that Shelties over 16 inches would not be shown.

England too had problems with size and finally the limit was revised to reflect an ideal of 14½ inches for males, 14 inches for bitches, with any dog more than one inch above to be severely penalized. The English Standard keeps this ideal height yet today; but in 1959 the American Standard was revised to specify a 13 to 16-inch size limit for either sex.

Ch. Tiny Toby of Walnut Hall, ASSA Best of Breed in 1960.

Ch. Shelteland Little Tartan.

A brief discussion of the strong points of some of the major lines is presented. Of course, similar qualities may also be found in other lines or kennels not described, and not all the dogs in a line will have a particular quality. Still, the founding breeder of each line began with a general idea of the traits he wanted to stabilize in the breed, and generations of selecting for these traits has tended to fix these qualities in a majority of his dogs.

PAGE'S HILL

Page's Hill kennel was founded in 1929 when William W. Gallagher obtained the English import, *Ch. Helensdale*

Laddie. Mr. Gallagher was a great supporter of the breed and active in the American Shetland Sheepdog Association (ASSA) for many years. In later years the kennel was first managed by and later transferred to Mr. J. Nate Levine, who continued the line into the present generation. Levine was a very successful and well known handler who had formerly handled Shelties for Mrs. Dreer of Anahassitt. Over a forty-year period Page's Hill bred approximately 69 champions.

Page's Hill foundation stock had Collie crosses close up, hence the markedly improved Collie type they consistently produced. They also produced the first red sable, Kim O' Page's Hill. Prior to this all the sables were dark mahogany with black shading.

A few of the best know Page's Hill dogs include:

Ch. Mowgli (produced by breeding Jean of Anahasset back to her sire, Ch. Wee Laird of Downfield), sire of 19 champions.

Ch. Mountaineer O' Page's Hill, sire of 22 champions, an impressive dog of almost perfect Collie type.

Ch. Windrush of Page's Hill, a typey, perfectly balanced Sheltie whose head photo is still used on the ASSA Official Standard. He is the only Sheltie to date to win the working group at Westminister KC. He was sterile.

Ch. Dark Miss o'Page's Hill.

Imported Ch. Peabody Pan, sire of Merrymaker.

Ch. Mountaineer O'Page's Hill.

Ch. Merrymaker of Pocono C.D., sire of 25 champions.

Ch. Merry Meddler of Pocono, sire of 21 champions.

Ch. Bil Bo Dot Blue Flag of Pocono, sire of 14 champions.

POCONO

Betty Whelen, formerly a Collie breeder, purchased her first Sheltie, *Ch. Syncopating Sue of Anahassit*, in 1933. She is one of the few early breeders still actively breeding and showing Shelties.

Betty's fascination with blue merle Collies, which she formerly bred, led her to establish a merle line in Shelties by importing *Peabody Silver Phantasy* from England in 1934. This lovely-colored small blue became the foundation of most of the blues in the U.S. today. Bred to Artful Dodger of Anahassit, she produced *Grey Mist of Pocono*, who was the sire of the first American-bred champion, *Sea Isle Merle Legacy. Ch. Sea Isle Blue Legacy, Ch. Larkspur of Pocono* (dam of 16 champions and still the record holder for top producing bitch), and *Ch. Bil Bo Dot Blue Flag of Pocono* were the first three American-bred blue champions. Larkspur's blue daughter, *Ch. Larkspur's Replica* remains third in the list of top producing dams. Her son, *Ch. Blue Heritage of Pocono*, and his son, Ch. Tiny Toby of Walnut Hall, also deserve mention.

From Ch. Peabody Pan and Ch. Syncopating Sue of Anahassit came *Ch. Merry Maker of Pocono C.D.X.*, a small, refined dog, the pillar of Pocono's sable line. Merry Maker's tricolor son, *Ch. Merry Meddler of Pocono* (21 champions), and Meddler's son *Ch. Bil Bo Dot Blue Flag* (14 champions) all hold impressive records that stand today among the top producing sires. A sable son of Merry Maker, *Ch. Victory of Pocono*, sired Ch. Bogota Blaze, who is the sire of Ch. Sheltieland Kiltie of Sea Isle, whose daughters were used extensively with Ch. Nashcrest Golden Note.

Shelt-E-Ain Little Sir Echo.

Geronimo Prince Royal, ASSA Winners Dog, 1953.

Ch. Timberidge Temptation.

Ch. Shelt-E-Ain Black Knight.

SHELT-E-AIN

A line closely related in type to Pocono was Tobi Ain Brace's Shelt-E-Ain strain, which was particularly good in angulation and soundness, and nearly all representatives had perfect profiles. Tobi Ain Started with a bitch, *Indigo of Pocono*, by *Ch. Merry Meddler of Pocono.*

She bred *Indigo* to *Ch. Catmore Chum* to produce *Shelt-E-Ain Pirouette*, a lovely tri bitch who, when bred to *Ch. Timberidge Temptation* produced *Shelt-E-Ain Little Sir Echo*, and in a repeat of that breeding, *Nashcrest Rhythm,* dam of *Ch. Nashcrest Golden Note. Pirouette* bred to *Little Sir Echo* produced *Ch. Shelt-E-Ain Black Knight.*

Black Knight, bred to a *Pirouette* daughter, produced *Ch. Shelt-E-Ain Reflection O'Knight,* an influential sire behind many of the present day Pocono and Kiloren dogs. Among his outstanding offspring are *Ch. Kiloren Nightstorm O'Alandie, Ch. Blue Heritage of Pocono, Ch. Kiloren Silver Mist of Pocono,* and *Ch. Lingard Blue Boy.*

TIMBERIDGE AND GERONIMO

Timberidge kennel, located on the East Coast, and Geronimo kennel, on the West Coast, developed closely related lines. The two kennels traded stud dogs, among them *Ch. Geronimo Son Rey*, to make them available over a wider area.

Dorothy Allen Foster of Timberidge bred *Ch. Timberidge Temptress* to *Ch. Kalander Prince of Page's Hill* to produce *Ch. Timberidge Temptation*, one of the breed's top sires with 32 champions to his credit. Among them was *Ch. Geronimo Crown Prince,* sire of 13 champions.

Ch. Timberidge Target, a *Golden Note* son out of a *Temptation* grandaughter, was bred to a *Temptation* daughter to produce *Ch. Timberidge Typesetter, C.D.* Ch. Prince George O'Page's Hill ex a Merrymaker daughter) continued the basic idea of combining these two lines. The two dogs complimented each other in type and the Kiltie-Note crosses formed the winningest line of Shelties in the history of the breed in this country. Golden Note sired 29 champions; his son *Ch. Sea Isle Serenade* (a result of the Kiltie-Note cross) sired 29. Another Note son, Ch. Lingard Select Bruce, sired 42 champions, and Ch. Halstor's Peter Pumpkin, who is linebred on Kiltie and Note, became the breed's all time top producing sire with 153 champions.

Gray Mist of Pocono.

Ch. Sheltieland Kiltie O' Sea Isle.

Ch. Brown Acres Desert Dreamer, 1983 Champion.

Ch. Pixie Dell Epicure, 3 times BoB at Westminster.

Am. Can. Ch. JimJonArd Geronimo.

SEA ISLE

Misses Evelyn Davis and Mary Van Wagenan of Sea Isle met through their mutual friend Catherine Coleman Moore. Mary bred her first litter (by Grey Mist of Pocono) in 1936, to produce the first American bred blue merle champion, *Ch. Sea Isle Merle Legacy*. The Sea Isle prefix was registered in 1937.

The influence of the Sea Isle studs is most impressive. *Ch. Sheltieland Kiltie* (by Ch. Victory of Pocono out of a Mountaineer daughter) and *Ch. Nashcrest Golden Note* (by

BROWNE ACRES

Jess and Donna Browne's Browne Acres was founded in 1956 with two adult Shelties, *Am. Can. Ch. JimJonArd Geronimo* (sire of 8 champions) and *Timberidge Crown Jewel,* a 14½-inch daughter of Ch. Geronimo Crown Prince ex Ch. Timberidge Gold Standard. In four litters, Crown Jewel produced 5 champions and two non-champion daughters that produced 2 champions each.

Ch. JimJonArd Geronimo was of Page's Hill and Pixie Dell linage, a dark sable, 15½-inches with good bone and a harsh, stand-off coat. When bred to Crown Jewel, he produced *Chs. B.A. Blaze, Ch. B.A. Blossom,* and *B.A. Bewitching,* all three of whom became producers of champions.

Susie was sent to Ch. Some Trade O'Page's Hill to produce *Am. Can. Ch. B.A. Bette*. Later, Sea Isle lineage was brought in through Chs. Golden Note, Kiltie, and Serenade.

Ill health forced the Brownes to sell out in 1975. After Jess passed away, Donna later married Hugh Hutchison. She has recently co-bred a few litters using bitches heavy on her old stock.

ASTOLAT

Constance Hubbard registered Astolat Kennels in 1930 while breeding Collies, and added Shelties in 1934 when she purchased *Anahassitt Aphrodite.* A couple of years later she bought a puppy from Betty Whelen named *Astolat Lady Harlequin* (by Artful Dodger of Anahassit ex Ch. Adorable of Anahassitt), mainly because she was a little more than one half white. At the time her main interest was white Collies, and she went into Shelties hoping to perfect a strain of whites (the standard allowed them at that time). Harlequin was bred to a grandson of Ch. Aphrodite and produced *Astolat Snow White* (both Harlequin and Snow White were tri marked). Snow White bred to a grandson of Betty Whelen's Ch. Merrymaker who was a sable marked white produced *Snow Flurry*, also a tri-marked white, and when she was bred to Ch. Frigate' of Faunbrook, CD. she produced *Frigat's Emblem of Astolat*, a mahogany sable.

Ch. Astolat Emblem's Onyx, Ch. Astol at Golden Symbol, Ch. Waccabuc's Merry Mac, Ch. Astolat Lady Timothy, Ch. Astolat Gold Twist, Ch. Astolat Gold Touch, Ch. Astolat Enchantor, Int. Ch. Astolat Gold Award, CD., Ch. Astolat Galaxy, CD., are all descendents of Emblem.

Am. Can. Ch. Astolat Galaxy C.D., owned by Connie Hubbard, Astolat, an influential Peter son.

Ch. Frigate's Emblem of Astolat.

PIXIE DELL

Founded on pure Page's Hill, the Pixie Dell Shelties have continued as a unique line for many years. Mr. and Mrs. A. R. Miller were the founders, and Mrs. Miller continues the line to the present day though on a smaller scale than before. Mr. Miller became a respected judge and his unfortunate and untimely death occurred as he was serving as delegate to AKC from the American Shetland Sheepdog Association. Pixie Dell is best known in recent years for *Ch. Pixie Dell Epicure,* who was Best of Breed of Westminster for three consecutive years and was many times a group winner.

WALNUT HALL

Katherine and Willis Nichols' Walnut Hall was established in 1929 with *Jock of Walnut Hall*, purchased from Mrs. Dreer. The Nichols continued to be active throughout the 1970's. Most of the Walnut Hall dogs were handled by Nate Levine in the early days, and later by Betty Whelen.

Jock produced *Tiny Eve of Walnut Hall*, dam of three champions, the most significant being *Ch. Jack of Pocono*, who went to E-Danha Kennels.

Author's Footnote:

Readers who want more information on current bloodlines are referred to the Shetland Sheepdog magazines listed in the appendix—the best way to keep abreast of current activities and breeders. Many other breeders deserve to be represented here, but space and economics would not permit.

Cats and Shelties—more friends than enemies! The catlike agility and affectionate temperament of the Sheltie generally lead to friendship with the family kitty. This is Siasconset Windy Rose, four months, with friend. Owner, Wendy Louring. (Photo by Krook)

The Essence of Sheltie Character 2

The most distinctive, and certainly the most endearing, qualities of the Shetland Sheepdog are his temperament and personality. He abounds with charm, dignity and distinction—from pixie-like to regal. He's a bit of a snob, yet sweet and loveable. He is dependable, intelligent, sensible, eager to please, naturally well mannered—one of the most trainable of breeds. Because of these qualities he adapts to a variety of lifestyles and purposes.

Two words express the Sheltie's relationship to his owner—*sensitive and responsive.* A Sheltie lacking sensitivity and responsiveness, even though he may be friendly, lacks the very essence of Sheltie character.

Sensitivity is sometimes construed to mean that a dog is cowering and cannot take correction or discipline. While it is true that the Sheltie reacts negatively to harsh treatment, he should have a degree of self-assurance and toughness. However, he quickly senses when someone is displeased with him and rarely needs strong discipline.

Because of this sensitive nature the Sheltie isn't likely to become a nuisance. He is enthusiastic and playful when you are; unobtrusive when you are busy; concerned when you are ill or "blue." He is capable of developing a "caring" relationship and becomes very attached to his owner or owners.

Quick response to training and to his handler's directions while working was highly developed in the Island Sheltie. Today he remains responsive to training and to the words and requests of his master. At times his ability to understand and respond is purely amazing. The Sheltie seeks and expects response from you, and responds best when you respond to him. It takes proper training, socialization, and play on your part to enable your Sheltie to develop his personality to its fullest potential. If you cannot appreciate the refinements and communication of this kind of relationship between person and dog you might want to consider another breed.

These qualities of sensitivity and responsiveness, combined with a degree of protectiveness and intense loyalty, occasionally cause a Sheltie to single out one member of the family as "his person," and become aloof to the other members. The same qualities are responsible for his disdain of strangers. He simply will not lavish affection, or even attention, on a person he doesn't know and to whom he has no reason to respond.

THE SHELTIE CHARACTER

The Sheltie with the true "old fashioned" Sheltie character is capable of establishing a relationship with his master based on mutual respect and understanding, an equality in which both parties communicate without use of words exactly what is expected of the other. This Sheltie may seem to others to be "just another dog," because he "turns on" only to his special person. The relationship becomes obvious, though, when dog and man are working together. The dog is so receptive to that person, so eager, so happy, so communicative, that bystanders marvel at the teamwork.

"A dog is the only living creature that can bring out the best qualities of his master and forget the others."

Michael McDowell

There is a certain charisma about such Shelties. They have a dignity and self-confidence which makes them occasionally disdainful, demanding, and insistent of their rights. Yet they are loving, loyal, openly communicative and never sneaky. They have a very real sense of humor and exhibit a certain gaity without being foolish.

This truly exceptional old Sheltie character is, at best, hard to find these days. Sometimes it is evident in a young puppy, but more often it comes with maturity and a certain amount of encouragement. Once you've found this kind of character you will never want to settle for less. together if they have been handled correctly from puppyhood. Such qualities are inherited, but become more pronounced with encouragement.

Shelties are easy to live with. They love traveling, are quick to learn, and can live indoors or out equally well. They do prefer being close to the family and are very sensitive to neglect or punishment. A Sheltie that is not given attention or training by all members of the family may bond to only the person who takes care of him.

As a child's pet, Shelties excell. They are small, active, playful, and caring. However, they should be raised

Sir Lancelot Laurel of Kinni demonstrates that special Sheltie affection with owner Laurel Fisher.

Grinning is an inherited trait.

Playing frisbee is more than a game. Gaines Company sponsors annual contests. Good way to exercise, too!

Some Unique Traits

Many small, unique traits have helped endear the Sheltie to his admirers. Some Shelties grin; many cross their front legs when they lie down; some use their "hands" extensively, or wash their face like a cat. Most Shelties have a distinct language of whines, groans, grumbles, and warbles; some of mine "purr."

It was said that the original Island Shelties never barked except to sound a warning. Unfortunately this is not as true today; most Shelties are barkers. Shelties never fought; and it is still possible to kennel unneutered males

with children from a young age. The Sheltie that has been raised in an all-adult household is often frightened by a child's more abrupt movements.

Unlike some dog breeds, there is little difference in the temperament of male and female Shelties. For a pet, my personal preference is a male. Males have proven to be quieter, more stable, and easier to housebreak than females. They are equally intelligent. I have not experienced a male "marking" in the house except when a female was allowed on the carpet during her heat season.

Some Shelties are bolder than others; some are more demonstrative of their affection. Some are quiet and others more active; some like to greet strangers while others could care less about anyone except their beloved master. Within the range of acceptable temperament you will find a considerable variation from which to select a dog most suited to your personality and lifestyle.

TEMPERAMENT OR PERSONALITY

The qualities we call "Sheltie character" are a combination of the dog's temperament and his personality. *Temperament,* that quality which makes a dog high strung or nonchalant, boistrous or quiet, timid or outgoing, is inherited. It cannot be altered radically although it can be modified somewhat by training and socialization. *Personality,* the individual characteristics which each Sheltie acquires in relationship to his owner, is developed through association with humans. The correct temperament and a tendency to behave in a certain way must be inherited; these characteristics are more fully developed through socialization and association with humans.

Importance of Correct Temperament

No matter how much you pay for a dog, he is worthless unless you can genuinely enjoy him. This implies a dog that is fun to live with; one who is responsive and dedicated to his owner, and polite with strangers. He should have enough personality to be an interesting individual, enough restraint to be a gentleman, and enough poise to accompany you anywhere. In addition, he should have the personality and temperamental qualities necessary to fulfill whatever purpose you have in mind for him.

In their concentration on the physical perfection of a breed, breeders often skip over temperament much too lightly. Yet it is one of the characteristics which makes our breed so special, and it was developed to a very high degree by early breeders who selected more for intelligence and temperament than for type. Thus, many early Shelties were noted for exceptional character and temperament. These traits still characterize the breed today, but to a lesser degree I believe, and various temperament faults are beginning to appear.

I expect my Shelties to have correct temperament, to be versatile, trustworthy, and tough enough to take a few emotional shocks without permanent damage. I expect them to meet new and different situations without panic, and to meet strange people without cringing or running away. When I travel with my dogs I expect to be able to let them out without fear that they will disappear into the woods. If, after a reasonable time with me, the animal cannot be trusted, I am better off without him.

Some Temperament Faults

The Sheltie has on occasion been criticized for being shy. In past years this was a real problem in some lines, and we still see it too frequently today. No one likes a dog that has to be extracted from beneath the furniture every time you want to show him off. The Sheltie with correct temperament is naturally reserved but he should never show fear or run out of the room when a stranger enters. Most Shelties dislike having a stranger reach for them, but left to make the advances themselves in their own time, they will be friendly.

Just because Shelties are "sensitive" does not mean that they cannot be disciplined or roughhoused. Indeed a nervous, flighty Sheltie has a serious temperament fault. A Sheltie with correct temperament is *not* fragile. He is a steady, capable, trustworthy, tough little working dog. He should not fold up under discipline, rigorous training, or the usual family roughhousing. He should, instead, respond quickly, with an ability to sense approval as well as disapproval.

There is another extreme in temperament, too. In the effort to breed striking, showy Shelties that win not only in the breed ring, but in the group as well, breeders have created another fault—the "terrier" temperament. The dog with this temperament is *overly* friendly. In the ring his ears are always up; he is alert, animated, sparkling—a standout. But often he never tones down at home either—running, barking, scrapping and generally making a nervous wreck of his owner. This kind of temperament is every bit as incorrect as the shy, cringing Sheltie, and it should be just as heavily faulted; unfortunately though it is often encouraged by breeders who find that they have to win in order to make a reputation in the breed, and that they must breed this kind of dog in order to win.

So called "schitzy" Shelties occasionally crop up, although most breeders have enough foresight to eliminate these animals from their breeding program. These Shelties are totally unpredictable—friendly one minute and totally "freaked out" the next, often for no apparent reason. All the time and work in the world will not correct such temperaments, and the dog is unsuitable for any purpose.

HOW TO RECOGNIZE CORRECT TEMPERAMENT

The Sheltie, especially the puppy, who comes rushing to greet you and jumps in your lap is not the one most likely to have correct Sheltie temperament. They are always endearing though, and I picked my own first Sheltie because she was the boldest and most playful one in the litter. She kept this "go go" disposition all of her life, and made a wonderful obedience dog, but was an excitable, nervous, noisy and sometimes annoying pet.

The puppy that hides under the table and refuses to come out is not the perfect Sheltie either. With patience and gentle handling, he may make a lovely pet, and be quite suitable for a mature older couple or a shy child. But he probably won't be satisfactory in the obedience ring or in a family of robust children.

If you want the puppy with the most correct temperament, look instead for the one that seems responsive and interested, but not *immediately* lavish with his affection. He may be watchful, or he may go on about his business. He may seem aloof or even friendly, but *hesitant.* He will probably come up to investigate after a few minutes, but he may not want you to touch him until he makes the first move. Although he may not trust you, he should not be frightened or nervous.

In order for a puppy to have correct temperament at least one of his parents should have the desired characteristics. The relationship of the adult Sheltie to his owner is more important than his reaction to you, a stranger. He should be responsive, obedient, trusting, and observant. If he is not, either his temperament is incorrect or he is lacking in the socialization and training necessary to develop it properly.

Shelties are temperamentally suited to work with the handicapped. Alamo Reaves of Handi-Dog, Inc., with her Sheltie. (Photo by Frank Tinker)

Beyond obvious surface traits, it is difficult to evaluate the fine points of temperament in the ring. For only the extremes of shyness or aggressiveness are evident there. The dog who bites as a nervous response or the dog who collapses into his handler's arms when being examined is probably unsteady at home, too. The dog that behaves like a terrier is likely noisy and boisterous at all times. Most dogs can be taught to stand for examination and to look intently at a tidbit of food, but some of the more intelligent Shelties get bored with the whole production, and thus it becomes difficult to tell these from the unresponsive dogs who won't turn on for anyone or anything.

Ideally, a Sheltie should be alert and responsive enough to "show" without being jumpy and hyperactive. And, since the Sheltie is supposed to be reserved, judges should not expect him to be a "showing fool," but instead should fault the overaggressive dog as heavily as the shy one. Unfortunately this is not usually the case.

Temperament, Personality, and Age

If *you raise a puppy* from a young age you will be able to encourage the natural traits of temperament which in association with you becomes his personality. The kennel-raised dog will not have this opportunity and will have less personality than the dog raised as a house pet. But even this Sheltie, given attention and training, will pick up individual traits which make him an enjoyable companion.

Brought into his new home between seven and sixteen weeks of age, the normal puppy adjusts quickly, and automatically "tunes in" to your lifestyle. Before seven weeks he will not be ready to relate exclusively to humans and needs the companionship and support of his littermates. After sixteen weeks the puppy will probably be attached to his former owner, and may take a bit longer to adjust. Once he accepts you as *his* person, however, he will be just as satisfactory as a young puppy. Obedience training helps establish communication and it most quickly instills confidence in the older puppy.

An *older dog who has been kenneled all his life* is probably a creature of habit and will become very confused, perhaps frightened, when his routine vanishes and his security does not seem as certain. Don't force this dog; rather ignore him and let him make the advances. He will soon learn to appreciate his new role. Since initial relationships are very important, when in doubt, back off and let the Sheltie decide how fast to progress.

The *badly abused dog whose basic temperament is stable or the very confirmed kennel dog who suddenly has a change in role* may never regain the confidence and happy-go-lucky attitude we like to see, but he should learn to behave with dignity and steadiness if you give him time. Work gently and patiently with him.

Personality and Kennel Dogs

Does being raised in a kennel ruin a Sheltie? No. Not if proper socialization takes place, especially during puppyhood. Naturally, anyone owning a number of dogs must have kennel facilities, and it is a good bet that your puppy may have spent some or most of his young life in the kennel. This should not harm his ability to function as a pet, show, or obedience dog.

It has been said that large breeders select as breeding stock Shelties that do well in the kennel. To a certain extent this may be true; with Shelties the good kennel dogs are *sometimes* also those with the correct temperament. Nervous, noisy dogs are not appreciated in a kennel and may be eliminated, as well those that are not "easy keepers" that stay in healthy condition on a basic food ration. I have heard it said also that intelligent Shelties are troublemakers in the kennel, and while occasionally this may prove true, some of mine with the strongest herding instinct and the quickest intelligence are also the best behaved in the kennel—but the most anxious to be let out to accompany me. They seem very "hurt" or indignant at being left behind, but obedient and well-behaved nevertheless. Even perfect temperament can be wasted and the personality lost if a dog is *consistently* confined to a kennel.

We rotate on a regular basis those dogs that are in the house so that all become well adjusted house pets as well as show or breeding prospects. In addition, we try to expose all puppies to children, other dogs, car travel, dog shows or matches, downtown shopping, or any other outing on which they can accompany us. Without this kind of exposure, even puppies with perfect temperaments can become shy and uncertain.

Attention will make any dog better, and it will never ruin a Sheltie for working or showing. On the contrary, it usually makes them even more eager. Naturally, some dogs become our favorites and get more attention than others. It is these dogs, if they remain with us, that have the more developed personalities and are the most fun to live with.

Shelties and kids are a natural combination. It is best if the puppy is raised with children from a young age. (Photo by Lloyd Price)

Ch. Macdega Barwood Birthright, Macdega. (Photo by Krook)

The Sheltie's head is like a beautiful sculpture, smooth and clean. The head should be refined and its shape, when viewed from top...a long, blunt wedge tapering slightly from ears to nose. Top of skull should be flat. Cheeks should be flat and should merge smoothly into a well-rounded muzzle. Skull and muzzle of equal length. Eyes medium size with almond-shaped rims, set somewhat obliquely in the skull. Expression should be alert, gentle, intelligent, questioning.

Understanding the Standard

3

Any canine has a number of traits—size, proportions, head, coat, expression, temperament, movement, and balance—which combine to make him a unique individual. Any given breed of canine is also distinguished from all other breeds by a particular combination of traits which are shared by *all* worthy representatives of that breed. To insure that the Shetland Sheepdog remains a distinct breed, and does not resemble any of a dozen other breeds or mix-breeds, a method of evaluation has been devised—a word picture of the "ideal" Sheltie, written by the authorities on the breed and tested by time.

This "blueprint," known as the Official Standard, is the final authority for evaluating individual dogs. No dog will be perfect in every respect, but the closer to the Standard, the greater the dog.

Without reference to the Standard, the distinctive characteristics of the breed would be lost. Anyone who breeds inherits the responsibility of safeguarding the Sheltie breed from extinction or drastic change.

Since even the experts differ in their interpretation of each detail I will not try to overly restrict the meaning. I choose instead to use the Standard as a framework within which to work, rather than as an exact unyielding model to be copied. I will define general terms and point out some things taken for granted by the experienced breeder, but not obvious to the newcomer. More detailed discussions of some of the Shetland Sheepdog's characteristics appear in later chapters.

As your concept of perfection develops, try not to get so "hung up" on specific points that the overall dog called for in the Standard is lost. Moderation is usually best, and the *dog with the most virtues is generally better than the one with the least faults!*

A LOOK AT THE STANDARD

Official Standard for the Shetland Sheepdog

Preamble

The Shetland Sheepdog, like the Collie, traces to the Border Collie of Scotland, which, transported to the Shetland Islands and crossed with small, intelligent, longhaired breeds, was reduced to miniature proportions. Subsequently crosses were made from time to time with Collies. This breed now bears the same relationship in size and general appearance to the Rough Collie as the Shetland Pony does to some of the larger breeds of horses. Although the resemblance between the Shetland Sheepdog and the Rough Collie is marked, there are differences which may be noted.

General Description

The Shetland Sheepdog is a small, alert, rough-coated, longhaired working dog. He must be sound, agile and sturdy. The outline should be so symmetrical that no part appears out of proportion to the whole. Dogs should appear masculine; bitches feminine.

"It is reasonable to have perfection in our eye that we may always advance toward it, though we know it can never be reached."

Johnson

The correct, balanced outline.

Short neck, cobby, compact body giving a square outline.

Too high on leg. Another out-of-balance outline.

The preamble describes the history of the breed and thereby establishes a reason for particular traits. Bear in mind, for example, the work expected from the early Shelties and the terrain and climate in which they performed their tasks. Remember, too, that the Collie they should resemble *is the Collie of a few decades ago; not the more extreme show Collie of today.*

The differences between the two breeds are subtle, but real. The most obvious is in conformation of the head. The Sheltie should possess a more distinct stop than the Collie, and emphasis in the Collie Standard is on a longer, leaner head, and smaller eye than would be desirable in a Sheltie. Also, in Collies, extreme emphasis is placed on head qualities alone, while the Shetland Sheepdog Standard calls for *balance and symmetry first,* and second a more detailed, sound working dog with quality of head, expression, and beauty. The Sheltie Standard requires *all* these qualities in a good representative of the breed, and neglect in any area beyond reasonable limits constitutes severe deviation from the Standard.

A key word is found in the second sentence of the General Description. In most places the Standard says that a Sheltie "should be, " but this sentence says he "*must be* sound, agile, and sturdy." This "must," therefore, ought to be considered a basic criteria upon which to build a beautiful Sheltie.

The difference between the Collie and Sheltie is accurately shown in the analogy used in the preamble. A Shetland Pony expanded to a full sized horse would have the proportions of a draft animal. Likewise a "blown-up" Sheltie would be too heavy and coarse to make a good Collie. However a "miniature Collie" would be too frail and refined to be a good Sheltie. Indeed, while the resemblance between the two breeds is pronounced, they should never be identical in proportion to size.

Size

The Shetland Sheepdog should stand between 13 and 16 inches at the shoulder. Note: Height is determined by a line perpendicular to the ground from the top of the shoulder blades, the dog standing naturally, with forelegs parallel to line of measurement.

Disqualification. *Heights below or above the desired size range are to be disqualified from the show ring.*

(For a complete discussion on size refer to chapter 6.)

Coat

The coat should be double, the outer coat consisting of long, straight, harsh hair; the undercoat short, furry, and so dense as to give the entire coat its "stand-off" quality. The hair on face, tips of ears and feet should be smooth. Mane and frill should be abundant, and particularly impressive in males. The forelegs well feathered, the hind legs heavily so, but smooth below the hock joint. Hair on tail profuse. Note: Excess hair on ears, feet, and on hocks may be trimmed for the show ring.

Note the elegant neck and outline. Ch. September Fair Share, owned by Barbara Linden.

Faults. *Coat short or flat, in whole or in part; wavy, curly, soft or silky. Lack of undercoat. Smooth-coated specimens.*

Coat is probably of the correct "harsh" texture if it tends to repel water. Some coats are profuse but soft and fluffy. While these may look impressive, they are harder to maintain and are a disadvantage to a working dog because they soak up water like a sponge and tangle easily in the underbrush. A correct coat is also fitted to the dog. If he looks like a haystack with legs and face peeking out he either has too much coat or he is improperly groomed. A beautiful coat finishes the picture of an otherwise beautifully balanced dog.

Bitches should be feminine. Note the lovely shoulder angulation, depth of sternum, and placement of head and neck in relation to the forelegs. Ch. Malpsh Count Your Blessings, owned by Betty Howarth and Macdega. (Photo by Krook)

Males should be masculine. Am. Can. Ch. Banchory Formal Notice, sire of Best in Show winners. Owned by Banchory (Photo by Krook)

Color

Black, blue merle, and sable (ranging from golden through mahogany); marked with varying amounts of white and/or tan.

Faults. *Rustiness in a black or a blue coat. Washed out or degenerate colors, such as pale sable and faded blue. Self-color in the case of blue merle, that is, without any merling or mottling and generally appearing as a faded or dilute tri-color. Conspicuous white body spots. Specimens with more than 50 percent white shall be so severely penalized as to effectively eliminate them from competition.*

Disqualification. *Brindle.*

White Shelties are discouraged because they are difficult for sheep to distinguish and therefore are ineffective as sheepdogs. Brindle is now virtually extinct. All recognized colors are equally acceptable. Refer to chapter 18 for more detailed information on color.

Temperament

The Shetland Sheepdog is intensely loyal, affectionate, and responsive to his owner. However, he may be reserved toward strangers but not to the point of showing fear or cringing in the ring.

Faults. *Shyness, timidity, or nervousness. Stubborness, snappiness, or ill temper.*

Temperament is an extremely important consideration in the Sheltie and warrants more space than can be given in this chapter. Please refer to chapter 2.

Head

The head should be refined and its shape, when viewed from top or side, be a long, blunt wedge tapering slightly from ears to nose, which must be black.

Correct profile. Note flat, parallel planes, well-defined stop, and depth and finish of underjaw.

Overfilled stop.

Deep through throat, planes not parallel.

Skull and Muzzle

Top of skull should be flat, showing no prominence at nuchal crest (the top of the occiput). Cheeks should be flat and should merge smoothly into a well-rounded muzzle. Skull and muzzle should be of equal length, balance point being inner corner of eye. In profile the top line of skull should parallel the top line of muzzle, but on a higher plane due to the presence of a slight but definite stop. Jaws clean and powerful. The deep, well-developed under-jaw, rounded at chin, should extend to base of nostril. Lips tight. Upper and lower lips must meet and fit smoothly together all the way around. Teeth level and evenly spaced. Scissors bite.

Faults. *Too-angled head. Too prominent stop, or no stop. Overfill below, between, or above eyes. Prominent nuchal crest. Domed skull. Prominent cheekbones. Snipy muzzle. Short, receding, or shallow under-jaw, lacking breadth and depth. Overshot or undershot, missing or crooked teeth. Teeth visible when mouth is closed.*

The section on head is the most heavily interpreted of any part of the Standard. What is "smooth," "molded," "flat," or "moderately lean" is difficult to describe and impossible to confine to one ideal. Refer to chapter 4 for reasoning on why heads with different proportions can be considered correct.

A correct head is a thing of beauty. It appears to have been cast from a solid piece without joints or seams, and it should be approximately the same shape viewed from the top or the side. A head excessively deep from topskull to throat is as undesirable as a grossly broad one. The Standard allows for some variation of actual proportions, but it is quite specific concerning profile and shape. You must *feel* the head with your hands to determine cleanness, and once you have done so with a really fine head you will be able to appreciate a good head with its strengths and refinement. Proportion of parts of the head to one another and to the body must be maintained.

Cleanness of head is more difficult to achieve than excessive leanness and is much more desirable. The head is a combination of several exacting parts and any one of these may contain enough faults to destroy the overall look. A receding backskull, bump over the eyebrows, or poor stop can produce an overall poor head regardless of expression. *Flatness on the top and sides* of the head is in danger of being lost, and yet this is absolutely essential to correct head type. This is something that cannot be seen. It must be *felt*. Learn to place your hands on either side of the head, and run your fingers over the topskull. There should be no ridge along the side of the skull from the corner of the eye to the outside corner of the ear, no prominent bumps or holes below the eye, and no groove down the center of the forehead. The topskull should be flat, with no prominent bumps or ridges. The muzzle should blend smoothly into the backskull. A head that flares at the backskull is called "two-piece." It feels as

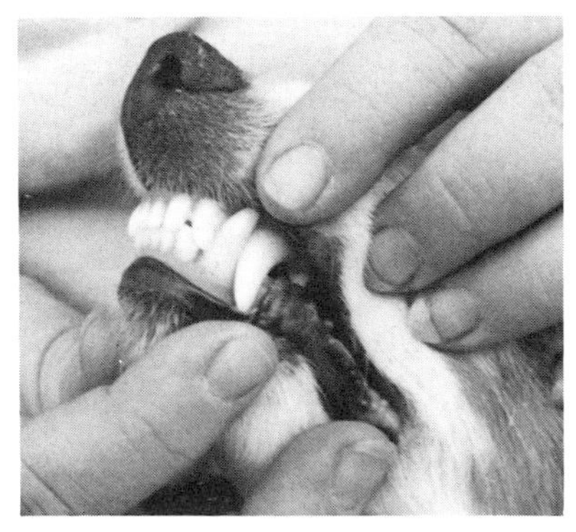

Correct scissors bite.

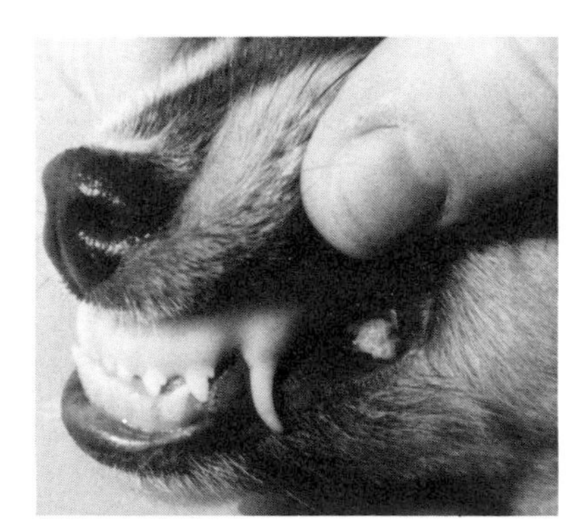

Underbite.

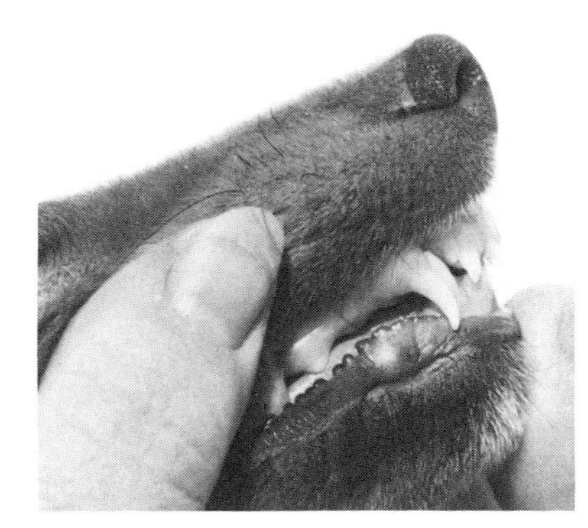

Overbite.

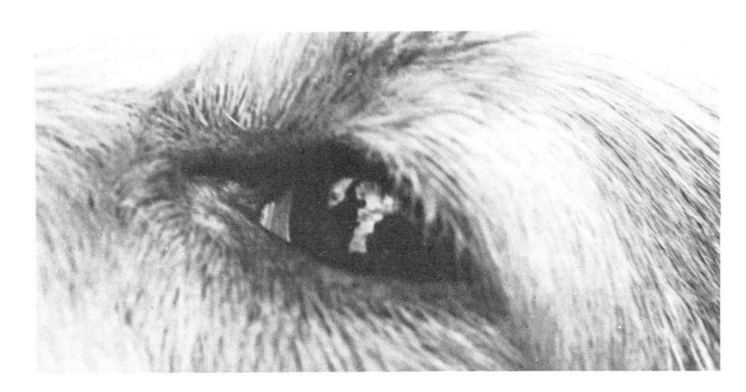

The correct eye—medium size with dark, almond-shaped rims. Note the dark haw which is barely visible. White haws can detract from the expression. It is the eye rims which create the almond shape; the eyeball itself is always round.

if the muzzle were plugged onto a round, flared backskull. This section of the Standard cannot be reread too often.

Shelties should have 16 premolars, 4 on each side top and bottom. Missing or extra teeth are faulted.

Eyes

Medium size with dark, almond-shaped rims, set somewhat obliquely in skull. Color must be dark, with blue or merle eyes permissible in blue merles only.

Faults. *Light, round, large or too small. Prominent haws.*

Eyes have four variables. In order of importance of how they affect expression these are shape, set or placement in the skull, color, and size. Shape should be almond; any tendency to roundness creates a blank or sharp expression, both of which are incorrect. The placement should be slightly oblique; neither too close together nor too far apart. This will produce the sweetness and inquiring look desired. A correct eye produces an obvious look of intelligence. Preferred color is brown (except in blue merles where a partially or completely blue eye is acceptable). Yellow eyes are abhorred because they distort expression, and black eyes (especially the tiny round ones) look foxy and hard. The darker browns gives the best expression. Size of the eyes should be medium. Large eyes are obviously faulted, and the tiny shoebutton eyes invite a host of eye defects due to damaged nerves and insufficient space. Small eyes are now in style, but again, extremes are to be avoided.

Ears

Small and flexible, placed high, carried three-fourths erect, with tips breaking forward. When in repose the ears fold lengthwise and are thrown back into the frill.

Faults. *Set too low. Hound, prick, bat, twisted ears. Leather too thick or too thin.*

Ears affect expression to a lesser degree than eyes, but are important nonetheless. They should be small, set high on the head, and tip forward. It is not necessary that they be so highset that they touch on top. In fact this usually indicates too narrow or too rounded a skull. A break that is too low or too high is undesirable, but, unless extreme, the break affects expression less than the set of the ear on the skull. Some Shelties have excellent set and break to the ears, but poor carriage. In other words they don't use their ears well, even though they could do so if they wanted. Ear carriage is important in a show dog and may reflect temperament. (Refer to chapter 14.)

Correct ears, three-fourths erect, set high on head.

Low or hound ears.

Wideset ears tipping to side.

Expression

Contours and chiseling of the head, the shape, set and use of ears, the placement, shape and color of the eyes, combine to produce expression. Normally the expression should be alert, gentle, intelligent and questioning. Toward strangers the eyes should show watchfulness and reserve, but no fear.

Expression, influenced by head shape, eyes, ears, and temperament, is the characteristic which differentiates a Sheltie from other breeds more than any other consideration. The soul and character of the Sheltie are evident in his expression. It can convey dignity, graciousness, a sense of humor, and even, on occasion, superiority; and above all, intelligence and understanding. A blank, fearful, hard, or devious look is not typical of the breed. Temperament is depicted in the expression, both through the eyes and the use of the ears.

An aura of communication and affection should be seen when a Sheltie relates to his owner. This may not be evident to a stranger trying to "bait" the dog. One must earn the favor of the self-respecting little Sheltie!

The Sheltie expression! Ch. Birch Hollow Once Upon A Time, one of the breed's top winning bitches, owned by Mildred Nichol.

Neck

Neck should be muscular, arched, and of sufficient length to carry the head proudly.

Faults. *Too short and thick.*

Length of neck provides elegance as well as helping overall balance. A long arched neck is highly desirable and usually accompanies a good shoulder. A long neck also makes the back appear shorter.

Body

In over-all appearance the body should appear moderately long as measured from shoulder joint to ischium (rearmost extremity of the pelvic bone), but much of this length is actually due to the proper angulation and breadth of the shoulder and hindquarter, as the back itself should be comparatively short. Back should be level and strongly muscled. Chest should be deep, the brisket reaching to point of elbow. The ribs should be well sprung, but flattened at their lower half to allow free play of the foreleg and shoulder. Abdomen moderately tucked up.

Faults. *Back too long, too short, swaying or roached. Barrel ribs. Slab-side. Chest narrow and/or too shallow.*

Again an eye for balance is needed to determine correct body proportions. The dog should be rectangular rather than square in body. This section is self-explanatory but sometimes overlooked. Good body proportions are as necessary to a good Sheltie as the specifics of head.

The overall outline of the Sheltie is what makes it "pretty," elegant, and uniquely Sheltie, and must not be overlooked. Long bodies, short necks, overly large heads, legginess, or exaggerated compactness create imbalance and destroy the desired outline. Straight shoulders force the front assembly of the dog too far forward so that the forelegs are almost under the dog's ears, thus destroying outline and balance. Over-angulated rears create lack of balance because the legs are not under the dog as they should be.

Forequarters

From the withers the shoulder blades should slope at a 45-degree angle forward and downward to the shoulder joints. At the withers they are separated only by the vertebra, but they must slope outward sufficiently to accommodate the desired spring of rib. The upper arm should join the shoulder blade at as nearly as possible a right angle. Elbow joint should be equidistant from the ground or from the withers. Forelegs straight viewed from all angles, muscular and clean, and of strong bone. Pasterns very strong, sinewy and flexible. Dewclaws may be removed.

Faults. *Insufficient angulation between shoulder and upper arm. Upper arm too short. Lack of outward slope of shoulders. Loose shoulders. Turning in or out of elbows. Crooked legs. Light bone.*

Straight front assembly and short upper arms are probably the most prevalent structural faults seen in recent years. Breeders need to constantly be aware of these problems and strive to correct them. Multi-genetic factors make faulty front assembly extremely difficult to breed out. Incorrect front structure creates a multitude of gait faults.

Feet (front and hind)

Feet should be oval and compact with the toes well arched and fitting tightly together. Pads deep and tough, nails hard and strong.

Faults. *Feet turning in or out. Splay-feet. Hare-feet. Cat-feet.*

Hindquarters

There should be a slight arch at the loins, and the croup should slope gradually to the rear. The hip-bone (pelvis) should be set at a 30-degree angle to the spine. The thigh should be broad and muscular. The thighbone should be set into the pelvis at a right angle corresponding to the angle of the shoulder blade and upper arm. Stifle bones join the thighbone and should be distinctly angled at the stifle joint. The over-all length of the stifle should at least equal the length of the thighbone, and preferably should slightly exceed it. Hock joint should be clean-cut, angular, sinewy, with good bone and strong ligamentation. The hock (metatarsus) should be short and straight viewed from all angles. Dewclaws should be removed. Feet (see Forequarters).

THE SHELTIE SKELETON

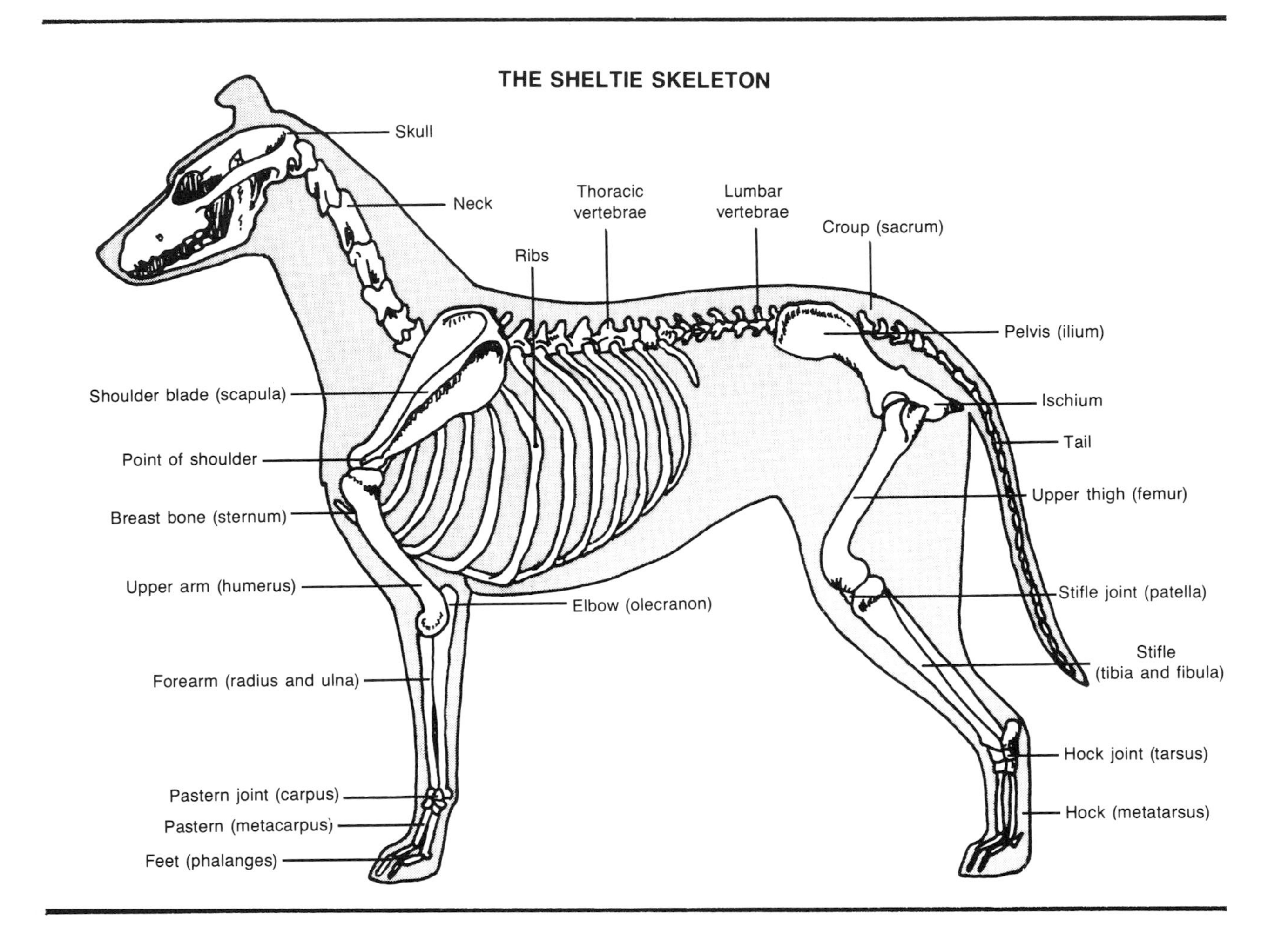

Faults. *Croup higher than withers. Croup too straight or too steep. Narrow thighs. Cowhocks. Hocks turning out. Poorly defined hock joint. Feet (see Forequarters).*

Tail

The tail should be sufficiently long so that when it is laid along the back edge of the hind legs the last vertibra will reach the hock joint. Carriage of tail at rest is straight down or in a slight upward curve. When the dog is alert the tail is normally lifted, but it should not be curved forward over the back.

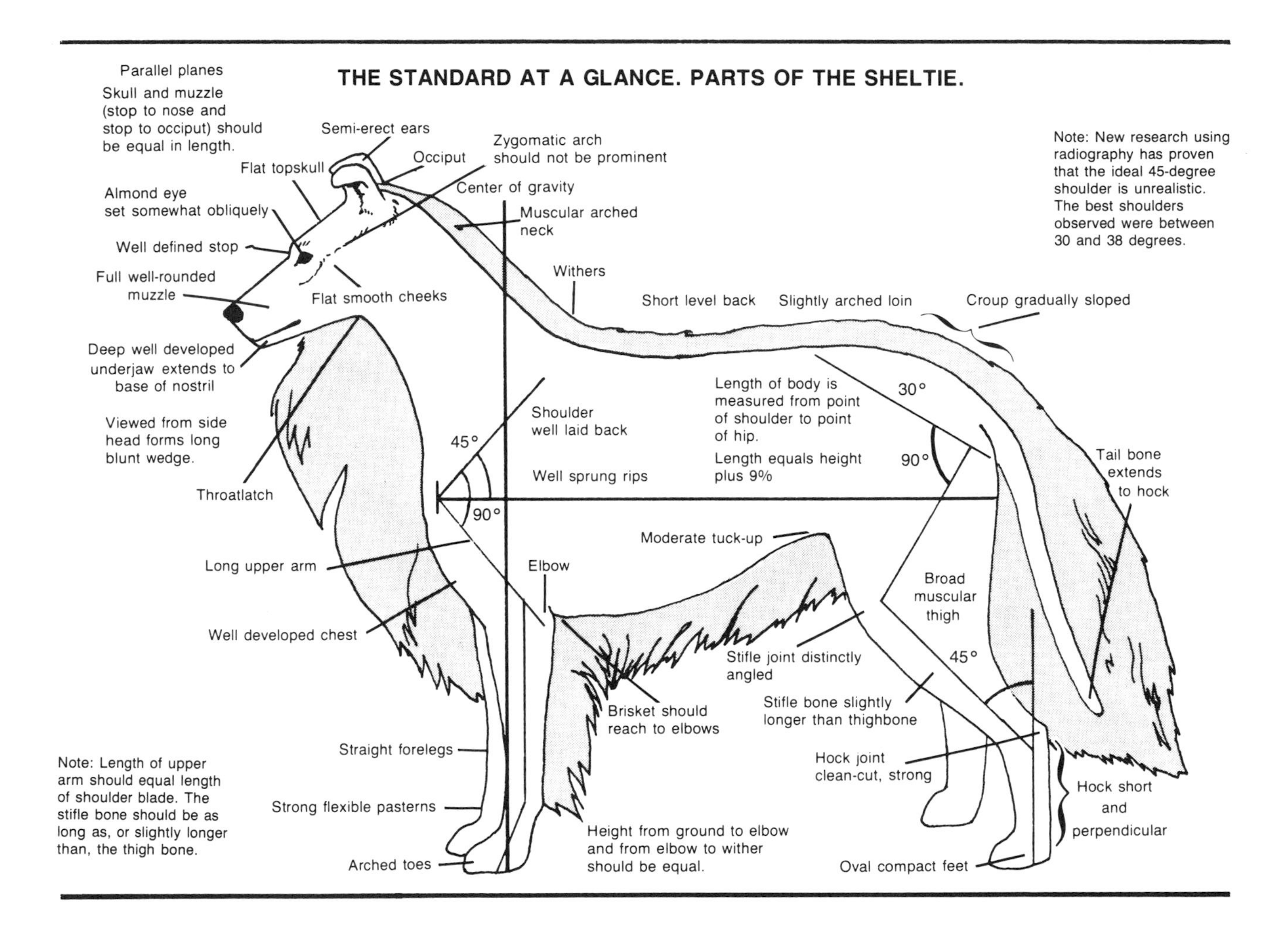

Faults. *Too short. Twisted at end.*

Gait

The trotting gait of the Shetland Sheepdog should denote speed and smoothness. There should be no jerkiness, nor stiff, stilted, up-and-down movement. The drive should be from the rear, true and straight, dependent upon correct angulation, musculation, and ligamentation of the entire hindquarter, thus allowing the dog to reach well under his body with his hind foot and propel himself forward. Reach of stride of the foreleg is dependent upon correct angulation, musculation and ligamentation of the forequarters, together with correct width of chest and construction of rib cage. The foot should be lifted only enough to clear the ground as the leg swings forward. Viewed from the front, both forelegs and hind legs should move forward almost perpendicular to the ground at the walk, slanting a little inward at a slow trot, until at a swift trot the feet are brought so far inward toward center line of body that the tracks left show two parallel lines of footprints actually touching a center line at their inner edges. There should be no crossing of the feet nor throwing of the weight from side to side.

Short hocks and sloping croups contribute to correct outline as well as to correct structure and movement. Level croups with accompanying high tail set and high (long) hocks are frequently observed faults. Hocks should be perpendicular to the ground when the dog is standing naturally. Sickle hocks (hocks bent forward from the hock joint like a sickle) do not allow the dog to extend fully when trotting. This is another fault which is appearing all too frequently.

Faults. *Stiff, short steps, with a choppy, jerky movement. Mincing steps, with a hopping up and down, or a* *balancing of weight from side to side (often erroneously admired as a "dancing gait" but permissible in young puppies). Lifting of front feet in hackney-like action, resulting in loss of speed and energy. Pacing gait.*

These last sections are quite specific in their requirements, and actual measurements can be taken for accuracy until one learns to recognize proper body and gait. The desired length of bones and angles of attachment are those which absorb shock best and provide maximum efficiency of gait with endurance. These are not abstract, like structed and should be recognized as such rather than being ignored in a breeding program.

COMPARATIVE VALUE OF FAULTS AND VIRTUES

It is the measure of outstanding virtues, and from a breeding standpoint, the hard to get qualities, that determine a good dog. It is better to have some faults along with great virtues, rather than few faults and mediocrity. The measure of an expert is his ability to see the "good"

SCALE OF POINTS

General Appearance	*Symmetry*	*10*	
	Temperament	*10*	
	Coat	*5*	*25*
Head	*Skull and stop*	*5*	
	Muzzle	*5*	
	Eyes, ears and expression	*10*	*20*
Body	*Neck and back*	*5*	
	Chest, ribs and brisket	*10*	
	Loin, croup, and tail	*5*	*20*
Forequarters	*Shoulder*	*10*	
	Forelegs and feet	*5*	*15*
Hindquarters	*Hip, thigh, and stifle*	*10*	
	Hocks and feet	*5*	*15*
Gait	*Gait—smoothness and lack of waste motion when trotting*	*5*	*5*
	Total		**100**

Disqualifications *Heights below or above the desired range, i.e., 13-16 inches. Brindle color.*

Approved May 12, 1959

expression, and are more a matter of science than of art. Proper structure may seem one of the hardest things to learn, but since it is simply a matter of study, there is no excuse for not learning the basics. The mechanics of gait will be thoroughly examined in chapter 5.

Feet seem insignificant, but a splayed or otherwise weak foot will break down under use. Such feet will also allow snow to build up between the toes and thorns to get between the pads. A neat oval (not round) foot is strong and functionally correct. Pads should be thick to absorb shock and protect the foot. A dog with correct feet and adequate exercise on a hard surface will usually wear the nails down naturally (at least to some degree). If the nails need constant attention the foot may not be properly con-

in a dog and weigh it objectively against the failings. Most novices can learn to fault a dog, and indeed, many breeders never progress beyond this point. It is their loss to never appreciate what some outstanding dogs with one obvious fault have to offer the breed.

There is a limit to the degree of fault which can be tolerated, even in an otherwise good dog, however, so here are a few guidelines for evaluating a dog.

Disqualifications

The most serious faults, and ones which virtually eliminate an animal from further consideration are those which would actually disqualify the dog from competition in the

When the dog is alert the tail is normally lifted, but should not be carried above the back.

show ring. These include oversize, undersize, brindle color, monorchidism or cryptorchidism, a dog which bites, an artificially presented dog (such as a dyed one), or a surgically altered dog. Monorchids or cryptorchids, by the way, are dogs whose testicles fail to descend to the normal position in the scrotum; these conditions disqualify a dog of any breed from the conformation ring. A virtual disqualification, though not a technical one, is the predominantly white Sheltie, or one of an unrecognized color. While such an animal is not barred from the ring, the Standard is worded such that he would usually place last in competition.

None of these conditions except the artificial presentation or the biting dog will restrict a dog from showing in obedience. An incorrectly entered dog may later have his wins disallowed.

Serious Faults

There are a number of faults which qualify as serious, although they do not result in disqualification. These include serious mouth faults (noticeably undershot or overshot bites or several missing teeth), extremely bad movement from one or more of the three angles from which gait is assessed, or severe head faults. A shy dog which won't stand for the judge, or one with any serious temperament fault (see chapter 2) is heavily faulted. Prick or hound ears, or any structural fault carried to extreme, are also considered major.

Minor Faults

To some degree every dog has one or more minor faults such as a short tail, slight gait problem, perhaps a little lack of angulation, or a shallow underjaw. A short neck, minor head faults, a gay tail, shorter coat, or a combination of things of this nature can influence the placement of a dog on any given day under any given judge. A multitude of relatively minor faults can knock a dog from competition, but in a moderate number and to a minor degree they are found on even the best dogs. To make him worthy of promoting, however, a dog must have many good points and a minimum of noticeable faults. Some judges, or for that matter some breeders, will put more emphasis on one point than another, and this varies with individual taste. Placings may vary from day to day, therefore, in identical competition under different judges.

Faults Which Can Be Corrected

The kind of fault which is most important for an exhibitor to recognize are the "correctable" ones. These include ears which are troublesome but not incorrigible, poor condition of coat or weight, a loose gait coming or going which can be improved by roadwork, or the appearance of a heavy head which is caused by excessive coat. Refer to chapters 13, 14, and 15 for practical advice in these areas.

Proper training, grooming, and health care can minimize most minor faults. Learn to recognize a good dog

Gay tails are a problem in some lines. Often accompany a flat croup. Occasionally we see a definite kink near the end of the tailbone. Note tail of dog on the right.

regardless of condition (this isn't always easy) and then condition and present the dog properly. But don't waste your time trying to make over a second rate individual.

When formulating your mental image of the ideal Sheltie, read the Standard over carefully several times. If something is confusing, study and observe until the image becomes clearer. The most important thing to remember is that it is the *whole dog* which you are considering, not just one segment. Balance is paramount and extremes are to be avoided. Your Shelties will have a far more lasting impact if you subscribe to the theory: The ideal Sheltie—a goal stressing MODERATION!

The Standard should be read and reread and committed to memory. Each section should formulate in your mind a mental image of the ideal Sheltie. If something is confusing, study, observe, and ask questions until the image becomes clear. Many successful breeders have related how, during their learning stage, they sat down with a more experienced breeder and went over every Sheltie they could get their hands upon, learning to recognize faults and virtues. You must put your hands on the dog. Skillful grooming and presentation, plus a heavy coat, can cover a multitude of problems. Muster the courage to ask breeders to go over their top winners and producers. You cannot recognize faults until you learn how the correct structure feels. Once you have felt a near-perfect head, shoulder, or body, you will more quickly recognize imperfection.

Most important—remember that it is the *whole dog* which you are considering, not just one segment. *Balance and harmony of all the parts are paramount and extremes are to be avoided.* Your Shelties will have far more lasting impact if you subscribe to the theory that *the ideal Sheltie is a goal stressing moderation.* Then within this framework look for the dog that possesses outstanding virtue in one or more areas. Appreciate the excellent, but imperfect, Shelties for what each can contribute, realizing that perfection is a goal to strive towards...not one we can easily achieve.

Note the lovely parallel planes, correct stop, and equal length of foreface and backskull. Ch. Banchory Strike Me Silver. (Photo by Krook)

Parallel planes. Foreface is longer than backskull and finish of underjaw is lacking, giving a pointy appearance to muzzle.

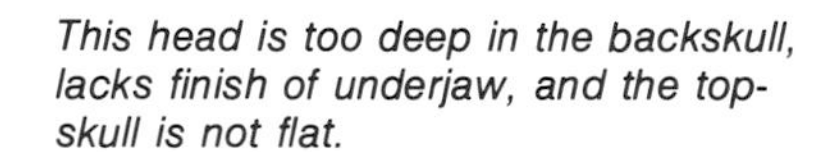

This head is too deep in the backskull, lacks finish of underjaw, and the topskull is not flat.

A "wedge" can be a piece of pie...

Or a blunt wedge—(most correct)...

Or a long, narrow wedge.

Light eye haws visible in this puppy often recede or darken when the dog is more mature. If they do not recede, they detract from the desired expression.

Light eyes on a tricolor are both incorrect and unattractive.

The Sheltie is not a reduced version of the Collie. A five-month Sheltie, front, and a six month old Collie. Note differences in length of head, stop, and body proportion. The Sheltie head should be more moderate, the stop is more definite, and he is proportionately shorter in leg. The head is not as large in relation to the body.

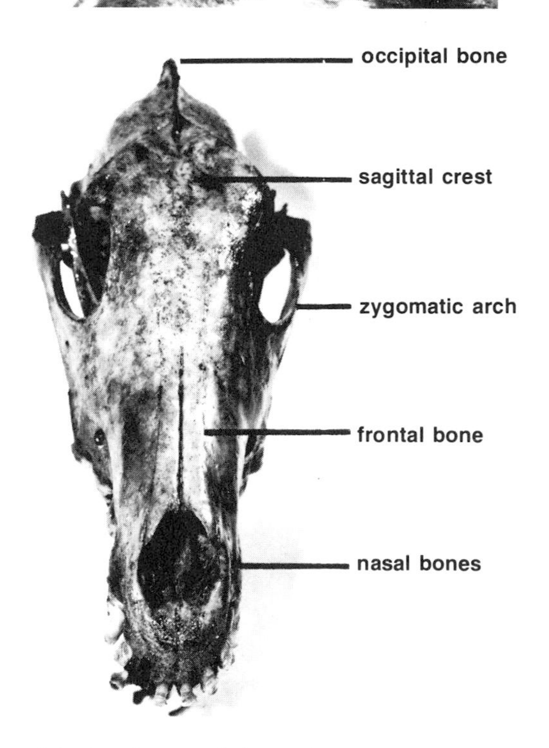

Parts of the head are easily located on this skeleton of the Collie's head. (From **Collie Concept** by Roos)

Note the almond shaped, dark eyes, full rounded muzzle, and soft expression on this young male.

Examine the head from the side. Look for parallel planes, bumps or holes in the topskull, a dish face, or roman nose.

Feel the zygomatic arch (bone under the eye) and the backskull to determine flatness.

To determine length of loin, find the last rib and the point of the hip. The area in between is the loin.

To find the shoulder angle, locate the point of the shoulder and the withers. Then run your hand along the ridge in the shoulder blade.

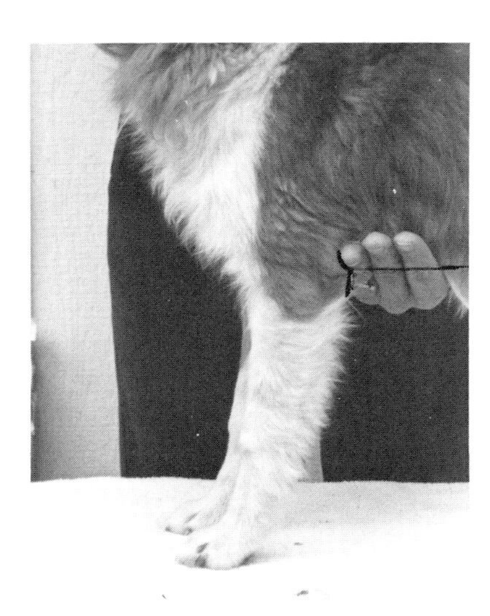

The chest should come to the elbow or below.

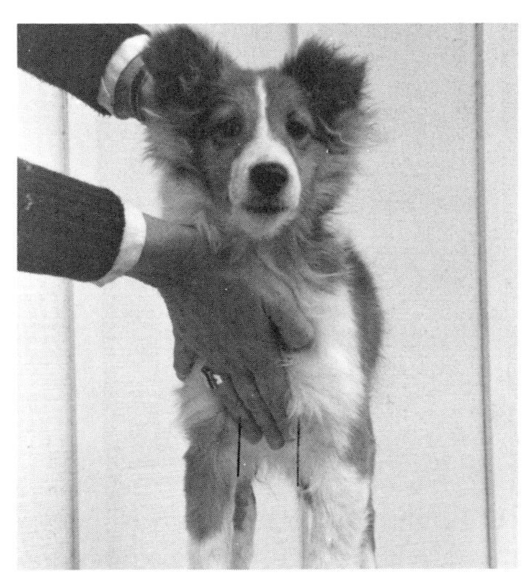

Chest should be broad enough to allow three fingers between forelegs.

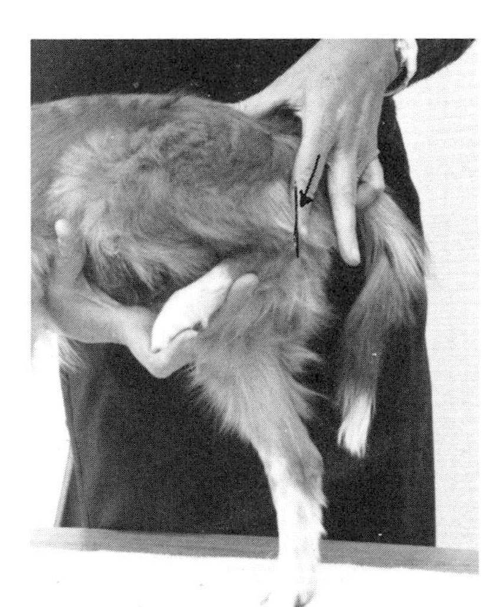

Lift hock straight up. If rear angulation is correct, hock joint will touch ischium.

The pixielike expression, small almond eyes, semi-erect, high-set ears, and full rounded muzzle contribute to what we call a "typey" head. Ch. Rorralore Sportin' Chance C.D., Best in Show winner and sire of champions, owned by Charlotte Clem McGowan. (Photo by Krook.)

The Standard and Type 4

The word "type" is one of the most used, abused, and misunderstood terms in the dog world, yet it is one of the first and most frequently used terms you will hear. Type is a vital element in evaluating a Sheltie, and anyone aspiring to breed, judge, or select a prospect for show or breeding must understand what it is and be able to identify it. Just what is a "typey" Sheltie? Since there are two different schools of thought on what constitutes "type," the answer to that question is a problem that faces every fancier.

Many breeders and judges define "type" simply as *those characteristics which set a breed apart from other breeds and make it distinctive.* In this sense, type in Shelties would be mainly overall appearance, shape of the head, expression, coat, and temperament. A "typey" Sheltie would be one that looks like a Sheltie instead of another breed; one that has a characteristic general outline, with the greatest emphasis given to head and expression. (Actually the Sheltie's most distinctive feature is his temperament, but unfortunately it is virtually impossible to evaluate in the show ring so is given less attention by judges. Breeders, however, should consider it as essential as the other elements of type.)

This definition has the advantage of preserving the undeniably important Sheltie head and expression, and it helps to balance the tendency of some all-breed judges who stress soundness because they lack knowledge of the finer points of the breed. Some major disadvantages are: it does not take soundness (correct structure) or gait into account; it is too easy for its proponents to become merely "head-hunters" who care little for the rest of the dog as long as he makes a pretty picture. For example, a Sheltie may have severe structural faults which are nevertheless hidden by a heavy coat and clever grooming. This leads to the *separation of type and soundness* and to the argument of "which is more important, type or soundness?"

The other main theory of "type" is *"the sum total of the characteristics called for in the breed standard."* This is a much broader definition than the first one and encompasses not only breed-definition traits but also structural traits and gait requirements shared with other breeds as well. Under this definition a typey Sheltie would have the characteristic outline, head, expression, coat, and temperament just as under the first definition, but *in addition, he would have a strong degree of correct structural traits and proper gait as well.* Here the Sheltie is considered as a *whole* dog, and since soundness is included as an element of type, the "type vs. soundness" argument evaporates.

Which of these definitions is correct? There is nothing wrong, per se, with the first. Its danger lies in overlooking soundness and concentrating on *parts* of the Sheltie instead of the whole. If breed-distinguishing characteristics were all that were necessary the standard could retain the paragraphs on general appearance, head, expression, coat, and temperament and throw out the rest as nonessential. Since the standard goes into structural traits at great length, even though they may be applied to other breeds as well, they should be considered a necessary part of a Sheltie who looks like a Sheltie *should.*

This chapter was contributed by breeder-judge Jo Parker.

Furthermore, the Sheltie was developed as a working dog and his structural traits are ones that enable him to do his job well and without undue effort or exhaustion, and thus are the very essence of the dog. So, I would argue strongly that the most accurate definition of type would be the second. A typey Sheltie would be one that shows a preponderance of those characteristics which would be considered correct under the *entire* breed standard.

Anyone planning to breed Shelties should take seriously the second definition. This will help them avoid falling into the trap of over-accenting any one feature at the expense of others. Fads exaggerating the importance of some particular feature come and go in any breed. An *exhibitor* might want to select a dog for showing that has characteristics currently popular, but a *breeder* must have a longer range goal in sight. The breeders who survive the fads and continue to be successful are the ones that stress the whole dog.

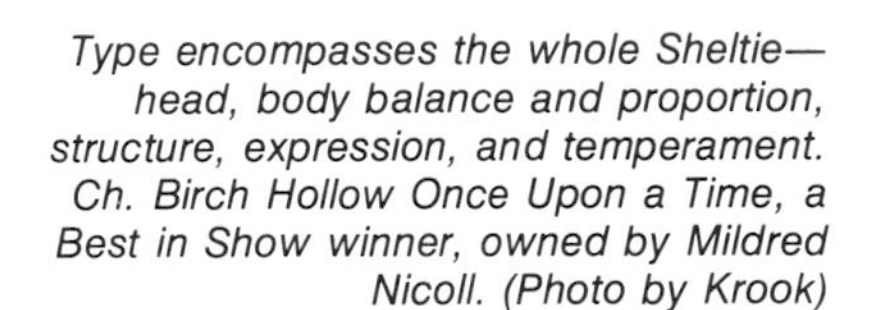

Type encompasses the whole Sheltie—head, body balance and proportion, structure, expression, and temperament. Ch. Birch Hollow Once Upon a Time, a Best in Show winner, owned by Mildred Nicoll. (Photo by Krook)

A sound Sheltie is not always "typey." This bitch has an excellent shoulder, long upper arm that sets legs well under body, matching rear angulation, hock well let down and perpendicular to ground. Neck is arched and sets into shoulders correctly. She lacks the fine detail of head and expression that create a "typey" appearance.

TYPE VS. SOUNDNESS

While it is possible to go into all kinds of dictionary definitions of soundness, the term among dog fanciers usually means correct body structure including bones, skeletal angles, muscles and ligaments, as well as correct gait. Actually, gait itself is not soundness but is a *measure* of soundness. Proper gait is not possible without proper structure, and faults will be revealed in gaiting that might be hidden while the dog is posed.

The argument of type vs. soundness is precipitated by those who use the first definition of type, which in effect breaks the Sheltie down into two separate compartments: traits which are Sheltie only and called "type," and traits which are common to nearly all breeds and are called "soundness." The question must then arise as to which of these compartments is more important. The answer should, of course, be neither. Anyone using the first definition must realize that *both* elements are important in equal proportion as they are two sides of the same coin.

The Sheltie should be seen as a whole dog. Correct body structure then becomes as integral a part of type as is correct head. Both are essential if a Sheltie is to be what the standard says he should be. While no dog is perfect, one that is excellent in head and very faulty in body is just as lacking in type as one that is excellent in body and very faulty in head. The typey Sheltie should be average or better in both head and body traits as well as have a characteristic temperament. The nearer to perfection he is in both head and body, the better the dog.

THE FINE POINTS OF TYPE

What does a typey Sheltie actually look like? Even the pros do not agree! The standard gives a word picture and it is up to us to fill in the flesh and blood. Judging a dog is essentially subjective rather than objective, but any personal opinion must be formed within the framework of the standard.

Some features of the standard are very definite and not open to individual interpretation. These are mainly the paragraphs on body structure; here exact specifications and angles are given. Adherence to them constitutes soundness and a dog either meets these requirements or he does not, although there can be differences in the degree of deviation from perfection. Learning about structure is just a matter of study.

Other requirements are less explicit. How long and wide is "a long blunt wedge?" How big is a "medium sized eye?" How long is a "moderately long body?" The paragraph on expression is especially open to interpretation, yet it is a vital part of type. It is extremely difficult to put into words, but very easy to see if present. Place two dogs side by side. If one has correct expression and the other does not, the correct one is obvious.

The photo used on the ASSA Standard brochure: as an example of Sheltie type and expression. Ch. Windrush O'Pages Hill.

An appealing puppy lacking in type due to round eye, short neck, and straight angulation.

This puppy, about the same age as the male at left, is much more typey. Body is long at this age. Siasconset Montage September Morn. (Photo by Dear)

Good expression gives a sweet, gentle, yet alert look. Hardness, sharpness, apprehension, fearfulness, or even a blankness all fail to show true Sheltie type. One may have to look at many dogs before finding a really wonderful expression, but once seen it is unmistakable and unforgettable

Quite a few of the other non-explicit characteristics are dependent upon balance to bring them into focus. It is very significant that the standard says "no part should appear out of proportion to the whole." Look at as many Shelties as possible and see which ones have that all-of-a-piece look. Here an artistic sense or an "eye for a dog" comes in. You may be born with it, but you can also develop it.

While the failure of the standard to make every feature into an exact blueprint may be confusing to the novice, it has the great advantage of preventing a machine-stamped look. It enables a breeder to exercise his talents as a creative artist, as long as he keeps within the framework of the standard. It allows each Sheltie to have an individualistic appearance.

You must turn the word picture of the standard into a mental picture of your *ideal* dog, for this will be your basis for judging—for comparing dogs against each other or against the standard. This will provide the goal of perfection towards which you will direct your breeding program. To do this, you will have to compare many, many Shelties with the standard and see where each one fits or deviates. Gradually, your mental picture is built and becomes your individual interpretation of type. This explains why judges will place the same dogs differently or why breeders prefer one line over another.

Breeding to type is a work of art, not an exact science. As breeders exercise this art there will be differences in the overall look of the various prominent bloodlines. Even though perfection is the goal, it is never quite reached and you as a breeder will have to decide which virtues must come first, and which faults you can live with and which are intolerable. And so, your line evolves and becomes distinctive.

SUB-TYPES

Another usage of the term "type" refers to differences in individuals or bloodlines and may be defined as a synonym for "sort." It is actually a misuse of the term "type." Thus we hear about Shelties who are "Collie-type," "moderate-type," "old-fashioned-type," "Sea Isle type," "Pocono type." The differences in individuals or bloodlines are actually sub-types, and as long as they are kept within the standard and not carried to extremes they may be acceptable.

As we discussed previously, the Sheltie is derived from several different breeds and throwbacks in type to some of the ancestors still crop up. Sheltie heads originally were much shorter, broader, and coarser than we see today. Breeders worked toward a longer, leaner head more nearly resembling that of the early Collie. This more refined head was often referred to as "Collie-type," while the shorter, broader head was "old-fashioned type."

Today the term "Collie-type" is often a misnomer for the exaggerated, overlong head, usually lacking in fullness of muzzle, faulty in profile, and accompanied by a rangy body. This would actually be considered faulty in a Collie and it is certainly not correct in a Sheltie. "Collie-type" may also refer to a correct head that is truly an ideal Collie in miniature.

The term "old-fashioned" is often used to refer to a shorter head and broader skull, often with good profile and flat topskull, sometimes accompanied by a too deep stop and a too round eye, usually with a stockier, wider ribbed body. Though the term is often used scornfully, this dog may actually be closer to the standard than the so-called Collie-type if the stop, topskull, and eye are correct.

The "moderate-type" is somewhere in between these two and is usually closer to being a balanced, refined dog. However, a tendency to either the longer, leaner head or the shorter, wider head, if *not extreme* and if *kept in balance with the body,* is acceptable. Moderation is not necessarily a guarantee of good type.

A short head does not have to be wide; nor is a long head automatically a lean one. Many people make the mistake of equating any shorter head with old-fashioned type. On the contrary, a shorter head which is also lean and clean can be exquisitely typey when it is in balance

An unacceptable subtype showing Pomeranian characteristics.

with the body. A long head, on the other hand, may be utterly lacking in type if it is broad, bumpy, two-angled, or lacking expression or proper planes. A long, lean head on a short cobby body would be lacking in type and balance as would a short head on a long body, a small head on a large body, or a large head on a small body.

A "Pomeranian type" would be a throwback to long-ago ancestors—domed in skull with a foxy muzzle, small round eye, and a too short body. A "Spaniel type" is likewise a throwback and has his ancestor's round, too-full eye, low ears, and silky coat with a tendency to curl. Both of these are *unacceptable* sub-types.

Some so-called sub-types are accompanied by so many faults that they actually have no type at all. These often occur when a breeder is breeding for certain characteristics at the expense of all others. For example, in the effort to produce a longer, leaner head, the breeder may at the same time produce a dog with a rounded, receding backskull, a long sliding stop ending halfway down the muzzle, and a shallow, short underjaw. Even if correct eyes and ears produce a good expression, this is not a typey head.

Another example—a breeder wants to shorten the body, but in doing so he ends up with a dog that is square instead of being slightly longer than he is tall, who lacks angulation front and rear, and who has a short, thick neck and barrel ribs. The breeder has achieved his objective but lost correct type altogether.

Type can also be lost both through the number of faults present or through the degree of a single fault. A collection of minor faults can be as bad as a single, severe major fault. Either way the dog falls enough short of the standard to be completely lacking in type.

To sum up, a typey Sheltie is well balanced, sturdy yet agile, with a fitted, double coat; he has a smooth, wedge shaped head with good planes; a sweet expression and correct temperament; and a body correct enough to move effortlessly and gracefully. The picture he makes, *standing and in motion,* is pleasing to the eye!

Anyone attending a major specialty show will note the variety of subtypes within the breed. Just a few examples are pictured. Top left, Ch. Knightwood's Wynborne Breeze; top right, Ch. Carmylie Polly Paintbrush. Bottom left, Ch. Macdega The Family Man; bottom right, Ch. Banchory Rebel Blue.

Ch. and O.T.Ch. Merriley's Steely Dan, co-owned by Karen Dickinson and Maryann Morley, is one of the all time great Shelties. Danny finished his American, Canadian, and Mexican C.D.s with scores over 195 which qualified him for Dog World Awards. Twice in Mexico he went High in Trial and Best in Show on the same day. He went on to earn Utility Dog degrees in the U.S., Canada, and Mexico. In the breed ring he won 3 All Breed Best in Shows, 19 group placements, and 64 Best of Breed awards. He has numerous High in Trial awards, both in the U.S. and Mexico, and in 1978 was first in the Gaines Western Regional Obedience Competition. He is the first multiple all-breed Best in Show dog with an O.T.Ch.

The beauty and correctness of Danny's smooth, flowing stride, level topline, and long reach are evident in this photo by Chris Osborn. Also note correct head and tail carriage.

See the Dog Trot 5

SOUNDNESS

"Soundness" is often used to mean a healthy, structurally functional animal, one who has not been injured and who has no defects which would affect his performance. It is also used in referring to solid, correct temperament. Any animal referred to as "sound" should have proper temperament, a healthy body, and functional gait or movement. Many dog people, however, use the term exclusively to describe gait, and it is this area of soundness with which we are concerned here.

Correct gait could be defined as "freedom of movement," and if this rather elusive "something" can be recognized, little else about gait need be known. It describes an action which in our breed is near floating in nature, and it is an important consideration in a working breed because it lessens fatigue and thereby makes the physical chore easier.

ANALYSIS OF GAIT

Gait is determined by both bone structure and musculature. The skeleton presents the framework and prescribes limitations within which muscles must function. Muscles and ligaments determine the efficiency with which a dog moves, but even the best muscling cannot exceed what the skeleton is able to do. A structurally inferior dog (determined by skeleton) will at best be handicapped. On the other hand, a good skeleton with poor muscling will not perform as expected.

Muscles have the advantage of flexibility because they can be conditioned to perform better or worse than they would without conditioning (refer to chapter 9 for instructions on road work).

Ligaments determine tightness of the joints, and tendons control the attachment of each individual muscle to the skeleton. Ideal ligamentation allows the joint to move freely without restriction, while holding it in the position in which it was intended to operate and preventing unnecessary play. Ligamentation is less able to be modified than musculature.

There are usually two kinds of gait variations from the ideal. One type is the dog who is a "dry" or "tight" mover. He usually has no sloppiness to the coming and going motion, but may be *restricted or "cramped" in reach and drive.* This animal is not necessarily true coming and going, but he is not loose in movement. Sometimes the "dry" dog also lacks angulation, compounding the problem. If he does have ample angulation he will usually loosen up and move more freely after he is warmed up. This type of Sheltie shows best immediately after being exercised at a trot.

The other variation is seen in the loose or "spongy" dog who has a beautiful, floating side gait, but *moves sloppily coming and going.* This dog may need continual road work to keep in shape. He must be tuned like a fine athlete so his muscles can compensate for the looser ligaments.

"Nothing reflects more clearly the faults in structure than the gait."

Dorothy Allen Foster, 1945

If one must choose between these two less-than-perfect animals, a slightly loose dog is preferable. With conditioning, this dog may approximate the ideal. As with any fault, it is not so much the nature but the degree which matters.

MECHANICS OF GAIT

All evaluations of gait are made with the dog at a trot since this is his most natural and efficient speed. An individual moving correctly at a trot invariably moves well at the other gaits. Gait is assessed from three angles—rear (dog going away from the viewer), front (dog approaching head-on), and side.

Balanced side gait is the most difficult aspect for a beginner to recognize, but to the practiced eye, it becomes the most obvious component of a properly moving Sheltie. For maximum efficiency in side gait, every structural part must be correct from the ears back. Angulation especially determines the length of reach and drive. This establishes how tireless the Sheltie will be; it ranks him as an efficient working dog instead of a prancing toy and assures his ability to keep up in any physical endeavor. When the angulation of both shoulder and pelvis are approximately the same, the dog's gait as viewed from the side will be "balanced." When the angles of shoulder blade and pelvis differ greatly, movement will be out of balance and corresponding gait faults will be observed.

Recognizing proper front action can take time to learn. Rear movement, the easiest to evaluate, is probably of least importance in determining efficient movement over all. A Sheltie with poor angulation can still move well front and rear because straightness of the legs is the only consideration there. Good legs are highly desirable but by themselves they are not sufficient to make a sound Sheltie.

REAR OR "GOING AWAY"

The primary function of the dog's rear legs is to produce the drive which propels the body forward. However, the Standard also calls for the stance to be square and the gait true going away. A dog whose stance is less than perfect but who moves well is a superior individual to one who stands correctly and cannot move properly. Stance can always be trained or stacked, but movement is proof of structure.

To determine how well a dog is tracking in rear, draw an imaginary line down the back of each hind leg from hip to hock to foot. When the dog is standing these lines should be straight, vertical and parallel to each other. A deviation at the hock or foot, either in or out, indicates a weakness. When the animal is moving, these lines should remain straight but come together in a "V" shape as speed increases. The inside edges of the feet converge on a center line, thus the term "singletrack" describing correct gait in a Sheltie.

Rear Faults

Hocking out. The hocks turn out as the dog moves. Sometimes accompanied by a rolling motion at the hock joint which may occur in one or both hocks. Probably the most serious of the rear faults because it puts terrific stress on the ligaments and is likely to restrict drive of the hindquarters.

Cow Hocks. The other extreme is also to be avoided. This term is used when the hocks turn in and the feet turn out. If the legs are straight at the hocks but the feet turn outward the dog is said to "toe out." True cow hocks exhibit both problems. A "close parallel rear" is one which in motion is parallel from hock to foot with an angle at the hock. This condition is often accompanied by a narrow pelvis.

Correct singletrack viewed from the rear.
Ch. Knightwood's Wynborne Breeze, a top-winning, beautifully moving bitch belonging to Nancy Lee Marshall. Note how the legs converge toward a center line as she trots. (Callea photo.)

Toeing out. To a lesser degree than cow hocks, toeing out and close rears are undesirable. In both cases the efficiency of gait is not badly restricted. Toeing out sometimes affects stance only, whereas a close parallel rear is obvious in motion. This fault usually accompanies a narrow pelvis.

Crossing over. The feet overstep the center line, actually crossing when gaiting, and the entire rear of the dog usually bounces from side to side as the center of gravity is shifted with each step. This fault is move obvious with increased speed.

The wide parallel rear. A Sheltie with this fault often (though not necessarily) stands perfectly; in fact, he is often touted as not being able to stand wrong. He is built like a table with unyielding vertical legs which remain the same distance apart at the feet in a swift trot as when standing. Wide parallel movement is more obvious at a slow gait because the fast trot will force the legs closer for balance.

This fault is quite common. It is even admired by some breeders and judges as well as by beginners who do not bother to learn proper structure for a Sheltie. A dog moving wide in rear lacks agility to turn by not being able to pivot readily from the center line. Occasionally a wide mover, particularly one who is wide both front and rear, develops a characteristic "roll" from throwing the weight from side to side. He varies from the individual who hocks out in that the hocks remain in line and appear strong. Wide rears rarely affect side gait.

Hocking out.

Toeing out.

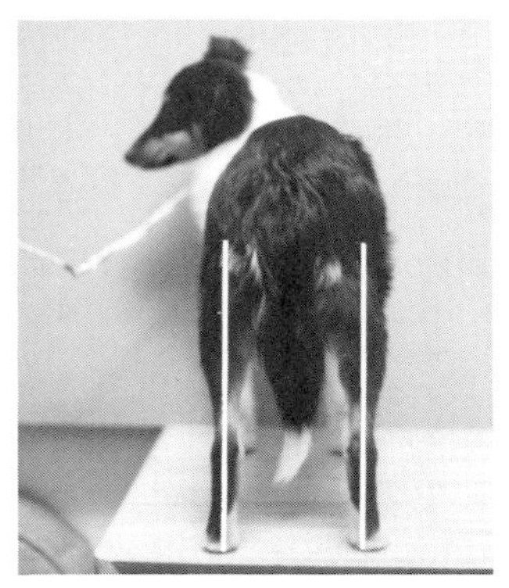

Correct rear stance.

Crossing over and crabbing.

Wide parallel rear.

Left, cowhocks; right, close parallel rear and toeing out slightly.

FRONT OR "COMING" GAIT

Shelties should also single-track in front at a brisk trot. The legs should be in straight parallel lines from elbows to pasterns to feet when the dog stands.

Correct front action is partially dependent on correct rib spring. Proper ribs are rounded at the top half to allow plenty of room for heart and lungs, but flattened on the bottom half to allow unrestricted swing of the front leg backward along the side of the dog. If the sides are too rounded (barrel-ribbed) or too flat (slab-sided) the plane in which the elbow moves is distorted and some of the efficiency in gait destroyed. Barrel-ribs often lack depth and cause the elbows to swing out to go around the interference. A slab-sided individual lacks substance and appears frail. Although a normal condition in a young dog, slab-sidedness usually causes faulty front action because of inadequate support for the front.

Correct singletrack from the front. "Breeze," (Callea photo.)

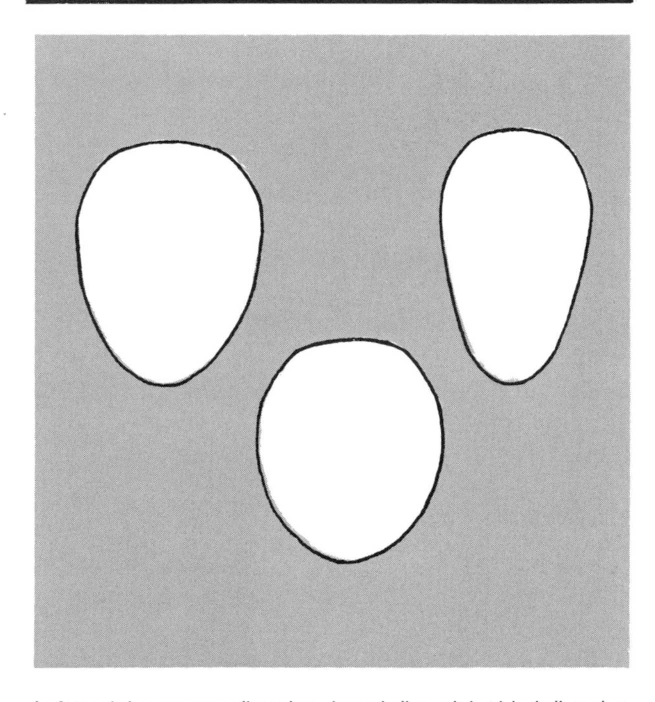

Left to right: correct ribspring, barrel ribs, slab-sided ribspring.

Front Faults

Poor fronts have been a problem in all breeds and particularly so in Shelties. Once lost from a bloodline, correct front structure is difficult to regain, but once obtained it can be reproduced consistently with a little effort. Unfortunately, straight shoulders and short upper arms seem to be increasing rather than decreasing in frequency, while crooked legs and gross movement faults have improved in recent years. Breeders need to be aware of these trends and seek to hold those improvements gained while concentrating on breeding out any new problems.

Crooked front legs. Somewhat comparable to cowhocks in the rear. The legs bow outward, come inward at the pasterns and then out again at the foot. A dog with a crooked front may move well, but he often has other front faults which complicate the issue. Carried to extreme, this fault is known as a "fiddle front."

Out at elbows. Related to hocking out. The elbows come out from the body rather than moving smoothly backward when the dog moves. This can be caused by excess weight on the dog, but is often a result of barrel ribs. Elbowing out is often found in conjunction with crooked legs, toeing in, short upper arm, or loose ligamentation.

Crooked front.

Out at elbows.

Paddling. Throwing the *leg* in an outward circle from the elbow as the dog moves. A dog who paddles usually tracks wide.

Winging. Often erroneously called "paddling." While both faults involve throwing the feet outward, winging originates at the *pastern* rather than the elbow. Winging is more frequently seen than true paddling.

Crossing over. The same as crossing in the rear. The feet pass beyond the center line and the center of gravity shifts causing a choppy, bouncing appearance. Crossing in front is usually due to a narrow chest.

A wide front. Does not move in a single track. The dog usually stands nicely, but the legs remain vertical and parallel when in motion. A condition similar to the wide parallel rear.

A narrow or "tied-in" front. A narrow chested dog that is too close or pinched at the elbows. The legs may or may not be straight, but they lack adequate support from the ribcage and chest. As a result, the front exhibits an egg beater motion or is thrown randomly from side to side. This type of front in a young dog may improve as the chest broadens with maturity. The feet often point outward.

Wide front.

Narrow or tied-in front.

Paddling.

Winging.

Crossing in front.

SIDE GAIT

Observation of side gait shows whether a dog is properly constructed. Correct side gait depends on proper structure, musculature, and ligamentation. Perhaps the most important element in side gait is balance, allowing for correct timing and agility. As a herding dog, the Sheltie must be able to cover ground with maximum speed and agility with the least possible effort. Since every wasted motion causes him to tire sooner, efficiency is a premium.

Correct trot with opposing diagonals moving in unison.

Balanced side gait lacking extension due to straight angulation.

Extension of the foreleg is limited by shoulder angulation. Note how at full extension the toe can extend no further than the line formed by the angle of the shoulder blade when the dog is standing.

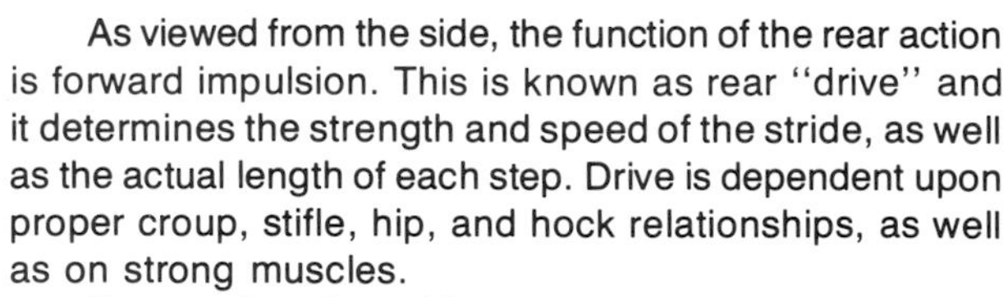

As viewed from the side, the function of the rear action is forward impulsion. This is known as rear "drive" and it determines the strength and speed of the stride, as well as the actual length of each step. Drive is dependent upon proper croup, stifle, hip, and hock relationships, as well as on strong muscles.

Front action viewed from the side is commonly referred to as "reach." The front must be able to keep up with the rear and move simultaneously with it to avoid interference with the stride. The skeletal part of the front assembly includes the shoulder lay-back, upper arm, leg, and pastern. Since the front assembly controls changes in direction and speed, it must be supple and move freely.

The Trot

At the trot a Sheltie should exhibit a two-beat gait with the right front and left hind legs moving together and the left front and right hind legs moving together. When fully extended the legs on the opposite side come together in a "V" with the hind foot leaving a print almost touching the mark left by the front foot on the same side. A dog of normal proportions moving at a very fast trot may overstep the front foot with the hind one. The trotting dog has two feet on the ground at a time (opposing diagonals) and must rely on his speed for balance.

The back should remain strong and level with little up and down or rolling motion. Imagine a glass of water resting on the back without a drop spilling as the dog moves.

The mechanics of the balanced trot are determined to a great extent by proper angulation. *Having the same angle at shoulder and stifle is most important.* Even if both are faulty (too straight) the rhythm of the gait is maintained, although with shorter and less efficient stride. A poorly angulated dog will require more steps to cover the same distance as a well-angulated one, and the effect will not be as smooth and effortless. The better the angulation at both ends of the dog, the better reach and drive he will have and the more efficiently he will move.

At his maximum reach in an extended trot, the Sheltie's front leg ideally extends as far forward as possible without undue upward swing. *The feet should just clear the ground.* The rear diagonal should also be at full forward thrust and for a split second all four feet should be off the ground. It is imperative that these two diagonal feet strike the ground simultaneously or rhythm, balance, and efficiency are destroyed. As the other pair of diagonals come forward, the hind leg swings backward creating drive for the forward propulsion of the dog.

As the leg passes the vertical on its way back, it begins the portion of the stride known as "follow-through." The hind leg should remain parallel to the opposite front leg and continue backward to maximum extension. The foot remains close to the ground with no wasted vertical motion. If the foot travels upward instead of back for the complete stride, the fault is known as a "kick-up." This is a deterrent to maximum drive because the foot leaves the ground too soon.

A dog with good angulation at one end and poor at the other will be unable to maintain proper timing. He must compensate in some way for the uncomfortable stress on his weak part, and will probably develop any of a number of gait deviations.

Faults of Side Gait

The *least severe* side fault is one in which the dog is *balanced but poorly angulated* and must take more steps to keep up. In this fault timing and cadence are still correct. More severe side faults are usually due to incorrect skeletal proportions. The cause of these faults can vary from unbalanced angulation to disproportionate length of individual bones.

A dog who has good rear angulation but inadequate shoulder lay-back is all too common a sight in many breeds, including Shelties. Although a dog with this fault may have good drive, the front cannot keep up. The dog loses cadence in his trot and throws his front feet in an attempt to keep them out of the way of the hind feet. Usual-

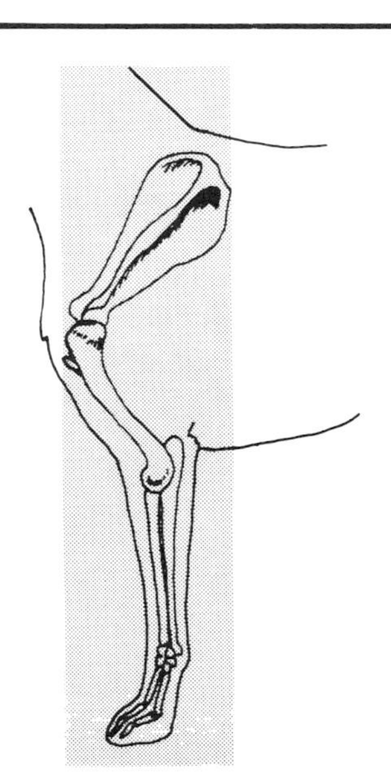

Correct angulation provides a deep brisket and heart area, and wide area for muscle attachment. Legs sit well back under the body.

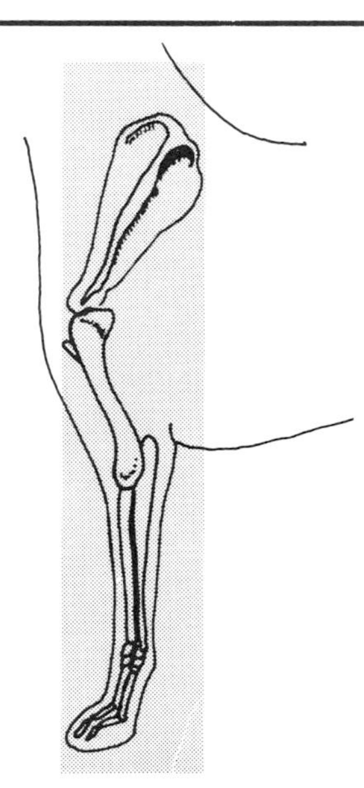

Straight shoulders provide less space for muscle attachment; less room for the heart. Legs fall too far forward, almost below ears.

Kicking up in rear.

Faulty side gait caused by straight shoulders.

Dwelling, sometimes called pounding.

Running downhill due to straight stifle.

ly the front feet are lifted too high in a jerky motion. In a severe case the hind feet strike the front legs and the dog looks as if he's trying to kick his chin; or, he may carry his rear along with very little drive. The shoulder is fairly rigid and lacks flexibility. Some individuals take short picky steps and lift the rear feet very high in order to expend the extra drive. In any case, the back bounces rather than remaining level when the animal is in motion.

When the synchronization of gait is disturbed, a dog may exhibit *"pounding"* or *"dwelling."* The front foot reaches full extension, hesitates in mid-air, then crashes through. His hind foot never reaches the print of the front one. Since the stride is shorter, power of the drive is severely reduced. Again timing is thrown off and efficiency is below par.

Hocks set too high. Often (but not always) accompanies straight stifles. When both faults appear, the dog is usually high in rear. The hind leg lacks flexibility and the stride is shortened. Kick-up occurs sometimes and is quite noticeable in a dog with high hocks.

Sickle Hocks. The sickle hock is shaped like a reaper's sickle. The hock bone actually curves forward

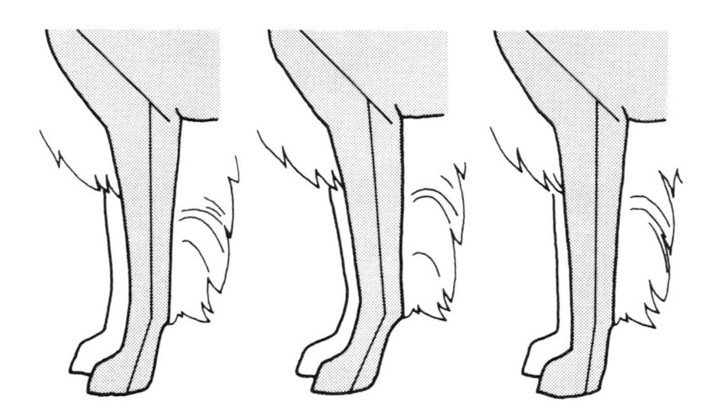

Left to right: correct, weak, and short pasterns.

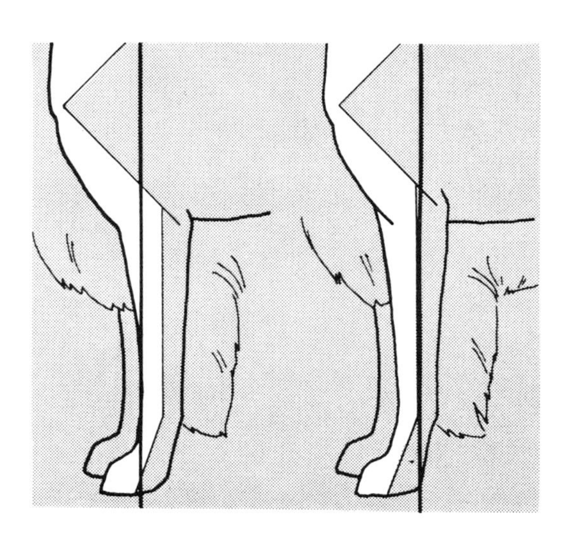

Left, correct upper arm; right, short upper arm.

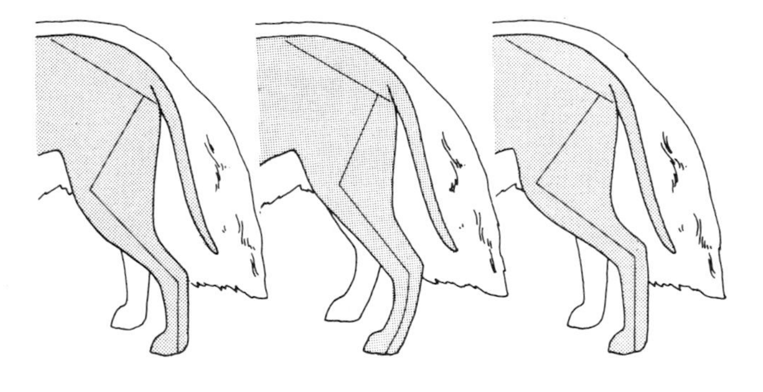

Left to right: correct hock; sickle hock; high hock.

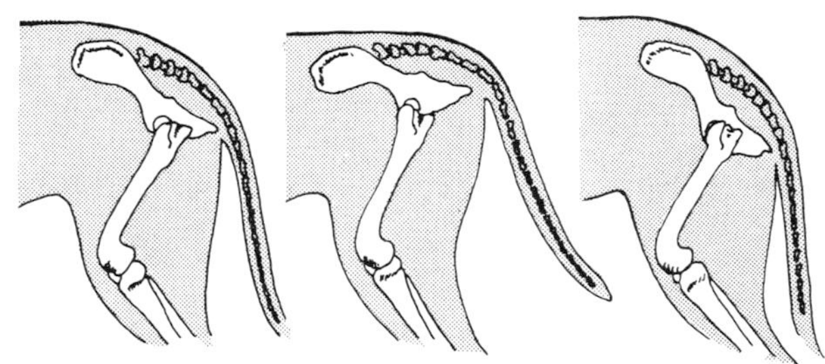

Left to right: correct, flat, and steep croup.

down after the hind leg has begun the next stride. This is extremely hard on the entire front assembly. It may be difficult to detect at first; watch for the diagonals moving together to indicate correct gait.

Likewise, *a dog better in shoulder than in stifle angulation* has problems. Probably he will appear to be running downhill even on the level because his rear remains higher than his withers as he moves. A dog straight in rear angulation usually has a kick-up or at least inadequate follow-

bringing the foot too far under the dog and making it impossible for the dog to stand naturally with the hock bone perpendicular to the ground. Rear drive and follow through is virtually impossible, and a stiff, stilted rear action results. Kick-up always occurs with sickle hocks. This fault is becoming very prevalent in Shelties.

Short upper arm. The upper arm should be equal in length to the shoulder blade. Regardless of angulation, a short upper arm throws the gait off. A hackney or prancing action, with the front feet lifted high, is often indicative of a short upper arm. Less common is the proportionally short stifle. This results in a choppy rear action, again lacking in follow-through.

Steep or Flat Croup. Flat croups are appearing with epidemic frequency in the breed, and while at first consideration the effect may seem mostly visual, the fault also creates gait abnormalities. The slope of the croup affects rear drive, rear extension, and tail carriage. The correct croup slopes down at about a 30 degree angle from the horizontal line of the backbone. This places the back legs correctly for balance and freedom of movement.

When the croup is flat, rear extension is limited. The dog may have drive, but he will lack agility in turning and maneuvering because his hindquarters are not under his body.

When the croup is too steep you will see the tail sticking up instead of blending into a smooth line from loin to rump. Rear drive is restricted because the legs are pulled too far under the body.

Incorrect pastern. The pastern is designed to absorb shock from the forequarters. It needs to be moderate in length and slope to perform its function efficiently. Too much slope results in a loose, extremely weak wrist. More frequently seen is the too-straight pastern similar to the pastern of a terrier. A steep pastern is usually short, and often occurs in conjunction with a straight shoulder. Either condition is restrictive and jarring puts strain on the entire front assembly. Under hard work this type of front will become sore and break down.

Pacing. Similar to trotting, except the legs on the same side, instead of the diagonals, move in unison. Sometimes a dog will pace quite rapidly. Unless the handler is aware of the difference in gait a dog may be allowed to remain in a pace in the show ring. Since structural analysis cannot be made from a pace, an individual who fails to trot readily will not be considered in a conformation class. A quick jerk to speed up the dog will usually put him into a trot.

Crabbing. The lack of alignment of the body in motion; the dog moves somewhat sideways with the rear tracking to left or right of the front. This last consideration of gait is more easily seen coming or going. In some instances crabbing is a way to avoid striking the front legs by the hind feet; the result of too short a body. The same effect can be caused by more angulation in rear than in front, or by showing a dog on an extremely taut/lead.

Anything which interferes with the desired smooth floating trot is faulty. The above are examples, but they do not cover every possibility for faults. The complex interrelationship between parts of the body can be easily disturbed, so care to breed only individuals who are correct in structure must be exercised.

Pacing. Note legs on same side moving together.

Crabbing. Note how the tight lead causes the dog to cross over and lift his foreleg too high.

Pawprints of opposing diagonals at a trot illustrate how the feet converge to touch a center line.

Who can resist the winsome appeal of a seven-week-old? Knightwood Country Girl, owned by Nancy Lee Marshall.

The Question of Size 6

Since 1952 the American Shetland Sheepdog Club has asked for a show Sheltie between 13 and 16 inches at the shoulder. Still, size is one of the most tenacious problems plaguing the breeder today, with both oversize and undersize Shelties appearing, sometimes in the same litter.

Why is size so difficult to control? There are many reasons. The Sheltie is still a young breed with many kinds of dogs in its background. Often the oversize animals strongly resemble their Collie ancestors, while the undersize ones may exhibit Pomeranian characteristics such as pinchy muzzles or domed skulls.

The English standard sets an "ideal" size of 14 inches for bitches and 14½ inches for males, thus giving breeders something very specific to work toward. Breeders in the United States have three inches to work with and, therefore, they tend to be less selective. If they do show a preference it is toward the heavier, taller, more impressive dog at the top of the standard because he stands out more in the show ring. While it is possible to produce excellent quality 14-inch bitches and 14½- or 15-inch males, American breeders seem to have little incentive to do so, and thus size continues to push and exceed the limit.

PRACTICAL ASPECTS OF BREEDING TO SIZE

It is impossible to breed 16-inch dogs and get all puppies within size, whether you breed two 16-inch dogs or a 16-inch one to a 14-inch one. It is a fact that the genes for size do not combine so that, for instance, a 16-inch Sheltie bred to a 14-inch would produce 15-inch puppies. Instead, the puppies will either inherit the genes for smallness or the genes for largeness. Some puppies in the litter will inherit genes for a size between the two parents—a throwback to some ancestor in the pedigree. Apparently size genes are recessive, probably linked with structural factors. Since breeders used Shelties ranging from 12 to 18 inches or more in the formation of the breed, these recessive genes are still carried in our dogs.

How Can You Breed for Moderate Size?

Can you possibly mate your dog with the hope of getting all insize puppies? There's no pat answer. Your only aids are common sense, a thorough knowledge of the genetic background of your Sheltie, and luck! Naturally, two medium size dogs, 14 to 15 inches at the shoulder, with a majority of medium size dogs in their pedigrees, will have the best chance of producing correct size puppies.

If your bitch is large (bordering on 16 inches) or tiny (just over 13 inches) don't choose the opposite extreme as her mate. Instead, pick the mid-size dog with a *majority of mid-size ancestors;* and if possible, make sure he is one known for producing medium size in a large percentage of his offspring.

There are some Shelties who predominantly control size. If you have one of these consider yourself lucky!

There are also those Shelties which beget predominantly large or predominantly very small puppies. A stud dog who is known to control size can be very valuable, and is, of course, the perfect choice for the bitch who is herself close to 16 inches or who tends to have large puppies. Likewise, the bitch who controls size is the perfect mate for one of the typey, larger males. Carefully planned, such breedings can help bring the more elegant type of Sheltie, seen most often in the larger animal, down to a more reasonable size.

How Do You Know If a Dog or Bitch Controls Size?

Only by trial breedings. If a bitch has been bred to two males between 15½ and 16 inches, and both males have a record of producing large or oversize puppies, yet this particular bitch raises litters of 15-inch Shelties, she is probably dominant for smaller size. If a male, bred to many bitches of different lines and sizes, produces almost all insize puppies even though some of the bitches have a record of producing big offspring, he should be considered dominant for correct size. In my experience, dogs that control size are themselves on the small side, with one or both parents small and also known for controlling size.

However, don't assume that just because a dog is small he or she will control size. You will only know after several litters. The genotype may be entirely opposite of the phenotype. In my own kennel I have a 13½-inch bitch who consistently controls size, a 14-inch bitch who has produced a high percentage of oversize pups, and a 15½-inch bitch who has yet to produce a puppy over 15 inches tall.

When Is a Sheltie Too Large or Too Small to Breed?

Generally speaking, when it is over or under the limitation of the Standard. However, in actual practice there are many other considerations. In my own breeding program I eliminate those dogs or bitches that produce too high a percentage of oversize or undersize puppies. They simply aren't worth the effort. Some small Shelties will produce puppies even smaller than themselves, thus under the Standard. Other small ones produce correct size but the strain of producing a litter may be very hard on them. The pelvis may be so small that whelping is difficult, if not impossible.

The most taxing problem is created by the oversize dog. Many Shelties barely over 16 inches are glamorous, typey dogs that, except for size, are an asset to the breed. This type of Sheltie was used extensively to set type in the breed's early years. Many foundation dogs in all the popular lines were at or over the 16-inch limit. One-quarter-inch seems so minute but can cause many problems down the line.

Occasionally, however, breeders still use an especially exquisite oversize Sheltie, but they would be the first to admit that once size is introduced back into a line it is very difficult to breed out. The only justifiable reason—if indeed there is *any* justifiable reason—for using an over or undersize Sheltie is because he has extremely desirable, extremely hard-to-get qualities that are impossible to find in a suitable insize dog. Even then, such breedings should be made only by experienced breeders who will carefully eliminate all outsize dogs from being bred.

HOW TO MEASURE

In working with any breed with size limitations, it is essential to obtain precise measurements. This requires some knowledge of breed structure.

Height is determined by distance from the point of the withers (or shoulder blade) to the ground, with the dog standing squarely. The legs should parallel the line of measure with the front feet in front of, not in line with, a vertical line dropping from the point of the withers. First you must find the point of the withers and part the hair so that excess hair doesn't raise the measurement. Stand the dog squarely in a relaxed, natural position, with his head held naturally, not pulled up or ducked.

Measurements will vary according to how the dog is standing, if he is tense, frightened, or relaxed, and how much weight and coat he is carrying. Any dog between 15½ and 16-inches should be trained to stand for measuring, and should not be allowed to become overweight. A small area of hair may be thinned or removed over the point of the shoulder where the wicket rests. When showing, try not to position a large dog too close to a small Sheltie, nor a 14½-inch male between two large dogs.

Measuring at Shows

More and more, judges are being encouraged to use the wicket to determine whether a dog being exhibited is oversize. The AKC rule book states that "In those breeds where certain heights are specified in the standard as disqualifications,... the judge shall have the authority to make a determination as to whether any dog measures within the specified limits provided such a determination has not been made previously during the competition at the show."

Furthermore, a *competing exhibitor or handler then in the ring* may request a measurement prior to the time the judge has marked his book and the judge must comply with the request provided a measurement has not been made previously during the competition.

The rules further state that:

> "If the judge finds that the dog's height is in accord with the breed standard or the conditions of the class, he shall mark his judge's book "Measured in."
>
> If the judge finds that the dog's height is not in accord with the breed standard, he shall disqualify the dog, marking his judge's book "Measured out - disqualified." A dog that has thus been

disqualified by three different judges may not again be shown."

As of October 1, 1974, AKC rules state that at shows dogs will be measured only during judging. The judge will make the height determination while the dog is correctly stacked by the handler. The judge will determine *only* whether the dog is *insize*, not his actual height in inches, by the use of a wicket. This device looks much like an oversize croquet wicket. If the dog is 16 inches or less, the 16-inch wicket will touch the floor. If the legs of the wicket do not touch the floor the dog is oversize.

Size variations can be extreme. Top left: young littermates. Center: father and daughter. Bottom: half-grown littermates.

Stand the Sheltie squarely and position the crossbar of the measuring standard directly over the high point of the withers.

A wicket can also be used to check minimum height. If the 13-inch wicket does not touch the floor, the Sheltie is within the lower size limit, or over 13 inches.

Use of the wicket is fast and simple. After the handler has positioned the dog and parted the hair, the judge will place his hand on the dog's shoulders to determine the high point. When he has found this point the judge brings the wicket up quickly from behind the dog, over the dog's back, and lowers it so the crosspiece is directly over the point of the shoulder.

If a measurement is called on your dog, remain calm. *You* have the right to pick where the dog will be measured—on the floor or on a table. The best spot is a bare, level floor with no matting. If a dog is being shown on grass request a measurement on a cement walk, or on a board or table. Set the dog carefully and allow him to relax. Part the hair over the point of the shoulder and separate it down to the skin.

Remember that the judge cannot take the dog from you to measure. You should hold the dog's head in a natural position. The judge may request that you readjust the position of the legs and he may touch the withers while bringing the wicket forward. You have the right to request that another person handle the dog for the measurement, or to request the presence of the AKC representative at ringside. *You* give the okay for the wicket to be placed. Don't allow the judge to rush you.

The judge must use a wicket that meets AKC requirements, and the only requirement is that the wicket *touch* the floor. If an adjustable wicket is used, you may challenge its height after the measurement. Some wickets have been found to vary as much as one-fourth inch.

If the dog will not stand for measurement, the judge may excuse it for temperament.

OTHER METHODS OF MEASURING

The measuring device used by most breeders is a guillotine-like device known as a measuring "standard." Depending on the size standard you buy, it will measure anything from a six-inch puppy to a Saint Bernard. The one used by most Sheltie owners goes from about eight to 17 inches.

The Sheltie isn't particularly fond of this device and usually needs a little training and encouragement before he will walk under it and stand squarely. Once he is standing squarely between the uprights, the bar is lowered over the point of the withers and a setscrew tightened to hold the bar in place. The measurement can then be read with the standard in place or lifted off the dog.

Variation in the way the dog holds his head, places his feet, or moves his neck can cause measurements with a standard to vary as much as an inch. If measurements are critical it is best to take several in a row and average them.

Lacking a measuring standard, you can construct a makeshift device with a yardstick and a small carpenter's square. Position the square so one side is flat against the yardstick and secure it with a piece of wire so that it will move up and down without coming apart. When the puppy is standing squarely, place the yardstick in a line with his shoulder. Take the reading from the underside of the arm of the square. While not completely accurate, this method will suffice for checking a puppy's growth rate or getting a general idea of the height of a Sheltie.

Another method used by some people is to stand the dog next to any vertical surface, such as a wall. Lay a bar across the dog's shoulder blade, keeping it as level as possible, and make a mark on the wall where the underside of the bar falls. Measure to this point.

PREDICTING SIZE

Puppies do not grow at the same rate. Some will spurt at three to four months; some are large at eight weeks but grow slowly after that and are within size by 12 weeks; others keep growing at a slow but steady rate until they are a year of age or over. The runt at birth may end up being the tallest, and the fat, big boned puppy may suddenly "go off" and become fine boned and small at three months. Such are the woes of a Sheltie breeder!

Breeders have developed several guidelines which are helpful in predicting the adult size of a Shelitie. Again, some puppies grow fast early while others spurt at a much later age, but if the puppy is consistently under the charts through his first four or six months he will probably stay insize. If he is over at an early age and drops under by three or four months, he will also usually stay in. The ones to worry about are the puppies that stay right on the top measurements through the first four or six months, and the puppies who suddenly spurt over the charts in their third or fourth months. The final height of these Shelties will simply depend on the age at which they stop growing. Usually this is about eight months, but some lines grow until over a year.

One theory says that if you measure the length of the leg from elbow to floor when a puppy is three months old and double that measure, you will arrive at adult height. The following growth is more dependable.

GROWTH GUIDELINES FROM OTHER BREEDERS

Barwood

6 wks.....8″ risky
7 wks....8″ ideal
3 mos....11½″ maximum

Major culling at 3 mos. Any pup with huge head, huge feet, lots of bone, will probably go over. Pups that are 12″ at 3 mos. but medium bone, very balanced, and shorter on leg may stay in size.

Males that are over 15¼″ at 6 mos. are in danger of going oversize. Ideal is 14¼ - 14½″.

From the 1981-82 *ASSA Handbook.*

September

In evaluating puppies, we consider head size, bone density and actual body weight, as well as measurements. Most of our Shelties reach their full height by seven to eight months of age. They tend to appear very immature at this age, however, and generally complete their full mature appearance at approximately two years of age. Our best puppies stay in balance through the entire growth period.

	IDEAL	MAXIMUM
6 weeks	7"-7½"	7¾"
7 weeks	7½"-8"	8¼"
8 weeks	8½"-8¾"	9"
9 weeks	9"-9½"	9¾"
10 weeks	9½"-10"	10½"
3 mos.	10½"-11"	11¾"
4 mos.	12"-12½"	13¼"
5 mos.	13¼"-14"	14¼"
6 mos.	13½"-14¼"	15"

Sea Isle

6 wks...7¾"
7 wks...8¼"
2 mos...9"
10 wks...9½-10"
3 mos...11½"
4 mos...13"
5 mos...14"
6 mos...14¾"

Macdega

10″ top limit at 10 wks. most accurate indicator. Males usually finish growing at 8 mos., bitches earlier. Consider head size, knuckles, and basic body proportions.

Rorralore

Ultimate guide is not to exceed 10″ at 10 wks. Also, watch for rapid growth between four and five months. If a puppy is shooting up at this age it probably will not stay in size; if it is slowing down it probably will stay in.

SHELTIE GROWTH CHART

This chart, adapted by Phyllis Holst from tables kept by Evelyn Davis (Sea Isle) and Jo Parker (Parcana) shows maximum height for puppies expected to mature under 16 inches. You may want to copy it and chart the growth rate of your own litters.

There is no chart available showing growth rate on small Shelties that can be expected to mature in size. With either over or undersize, a great deal depends upon the age at which the puppy stops growing. For some this is as early as six months, while others continue to grow up to eighteen months. The most reliable indication that growth will continue are big knuckles at the pastern joint.

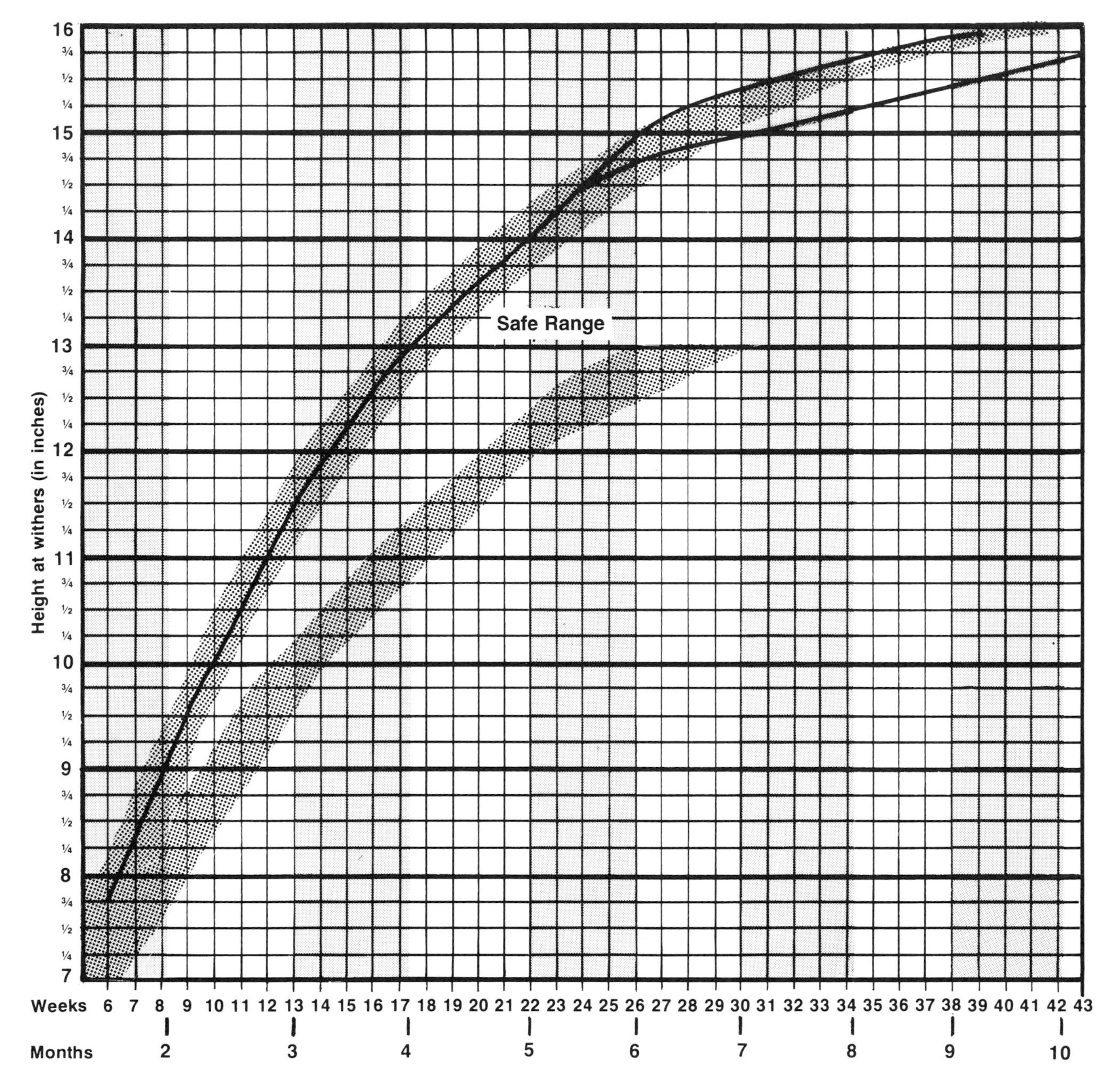

Screened area shows Nobel growth chart for top and bottom sizes imposed over Sea Isle chart.

Note - Both Parker and Davis list 9½ inches at 10 weeks.

Oh, really! Siasconset The Garden Party, left, and Siasconset Secret Gardens, four month old litter sisters by Ch. Northcountry Westering Son. Owner, Wendy Louring. (Photo by Krook)

Those Darn Ears 7

The correct Sheltie ear is beautiful. It contributes to a soft, intelligent expression and gives an alert look to the entire dog. It is set high, opening forward, semi-erect. The top third of the leather breaks forward with no inclination to turn to the sides. The ear itself is small in relation to the head; the leather strong, yet flexible, and of medium thickness.

Shelties have one of the more functional types of ears in dogdom. The semi-erect ear is useful as well as being aesthetically pleasing. The erect base of the ear works as a scope to trap sounds, providing very acute hearing. The set of the ear allows for mobility, and again, the ability to catch more sound waves. The forward break causes rain to run off, protecting the delicate inner ear without the necessity of pinning the ear (which handicaps the hearing).

Because ears are extremely noticeable on a Sheltie, any deviation from the ideal is readily detected even by an untrained eye, and therefore specifications for proper ears are more exacting than in many breeds. This is unfortunate because it puts disproportionate emphasis on the ear.

Ears must be kept in proper perspective. All other things being equal, in show competition a dog with correct natural ears ought not lose to a dog whose ears have been "manufactured" to more than natural perfection. Ears should *not* touch on top of the head and should *not* appear as if they've been cast from concrete. This is a current fad encouraged by a few breeders and judges who place unrealistic emphasis on earset and showmanship.

The ear which never needs to be corrected is convenient; and more important, it is correct in a breeding dog. For decades the original working dogs exhibited a fair percentage of individuals with natural semi-erect ears. Can we not expect at least as much from our show dogs who have become so much more standardized in other respects?

HEREDITY VS. ARTIFICIAL CORRECTION

Unfortunately for the breeder, ears can be difficult. They are influenced not only by heredity, but also by emotional stress, teething, puberty, coat loss, temperature, hormone changes, calcium assimilation, humidity, and age. And to top this off, they rarely inherit as predicted.

Some ears are perfect regardless of the environment and others are utterly hopeless. The majority of ears, however, can be helped at crucial times—especially during teething from about 10 weeks of age to nine months.

A few breeders feel strongly that ears should never be touched. By showing and eventually breeding dogs that have had their ears fixed, these breeders believe, the occurrence of problem ears in the breed will increase, while breeding only those individuals with perfectly natural ears will help to breed out the problem. Unfortunately this is not always feasible. For one reason, dogs from several generations of natural-eared Shelties may show up with problem ears. For another, ears are affected by physiological, environmental, and stress factors. Furthermore, if you have achieved many goals in your breeding program, should you eliminate a dog with incorrect ears and thus lose some more important virtues you have gained? Of course not. A more realistic position, it seems to me, would be to value and breed for correct ears. Apply corrective measures to those with less than perfect ears, and eliminate from a breeding program any dog that consistently produces very low or very persistent prick ears.

Surgical correction is undesirable and is forbidden by AKC for show dogs. It is, however, perfectly legitimate to try to improve the appearance of a dog by working on his ears. In the case of a breeding dog, this should be acknowledged openly if the question arises.

For aesthetic reasons, many pet owners will also want to apply corrective treatment to a Sheltie with incorrect earset. To me, a Sheltie is much more attractive with the correctly tipped tulip ear, and I encourage you to persist in learning these techniques and applying them, but with the realization that some Shelties are sold to pet homes because they have poor earset.

WHICH FAULTS ARE CORRECTABLE?

The appearance of the ear is affected by size, thickness of leather, placement of the head, carriage, flexibility, degree and angle of tipping. Size and thickness are inherited and cannot be altered. Earset, carriage, and flexibility can only be slightly modified. Tipping is the element most easily corrected and the least completely controlled by heredity.

A very tiny, thick ear which is prick (completely upright with no forward break) is difficult to correct, especially if it has been up for several months. Likewise, a very thin, weak ear will probably not respond to bracing. The character of the ear cannot be changed. All we can do is hold an ear in position until the cartilage stiffens and fixes the ear in the right position. If the cartilage has already hardened, or if it never stiffens enough to hold the ear in the correct tulip shape, the most we can hope for is temporary correction that will allow the dog to be shown with some success.

SOME GENERAL PRECAUTIONS

1. Any work on ears refers to the ear leather only. Be very careful to keep any hair or foreign substance from entering the delicate ear canal. Hearing is delicate and far more important than outward appearance. Small cotton balls can be placed in the ear while trimming, bathing, or applying foreign substances.
2. Before moleskin or tape can be applied, the ear must be free of grease or wax. Clean the ear leather with rubbing alcohol and cotton.
3. Moisture and cold will cause ears to stiffen, therefore never wet prick ears. Bathe them with waterless shampoo or clean the hair with *Fuller's Earth*.
4. Grease and heat tend to make ears tip lower, but when greasy softeners get very cold they do not penetrate and do more harm than good.
5. The ear leather has only minimal circulation. If you cut off circulation by bending the tip too sharply, the cartilage will die. If this happens the eartip can be lost.
6. The short, thick hair on the eartip serves as a natural weight. Trimming or shaving an ear may help a heavy or low ear, but it can also cause one with a tendency to prick to do so.
7. A dog with drop ears is much more subject to ear infections. Artificially blocking the airflow to the ear canal with braces or tape can also cause problems. Do not block the ear canal.

Ch. Beltane Color Me Pretty, a Sportin Chance daughter owned by Barbara Curry, exhibits correct natural earset, soft almond eyes, and a clean, correctly proportioned headpiece.

SETTING EARS ON A PUPPY

The easiest, simplest, and quickest method of ensuring that your Sheltie matures with a beautiful earset is to train the earset when the puppy is young—four to twelve weeks. At four weeks of age the ears should begin to pull up on top of the skull and should tip forward. The fold is about halfway down. High-tipped ears at this age are likely to become prick ears later. Low-breaking ears may come up on their own, but low set ears may be helped by glueing the hair on the inside edge of the ear together to pull the ears higher

At seven weeks, low-breaking ears should have come up to at least the half-way point. If they haven't, they should be corrected.

Ears that are not perfect at this age can be corrected by either tapeing or glueing. Generally glueing is less irritating to the puppy. Leave the glue or brace in place until it comes loose on its own, then wait to see if the ears hold the correct position or if they need further work. If other puppies chew on the braces, apply *Bitter Apple®* to the brace and to the hair around the ear.

The puppy "fuzz" on some puppies' ears can be prolific. Sometimes all that is needed to correct earset on these puppies is to trim the excess hair off the tip and back of the ear. Excess hair at the base of the ear can force the ears to set wide apart. Always remove the thick hair in this area with thinning shears.

Many times all it takes at this young age is a few weeks of bracing or glueing for the ears to grow into a beautiful, natural position. Be careful not to over-correct. I have braced low ears too early or folded the brace too high (toward the tip) and ended up with prick ears.

Ch. Mainstay Once Upon a Time at five months of age has moleskin braces to help shape his beautiful ear set.

Most Sheltie puppies benefit from having their ears held in position when they are young. This lovely pup by Shadow Hill's Double Trouble has the ears glued on top. (Photo by Krook)

PRICK EARS

The keys to success with prick ears are two-fold: correct them before they have been up more than a few days and persevere until they finally stay over. Mechanical assistance may be needed from a young age all through the teething stage (to nine months of age), and during periods of stress throughout the Sheltie's lifetime.

Many basically correct ears will "fly" on particularly cold days, when too much calcium is fed, when a bitch comes in season, when a Sheltie loses coat, or as a result of physical or emotional stress of any kind. Ears that temporarily go prick as a result of cold weather, wind, or water should tip again within a few hours after the cause is removed.

Over-correction can cause problems, too, so if your Sheltie's perfect ears suddenly go prick, wait three or four days to see if this is temporary. If they stay up, or if they go up again after having glue or braces removed, apply correction quickly or all your time and energy may be wasted. Stop working on a prick ear only when it remains tipped for several weeks without assistance.

Many methods are used for correcting prick ears, including:

1. Moleskin or tape braces
2. Glueing
3. Weights
4. Softeners
5. Combinations of the above.

Personally I prefer bracing or glueing to correct most ear problems. Try a method. If it doesn't work, try another method until you find what works best for your particular Sheltie.

Glueing Ears

A less irritating method of holding the ear in position is to glue it over with surgical or fabric glue. Place a drop of glue on the *hair* at the tip of the ear. Fold the ear about halfway down, pressing the glue on the eartip against the long hairs growing at the base in front of the ear. Hold the hair together until the glue has firmly set. If the ears need to be higher on the head, gather a few hairs from the inside edge of both ears, welding them together in the center with a drop of glue. Hold until the glue has dried. Comb out any excess glue and stray hairs caught in the brace using a flea comb. If a sharper crease is needed, comb the hair on both edges of the ear outward and, folding the ear so it tips correctly, glue the hair at both sides of the ear to hold it in place. *NEVER glue skin to skin or hair to skin.* Be especially careful when removing the glue—you can pull away part of the ear leather. *Detacol* or similar surgical tape removers will loosen the adhesive.

The ears of this dog barely tip. Expression is often improved by working with the ears to encourage the ears to tip one-third of the way down.

Some prick ears are impossible to correct.

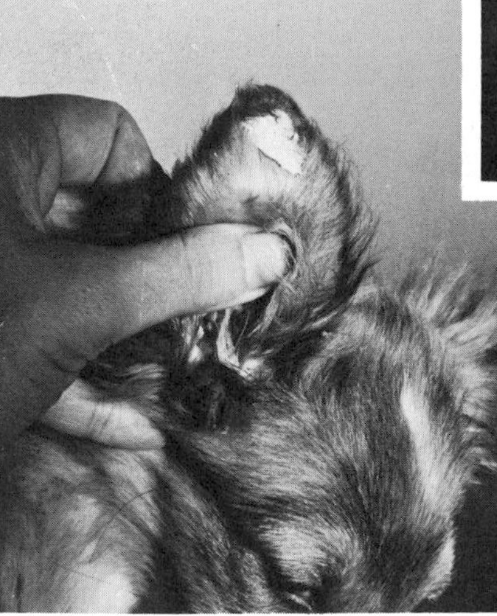

Antiphlogistine applied to the eartip for weight. Powder the "mud" to keep it from being sticky.

Roll masking tape and attach to eartip for weight.

Moleskin Brace

Braces are used to correct all kinds of incorrect earset. Braces shape the ear and hold it in the correct position until the cartilage has hardened. Follow the instructions under low ears, except no hairpin or extra bracing material is needed. Fold the moleskin over where the ear should crease. Be sure not to fold it over too sharply. Running a straw or matchstick between the moleskin where it is folded will prevent the circulation from being cut off. Glue the moleskin to itself with surgical adhesive or *Speed Sew*.

Softeners

A reasonably flexible ear may require only the application of a softener such as *Cuticura*®, glycerine, *Ears Beauti-*

ful™, Neatsfoot Oil, Bag Balm, or various hand lotions. These products penetrate the ear leather, making it more pliable. At the same time, dirt and grease that accumulate on the ear as the result of their use add some weight.

Softeners are applied on the under side of the ear. Start at the break and work toward the tip of the ear. Rub in throughly. Fold the ear in the desired position and massage the crease. Leave your Sheltie in a warm location. After a few hours the ear should come over. If it is still pricked, a second application is in order. Thereafter, apply twice a day or as needed. For extremely stubborn ears apply the substance also to the top (hairy) surface of the eartip.

Most of these substances can be removed before a show by working *Fuller's Earth* or grooming powder into the area, then combing it out with a flea comb. A small toothbrush is also helpful. Brush carefully, separating each hair as you brush. Waterless handcleaners such as *Goop*™ will also remove greasy softeners, but the ears must be cleaned afterward with *Fuller's Earth*.

Softener Plus Weight

More severe products provide softening plus weight. *Hooflex* or *Pine Tar* are two of the most common. Either can be painted onto the ear tip *above the crease* with a small paintbrush or a cotton swab. Use sparingly. Wait twelve hours to see if the ear comes over. If not, reapply. If you apply enough pine tar to make the ear tip over immediately, it may hang like a hound's ear after a few days. These products work slowly over a period of several days, and best results are obtained by leaving them on for several weeks until they wear off naturally. Hand cleaners effectively remove *Hooflex*.

Pine tar works well in hot weather, but can cause frostbite during cold weather. It is difficult to remove so use it only on a dog that will not be exhibited for several months. As pine tar will harden, *do not apply it on the crease*. Softeners may be applied over the tar periodically to keep it flexible.

Once it has dried, pine tar blends with the ear so well that it is easy to forget it is there. In cold weather, however, it acts as a conductor for cold and the ear is extremely susceptible to frostbite. Pine tar freezes easily, cracking and forming lesions on the ear which may not show because they are under the tar.

Weights

Other methods are generally superior to the use of weight to cause the ear to tip. Weight used by itself strengthens cartilage rather than weakens it, so some type of lubricant must be used in conjunction with the weight.

Antiphlogistine is a putty-like substance which can be used. Found in drugstores (as a mud pack for use on wounds), it is applied to the underside of the very tip of the ear. Chalk, powder, or even dust pressed on top of the mud will keep it from flying off or sticking to the coat. After the first application has dried, more can be added if necessary to bring the tip over. If the ear comes over too far, chip the antiphlogistine off a little at a time until the desired tipping is achieved. The substance can be removed with a flea comb and any remnants cleaned with waterless shampoo.

Temporary weights to help keep an ear over before a show can be created by forming a roll with tape, leaving one-half inch exposed with which to attach it to the ear. Masking tape will stay on for a short time and removes without a trace.

Wideset ears often break low as well. This type of ear may be helped by applying moleskin braces while the puppy is quite young. Even then, correct earset will be difficult, if not impossible, to achieve.

HEAVY OR LOW-BREAKING EARS

Heavy ears are set correctly on the head but break lower than is desired. On a puppy under four months of age the ears should break about halfway down, but on an adult only the top third of the ear should be tipped. Puppy ears that break further than halfway down or that hang down from the base need assistance.

Heavy or low-breaking ears are more difficult to correct than prick ears. Some are incorrigible. They also seem to inherit more directly than prick ears and a Sheltie that throws low ears can be a detriment to a breeding program.

Some ears break low because the ear leather is very weak and thin. This ear may have no definite break at all. Lack of strength in the cartilage is the real problem. The other type of low-breaking ear is large and heavy. This ear is more easily corrected by bracing.

Low-breaking or heavy ears in puppies may be corrected by clipping the hair and glueing the eartip in the correct position when the pup is between seven and twelve weeks of age. Later, all that may be required is to trim any excess hair which weights the ear down.

Massage may strengthen this type of ear. Grasp the base of the ear with your thumb and forefinger, stroking the front of the ear firmly upward to the break with your thumb. Continue with long strokes, always upward in direction. Repeat several times a day to stimulate circulation without breaking down cartilage. Since both cold and moisture tend to stiffen cartilage, apply rubbing alcohol and continue massaging for a few more minutes.

LOW SET EARS

Ears that are set too low or too wide on the head are also a problem. If they tip correctly, you may be able to encourage the dog to pull them up by pulling the ears higher and glueing them in position. This encourages the dog to use the ears and strengthens the proper muscles.

Low breaking or hound ears must be braced consistently for several months.

The left ear on this pup needs bracing to correct the low break.

Wideset ears or ears that tip out may be corrected by glueing the hair at the base of the ears to pull the ears up.

Correctly glued ears tip forward correctly and are centered on head.

Leave as much hair as possible on the bottom of the ear. Separate tufts on the inner edges of each ear. Twist each tuft between your thumb and forefinger to hold the hair together. Apply a small amount of adhesive and twist it into the hair. Allow it to partially dry, then twist the two tufts together, pulling the ears into the correct position. If the ears are really wideset, correct them a little at a time, gradually pulling them higher each time the glue is redone. Sometimes the effect will not be quite right and another tuft must be pulled from the back of the ear to keep them facing forward.

APPLYING A MOLESKIN BRACE

Braces are used to correct nearly every kind of ear problem because they literally form the ear into the correct position and hold it there until it confirms to the shape of the brace. Ears that are constantly in braces tend to have an unnatural appearance when the brace is removed. Most dogs tolerate a moleskin brace fairly well, and it should remain in position anywhere from one to four or five weeks. A few dogs seem to be allergic to the moleskin. Their ears become red and irritated and scabs may form after the braces have been removed. Glueing is the only alternative for these dogs.

The items you will need include: a box of Dr. Scholl's Moleskin, scissors, a package of hair pins (the old fashioned kind the hairdressers use to pin curls in place—not bobby pins), a can of engine starting fluid or a cigarette lighter, and surgical adhesive.

Take a sheet of moleskin, fold it in half, hold it in front of one ear and measure width and length. Cut an egg-shaped piece that will cover the entire inside of the ear, but is not wide enough to extend over the hairy edges. Cut out a small area in one corner for the bony cartilage at the inner edge of the ear. Hold the piece in place and trim to fit if necessary.

Now that you have the pieces cut, one will fit the left ear, the other the right ear. Next, clean the inside of the ear leather thoroughly with rubbing alcohol. Let the ears dry completely, about ten minutes. Trim all excess hair from the inside of the ear leather so it won't pull.

Recheck to make sure the moleskin fits correctly, then remove the backing from one piece. Moleskin is not sticky enough, so there are several methods you can use to make it stickier. One is to spray it with engine starting fluid and let it set for a few moments until the glue becomes very sticky. Or, you can pour a small amount of lighter fluid on the backing to increase adhesion. Another method is to use the cigarette lighter to heat the backing until it partially melts and becomes sticky. The backing will turn black. Let it cool before applying.

Press the moleskin to the inside of the ear, using your thumb and fingers to smooth and press from the center out. Make sure there are no folds or bumps in the moleskin and that it is adhering well. Repeat with the other ear.

Pull out any stray hairs that are caught in the ear braces or crossbrace. Let the Sheltie sit on the table for five or ten minutes to give the brace a chance to stick. Then, cut a one-half-inch piece of moleskin to be used as a cross brace. Cut one and a half inches of backing from one end and position it at the base of the ear as shown. (Use engine starting fluid or adhesive to make it stick). Hold in place for a minute, then pull the opposite ear into position and cut the backing off that end of the brace. Glue it across the ear and hold until the glue has set.

To form the correct tipping, the moleskin can be bent where the crease should be or it can be glued to itself or to the hair at the base of the ear. An alternative method is to cut a half-inch strip of silver duct tape and roll it sticky side out. Fold the eartip over the roll.

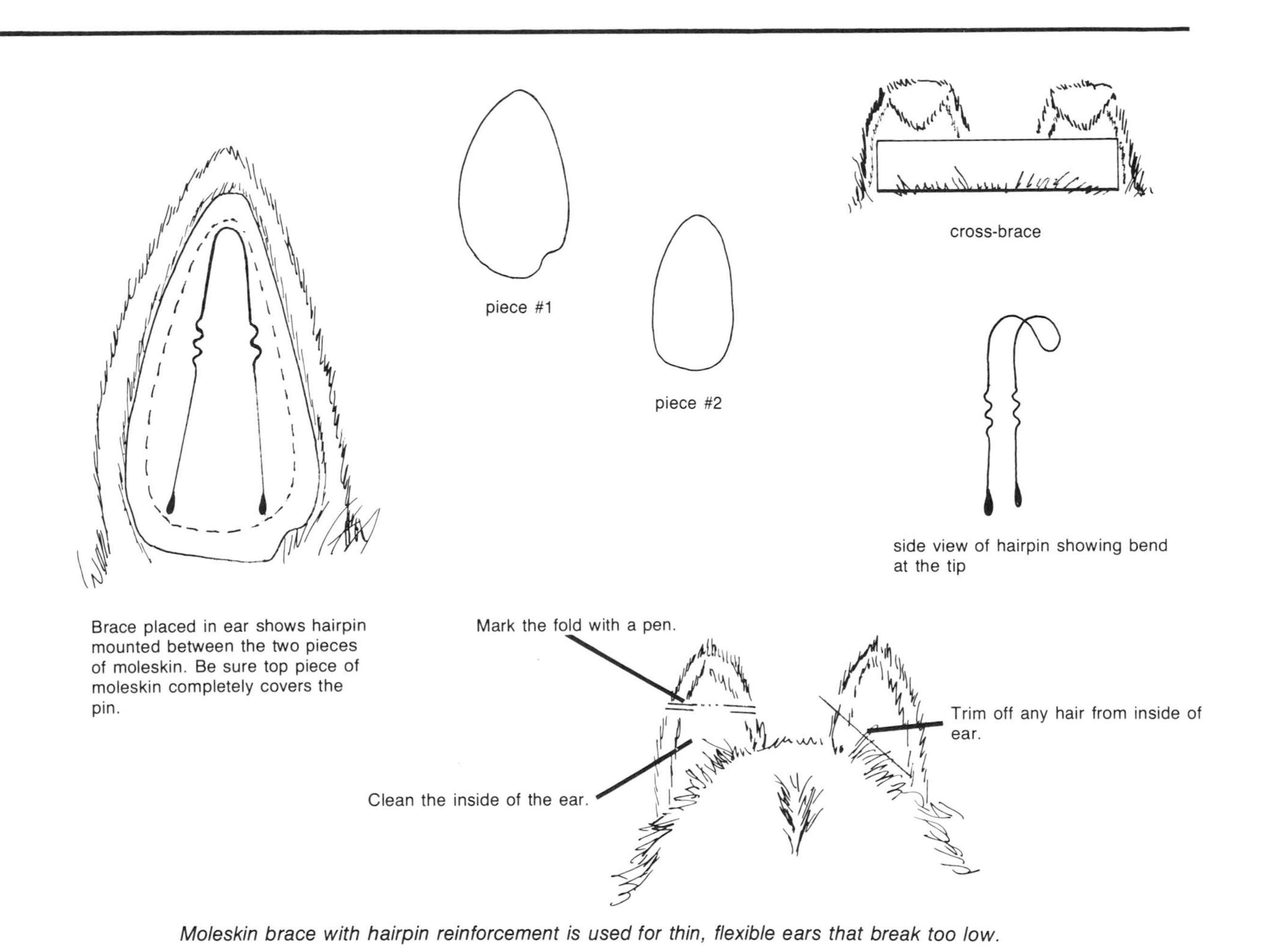

Moleskin brace with hairpin reinforcement is used for thin, flexible ears that break too low.

Weaker ears will benefit by cutting two identical pieces of moleskin and placing a hairpin between the layers as illustrated. The moleskin must be large enough to cover the hairpin, or, if not, trim the prongs of the hairpin to shorten it. The hairpin then can be bent to form the tip.

An alternate method of forming a crossbrace is cut a strip with two half-circles, one at either end, which reinforces the brace at the base. For puppies, some people thread yarn through the inside corner of the brace and tie it in a bow between the ears. The yarn can be tightened gradually to bring the ears closer together. Clean off any remaining glue with adhesive remover, alcohol, or *Fuller's Earth* and a flea comb. Rub glycerine on the ear to remove cleaning fluids. If the ears now appear to have the correct set, leave the braces off until a problem recurs. If the correct set has not been achieved, redo the braces the following day. Some Shelties need to have their ears braced throughout their first year.

Be especially careful not to get adhesive remover, lighter fluid, or powder into the ear cavity. This can be extremely irritating, or even cause infection or deafness.

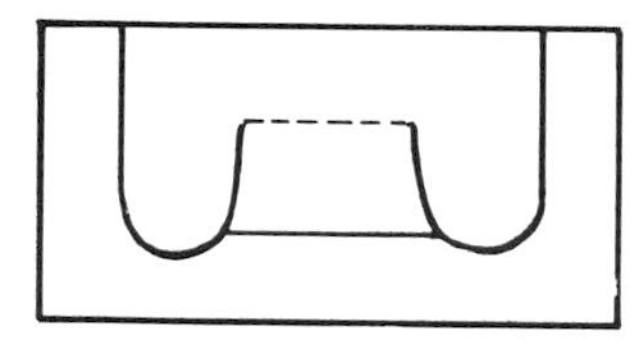

Cut cross-brace from a piece of moleskin. Fold back center flap on dotted line.

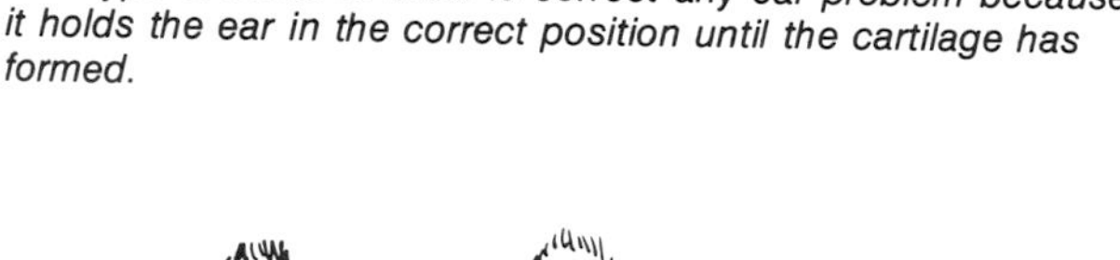

This type of brace is used to correct any ear problem because it holds the ear in the correct position until the cartilage has formed.

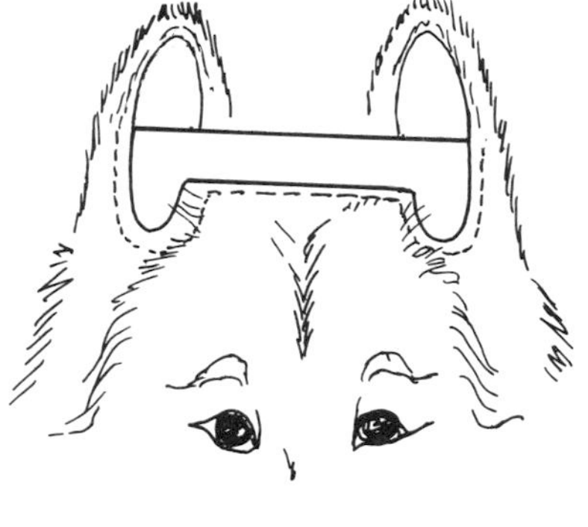

Mount crossbrace as indicated. Then fold tips over and glue.

If the dog pulls off the braces, wrap the ears with adhesive or masking tape.

The finished brace in place. If ears tip naturally, you may not need to glue the tips down.

Braces should be left in place until they begin to come lose or pull out of position. If your Sheltie tears at the braces, the entire ear and brace can be wrapped with wide adehesive tape to keep them in place. If he tends to pull the ears forward, twist and glue strands of hair at the back of the ears to keep them upright.

Braces must be removed very carefully, pulling from the bottom to the tip, using a surgical adhesive bandage remover under the edge of the moleskin to loosen them gradually.

EARS THAT TIP OUTWARD OR BACKWARD

An ear which tips naturally but to the outside can often be helped with a strategically placed weight. Place weight on the opposite side from which the ear leans to bring it forward.

The ear which folds diagonally from the base, or which tips lower on the outside than on the inside will require a moleskin brace reinforced with a hairpin or other additional support.

If an ear tends to tip backward, weight will only make it worse. Glue or braces are the best corrective measures.

A variation from glueing that one breeder shared is using denture cream to stick the eartip down. She shaves the inside of the ear to remove all hair, making the ear more flexible. Then she cleans the ear leather with alcohol and applies a dab of denture cream. She reports that denture cream will hold the ear together for several days, after which the application must be repeated. Dried denture cream is removed with a flea comb just as is antiphlogistine.

folded back into the frill to keep out rain or wind. The danger of infection or rejection by the dog's system is high. Priorities seem a bit warped when the superficial look of an ear is more important than the health of the dog.

Another practice that is illegal in the show ring is "loading" ears with powdered lead, iron filings, or diamond dust. Some handlers are adept at this, but many judges are equally adept in detecting loaded ears.

The goal to strive for.... Side view of correct earset. Knightwood Zephyr, owned by Nancy Lee Marshall. (Photo by Jan)

UNACCEPTABLE EAR CORRECTION

Any correction which permanently alters the ear by artificial means is banned from the show ring and should be avoided. Such methods include surgically breaking the ear cartilage of a prick ear, implanting silver wire or cartilage to strengthen ears, etc. They are often easy to detect by touch and produce a stiff, artificial effect. Often the ears are forced to remain in an upright position and cannot be

Ch. Hyalti Prince Hottentot C.D.X., Arrowhead Cinnamon Spice, and Arrowhead On Target, C.D.X., owned by Elizabeth Hall, relax for their portrait.

For Beauty's Sake 8

Shetland Sheepdogs do not require heavy grooming, and it need not be daily unless you have the time or are conditioning the dog for show. But some weekly routine grooming care is necessary if you want to maintain him in optimum condition.

Recently a new Sheltie owner was watching me groom. He commented in amazement on how willingly my Sheltie stood to have this teeth cleaned, and remarked that his terrier would not permit such handling. It's really quite natural for a Sheltie to be so patient. Shelties are a joy; they actually seem to expect and appreciate being groomed and cared for, and are very patient and tolerant with their owners. The daily care and management of your Sheltie will provide a bond of loving companionship between you.

GROOMING TOOLS AND EQUIPMENT

A few basic tools are needed by the pet owner. They include a pin brush, slicker brush, flea comb, and a toenail clipper. Scissors, a spray bottle, and a tooth scaler are necessary if you want to do more.

A convenient work area is important. It should be a comfortable height for the groomer and provide non-slip footing for the Sheltie. For years I used a rubber mat placed on top of my clothes dryer. A typing table, chest, utility table, or the top of a large crate are other possibilities. Rubber mats provide the best footing and are not damaged by water. Indoor/outdoor carpeting is an alternative. If you plan to show, invest in a good grooming table with folding legs and a grooming arm with which to secure the dog. If you are the "do-it-yourself" type you can purchase the legs and construct the top from plywood covered with rubber or carpeting.

Exhibitors will need a grooming box of some sort in which to carry their tools. These range from expensive professional models to tackle boxes or an assortment of handmade types.

BRUSHING

Brushing is the most important aspect of grooming. Done properly it cleans and stimulates the hair; done improperly it will break and pull out the coat. Every inch of the body should be brushed from the skin out. It is tempting to skimp on brushing, but this always shows in a lack of smoothness, finish, and the glowing shine which a diligent groomer achieves.

At least a thorough weekly brushing is a necessity.

Unless you have just bathed your Sheltie, always dampen the coat before brushing. Between baths, a good method is to spray the dog with a waterless shampoo such as *Self-Rinse Plus*® or *Kote-Glo*™, and towel dry. This removes dust and brings a gloss back into the coat.

Teach your dog to lie on either side for grooming. Brushing, if thorough, takes one-half hour per dog. He might as well learn to be comfortable.

Linebrushing is a basic technique for grooming long coated breeds. Using a metal pin brush or a combination pin and bristle brush, start at the neck and separate the coat in a line down to the skin. Spray with water and brush against the lay of the coat, one thin layer of hair at a time. Then make a new part and spray again. Dampen the undercoat to make the hair stand off and prevent breakage. For a finished look, go back through the coat a second time, holding the hair down firmly with one hand as you take the brush and pull out a section of hair and flick it backward, making it literally stand on end. Moisten the hair again as you work, and proceed section by section over the entire body.

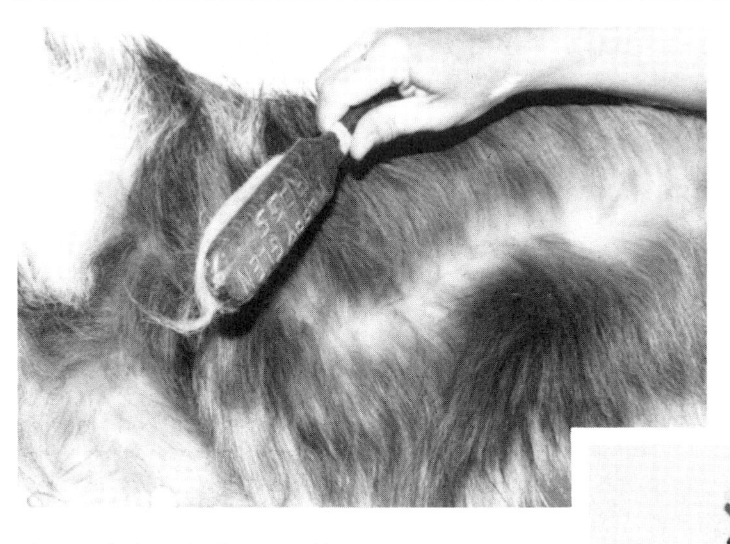

Line brush, layer by layer, working from the head back, lifting and separating the hair. Always spray with water before brushing.

Basic grooming tools: pin brush, slicker brush, flea comb, scissors, spray bottle, shampoo, and tooth scaler.

Brush the tail against the grain, all the way around until every hair stands out. Placing your hand on the thigh, lift up a section of hair and brush it out and down, giving a look of fullness to the pants. Using a comb or a light touch with the slicker brush, moisten the hair on face and head and shape the hair on the backskull and ears to frame the face. Hair at the side of the head should be brushed up toward the ears. A receding backskull is disguised if, each time you brush, you brush the hair at the back of the topskull straight up. Curl the dampened ruff around your hand to frame the face.

Shape the topline and croup by brushing the hair to form a level back and a sloping croup. If your dog is too high in the rear or too flat in the croup, or simply has a big puff of hair on the rear, remove some of the undercoat on the rump with a thinning shears. Smooth and spray the hair, pulling it down and shaping it layer by layer with the brush. A weak topline can be improved by standing the back hairs straight up or even doing a little backcombing.

The ruff is always brushed straight up. Moisten the undercoat and backcomb or backbrush at the roots to make the hair stand out all around the neck. If the hair at the back of the ears still looks straggly, clean it with *Fuller's Earth* powder. Shake the powder into the coat, let it sit for a few minutes, then remove every trace with a soft bristle brush.

Brush the hair on the legs so that every hair stands out, and brush the feathering back and towards the body. Comb the hairs on the inside of the stifle down to accentuate angulation. Shape the coat so it "fits" the body, and mist lightly overall with water or coat polish.

Blowing The Coat

As an alternative to linebrushing, some exhibitors are using livestock blowers to lineblow the coat. The method is the same as for brushing except the powerful blower nozzle is used to separate the coat in layers, blowing against the grain. The blower, which produces little or no heat, has the advantage of cleaning the dry coat without breaking it, and creates an airy, lifted appearance. A second time through misting with water which is simultaneously blown into the undercoat produces a full, healthy-looking coat. After blowing, the coat is shaped into the correct lay with a pin brush.

Three kinds of nail tools commonly used: a guillotine type, a Resco clipper; and the alternative, a nail grinder.

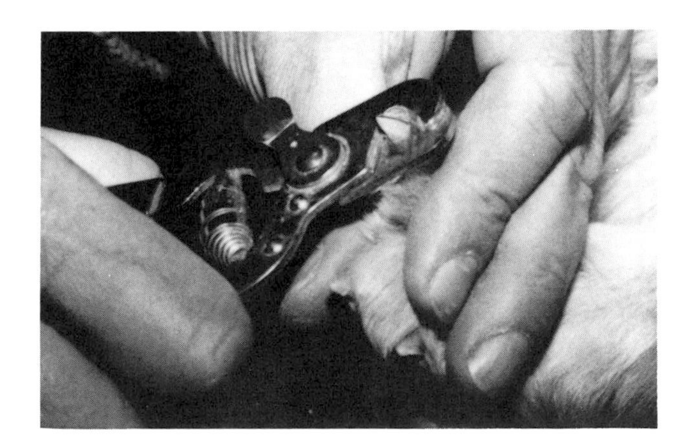

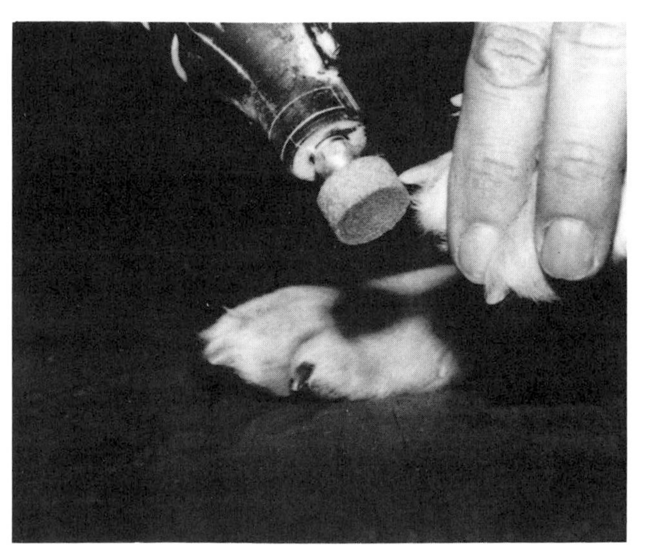

Move the grinder over the nail, rounding it. Keep the wheel away from long body coat or it will quickly become entangled.

Most people prefer a clipper with two cutting edges. Note the angle at which it is held.

ROUTINE GROOMING

Toenails

Long toenails allow mud and ice to accumulate between the toes. The foot splays and footing then becomes difficult. Also long toenails may force the dog's weight onto his heels. Eventually, the foot becomes tender, breaks down, and then is ruined for showing.

Ideally the nails should be cut every seven to 10 days and kept short enough that the nail does not touch the floor when the Sheltie is standing squarely. If your Sheltie has dewclaws (the claw sometimes found on the inside of the leg) cut these too so that they do not grow long and curled and snag in grass, fences, or carpets.

There are several kinds of dog nail clippers on the market, all of which work well. Hold the paw and clipper as illustrated, cutting the nail almost to, but not into, the blood line. On a white or clear nail the blood line can easily be seen as the pink area, but it is impossible to see on a black nail. The safest technique on these nails is to cut away just the hooked part of the nail.

The "quick," or blood line, recedes after cutting. If the nails have been allowed to grow extremely long the quick will be much further out and you will have to be careful to cut only a tiny bit of the nail at a time, repeating the process every few days until the nail is back to correct length. If you should accidently cut into the blood line you can stop the bleeding with a dab of *Quick Stop®* or other styptic, or a little powdered alum.

Shelties in general have little trouble with their feet. Excessive hair between the toes of some Shelties tends to accumulate grass seeds and dirt and should be removed carefully with a blunt nosed scissors. Occasionally Shelties will get a bit too inquisitive and pick up a splinter or a cactus spine which can be removed with tweezers and the foot swabbed with alcohol. If the pad gets sore or cracked, rub it with lanolin lotion or with one of the commercial preparations available for toughening pads such as *Tuf-Foot*® or *Pad-Kote*®.

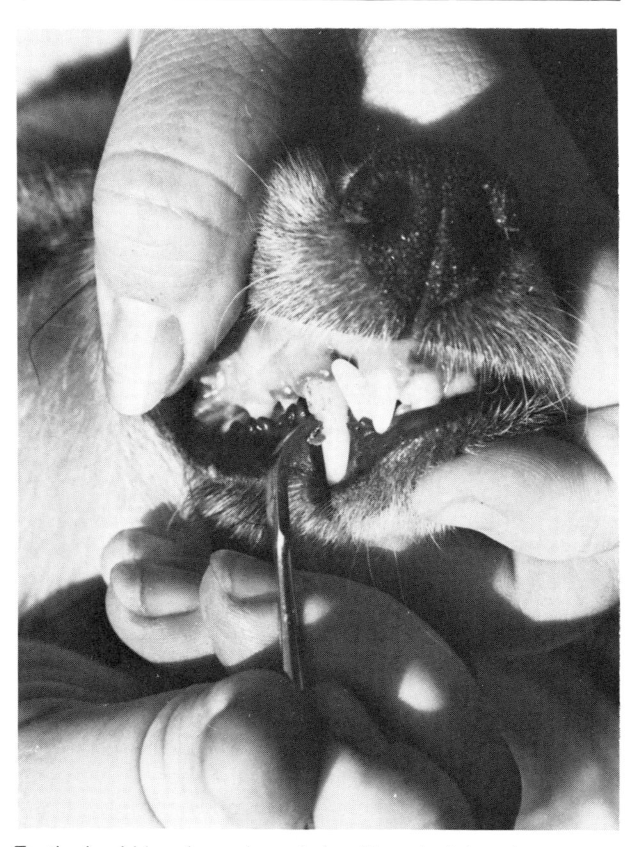

Teeth should be cleaned regularly with a dental scaler.

Ears

Like children, Shelties sometimes have dirty ears that need to be washed. Water in the inner ear can cause problems, so use alcohol on a cotton swab to clean the ear itself and the inside of the ear flap. Never probe deeply into the ear or let alcohol run down into the ear cavity.

Scratching or digging at the ear, evidence of pain on the side of the head, or tilting the head to one side may indicate ear problems or ear mites.

Teeth

When tartar forms on a dog's teeth, gum problems set in just as with human teeth. Puppies clean their teeth by chewing, but adult dogs generally need some assistance to keep their teeth clean and healthy. Bones (big joint or leg bones, *not* splintery chop or chicken bones), along with *Milkbone*®, rawhide chews and dry kibble, will help keep your Sheltie's teeth in good condition. Monthly cleaning is recommended. If you clean the teeth regularly you will never have to worry about having it done under anesthesia by your veterinarian.

Cleaning takes only 10 or 15 minutes. You will need a dental scaler available from your dentist or through a veterinary supply house. Beginning with the upper incisors, hold the lips out of the way with one hand and scrape from just under the gum downward, using short, firm strokes. Get under the gum without cutting it, and take care not to jab the scraper into the tongue or lower jaw as you come down. The tartar will chip off in flakes. Clean all the top teeth to the very back, scraping the surface thoroughly inside and outside. Then do the bottom row, scraping from the gums upward.

Rinse the scaler in oral antiseptic several times during cleaning, and soak the tool after the job is finished. Complete cleaning by polishing the teeth with powdered pumice or *Pearl Drops*® tooth polish on a gauze pad. Then swab the gums and teeth with oral antiseptic, using a gentle but firm rolling motion to stimulate gums. Weekly or even daily brushing with a soft toothbrush and a human toothpaste will prevent rebuildup of plaque.

If your dog develops bad breath between cleaning, swabbing teeth and gums with baking soda or with a product called *Happy Breath*® should help. If the odor persists suspect a digestive problem or infected tonsils, and call it to the attention of your veterinarian.

Anal Glands

The anal glands are two small glands located below and on either side of the anus. They secrete a lubricant that enables the dog to expel feces more easily. Occasionally these glands become clogged, accumulating a foul smelling mass. Irritation of the glands results.

Clogging may be caused by injury to the region, bacterial infection, or migrating of segments of tapeworm into the ducts of the glands. Obesity and lack of muscular tone may be contributing factors in old dogs. Chronically soft feces will also cause retention of the fluid. Closely confined dogs appear to have more difficulty than dogs that are active.

The most common early sign of anal irritation is licking or biting at the perineum. As the condition progresses the dog may drag his anus across the floor or rub it against any rough surface. If glands become severely clogged infection will set in and sacs may abscess. The only way to correct the abscess is to have the glands removed by surgery.

Removing the accumulation regularly will prevent impaction and will make your Sheltie feel better and even look more sparky. Seize the tail with the left hand and encircle its base with the thumb and forefinger of your right hand. Press the anus firmly between thumb and finger, expelling the anal fluid. The dog will flinch a little, which is to be expected. Repeating once a month should be enough to keep the glands cleaned out. Be sure to empty both glands.

Eyes

A Sheltie's eyes are his most expressive feature. If he is healthy and happy they mirror his condition beautifully. If the eyes are dull or dazed this may indicate a physical problem. A blow to the eyeball, dust, pollen, weed seeds in the eye, or an infection can cause the eyes to water or accumulate pus. Prolonged watering or irritation of the eyes can lead to permanent, serious injury, even to the point of causing blindness if not properly treated.

Treat the eyes carefully and only when necessary. The best solution is a mild salt water solution made by adding ¼ teaspoon of sodium chloride (salt) to ½ cup of water. Artificial tears for contact lens wearers are also a good eyewash. Medicated drops or ointment should be used only on the advice of a veterinarian. Medications given for one condition can easily complicate a different condition.

If you ever notice a blue haze over your Sheltie's eyes, get him to a veterinarian immediately. It could be a reaction to a hepatitis shot or an indication of any number of serious conditions. Dilated pupils that do not respond to light may also indicate serious eye problems, although some medications will cause the pupil to dilate.

SHEDDING

Shetland Sheepdogs do shed, usually in the summer or early fall. Unspayed bitches usually shed about two months after each estrous cycle. The undercoat comes out in handfuls, and the only thing you can do is get rid of the old, dead hair as quickly as possible. Bathing with warm water will help loosen the hair. Use slicker brush or shedding blade to pull out the clumped undercoat, then follow with a thorough brushing using the pin brush. New coat takes two to four months to come in completely.

REMOVING MATS

Most Sheltie's coats do not mat easily except for the soft hair behind the ears. This area must be groomed frequently to prevent tangling. Clean the area and remove oiliness by sprinkling with baby powder, grooming powder, cornstarch or *Fuller's Earth*. Brush it out with a soft bristle brush.

If mats do form, or if your Sheltie gets into sticktights or burrs, saturate the matted area with *No More Tangles*, a product for children, or any tangle remover sold at the pet supply stores. Let the detangler sit for a few minutes and then attempt to comb out the mat with a wide-toothed comb. Reapplication of the detangler may be necessary. If the mat still does not come out, clip as small an area as possible with the thinning shears until the mat is free and can be combed away.

Always remove mats and tangles *before* bathing.

BATHING

Bathe your Sheltie when he needs it, but no more often than necessary. If you use a good dog shampoo followed by conditioner, and are sure to rinse all the soap out, frequent bathing should not harm the coat. Dry the dog thoroughly.

Any number of good dog shampoos are available, some even designed for a specific coat color—black, copper, blue or white. For show dogs, a moisturizing shampoo helps keep the coat from breaking, and a texturizing shampoo can help build body before a show. Deyoannes, Inc., manufactures some excellent shampoo and conditioning products for coated breeds under the brand name of *Cindra*. There are many other excellent ones to experiment with. The pet owner however, need only choose any good basic pet shampoo or human baby shampoo. A medicated flea shampoo should be used regularly in areas where fleas, lice, or ticks are a problem.

Many people use the bathtub or shower stall for bathing, or stand the dog in the kitchen sink astraddle the divider, using the dish sprayer to rinse him. If you decide to build a special grooming area, a large laundry sink is a good investment. Better still, purchase a small bathtub such as the ones used in camp trailers and raise it to a comfortable working height by building a platform. Rubber non-skid material must be placed on the bottom.

Plug your Sheltie's ears with cotton and wet him thoroughly with tepid or lukewarm (not warm or hot) water. Warm water causes the undercoat to come out. Wet the coat thoroughly, face to tail, lifting the top coat to be sure the water penetrates to the skin. Leave the dog standing in a few inches of water to soak any mud from between the toes.

Next, lather the entire body with shampoo, paying particular attention to the belly, back of elbows, anal area, and inside of elbows and thighs. Suds can be worked between the palms and wiped over the face.

Rinse the head and ears, then down the neck, chest, back, sides, rear legs, and tail. Shampoo all except the face a second time, and rinse until all traces of shampoo have been removed. Three tablespoons of vinegar to a quart of water as a final rinse will bring out the red highlights in a sable coat. One or two drops of laundry bluing added to a quart of water will brighten the white collar and feet. There should be just enough bluing to tint the hair a very, very light blue. It will dry a bright white.

Dry, broken, sun or wind damaged coats can be helped by a moisturizer. Any number of human hair products may be used, as well as those marketed specifically for dogs. If the coat is too soft, stale beer makes an inexpensive texturizer. Mix it half-and-half with water and use as a final rinse. Don't rinse out. The smell will disappear when it dries.

If you are showing your Sheltie, experiment with various products until you find what works best for his particular coat and until you determine how far ahead of a show you need to bathe him for best results.

Drying After A Bath

Drain any standing water and wring out the long hair on legs, belly, chest and tail. Wrap the dog in a towel and blot the excess water. Don't rub the coat as this loosens undercoat. In warm weather I let the dog dry partially in an exercise pen placed over grass or outdoor carpet. (Never put a wet dog where he will chill or be exposed to draft.) Otherwise, use a hair dryer and a pin brush and fluff the coat lightly until damp-dry.

When the outercoat is partially dry, use the pin brush to work against the coat in layers, blowing and brushing until the undercoat is completely dried. Then brush the coat back into its natural lay. Do not allow a part to form down the back.

Untrimmed ears give the Sheltie a ragged, unkept look.

TRIMMING THE PET SHELTIE

Most pet owners do not want to spend much time on trimming, but a minimal amount will give your Sheltie a neater appearance and increase his comfort. Never clip a Sheltie's body coat (except in case of severe skin disease). The double coat insulates against heat as well as cold.

Many Shelties have feet that look like overgrown clumps of hair. Not only is this uncomfortable; it collects dirt and gravel, interferes with movement and makes toenail clipping difficult. Clip the excess hair from the bottom of the pads, laying the scissors flat against the pad. Then shape the foot into an oval by trimming around the outside edge with either a straight or curved shears. Use the largest pair you have; a small scissors will produce a choppy look.

Very carefully trim around the anus and genitals. Trimming should not be noticeable, but should remove a layer of hair which does soil easily.

If you wish to further neaten up your dog, refer to the section on show grooming for instructions on trimming the hocks and ears. Evening up the hair on these areas will make a tremendous difference in your Sheltie's appearance and enhance your pride in him.

GROOMING THE SHOW DOG

Successful grooming achieves neatness and minimizes faults. The well-trimmed dog never looks trimmed. Overtrimming creates a harsh appearance and often draws attention to deficiencies instead of de-emphasizing them. Subtle trimming takes practice. Although a good judge knows all the tricks, he or she has only a few minutes to examine each dog and therefore places much emphasis on overall appeal.

An eye for the balanced Sheltie plays an important part in determining how much and what type of trimming should be done. Grooming is unique for each individual. The groomer must be able to picture the ideal Sheltie called for in the Standard and then attempt to create that ideal in the individual being groomed. Maximize good qualities and minimize faults without being obvious.

Grooming cannot be taught in a book. If at all possible, find an experienced groomer who will teach you personally. Watch the various breeders and handlers groom before a show. Everyone has their own technique, and you'll pick up an idea or two from each of them. Then practice on your own Sheltie far in advance of any show. It is impossible to put hair back if you create a hole or take off too much. Practice on pet Shelties—your own and anyone else's you can appropriate. Practice, and practice, and practice. Ask for advice and criticism. Experiment. Watch how people in other breeds groom. You can pick up skills and techniques from any good groomer, regardless of breed.

A lot of sculpturing and overtrimming is being done. It is up to the individual to decide just how far he or she wants to go in the creation of the "cosmetic Sheltie." Just remember that the show ring was originally meant to be the proving ground for breeding stock. The beautifully created picture you see in the ring may hold many surprises for the breeder. What you see may not be what you get! The only way to reverse this situation is to opt for a more natural show dog. Every exhibitor plays a part in what direction the breed will take in this regard.

TRIMMING THE HEAD

The head is the most important and most difficult to trim. The additional tools you will need include a Fromm Mini Thinner (or equivalent), a straight 6- to 8-inch high quality shears, a small 4-inch shears for whiskers and small areas, a stripping comb or stripping stone, and a flea comb. Clippers are handy for use on the throatlatch. A 46-tooth single sided thinning shears may also come in handy. Other items may be added as you experiment.

Lip Line

Neaten the lip line and create the illusion of deeper underjaw by cutting a straight line along the top lip with the long shears, trimming the hair to the skin. Be very careful not to cut the lip itself. Once I accidently cut the tongue. It bled frighteningly, and afterward I became a much more cautious trimmer.

Even up the hair along the bottom lip also, and, using the mini-thinner, smooth any unruly hairs at the back corner where the lips meet.

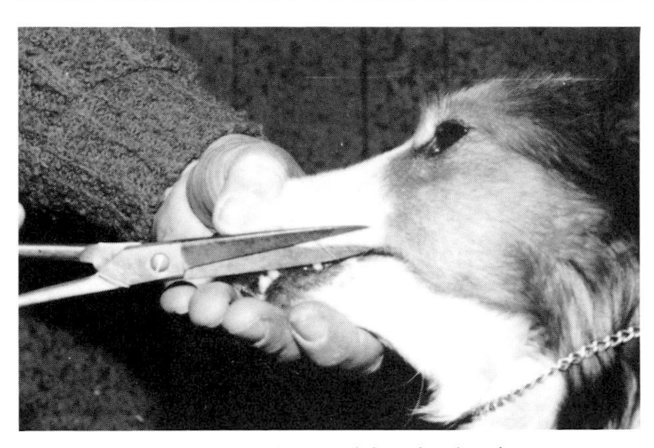

Trim along the lip line with a straight-edged scissors.

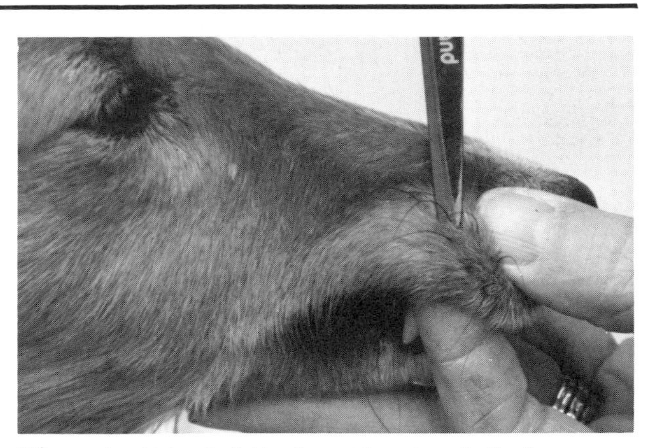

Trim each whisker individually, cutting clear to the base.

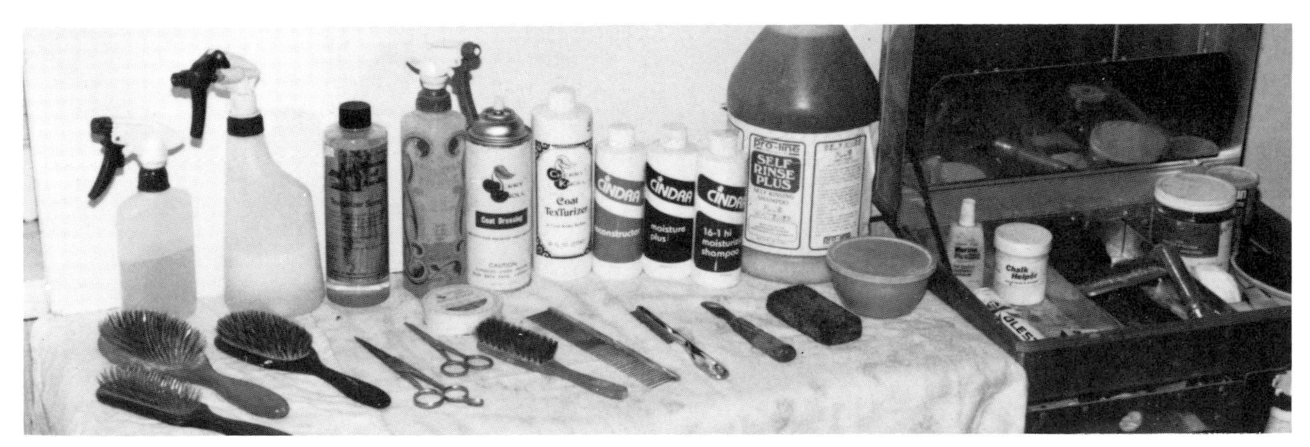

Show grooming equipment: various shears, combs, and brushes; Mini-Thinner; stripping stone; stripping knife; chalk. Back row: coat texturizer, coat conditioner, waterless shampoo.

Whiskers

Start by removing each whisker at the base. Insert your finger and thumb under the lip, holding the dog firmly by the teeth. Pooch out the whiskers so they stand straight out. With your small scissors, remove each one individually at the root. Be careful not to create holes by cutting away surrounding hair coat. Remove the large whiskers at the back of the cheeks and the long eyebrow hairs in the same manner.

Jawline

Using a clipper or your mini-thinner, trim the back half of the underjaw and the throatlatch. A Sheltie with a short head or deep backskull can be greatly improved by removing as much hair as possible. Trim an area the width of the jaw, and blend into the sides of the face and the ruff. On short-headed Shelties, continue trimming an inch or more into the ruff. Use a small show lead the same color as the hair to pull up a sagging throatlatch.

If the dog has a long, lean head, leave more hair at the throatlatch, but neaten and blend nicely into the face framing and ruff.

Smooth the tnroat and underjaw with a stripping blade or stone. Do not trim the front half of the underjaw except to remove whiskers and even the hair. You want to create the illusion of depth here.

If your Sheltie lacks finish of underjaw, the day before the show, rub a small amount of *Kolestral*™ into the hair and pack it with chalk. Repeat several times if necessary, brushing out any loose chalk before ring time. Using a small stiff-bristled chalk brush or toothbrush, brush so that every hair stands straight out.

The untrimmed throat creates the illusion of depth in the backskull.

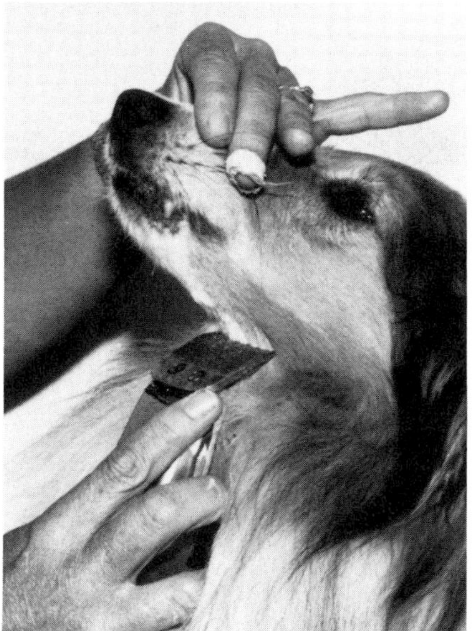

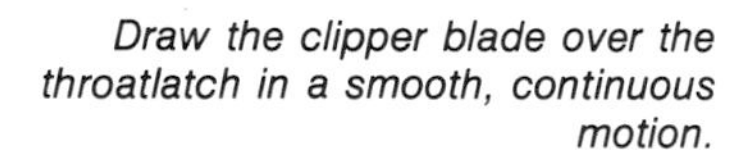

Draw the clipper blade over the throatlatch in a smooth, continuous motion.

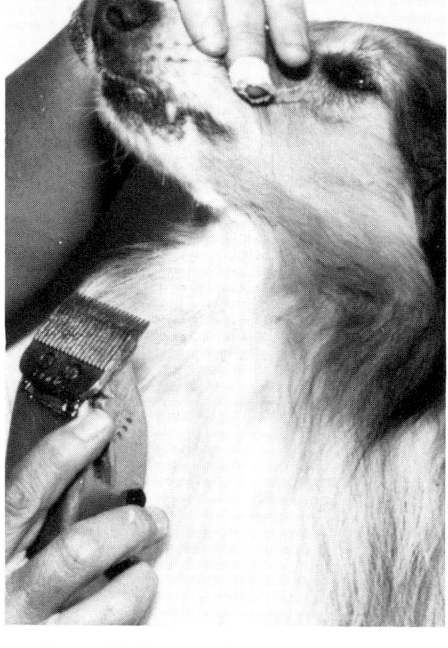

Use a #4 blade or the longest setting on an adjustable clippers. Hold clipper as illustrated.

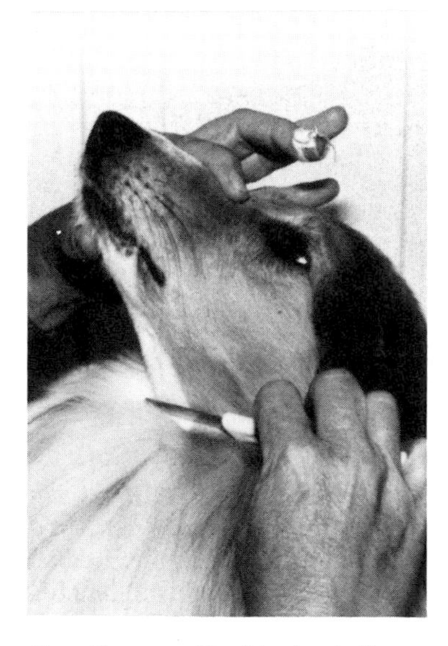

Smooth area with stripping knife.

The finished throat is smooth and blends nicely into neckline.

The Topskull

The topskull should be flat. To achieve this look, moisten the hair with water or hairsetting gel and comb it forward so that every hair stands on end. Hold the mini-thinner parallel to the line created by the top of the muzzle and trim the hair about one-fourth-inch to one-half-inch from the skull. All that should be trimmed is the area just above the eyes and the center front of the topskull. Be careful to hold the scissors parallel to the plane of the muzzle. Finish by combing the hair back into a natural position.

Head trimming should be done two or three weeks prior to a show in order to look natural in the ring. You will remove some of the dark mask on a sable when you trim, so this needs time to grow back. Otherwise the mask must be touched up by cosmetic means which are against AKC regulations.

An alternate method used on dogs with good head planes that need only to have a hairy skull thinned is, comb the hair up as before and bring the mini-thinner in from the back. Press the blades against the skull and thin the hair one snip at a time. Comb out and repeat until the hairy-headed look is gone and the topskull appears smooth.

Still another method, much more time consuming but also much more natural and preferred by many professionals, is to use a stripping stone or comb to gradually remove the undercoat on the top and sides of the skull and at the stop. The stone or stripper must be held perfectly flat to create a smooth, level line. It takes daily use over a period of several weeks to thin a hairy skull in this manner.

Moisten the hair at the occiput with setting gel and brush forward so every hair stands upright. The appearance of a good skull can be enhanced or the receding backskull hidden by training this hair to stand up. Smooth the topskull, blending the coat into the upright hair at the occiput and ruff. Any stiffness from the setting gel must be brushed out before showing.

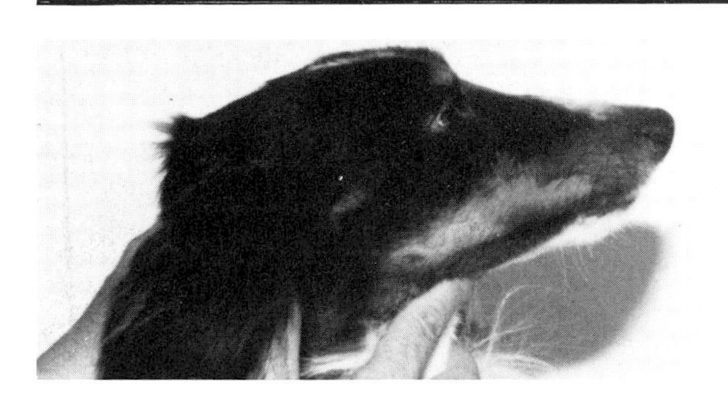

The untrimmed topskull.

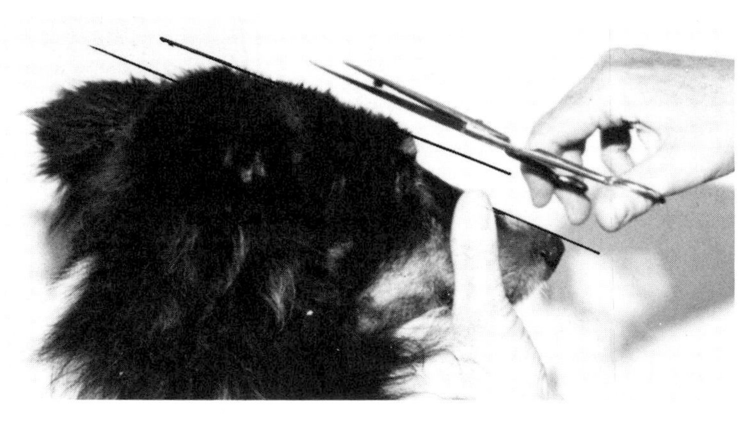

Brush hair straight up and trim in a line parallel to foreface.

Brush the coat upward at the occiput. Note vast improvement in appearance of head planes.

Sides of the Head

The sides of the head should give the appearance of a smooth, single plane, tapering from muzzle to backskull. Minimize any bumps by trimming. The feel of the skull will not change, but the impression at first glance will be improved. Holes can be covered by combing the hair upward and packing with *Kolestral* and chalk. Again, brush out all chalk before showing. The hair will still hold some body.

Using the back corner of the eye as a pivot point, bury your mini-thinner at the root of the hairs and thin the undercoat as needed to smooth and narrow the backskull. Some Shelties are tremendously hairy in this area, giving the appearance of a heavy, wide backskull. Thin as illustrated, a little at a time, preferably over several sessions, being careful not to remove too much or to create a choppy, trimmed appearance. A stripper may be used in lieu of the thinning shears.

Occasionally a dog will have puffs of hair below the eyes or on the sides of the muzzle. These should be removed in the same way with a series of cuts in the direction of the hair growth. The object is always to thin the undercoat, not to shave the head or chop the topcoat.

Don't worry about exposing the lighter undercoat. If you do your trimming several weeks in advance of a show, this will have darkened again. Rub in a little colored chalk or wipe the light area with a wet teabag to give temporary color. By the time the dog is shown it will have worn off. Experiment to determine how long it takes a particular dog to regain the soft, natural look and yet retain the advantages of trimming. This can vary from one to five weeks depending on the color of the dog, the severity of trimming needed, and the head type. An expert groomer may be able to trim a dog the same day he is shown.

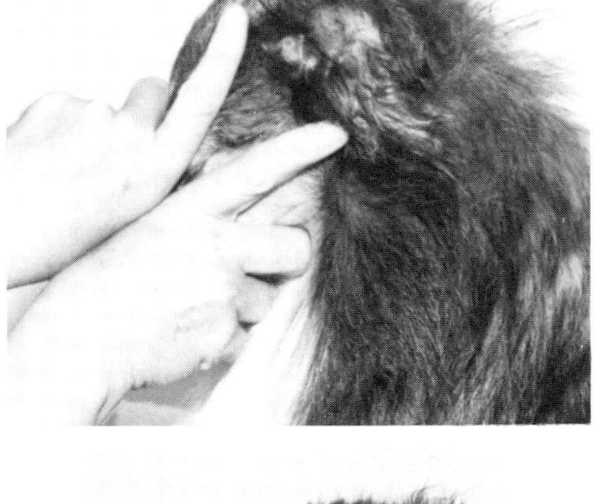

Thin backskull in a V-shape as shown.

Continue down the checks to the bottom of the "V".

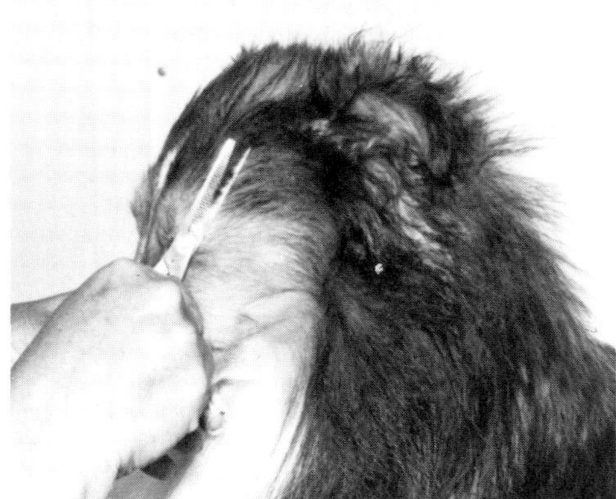

Holding thinning shears at the base of the hairs, start trimming at the top of the "V"

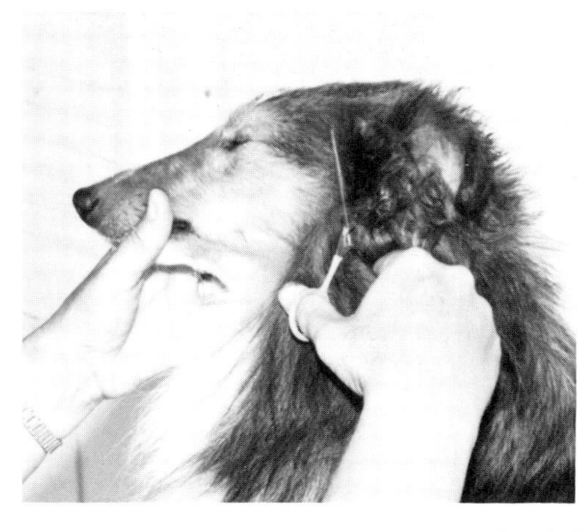

Go back over the entire area, holding mini-thinner in vertical position.

Ears

Ear trimming requires the most individualized treatment. Removing too much hair gives the Sheltie a harsh, naked look, the ears sticking up like some foreign appendage. Too little trimming destroys the neat, finished look and sharpness of expression we like to see. Trimming the first ear is easy compared to making the second one match. Sometimes it helps to match cut for cut from one side to the other.

Start by rounding the eartip with your curved shears, or mini-thinner. If the ear is heavy and tips too far forward trim this fairly short. Use the mini-thinner to shorten and smooth the hair on the top of the eartip to create a higher tip. If the ear tips normally, do not shorten the hair, just round it off, giving it a tidy, clean line. If the ears tip out, reshape the tip slightly, moving the centerpoint to the inside.

Next, remove the light colored hair from the inside edge of the ear with the thinners. Neaten the outside edge of the ear by cutting off any stray hairs. Remove the tuft of fine, soft hair that grows forward at the inside base of the ear.

Smooth back the facial hair in front of the ear and trim any uneven ends. Do not remove this patch of hair or your Sheltie will look bald and unnatural. If fine, light hairs are sticking out in every direction, pluck these out with your fingertips. Train the remaining hair to fall back into the face framing.

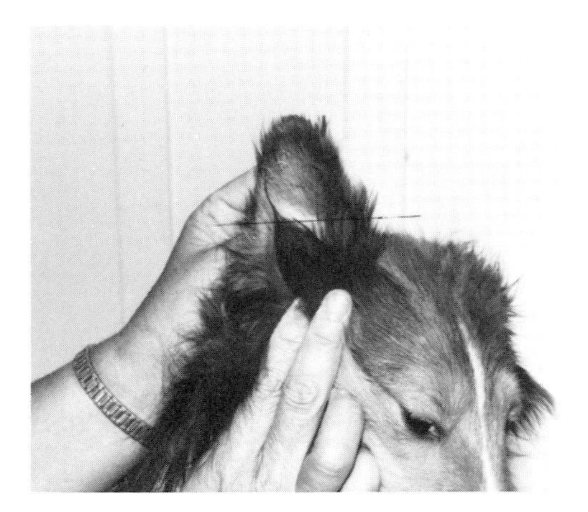

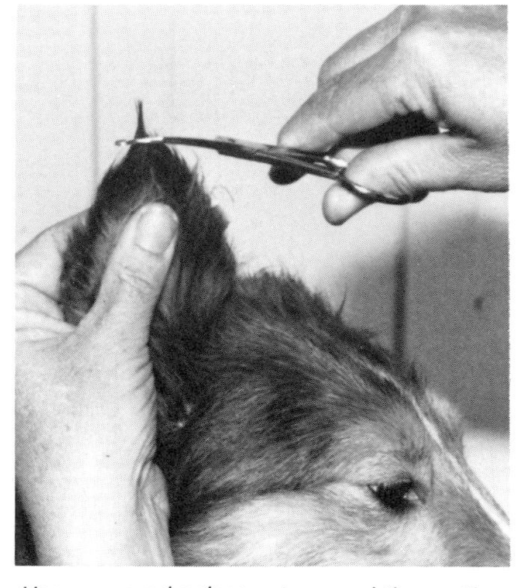

Use a curved scissors to round the eartip.

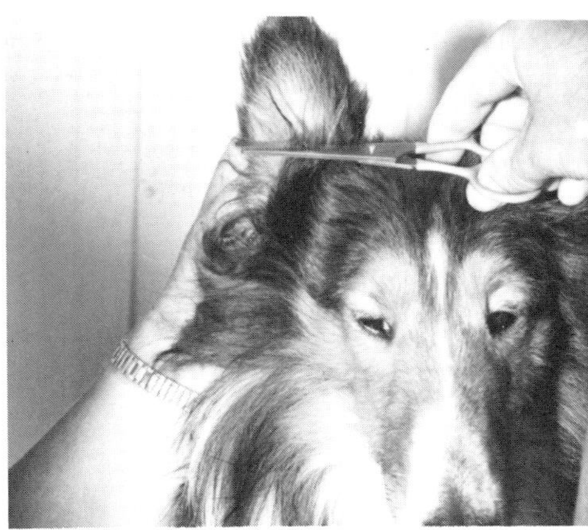

Trim any hair that extends more than halfway up in front of the ear and blend the rest into the face framing. Pluck light, fine hairs out with fingertips.

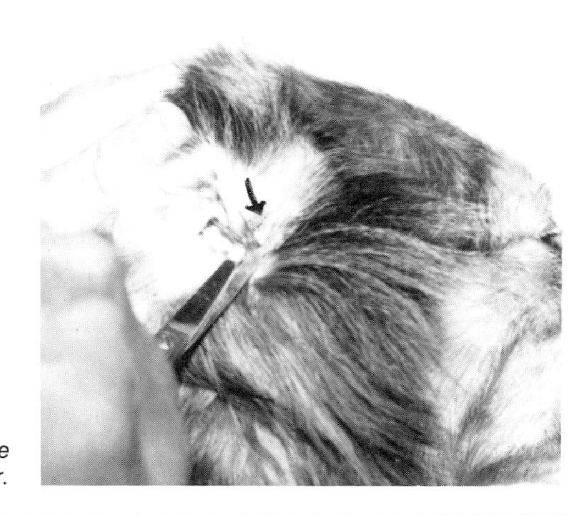

Remove hair that grows straight up from the boney ridge at the inside base of the ear.

Next, even up the hair framing the head and ears. Do very little trimming here except to even out the length and shape the framing. Comb the hair at the sides of the head out and upward, bending it around your hand to create a nice frame. Pluck out any unruly light hairs that offend.

Next, pull one ear straight out from the skull (see illustration) and with the mini-thinners trim the tufts of hair at the inside corner of the ear. Blend into a straight line with the topskull. Comb the hair on the front half of the ear forward and trim again. Repeat with the other ear.

Finally, from the side, pull the ear up into the correct position and hold it by the tip. Comb the long hair on the back of the ear up, misting with water if necessary to make it stay erect. The area must be well groomed so that every hair is standing on end. Trim from the tip back into the frill, creating a smooth line along the top and side of the ear. Blend and smooth until all heaviness is gone and the ear blends nicely into the ruff. Soft, fluffy hairs that give a messy, ungroomed look should be plucked by hand.

Finally, with the ear tipped forward, use the mini-thinner to even and smooth the hair on the top of the ear, creating a straight line across the tip. Smooth with multiple, quick snips until the hair is as level as a newly mowed lawn.

Remember—do not remove too much at a time. If your Sheltie has not been trimmed for some time, do it in several steps with a day or two in between for observa-

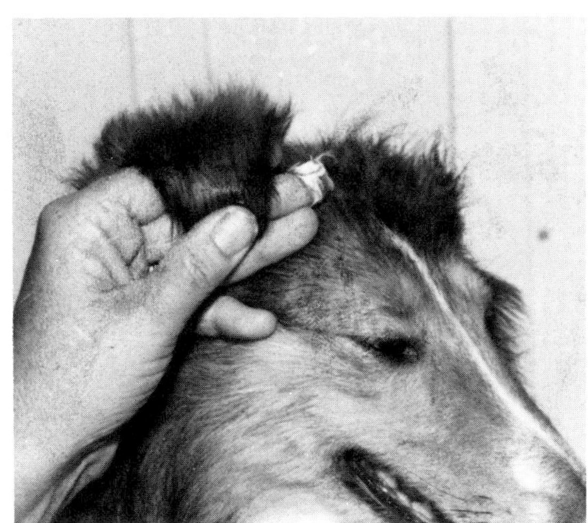

Fold eartip at its natural bend.

Hold ear straight out and trim top inner edge even with hair on topskull.

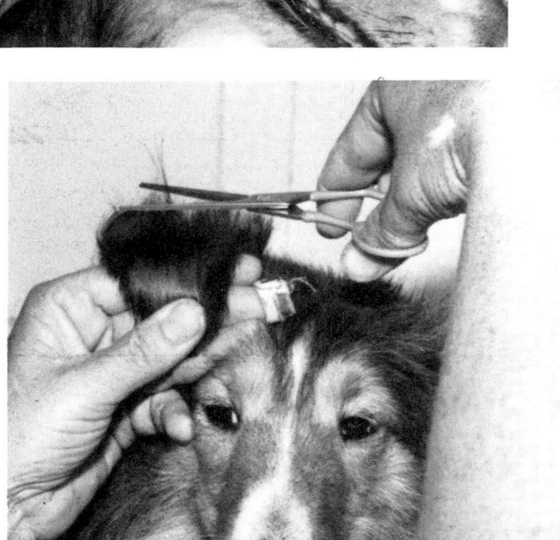

Trim off any hair from top or back of ear that extends above the fold.

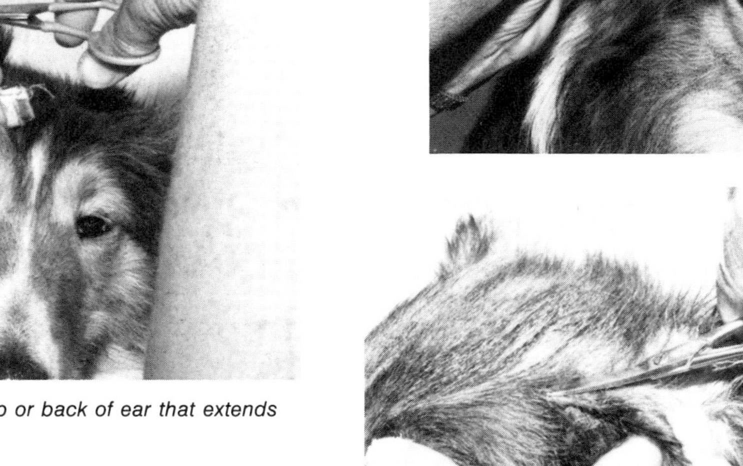

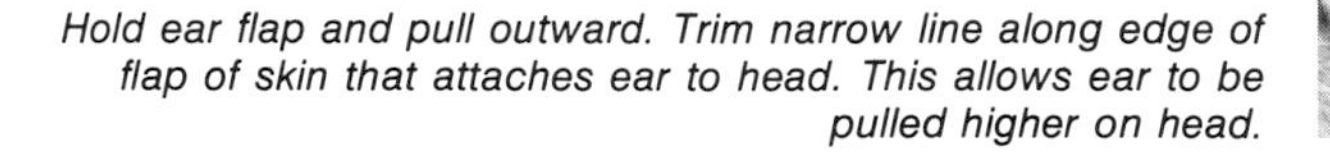

Hold ear flap and pull outward. Trim narrow line along edge of flap of skin that attaches ear to head. This allows ear to be pulled higher on head.

tion. Don't destroy the face framing or remove the hair in front of the ears. Remove as little hair as possible from the tip of a potential prick ear and do not wet this ear.

After trimming, dust the back of the ears with *Fuller's Earth* and brush until every hair is separated and standing up. This area should be brushed several times just before a show.

As with all other trimming, experiment well in advance of a show to determine what looks best for your Sheltie. Small ears generally need more trimming than large ears. Leaving a few longer strands of hair at the inside base of the ear is sometimes beneficial for a dog with ears that turn out or are wide-set. Wideset ears are also helped by thinning the hair at the inside base, thus providing space in which the ear can set. Make an "X" with your thinning shears, one half of the "X" in front of the ear and the other cut where the base of the flap meets the skull.

Examine untrimmed ear from side (line indicates trim line). Remove excess hair from back of ear, slanting thinner downward to blend into ruff.

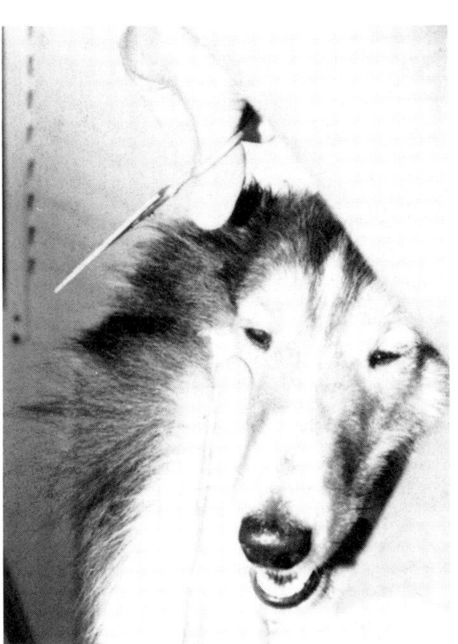

Even the tips of face framing hair.

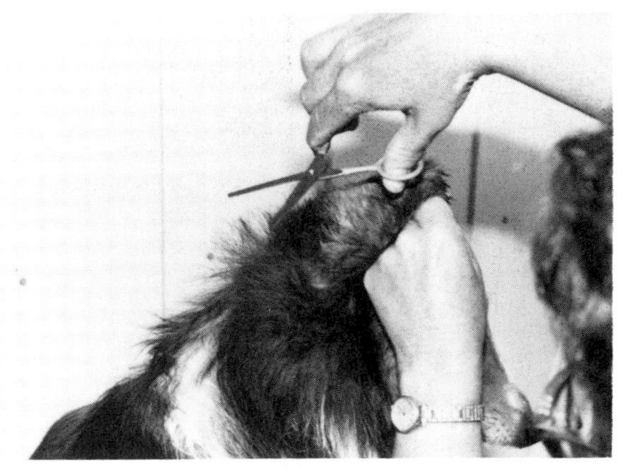

The Stop

Stops can be improved by removing undercoat with a stripping stone or thinning shears. This must be done a little at a time over a period of a week. Remove the undercoat to a point even with the corners of the eyes. Do not thin the hair between the eyes.

Sometimes an uneven top line on the muzzle needs trimming slightly to improve appearance. Another added touch is removing the tiny tufts of hair that grow at the corner of each eye with the mini-thinner or blunt-nosed scissors.

Final Touchup

Chalk any white markings with a chalk block. (Brush out the excess before entering the ring.) With moistened hands, smooth the hair on the face and head, shaping the hair to create the appearance of a smooth, clean backskull, a level topskull, and parallel planes. Make sure any remaining stiffener or setting lotion is brushed out. Fluff the hair behind the ears and shape the face framing. Make sure the collar has been set into the ruff by parting the hair, tightening the leash, and pulling out any hairs that are caught. Brush the hair out so the part doesn't show

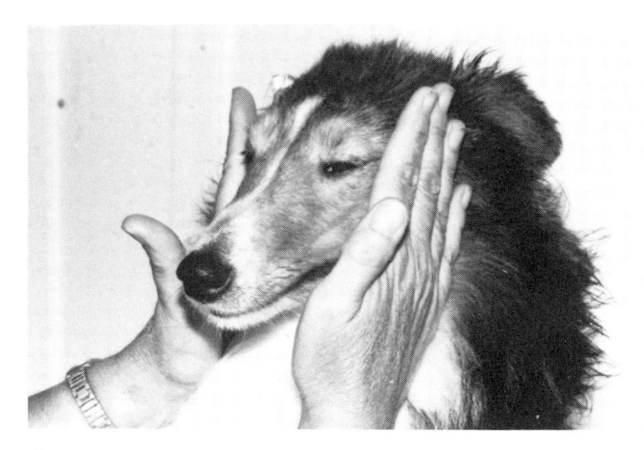

Smooth sides of backskull with setting gel and comb hair up, toward the ears. All stiffeners must be brushed out before going to ring.

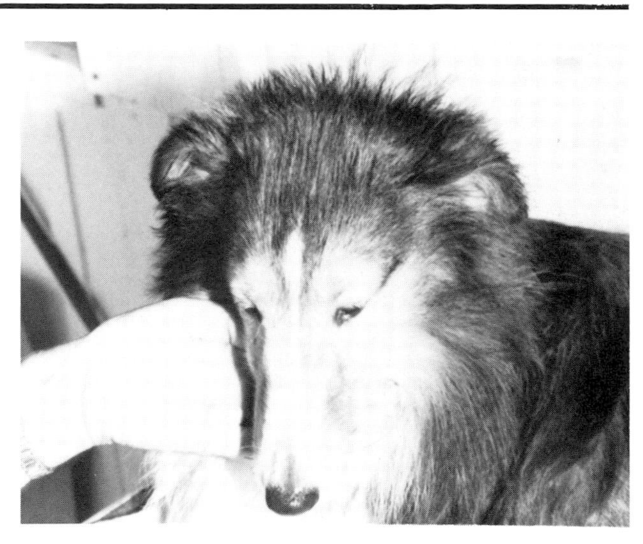

Using setting gel, train hair on topskull straight back, hair at neckline to stand up.

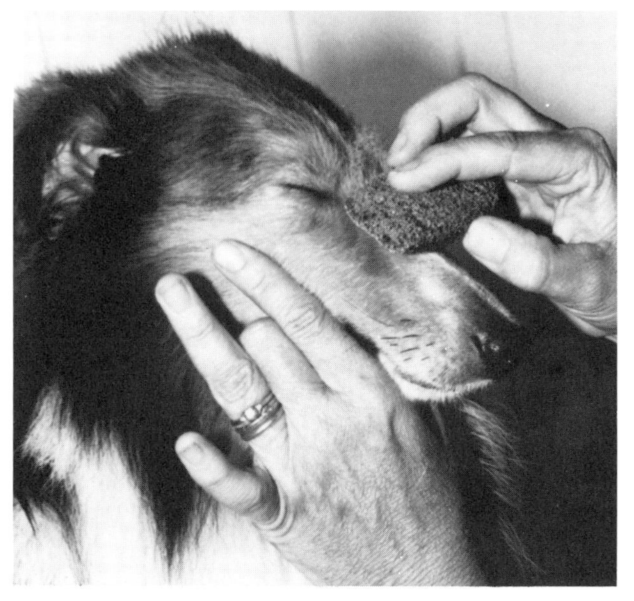

A stripping stone is used to clean the stop.

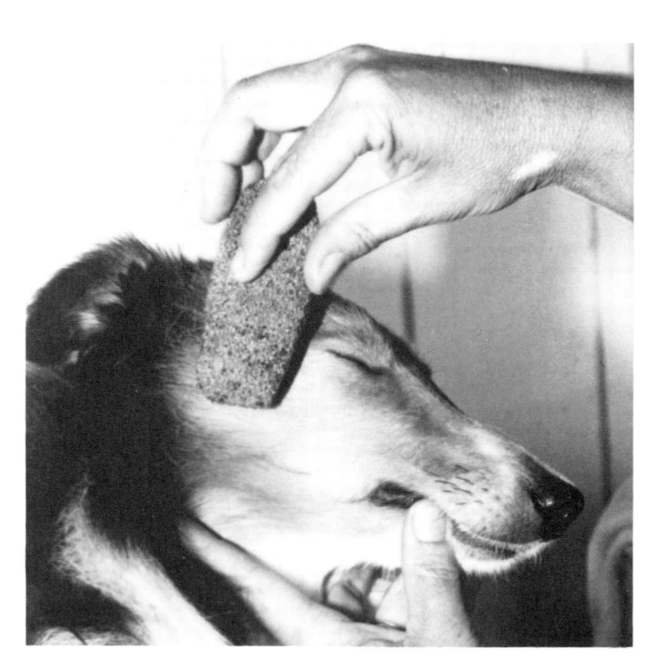

A stripping stone removes undercoat and smooths the skull.

and the collar is buried under the coat without a trace except where the lead emerges.

TRIMMING LEGS AND FEET

After the nails have been clipped or ground, the hair around the feet should be trimmed. Using a long curved shears, if you have one (a long straight pair if not), trim the hair around the side of the pad as shown. Then lift the foot and trim the hair underneath and between the pads.

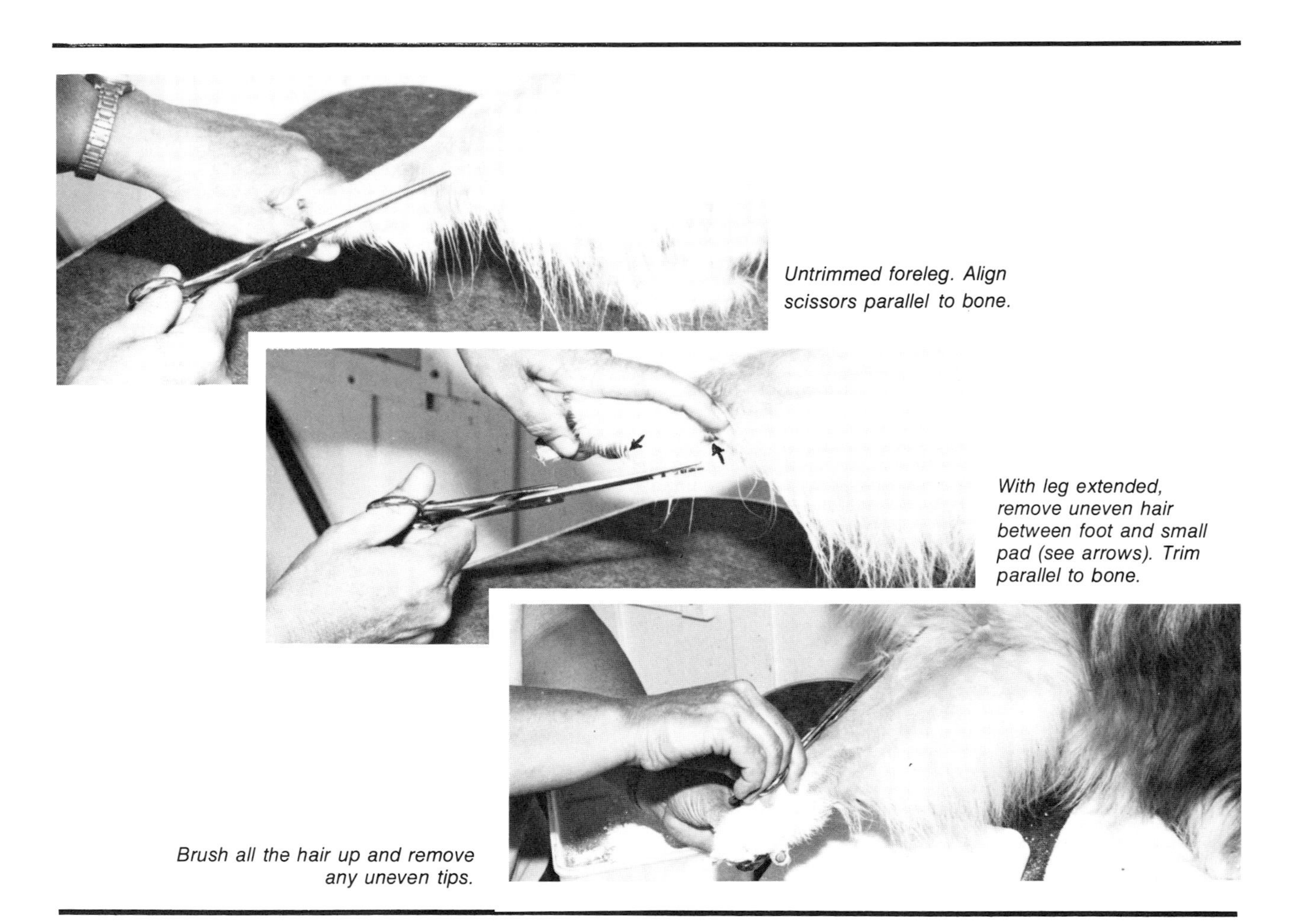

Untrimmed foreleg. Align scissors parallel to bone.

With leg extended, remove uneven hair between foot and small pad (see arrows). Trim parallel to bone.

Brush all the hair up and remove any uneven tips.

Finally, comb the hair on the top of the foot and between the pads up. Trim and shape the pad with the mini-thinners. Round off the front of the toes using the thinner, and, if desired, create a slightly longer foot by thinning the hair at the bend where foot meets pastern (see photos). Remember, the correct foot is a tight oval in shape.

Forelegs

Using the largest scissors available, lift the front leg and extend it forward. Starting at just behind the pad, trim the hair between the pad and the pastern joint. Create a straight line from foot to the small pad at the back of the leg, but not above it. The rest of the foreleg furnishings are left as long as they grow. They may be evened slightly if desired.

If there is a profuse clump of hair growing at the elbow, thin this on the inside to avoid the illusion of elbowing out. If your dog has this physical problem, thin the fringe in this area somewhat and brush it back into the body coat. Use hairspray or setting lotion to train the hair to curve back under the body. Of course, any foreign substance must be removed before you show.

Hocks

Hocks are trimmed below the hock joint. Moisten the hair on the legs and comb so that every hair is standing straight out. With the Sheltie standing naturally on the table, comb the hair back and trim a straight vertical line from just below the hock joint to the ground. Next, comb the hair to the inside of the leg and once again trim in a straight line. Repeat, combing the hair to the outside. This creates a smooth, rounded appearance. Continue to smooth and round until the leg appears finished. Hair on the hock should be between one-fourth and one-half inch in length when you are finished. More length creates the illusion of heavier bone.

Brush the tuft of hair that you left on the hock joint down, blending it into the pants.

Next, extend the leg backward, lifting the foot. Trim at an angle from the back of the pad to remove any straggly hairs.

If a dog lacks rear angulation, thin in front of the hock, taking the coat nearly to the skin. If the dog places the leg too far forward, trim the hair longer at the foot than at the hock joint.

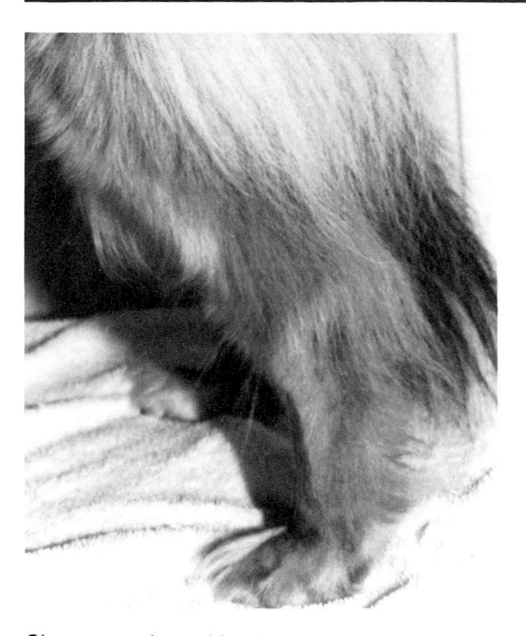

Shaggy, untrimmed hock.

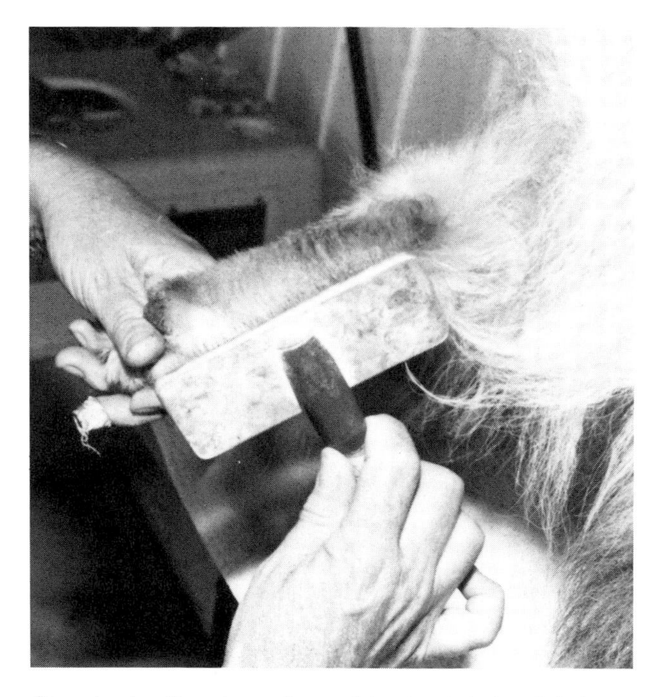

Spray hock with water and use slicker brush to brush hair to one side.

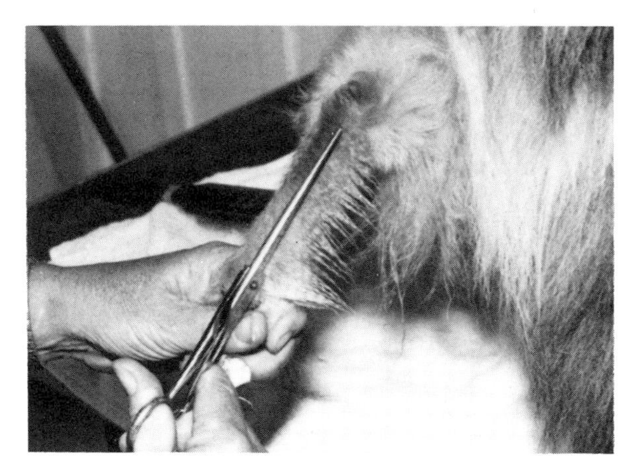

Align shears with center of hock bone.

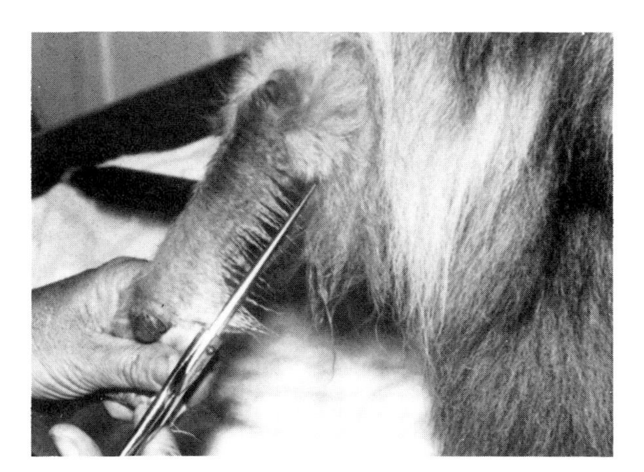

Bring shears straight over to longest hairs and cut.

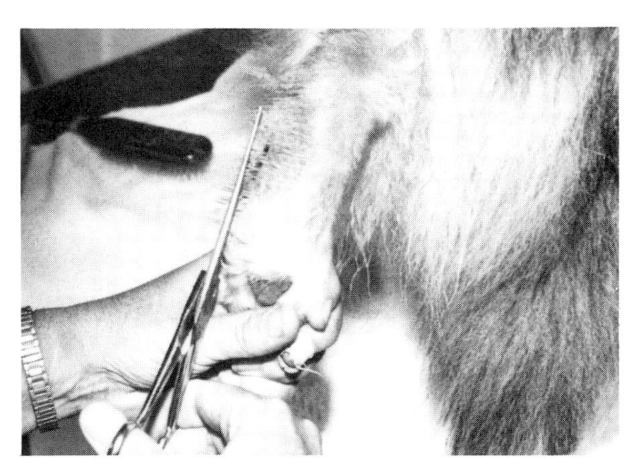

Repeat above steps on the opposite side of the leg.

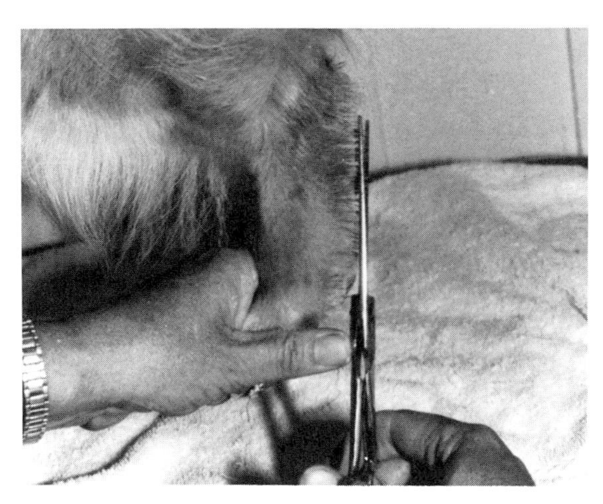

Now brush hair straight back, align shears parallel to leg bone and trim again.

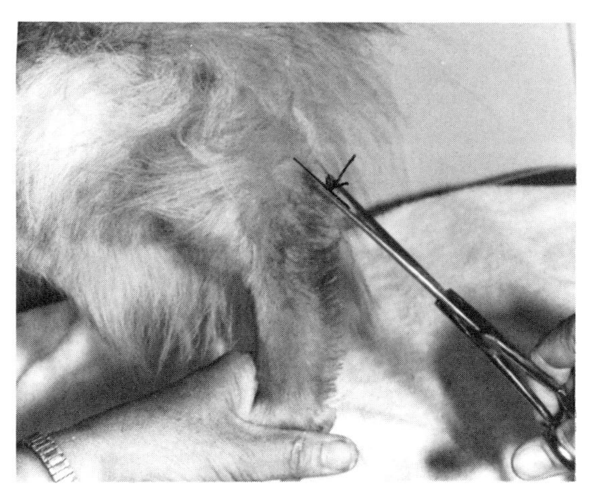

Use thinning shears to create illusion of a lower hock by trimming at an angle directly above the joint.

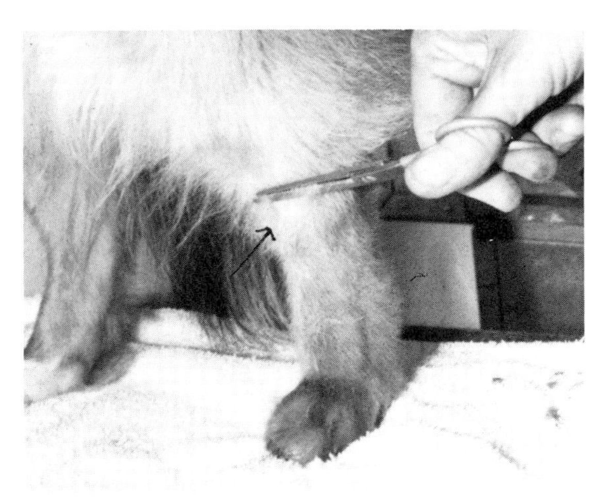

Thin puff of hair at the inside of hock joint. Round and blend into the leg and stifle.

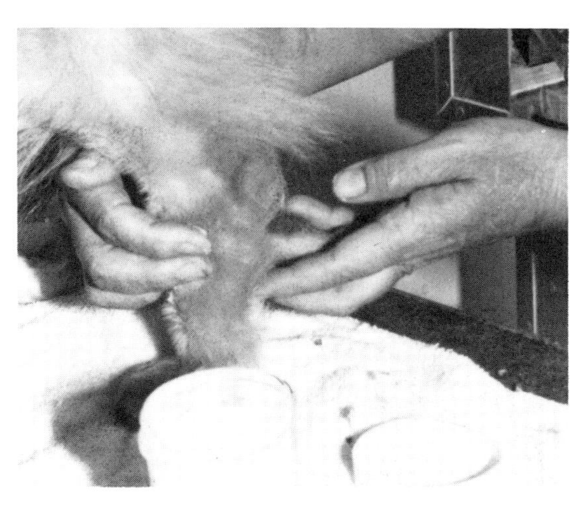

Rub a small amount of Kolestrol, Chalk Mate, or similar binding agent on hands and work clear to skin. Brush hair up with slicker.

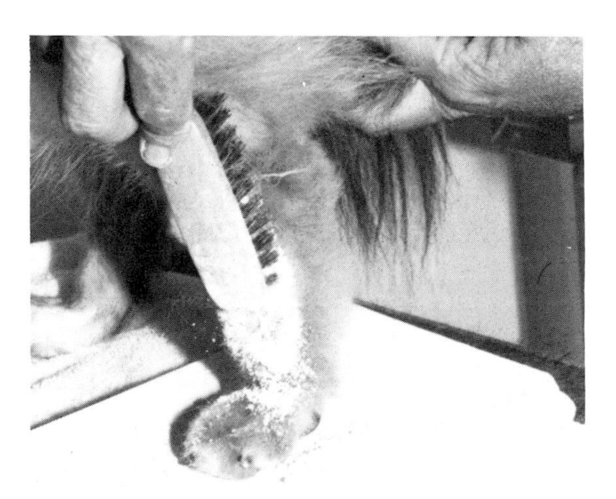

Pack chalk clear to the skin. Let dry for an hour or more.

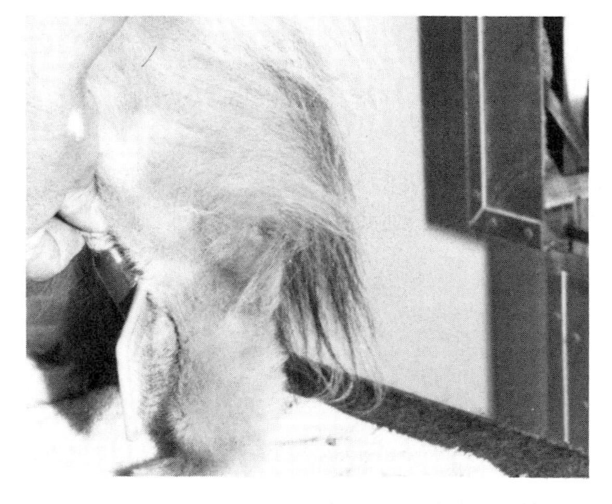

When hock is dry, brush out all excess chalk, making hair stand straight out around the leg.

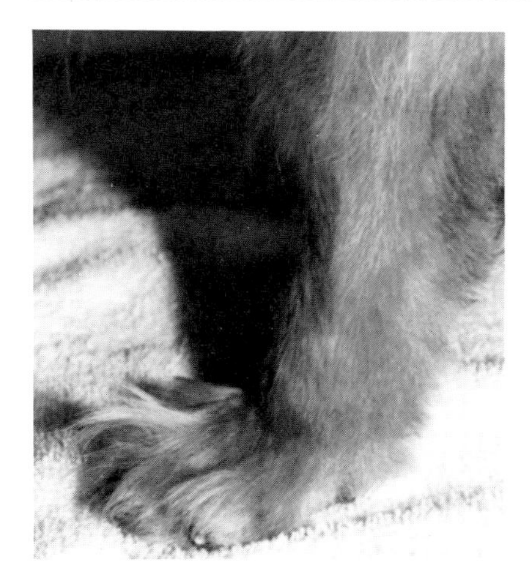

The untrimmed foot.

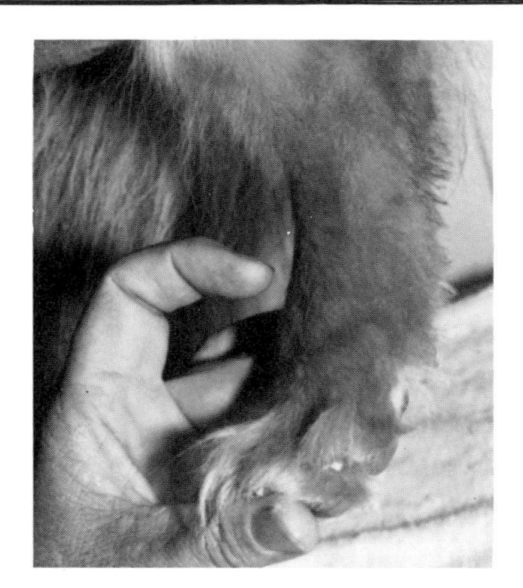

Pick up foot and push pads back with thumb. Keep middle finger behind the pad and squeeze.

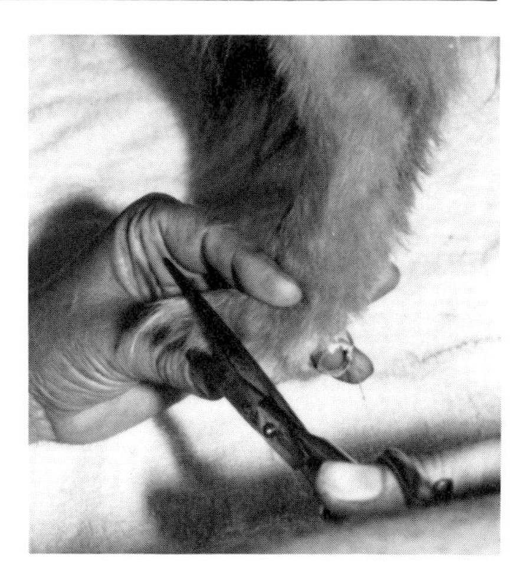

After cutting toenails, trim hair level with nails. Do not trim on top of nails.

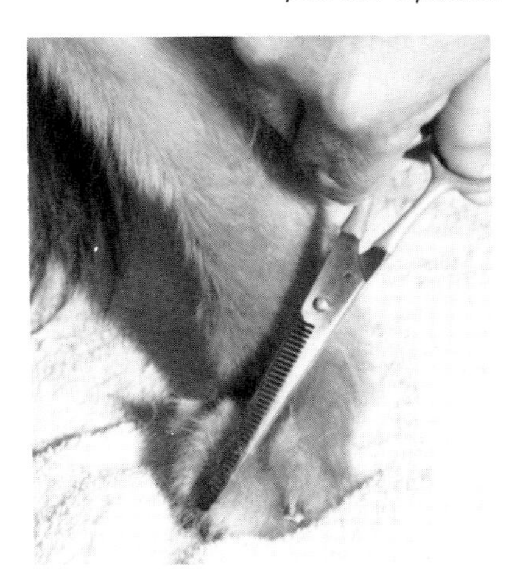

Using slicker, brush hair between toes up. Trim anything above the top of the foot.

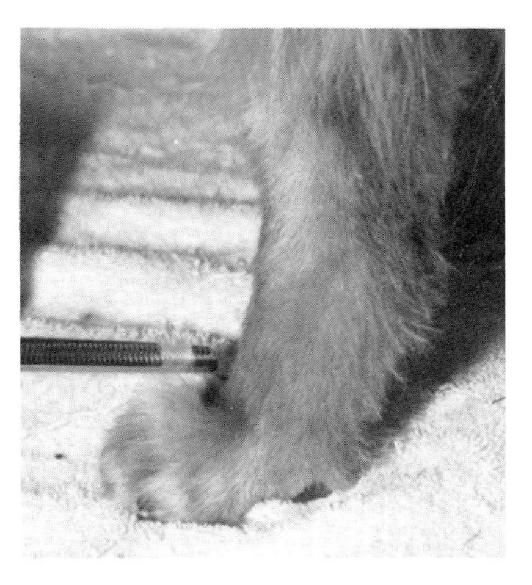

Trim around the foot as illustrated, rounding as you go.

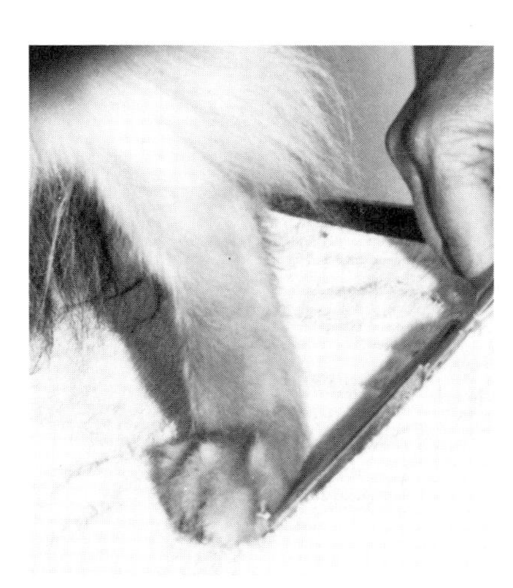

Set foot on floor and trim around the base as illustrated.

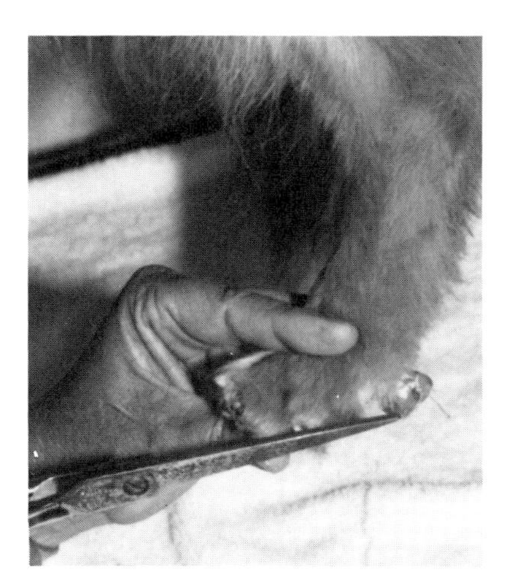

Trim hair from between pads if necessary and trim all hair on bottom of foot even with pads.

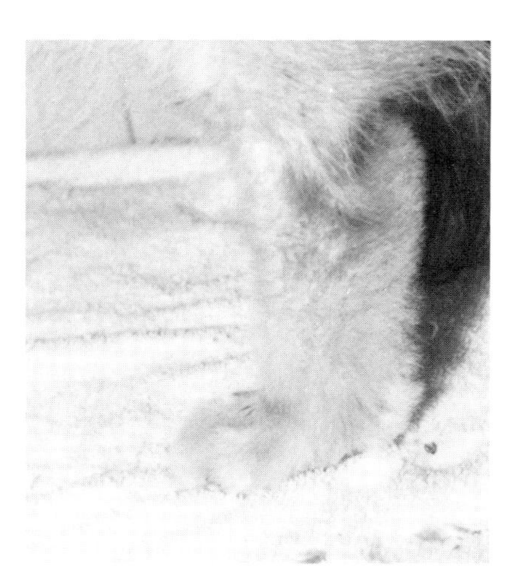

The finished hock and stifle is neat and gives impression of a low hock and plenty of bone.

OUTLINE

The final step in show grooming is to step back and assess the dog's outline. If he is high in rear or appears to be so because of profuse coat on the croup, remove the undercoat with thinning shears or stripping comb. Shape the croup by using your single-sided thinning shears to remove the undercoat from the area on each side of the base of the tail.

Comb the hair on the back up to correct a weak topline, or down on the back and up on the withers to correct a slightly roached back.

Experiment with combing the ruff and shoulder coat until you find the method that gives your dog the most elegance and balance. Backcomb if necessary, using a medium-tooth comb or a small human hairbrush made for this purpose.

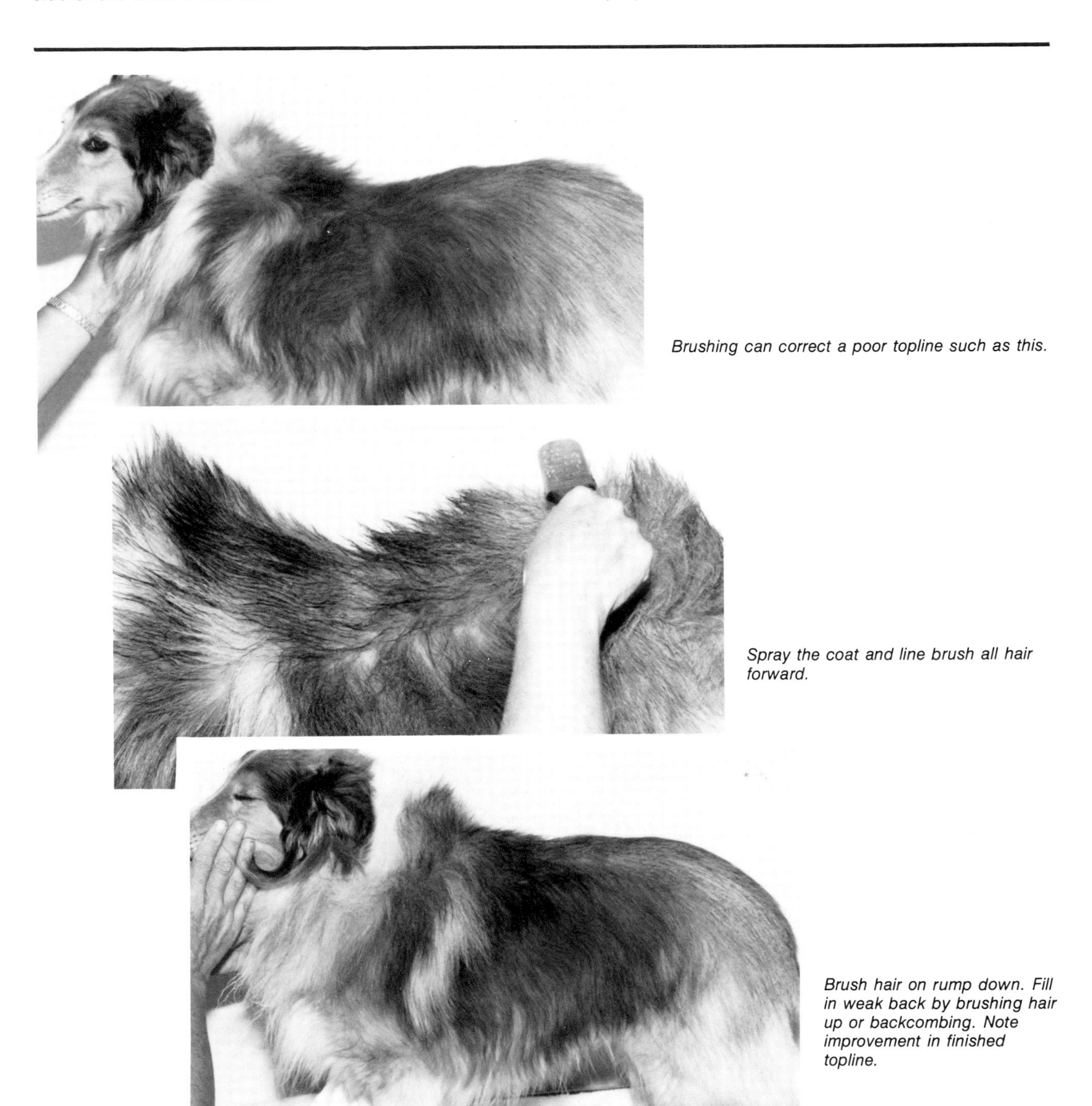

Brushing can correct a poor topline such as this.

Spray the coat and line brush all hair forward.

Brush hair on rump down. Fill in weak back by brushing hair up or backcombing. Note improvement in finished topline.

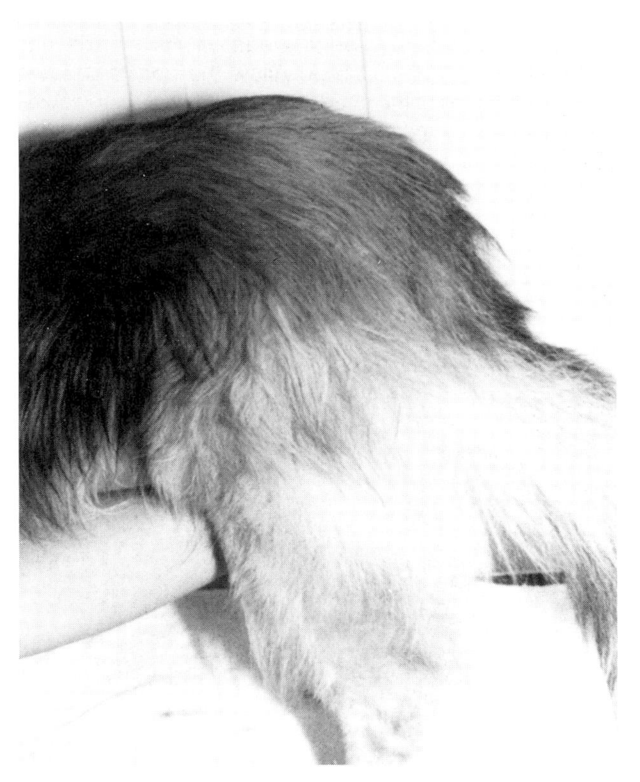

Excess undercoat can create impression of high tailset or rear.

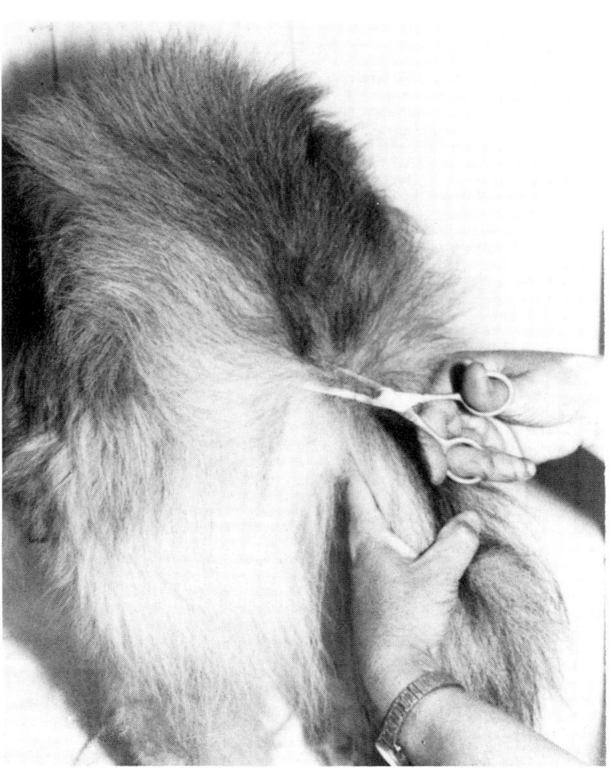

To correct, thin in a "V" at base of tail. Work thinners down to base of hair and take several quick snips.

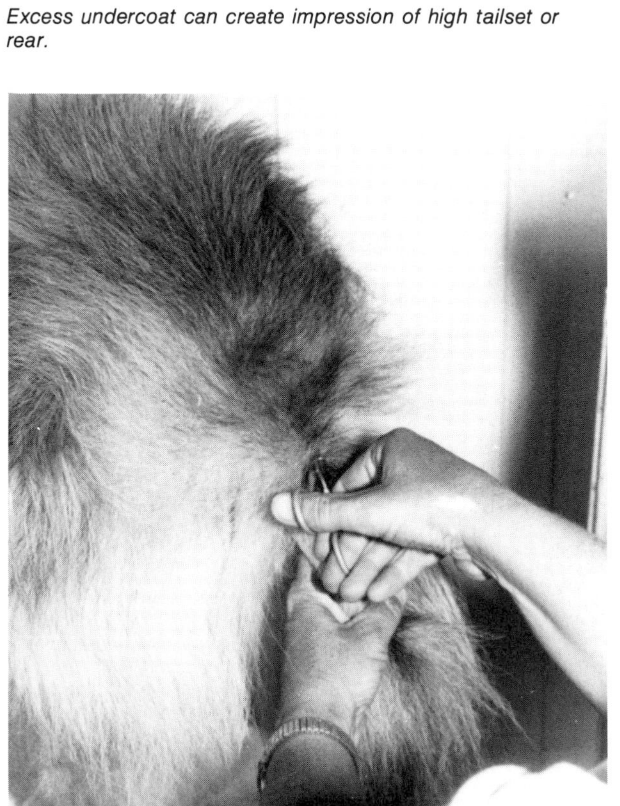

Now trim the other direction, completing the "V".

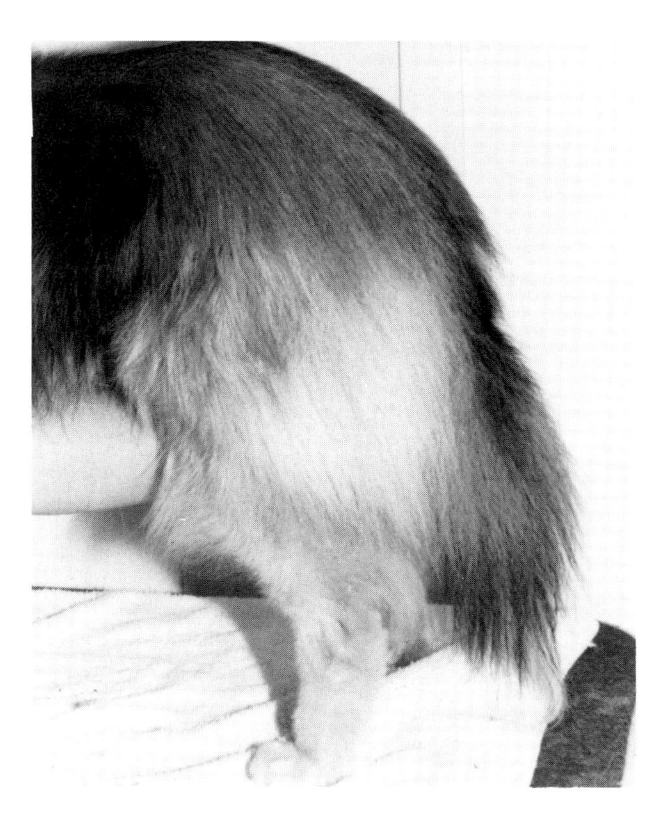

Correct rump and tail after trimming.

GROOMING AT THE SHOW

You have arrived at the show with the dog clean and trimmed. Check the teeth and ears to make sure they are also clean.

Early on the day of the show, re-wash the dog's white feet and legs. I have found that a brightening type or *Orvus*™ livestock shampoo works well for this. Carry a small plastic bucket or container and immerse the legs, one at a time. When damp dry, apply *Chalk Mate*™ or *Kolestral*®, working a small amount onto your palms and transferring it to the legs and feet. Using powdered grooming chalk and a small, stiff bristle brush, work the powder into the undercoat of the legs, brushing against the lay of the hair. Chalk any white areas on the muzzle and underjaw with a chalk block. Allow the dog to dry and remove all traces of the chalk with a bristle brush or blower.

Then, spray the coat with water and linebrush. Make sure every hair is separated and that there are no clumps or parts. Arrange the outline of the coat just before going to ringside. Placing a damp, folded towel over the dog's rump will improve the croup and top-line. Continue lightly misting and shaping the coat periodically until time to enter the ring.

Thin or strip undercoat as needed.

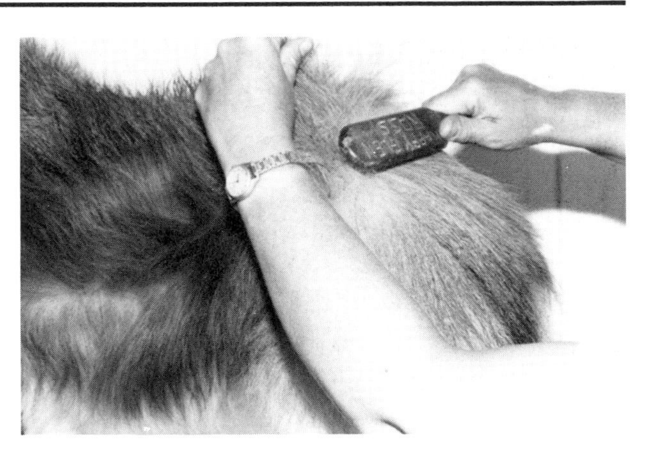

Linebrush hair on rump down.

After linebrushing rump and back in place, mist lightly with water and lay a folded towel over the rump to keep the hair in place.

Does your Sheltie have a healthy glow and vitality? It requires only a little attention and care. Ch. Knightwood Devon, owned by Nancy Lee Marshall, showing off.

Keeping Fit 9

A healthy Sheltie is a joy to behold—full of energy, vitality, and bloom. Keeping him in that condition includes daily maintenance and feeding, regular grooming, an immunization program, and an eye for observing abnormal behavior that may warn of health problems.

In order to recognize illness, we need to understand wellness—what is normal in the dog. Owners can usually tell if a dog is really sick by the symptoms he displays—vomiting, diarrhea, coughing, mucousy nostrils and eyes, or listlessness tell us the pet is ill. But observing the more subtle symptoms that occur early or with mild illness can be extremely important if optimum vitality is to be maintained.

A healthy Sheltie carries adequate weight but is not overweight. His eyes are bright and clear, his nose is neither hot or cold to touch, his coat is shiny and not dry or broken. He is alert and active, and should retain this activity into old age (past 10 years). Normal Shelties are happy, attentive, and playful. Dull, inattentive behavior is often a clue to illness.

The normal temperature in an adult dog is 101.5 to 102.5° F. Temperatures below 100° F. or above 103° F. are cause for a visit to your veterinary clinic. At rest, normal respiration rate is between 10 and 30 times per minute. During excitement, exercise, or stress the rate increases. Normal heart beat ranges from 80 to 140 beats per minute. Small puppies have a more rapid pulse. A normal pulse is steady and firm. You can measure the pulse by placing your fingers inside the rear leg where the leg meets the body. Count the beats for 15 seconds and multiply by four to measure beats per minute.

The healthy Sheltie has pink, firm gums which, if pressed, return quickly to the normal pink color. Pale or blue gums are symptomatic of shock or lack of oxygen.

Observe your dog's abdomen before and after eating to learn what is normal for him. The stomach should not gurgle or feel soft and hollow. Neither should it be distended abnormally as with bloat. He should not urinate too frequently or strain while urinating. Urine should be clear yellow in color. Cloudy or bloody urine is not normal. A sudden increase in the volume or frequency of urination or the amount of water consumed alert you to potential infection.

The teeth and gums should be healthy, with no bleeding and no visible tooth decay or inflamed gum tissue. Loose or decaying teeth should be removed to prevent infection.

Normal ears are free of excessive wax buildup and appear light pink inside. Redness, irritation, heat inside the ear or at the base, or blackish material accumulating in the ear are cause for a veterinary examination.

Keep a record of your dog's normal vital signs. If his average temperature is higher or lower than normal, make note of this. Also note recurring problems such as watery eyes, occasional sneezing or coughing, limping, or other abnormalities. Note the cause, if observed, and when and how often the problem occurs.

VACCINATIONS

The four most vicious killers of dogs are distemper, hepatitis, leptospirosis, and parvovirus. Luckily, you can provide your Sheltie with almost complete immunity through proper immunization.

Distemper is air borne and *no* dog is ever isolated from this virus, so be sure your puppy has his first DHL (distemper-hepatitis-leptospirosis) shot between six and eight weeks of age. At this time he is beginning to lose the immunity he had from his mother at birth. The shot will not "take" until the mother's immunity has left the puppy's system. This happens at different ages and it is impossible to predict, so a series of three shots is generally recommended. The second is generally given at 12 weeks and the third at 16 weeks. Thereafter it is important to give yearly boosters. Adult dogs are susceptible too, and the boosters must be continued throughout your Sheltie's lifetime. Immunization is a small price to pay to avoid the heartache and expense of treating any of these diseases. Parvovirus vaccinations may be given separately or combined with the DHL vaccine. Modified live vaccines are effective for one year after an initial series of three shots one month apart.

The only other vaccination your Sheltie needs is a rabies vaccination at six months of age. Most rabies shots are effective for two to three years, but your county or city laws will determine how often booster shots are required to insure protection from this public health menace. Certificate of rabies vaccination is a prerequisite for obtaining your city dog license or for obtaining a health certificate prior to interstate shipping.

SHELTIES ARE WHAT THEY EAT

Keeping any dog in peak condition requires first of all a well balanced diet—one containing all the nutrients, vitamins, minerals, protein, carbohydrates, and fat necessary not only to sustain life but to give the dog the extra sparkle and vigor that is a sign of good health.

Shelties, being an active, working breed (whether they actually work stock or not) seem to burn more calories than many small breeds and require more calories per pound of body weight than larger dogs. Yet most of them do not begin to eat the volume of food (usually three to four cups of dry food) that manufacturers recommend. *Therefore, higher fat content, lower bulk feeds are your best choice.* Actual working Shelties, bitches in whelp, and dogs kenneled outside during extremely cold weather, need an even more concentrated ration.

Kinds of Food

There are numerous brands of dog food available, some good and some not so good, These can be divided into three basic types—dry, semi-moist, and moist (canned). The best source of a balanced diet for your Sheltie is a good brand of dry food, one guaranteeing "a complete, balanced ration."

Dry Food. Dry food, or kibble, is the easiest to feed, the cheapest form, and generally the best complete food. It has an added advantage in that it helps to stimulate the dog's gums and clean his teeth while he eats. Kibble contains 23 to 28 percent protein, about 1500 to 1800 calories per pound, and 7 to 10 percent moisture. It comes in several forms.

The pellet form is very tightly compressed pellets and the palatability of these is not quite as good as some types. You may need to moisten this type to get your Sheltie to eat it. A more palatable form is the expanded food. This type is made in larger, less solid particles and sprayed with fat. It is especially good for self-feeding. A third form is the biscuit where the food is rolled out, baked, and broken into small pieces. The same process is used to make biscuit treats.

There is considerable variation in the many brands available; not all supply high quality protein or all of the essential nutrients. Read the labels carefully, or choose one of the old standbys recommended by breeders.

Since any kibble may be a little less palatable than moist food, some people mix canned food or meat with it. Others moisten it with water or broth, but this only has the effect of expanding the food so the dog eats less volume. Such additives should comprise no more than 25 percent of the ration or it will throw the carefully manufactured diet out of balance.

A Sheltie who learns to eat dry food, preferably self-fed, from puppyhood, will accept it readily without the addition of meat and will generally be less picky and stay in better weight than one who has to have his food "just so."

In the first edition, we recommended *Science Diet®* because it was a complete, high protein, high nutrient food that required no supplementation. *Science Diet Growth®* is still my personal choice for puppies. But in the past few years numerous new rations have been developed with rations formulated for puppies, lactating females, adult maintenance, and stress conditions. *Iams*™, *Breeder's Choice*™, *Nutro*™, and a number of other brand names cater to the dog show enthusiasts and breeders. The advantages of these foods are high caloric density, high protein, often high fat content, and better digestibility resulting in lower stool volume. No supplementation is needed with the possible exception of oil as a coat supplement. The disadvantages are the protein and/or fat content may be too high for some dogs, overfeeding may cause diarrhea, and some dogs will gain too much weight without getting the necessary bulk for healthy bowel function. Check with other breeders in your area as to availability and results they are getting with their ration. Then experiment until you find a food that works best for your dog(s) and stay with it. If cost or fat content of the high-nutrient feeds is a problem, consider mixing them with another dry food such as *Ken-L Biscuit®*, a cereal based ration.

Semi-Moist Foods. Sold as cellophane-wrapped patties, this food is also a complete and balanced ration, furnishing about 1400 calories per pound and 22 percent protein. It can be fed alone or in combination with kibble. It is a convenient general purpose ration and easy to carry when traveling, but is probably the most expensive type of dog food.

Moist or Canned Foods. Regular canned foods labeled a "complete" or "balanced" ration may be fed alone. They contain about 75 percent water, so a dog must eat a much larger volume of canned food than of dry food to obtain the same nutritional value. Canned foods provide only about 500 calories per pound of food; for most Shelties, who tend to eat only a small volume, this is not enough. This kind of food supplies about 10 percent protein, which converts to about 40 percent on a dry matter basis; but again, remember that a Sheltie would have to eat much more.

In addition to the "complete" canned foods, there are many *all meat rations which are not intended to be fed as a complete diet* but as a supplement to dry food. They furnish palatability and a little added protein when mixed with kibble. Be sure to note the differences when shopping for canned food.

The Prescription Diet line of canned food, available through your veterinarian, is a specially developed line of foods for dogs under specific stress situations. K/d, for dogs with kidney problems, was the first to be developed; followed by I/d for stomach and intestinal disorders; H/d for dogs with heart disease; R/d for overweight dogs; and P/d for dogs with high energy requirements. You may want to inquire about these for older or ill Shelties.

Shelties will do anything! This photo was taken as a promotional for a restaurant and bar owned by Roger and Norene Meltvedt, Rogene Shelties, Palmer, Alaska. (Hansen Photo.)

Where's the beef? (Photo by Lloyd Price.) Puppies at Keynote Shelties.

Oh, here comes Joe now! (Photo by Hansen.)

Supplements

If your Sheltie is eating a properly balanced commercial ration, vitamin-mineral supplements are rarely necessary except for puppies, pregnant or lactating bitches, or dogs which are doing poorly. Although some owners feed protein supplements to all their dogs, this is not necessary. If you want to add protein, however, the best way is to add whole cooked eggs (*raw egg white destroys biotin,* a necessary element, and should *not* be fed), whole or powdered cottage cheese, or raw or cooked beef. Liver is an ideal supplement containing B-complex and vitamins A and K. One teaspoon of chopped liver per day is maximum. Supplemental protein must never comprise more than 25 percent of your Sheltie's diet. Be sure he is eating the kibble as well as the protein. Prolonged diets of meat, especially organ meats, lead to an imbalance of calcium and phosphorus which can cause soft or deformed bones and other problems.

If you feed puppies one of the high-nutrient dry foods such as *Iams*™ or *Science Diet*® formulated for growth, they do not need additional supplements. Puppies fed an adult ration or a low quality feed may need additional calcium, vitamins, and minerals. Bone meal is a safe, inexpensive calcium supplement. Pregnant or lactating bitches on a low quality feed also need vitamin/mineral supplements.

New research is proving that oversupplementation, too much protein, and overnutrition can cause as many problems as a deficiency. Perhaps the pendulum has swung from one extreme to the other. Loose stools, diarrhea, constipation, poor digestion, dull, broken coats, and either hyper- or hypo-active temperaments can result from nutritional imbalance. Excess calcium has been indicated as a possible cause of hip dysplasia; too much fat causes kidney problems; lack of zinc can cause reproductive or skin problems. Tests are being developed to help veterinarians and researchers pinpoint nutritional imbalance and we are learning more in this area each year. A moderate diet and the use of natural foods and food supplements is recommended.

One discovery of note is the importance of the natural bacteria normally present in the digestive tract of humans and carnivorous animals. Lactobacillus acidophilus aids digestion and replaces these normal bacteria which can be destroyed by antibiotic treatment, disease, or stress. This is an important consideration for working dogs, dogs recuperating from surgery or taking antibiotics, and dogs suffering from gastrointestinal infections such as parvo or corona virus. Lactobacillus acidophilus can be purchased in liquid or powder form from a health food store. It is also present in yogurt and buttermilk, and is available in tube form in a product especially for dogs, *Or-Lac*®. You may want to keep some on hand when traveling. Many breeders and handlers recommend using lactobacillus as a preventative measure at the first sign of gastrointestinal upset.

When and How to Feed

Like all dogs, Shelties thrive on monotony in their diet. In fact, changes can easily lead to digestive upsets and poor eating habits. It is far better to select one basic ration and stick with it, feeding at the same time every day. Any changes should be made gradually over the period of a week.

Most Shelties do well on self-feeding (i.e., having food available at all times). Some breeders self-feed kibble while providing an additional meal of meat and supplements once a day. *Puppies* can be put on self-feeding at weaning time. If not on self-feeding, *puppies under three months* should be fed four times a day; then three times daily until six months; thereafter twice a day. *Adult dogs* do nicely on one meal a day unless they are light eaters or tend to be thin.

Some Shelties, like some horses, are "easy keepers" that stay sleek and fat on a minimum diet. Others, unfortunately, are picky eaters and go through several growth stages when they are extremely thin. This is particularly a problem with some dogs at about a year of age. Most of these dogs outgrow this phase by 16 months to two years, but a few never appear to reach peak condition. Fortunately, most Shelties are somewhere in between.

Definite symptoms of an allergic reaction to a foreign substance. Note lump between eyes and lumps under coat tufts throughout the body. This particular reaction was caused by using BenGay on the ears.

Adult Shelties need one to three cups of kibble, on an average, or three to four patties of semi-moist food, or two cans of moist food. Puppies are individuals and must be regulated accordingly. Unless on self-feeding, allow about 20 minutes for a dog to clean up his plate and then remove any leftover food. Water should be available at all times.

The best evidence that a ration is correct for your Sheltie is a steady weight gain in a puppy and a firm, well padded but not fat condition in an adult. Stools should be firm; constantly loose stools often result from overeating. Most dogs will skip a meal now and then, and this is of no concern. However, if your dog refuses more than one meal in a row he should be watched carefully for symptoms of illness.

Maintaining Correct Weight

A dog that is being exhibited and therefore traveling a lot, or one being used for breeding, is under a great deal of stress and may be difficult to keep in condition. *The Sheltie that is too thin* may be helped by switching to a food with a higher fat content or one in a more concentrated form. If this doesn't work try adding ¼ cup table cream per day to his ration for a month or so, or adding cooked rice, oatmeal, or bacon fat for extra fat and carbohydrate content. Usually thin dogs are also overactive and may need their exercise restricted.

The last resort for putting weight on a show dog who refuses to eat enough volume to maintain his weight is to force feed. Mix ½ cup cooked rice or oatmeal with one semi-moist food patty. Roll it into half-inch balls which can be stuffed down the Sheltie's throat like a pill. Feed him this amount, or as much as it takes to make his stomach feel distended and full, three times a day for two to four weeks. Immediately after feeding he should be let out to relieve himself, then confined to a small area or crate. After a few weeks his stomach should be able to accommodate this larger volume of food and he should already have gained some weight. You should then be able to return to feeding him from a bowl.

The *overweight dog* can also be a problem to condition because he tends to be sloppy in movement and tire easily. A fat dog is also prone to breeding difficulties, heat and skin problems, and to breaking down in the stifle. So, if you want a healthy Sheltie, keep his weight down.

A report issued by Ralston Purina Company[1] listed eight practical guidelines:

1. Reduce food intake by as much as 20 to 40% of the previous daily intake.
2. Feed smaller amounts more often. This helps satisfy the dog's appetite and keeps him from begging.
3. Avoid diets high in fat. There are several rations available specifically for the overweight dog, such as *Purina Fit and Trim*.
4. Do not feed table scraps.
5. Make sure plenty of fresh water is available at all times.
6. Do not add any supplements. (I personally feel that a vitamin mineral tablet may be advisable for the older dog that has had his food ration severely cut.)
7. With your veterinarian's guidance, establish a supervised physical exercise program for your dog.
8. Do not let the dog have access to garbage cans or other sources of additional food. (My old male is an artist at finding leftover food, spilled food around the crates, or getting into the cat food. When all these sources were carefully eliminated he began to lose.)

Most overweight dogs simply overeat. If they are on self-feeding they must be taken off and the amount of food carefully controlled. Don't, for example, allow them to have tidbits of food at the table. Fat dogs are often lazy dogs and a program of enforced exercise may be needed along with the reduction in calories. If the dog does not lose weight on this program, consult with your veterinarian about R/d Prescription Diet or about having tests done to rule out the possibility of a hormone malfunction. Thyroid deficiency, or malfunction of the adrenal, pituitary, pancreas, or reproductive glands will cause over- or underweight problems.

[1]*Canine Obesity*. Robert K. Mohrman. Senior Manager, Pet Nutrition and Care Research. Ralston Purina Co., St. Louis.

CONDITIONING THE SHOW DOG

The sparkle and bloom of the Sheltie who carries away the Best of Breed ribbon is more than a matter of good breeding and daily care—it is the result of a planned, regimented conditioning program. So, if you have dreams, like I once did, of taking your Sheltie out of your back yard the day before the show, bathing and brushing him, and walking off with the ribbons next day, forget it! Shelties do not reach this beautiful peak condition without a lot of work; but when they do reach it they not only look better, they will be healthier, happier, more willing to work, and more alert, too.

There are four major elements in conditioning—diet, daily care and grooming, coat conditioning, and exercise. Daily care and grooming have been discussed elsewhere, so here I will consider feeding, conditioning the coat, and exercise, with particular emphasis on conditioning for the show ring.

CONDITIONING THE SHELTIE'S COAT

A Sheltie's coat is his crowning glory and its density, texture, and condition can make or break him in the show ring. While the amount, texture, and length of coat are inherited, they do not reach their peak potential without a great deal of effort.

As we have already mentioned, nutrition is important to optimum coat growth. Another basic is grooming. Brushing stimulates hair growth and distributes natural oils. Frequent brushing, lightly and against the lay of the coat, is a must. Never brush a dry coat. It must always be sprayed with water. Dampen the coat thoroughly with a fine spray, work the moisture evenly through the coat with your hands, then brush until dry. In dry climates you may want to repeat the spraying several times a day. You should begin to see results in a month. Humidifiers and air conditioning in the kennel room are beneficial for show dogs kept in hot, dry climates.

Some exhibitors use livestock blowers instead of brushing. The blower removes dirt, stimulates the skin and hair follicles and causes less breakage. However, it can also dry the coat too much. The blower nozzle is moved over the dog in the same manner as you would linebrush, blowing against the lay of the hair.

Cleanliness is another important factor. Dirt causes more coat damage than anything else. Tall grass, weed seeds or burrs, and gravel used in kennel runs also cause coats to break. Frequent grooming will remove most of the dirt. If the coat is still dirty, use a waterless shampoo such as *Self-Rinse Plus®* . Spray it onto the coat, work in with your hands, and towel dry. Frequent baths removes natural oils from the show coat. If a bath is necessary, cool water and a moisturizing shampoo help prevent unnecessary coat loss.

Since the climate in Colorado is very dry, I have used just about every conceivable product for coat conditioning at one time or another. The same product will not work cool, humid room. Let them outside in the early morning or late evening. Sunscreen preparations are available at pet supply shops. If your black or blue Sheltie's coat turns rust-colored in the summer, this is also sunburn. Some breeders recommend a diet high in iron as a preventative. Blackstrap molasses is a good natural source of iron.

The general health of your Sheltie is also reflected in his coat. If, in spite of all your efforts at conditioning the coat remains dull and lifeless, look for other causes, such as worms, diet, illness, lack of exercise, hormone or thyroid deficiency.

The coat of blue merles is more brittle than other colors and tends to break easily. Ch. Heir Apparent of Karelane, owned by Elaine Samuels, is in lovely condition here. (Photo by Shafer)

Carrying heaving coat for a bitch and in excellent bloom and condition is Ch. Ardencaple Berridale Belove, a Ch. Gerthstone Jon Christopher daughter bred and owned by Jesse and Glennis Carroll Canden. (Photo by Krook)

for every dog, so the best advice I can offer is to experiment until you find one that works for you. There are numerous commercial coat conditioners for dogs, and as many more for humans. I have had good results by cleaning the coat with a spray containing waterless shampoo, toweling dry, and then spraying with distilled water or one of the coat conditioners. I prefer protein or moisturizing conditioners over coat oils. The oils tend to collect dirt, causing coat breakage.

In summer, a Sheltie's coat can get sunburned from too much exposure just as your own hair sometimes does. The hairs split and turn up on the ends and are extremely difficult to recondition. It may take as long as a year to restore a badly sunburned coat. For this reason, keep your Sheltie out of the summer sun as much as possible. Show dogs should be confined to a shaded run or a crate in a

Coat supplements. Normal skin and hair condition depend on an adequate supply of fatty acids. These are found in bacon drippings, vegetable oil, corn oil, safflower oil, soy oil, peanut oil, wheat germ oil, or in commercial coat supplements. Hamburger and other meat grease, with the exception of bacon grease, does not contain the needed fatty acids and has no benefit at all to a dog's coat; it simply adds calories.

There are many coat supplements on the market. Again it is best to experiment until you find one that works best for your dogs in your environment. Supplements may be either liquid or powder and should be given according to package directions. If you prefer to use one of the vegetable oils, start with one teaspoon per day and build up to one tablespoon per day for adults. An exception is wheat germ oil. This oil is so rich that one-fourth teaspoon is

Moderate coat such as this is perfectly acceptable in a bitch. Ch. Macdega Make Me Smile, dam of three champions, owned by Canden Shelties.

enough for a six-month-old Sheltie, and one-half to one teaspoon for an adult. I have used a combination of one cup wheat germ oil with twenty-four ounces each of safflower and peanut oil with some success.

With all the interest in health foods, attention has been given to natural vitamins and minerals. The B-complex vitamins (found in brewer's yeast), zinc, sea kelp, and pantothentic acid have been recommended as necessary for good coats by many health food enthusiasts.

EXERCISE AND ROAD WORK

No conditioning program is complete without a structured exercise program! Neither the kennel dog nor the house dog gets enough of the right kind of exercise. Shelties need at least one hour a day of romping together in a large area to keep in hard condition.

The best conditioning exercise, however, is conducted at the end of a leash—"road work." If it were possible to include movies in this book we could demonstrate the amazingly good muscle tone achieved by road work and the effect this has on a Sheltie's gait. The sloppy mover tightens up (sometimes beyond belief) and the basically correct moving dog becomes more perfect, smooth, and extended in reach. Good muscle tone also encourages sexual vigor in males and helps bitches conceive and whelp easier. It won't, however, correct the movement of an unsound or straightly angulated Sheltie but it will make the best of what he is capable.

Provided you progress gradually, road work may be started on a Sheltie as young as seven or eight months, but he must be worked much shorter distances than an adult. Adult Shelties should also be started gradually and slowly worked up to a maximum of two miles a day.

To be beneficial, road work must be started at least a month prior to showing. Work on a loose lead at a comfortable trotting speed for your dog. A Sheltie with correct angulation and therefore a long stride can naturally trot faster than one with steeper angulation and more restricted reach. Do not allow the dog to run or gallop as this uses entirely different muscles than those used for trotting.

The best surface for road work is grass or dirt, but a gravel road will do nicely too. If you gait on pavement, or cement, go shorter distances and be sure to watch for sore pads or lameness. Pavement is not a desirable surface to use and should be avoided if possible. The surface used for road work should be level. A slight uphill grade will help, but *never* trot a dog downhill as this can break down pasterns and shoulders. Keep the dog's nails as short as possible and treat the pads with a pad toughener if they get sore.

The first few days take your Sheltie about one-half mile at a speed of four to six miles per hour. You can trot with him or work him alongside your bicycle. If you have someone to help you, that person can drive your station wagon while you lead the dog from the tailgate. It is unsafe to tie a dog to the rear of a moving vehicle. Always sit in the back and lead him carefully behind.

After a week going one-half mile a day, gradually increase the distance to a mile a day by the end of the second week. Watch carefully to make sure you are not forcing the dog beyond what he can take. He should not come in completely exhausted, or want to stop and lie down during the session. Of course, if he does become stiff or lame, discontinue or shorten the workout until he recovers and then increase the distance more slowly.

Gradually increase the distance by about one-half mile per week until the dog can trot two miles a day without tiring. Working at this level every day for a month will put your Sheltie in the best possible muscle tone he can attain. Thereafter, working once or twice a week should maintain optimum condition. The dog will fall into a natural, easy, level trot—the kind you can admire by the hour.

If you own or show a number of dogs, you may want to invest in a treadmill or a dog-sized version of the "hotwalker" used for horses. Treadmills have an advantage during wet or icy weather. They also enable you to work one dog while grooming or feeding others, can be set for various speeds, inclined to encourage drive, and operate on timer for more precise conditioning. Disadvantages are cost and the fact that you, the handler, are deprived of exercising with your dog. I thoroughly enjoy running or bicycling with my Sheltie while the sun is just rising, birds are singing, and the dew is still on. It's physically and spiritually uplifting, and it encourages the delightful human-animal bond that develops responsiveness and attention in the show dog.

What a happy breed! Keynote Beyond Belief, right, and Keynote Endless Dream, owned by Shelby Price.

To Have and to Hold 10

Shelties, by and large, are a sturdy, happy-go-lucky lot not apt to cause you a lot of worry. But all dogs, like all children, are notably prone to accidents. Now that you have acquired your new companion, safeguarding him from the hazards of a dog's life will constitute one of your responsibilities.

KEEPING YOUR NEW SHELTIE

Shelties are amazingly quick and agile, a very pleasing trait most of the time, but this also enables them to skillfully dance right out of your reach or sight and disappear if they suddenly opt. A frightened Sheltie can be next to impossible to catch. Now, this shouldn't be a problem once you've owned the little creature for awhile, but when a Sheltie is first transferred to a new owner, the dog's nature being what it is, he is apt to be unaccepting and a bit frightened. Take a few precautions until your new Sheltie has accepted you as his new "parent."

Before you bring the new Sheltie home, check the yard for holes or broken wire near the ground or wide cracks in a board fence or around a gate. Patch these. An eight or ten week old Sheltie can squeeze through a hole no more than three inches wide. Older Shelties can go through hogwire or welded wire fences with ease. Solid board or chain link fences are recommended.

Since the Sheltie by nature is loyal to an owner to the point of being slow to accept a new owner, I do not trust a young puppy off leash for at least a week; nor one over six months for at least a month. During this time I'm especially careful to see that fences are tight and that the dog doesn't slip through an open gate or door. I once sold a one year old Sheltie on a noisy holiday weekend. The bustling family accidently let the dog slip by when the door was opened and he ran out onto the street. Immediately the entire family gave chase both on foot and horseback, and the frightened Sheltie fled into the fields and vanished.

Another buyer left her newly purchased adult Sheltie in an unfenced yard without a leash after she had him only a week. She thought he had accepted his new home, but a stray dog gave chase and he, too, disappeared in the maze of houses. Although the new owner sighted him several times, the dog only fled. He roamed the city for two weeks before I was finally able to locate him—thin, mussed, but alive. He came at a run and leaped into my arms for joy!

Most Shelties make a beautiful adjustment to a new home so long as accidents of this sort are not allowed to happen. Within a month (and many adjust more quickly) they should be confident and happy in their new situation.

Every Sheltie needs a place to call his own, whether box, crate, kennel, or dog house. The essential requirements are that he be dry, clean, and out of drafts. Your Sheltie will be happiest if his bed is close to yours, but he can also sleep outside, even in cold weather, if he has adequate shelter and warm bedding.

"What is lovely never dies,
But passes into other loveliness."

Thomas Aldrich
A Shadow of the Night

THE INDOOR SHELTIE

If your Sheltie is a house pet, he will like a box in one corner of the kitchen, bedroom, or basement, preferably where he will be near the family. Place the box away from any drafts or dampness. It should be large enough for him to stretch out comfortably, and it should be raised off the floor a few inches, with six or eight inch sides to further help prevent drafts. Bedding can be a covered pad, newspapers, or an old rug. Remember to change or clean the bedding often and disinfect the box with any good household disinfectant (use one that doesn't contain poisonous Phenol).

Sheltie owners have often told me that they lock their Sheltie in the bathroom at night or when they leave the house. Besides being damp, many bathrooms get much too hot if the furnace is running. The porch, utility room, basement, or even the garage is much more suitable. Better yet, buy a crate. Most Shelties enjoy the security it offers.

THOSE AWFUL CRATES!

The experience of crating isn't as bad as some dogs would like us to believe. In fact, Shelties who are used to being crated find a great deal of security in having a familiar place, especially when they're away from home. Crates are an invaluable aid to housebreaking, too, since the Sheltie detests messing his bed and will do his best to wait until he is let outside. You'll find the crate becomes your dog's seat belt when traveling, protecting him from sudden stops, and preventing him from jumping out the door when you stop. It could very well save his life someday. If the day comes when the crate-trained dog must be shipped, or travel with a handler, or stay overnight at the vet hospital, he will be able to take it in stride.

Crate training is easy. At first put the Sheltie in at feeding time and let him out when he finishes his meal. Gradually increase the time until he will stay quietly for several hours or overnight. Give a puppy a bone or chew toy to prevent boredom. If he barks or cries correct him immediately. If you baby him he'll take advantage of you.

Don't leave your Sheltie crated too long though; eight or nine hours is maximum for an adult, two or three hours for a puppy. If you must keep him crated over long periods be sure he has plenty of clean water available and daily exercise on a leash or in a run.

When selecting a crate, pick a size just large enough to allow the Sheltie to lie stretched out. Wire crates which allow the dog full view of his surroundings are perfect for kenneling in the house or in a warm car; but for confining a dog in drafty or cold areas, wooden or fiberglass enclosed crates are best.

IN THE DOGHOUSE

If you own only one to two Shelties and prefer to keep them outside, a simple doghouse will suffice. So will a shed, barn, or garage with an enclosed, well bedded box. Again, what matters most is that the quarters are dry and free of drafts. The doghouse should have a raised floor and a rubber or canvas door flap to keep out wind.

If the house is too small it will be uncomfortable; if too large it will be cold in winter. Ideally, the Sheltie should have a house about 20 x 30 inches, with the roof about eight inches higher than his back. One of the best designs I've seen was for a cement block doghouse with a raised floor and a removable shingled wood roof (which facilitated cleaning). This house is almost completely draft free due to the unique floor plan, and can be built to accommodate one or two dogs.

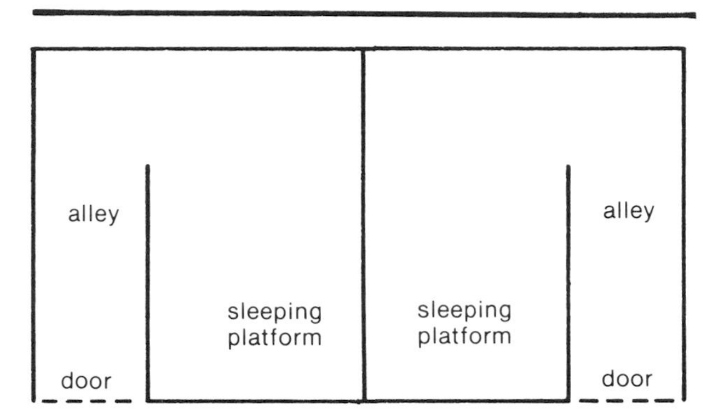

Design for a draft-free dog house.

BUILDING A KENNEL

Shelties can be raised quite well in kennels provided they are given frequent exposure to many other situations. I raise puppies in the house for the first two months or so, then handle them daily after they have been transferred to the kennel. All my Shelties have their turn at being house pets for a day at a time and look forward to "their day" with me. I kennel dogs in pairs in runs 4′ x 24′ and alternate them in larger runs. All the dogs spend several hours a week running free in larger areas or yards.

The kennel location will depend largely on convenience, but if possible it should be constructed with the runs sloping gently away from the building. If you have a choice, set the building north and south with runs on the east where they will get morning sunlight. Trees on the west and north of the kennel are fine, but do not place the kennel in an area so shaded by trees that the sun cannot shine in at least part of the day. Overly shady areas invite dampness and disease.

Either a wood or cement block structure is acceptable. Concrete floors, although they tend to be cold and damp, are easier to clean and disinfect. If you use poured concrete flooring, lay a sheet of heavy plastic before pouring the floor. This works wonders in keeping out moisture. You may also want to use wooden boxes or platforms in each stall for the dogs to sleep on. These can easily be removed for disinfecting and drying in the sun. Wood floors should be about a foot off the ground, made of a double layer of wood with plastic sandwiched between for insulation.

Ventilation of some type is a must. Fans at both ends of the building near the roof are best. Lacking these, shutter type ventilators at each end, with a tin vent pipe on the roof, will prevent drafts and let stale air out.

Kennel Runs

Long narrow pens encourage Shelties to run, but discourage the tendency to run in tight circles, a trait which herding breeds sometimes exhibit. A nice size for two Shelties is 4′ x 24′, but it can be wider. Concrete flooring in the runs is definitely easiest to clean, but it is hard on the dog's feet and shoulders and reflects heat in summer. Pea gravel is excellent for the feet, but harder to clean and care for.

Gravel should be layed about one foot deep. Some people put down a layer of lime, then a layer of coarse gravel, followed by a six inch layer of pea gravel. This top layer will need to be raked and turned frequently, and replaced every few years. Sprinkling the ground with salt before pouring the cement or gravel will kill roundworm larva and inhibit urine odors.

Hard dirt runs are the least desirable and the most difficult to clean. Dogs' urine and salt will kill grass, so eventually all you have is an impenetrable dirt surface that holds odors and is almost impossible to keep sanitary.

Cleanliness in the Kennel

Cleanliness is essential to any kennel; otherwise diseases, worms, and poor condition of the animals occur. Food and water dishes should be washed and disinfected daily. Stainless steel dishes excel for ease of cleaning, but you will find heavy rubber ones more indestructible from chewing puppies or freezing water.

The building and runs should be washed down spring, summer, and fall with a good germicidal disinfectant. If flies, mosquitoes, or hookworms are a problem, spraying the premises with Malathion will help. Be sure to follow the directions on the insecticide carefully and keep the dogs out of the area for 12 to 24 hours after spraying.

Rock runs can be difficult to keep wormfree. Sodium borate applied at the rate of 10 pounds per hundred square feet will help control hookworm larva. Heavy applications of stock salt washed in with hot water will control roundworms. Naturally, the most important part of sanitation and worm control is keeping feces picked up daily, preferably twice a day.

Disease control in the kennel is also facilitated by placing a foot high cement barrier at the base of the fencing between runs. (Sink it into the ground six inches if the runs are gravel.) This prevents urine and germs from one pen seeping into the pen next door. Boarding kennels use an eight foot high solid board fence a few feet outside the periphery of the kennel to help keep out airborne disease germs, as well as to cut down on noise and distraction.

NOISE CONTROL

Without a doubt, Shelties are one of the noisier breeds. They are almost all on the vocal side, and some will bark continuously. Since we live in an increasingly urban society with laws that penalize barking dogs, this can present a problem.

If your Sheltie barks at night, or just when the kids walk by on their way to and from school, confining him during this time may solve the problem. You can train most Shelties that barking is not allowed *if* you are home most of the day and take the time to make consistent corrections. A tin can filled with ten pennies and taped shut makes a good "throw can" for correcting a barker. Toss the can toward the dog, but do not hit him with it. Give the correction, "No Bark!" as you toss the can. Eventually just rattling the can may be all that's needed. Water pistols filled with ammonia water are also effective, or squirt the dog with the garden hose.

If you kennel a number of dogs or leave your dog outside while you are at work, debarking may be the only answer. This simple surgery, consisting of a short-acting anesthesia and a couple of quick snips to notch the vocal cord, cuts down on the volume of the noise but does not affect the dog's personality. To me, it seems much more humane than continually nagging a dog to be quiet. The dogs don't notice, or at least do not object. They still bark and you can hear them in the house or yard, but the sound does not carry.

There are a few drawbacks to consider before debarking. As with any surgery, there is some slight risk with anesthesia, and there is also a slight risk of uncontrolled bleeding from the surgery. Some Shelties are difficult to debark. The bark will not be softened that much, or they may have a raspy, hoarse-sounding bark. Sometimes the vocal cords will grow back in a few years and the surgery must be repeated. For all the risks, the reward is peace of mind for both you and your Sheltie—he can bark to his heart's content without getting yelled at, and you have no need to worry about complaints from the neighbors. Ask breeders in your area to recommend a veterinarian. Those that debark a number of dogs become quite expert at the surgery and you can expect a quieter, more permanent job.

IF YOUR SHELTIE IS LOST

If your Sheltie runs away, *do not* chase him. Try to keep him within your sight and call or whistle. Calling from a squatting position will sometimes seem less threatening to a dog. Or try walking away to see if he will follow you. If this fails, try to corner him quietly.

If your Sheltie should disappear from sight, you must act fast. Go to as many houses as possible in the area where the dog was last seen, asking the residents to watch for the dog and call you if he is spotted. Ask them not to try to catch the dog, but rather to call you if he is sighted, and not to call the dogcatcher. Call the humane society, the dog control officer, and the radio station to notify them of the loss. If the dog was recently purchased, by all means alert the former owner, especially if he lives nearby, as the dog may respond to him or may head for the former home. Run an ad in the local newspaper offering a reward and describing the dog ("resembles a small collie") giving color, sex, age, call name, location lost, and your phone number. Finally, call the city and county dog pounds and any veterinarians in the area. Then go home and wait. If the dog is lost for several days, keep repeating your calls to all sources to let them know that you are still looking. Searches such as this are generally successful. Shelties are intelligent and hardy and can survive amazing odds.

HAZARDS AT HOME

Like all canines, Shelties like to chew, and sometimes they are not very selective about what they chew. The best protection is to keep electrical cords, fiberglass insulation, chemicals, poisons, bones, or wood that might splinter, and other harmful substances out of your dog's reach. Anything that would constitute a hazard for a young child is also hazardous to puppies.

Poisonous substances to keep away from your Sheltie include bleach, antifreeze, cleaning fluid, gasoline, fungicide, insecticide, herbicide, tar, suntan lotion, wax, paint and paint remover, hair setting lotion or bleach, matches, mothballs, rat poison, shoe polish, crayons, detergent, disinfectant, aspirin and other drugs, and plants. Many houseplants are poisonous if eaten, especially dieffenbachia, philodendron, poinsettia, and mistletoe. Many bulbous plants are harmful, as are vines such as wisteria and sweet pea, and some bushes or hedge plants, including euonymous, rhododendron, laurel, and yew. Castor bean plants, especially the seed, or beans, are extremely poisonous. If you plant a hedge or screen around your kennel, keep the plants out of the dogs' reach.

In addition to swallowing harmful substances, puppies are apt to tip things over on themselves, get cut on glass, tin, or sharp objects, or get caught in tight places. They are fascinated by snakes, toads, porcupines, skunks, big dogs, and cats—any of which could harm them. Young puppies can easily wander away and find themselves lost. Their sense of direction is not very well developed until they are at least six months old. Common sense and a few precautions on your part are all it takes to insure your Sheltie a long, healthy life.

Some hazards are so common we hardly think about them. Leaving a choke chain on your Sheltie at night or while he's in the yard is one of them. I have heard about a number of dogs that strangled or suffered a broken neck as a result of getting a choke collar caught.

Hundreds of dogs die from heat stroke each year because thoughtless owners leave them locked in a car during hot weather. When temperatures outside approach 80° F. the temperature inside a closed car will rise to over 100° F. in as little as fifteen minutes. If you must leave your dog in the car, open several windows an inch for ventilation and give him plenty of water. Check frequently.

PREVENTING THEFT AND THE NATIONAL DOG REGISTRY

Dog theft is decidedly on the increase, especially in urban areas and around shows. Recently in this area a Sheltie puppy was stolen from an unlocked car while the family ran into a store for less than five minutes. Another was stolen from a backyard during the night while the family was at home; and an entire litter of puppies was taken in the same way.

The best prevention is never to leave your Sheltie unattended in an unlocked car or yard, even for a few minutes. This is sometimes impossible, though. Beyond that, the only security you can give him is to have him tattooed and registered with the National Dog Registry.

The primary problem with stolen dogs is the inability of law officers to make positive identification. Because of this, the National Dog Registry was established to solve the problem by permanently identifying dogs with a number that is already yours and will always be yours—your social security number. The number is tattooed on the right groin of every dog you own. Tattooing can be done by your veterinarian or at tattoo clinics sponsored by kennel clubs, often in conjunction with matches. Tattooing is painless, permanent, takes only a few minutes, and is inexpensive. You must then register your social security number, name, address, and telephone number one time with the National Dog Registry, 227 Stebbin Rd., Carmel, NY 10512 for a fee. Don't forget to let them know if your address or phone changes.

More than 1500 laboratories (that use animals for research), medical schools, and research centers have been asked to notify NDR if a dog bearing a social security number tattoo is delivered to them. Most state and local police and humane societies also cooperate. Even if your dog is stolen and you know where he is you cannot enforce the law and prove theft unless he is permanently identified.

NDR also supplies stickers for your crates, kennel, and car which warn "Tattooed Dogs, Registered with National Dog Registry," to help deter thefts. You can also purchase tags for your dog's collar bearing this warning. Keep the tattooed area clipped so the tattoo is visible.

BON VOYAGE—THE TRAVELING SHELTIE

Traveling with your dog requires you to observe all the safeguards discussed up to this point—doubly enforced. More dogs are lost during trips than at any other time.

Before you leave, put a leather collar with your dog's rabies tag and ID tag on your Sheltie and let him wear it for the duration of the trip. Be sure your Sheltie is given a drink of water and exercised about every three hours. Most Shelties love traveling once accustomed to it and do very nicely; but any traveling dog can get carsick, constipated, or develop diarrhea. Be prepared and carry a medicine chest, paper towels, a washcloth, and some *Dramamine*® tablets. These items will enable you to cope with just about any situation—and believe me, on a long trip you never know which it will be!

If possible carry a supply of drinking water from home. There is so much variation in our chemically treated water that a change can cause digestive upsets in dogs as well as humans. Take plenty of your Sheltie's regular diet too so you won't have to change rations enroute.

Planning to stay in a hotel or motel? Better write ahead to make sure they will accept dogs. While there, walk your Sheltie in back areas, not the front lawn, and leave your room without a trace of the dog's visit. This will help insure that the motel will continue to host doggy visitors. If you must leave your Sheltie in the room alone tie him securely or crate him so he can't go looking for you if the maid enters. If necessary to avoid accidents, carry your dog outside. You will find a box of *Baggies*® convenient. Invert the bag over your hand and use it to pick up droppings. It's sanitary and easy to dispose of. *Baggies*® are also useful for storing food or bait or filling with water and freezing for your ice chest.

Shelties love to go! (Photo by Price)

Hyalti Headliner enjoying a clean gravel run fenced with chain link.

Never leave your dog in a locked car with the windows up during warm weather.

FLYING THE FRIENDLY SKIES

Shipping a dog by air is probably more frightening to the novice owner than to the Sheltie. While shipping conditions are no doubt less than perfect, thousands of dogs are shipped each year, yet only a small percentage are harmed. These injuries generally could be prevented if the owner took proper precautions.

Cargo compartments where the dogs ride are sometimes not supplied with oxygen, heat, or air conditioning. The air in the compartment at the beginning of the flight is all the animals have to live on during the trip. Therefore the dog crate must have plenty of holes for cross ventilation and good air circulation. Temperature within the baggage compartment of an airplane sometimes varies considerably during the same flight. There is no way to avoid this possibility, but you can avoid major extremes by not shipping when the weather is below freezing or over 80 degrees. If you must ship in extremely cold weather try to schedule the dog for a midday flight; if it is very hot try to ship in early morning or late evening. Since puppies are more vulnerable than adults, I try never to ship a Sheltie less than three months of age.

Making Reservations

Always make reservations with the air freight office several days in advance because only a limited number of live animals can be taken on any given flight. Most breeders prefer air freight over air express as the dogs seem to be handled faster and more carefully by the freight offices. Choose a non-stop direct flight whenever possible, even if you have to drive a few extra miles to a different airport. If the dog must transfer, allow plenty of time between flights, usually two or three hours. If one or more transfers must be made, express many be preferable because only one company is responsible and express transfers have priority. If you are flying with the dog, you may be able to take a very small Sheltie on board with you. Check with the reservation desk for regulations.

The Crate

Prepare the shipping crate well in advance so nothing is overlooked and the dog can become familiar with it. A wooden crate is best in extreme weather. Fiberglass crates, providing they are well ventilated, are satisfactory except on extremely hot or cold days. *Never* ship in a wire crate because it does not provide adequate protection from crushing, flying objects, or draft, and it is very noisy. Metal crates are icy cold in winter and hot in summer.

Check to make sure the vent holes are not large enough to allow a nose, paw, or tail to slip through and be crushed. The crate should be large enough to allow the Sheltie to sit, stand, lie down, or turn around, but not so large that he can be thrown around in it. Place a thick layer of newspapers on the bottom with an inch of shredded paper on top of that. Be sure the latch is secure and for added safety provide a second snap or wire fastener.

The Label

Prepare a label which prominently indicates the city or *airport* at which the plane will land; this may be different from the address of the consignee. The name, address, and phone number of the person to whom the dog is going must also be prominently displayed. Place the label in a plastic sleeve and attach it securely to the top of the crate with strapping tape. If you want to attach an envelope containing a letter or papers, you may do this in the same way, or put it under the label. Attach another label permanently to the crate with the warning "Live Dog. Do Not Place Near Dry Ice." This is important since dry ice, used for packing perishable cargo, lets off fumes which can kill a dog.

Before the Flight

A day or two before shipping obtain a health certificate from your veterinarian. This is required by state laws and will be checked at the airport. Do not feed an adult dog for 12 hours before the flight, but give plenty of water and exercise. Place a buckled leather collar with ID tag around the dog's neck.

As soon as you have all information, you're sure the weather is favorable, and the reservations are made, call the person who will be receiving the dog and confirm shipment, giving departure and arrival times, airline, and flight number. Ask that they be at the airport shortly after the plane is due to arrive.

At the Airport

Get to the airport in plenty of time, usually one or two hours before scheduled departure time (check with the freight agent). Late arrival could cause your dog to be jammed in without adequate air space or placed close to harmful materials, or he might not get loaded at all.

If you're shipping more than one dog to the same place, don't do them any "favors" and put more than one dog in a crate so they will have company. *Put each dog in a separate crate.* If your Sheltie is very excitable you may want to give him a tranquilizer, but check with your veterinarian first. Generally it is better to avoid tranquilizers.

The freight agent will weigh your dog and write up an airbill. Be sure to give a declared valuation and insure the dog. Unless you do this, airlines will pay only a minimum figure in case of loss. You should also check the airbill carefully to see that the information is correct. Make sure the correct airbill is attached to your crate; fill the dog's pan with water, and leave the rest to the air freight office.

With these few precautions, your Sheltie will find the skyways generally safe and friendly.

CARING FOR THE OLDTIMER

Your Sheltie will probably live to a ripe old age - 13 to 15 years is average. While older dogs do have special requirements to keep them comfortable, a happy, healthy older dog is a tribute to your good care.

Old dogs, besides being excellent companions, often can contribute in training young stock. Many stories have been told of an old dog helping discipline a puppy in show, obedience, or herding routines. Keeping the older dog also allows the serious breeder to study the aging process in his particular line. An older dog—hale, hearty, and brimming with personality as most oldsters are—is living proof of the soundness of a kennel's stock. He is, in fact, a super-salesman who will do more to sell young puppies than any sales pitch a breeder might make.

The aging process in Shelties is so gradual you'll hardly notice the changes taking place. One day, though, you will realize that the hair on your pet's muzzle is greying and his step is a little less lively. The body processes of your Sheltie will slow down in every way—tissue repair, resistance to infection, recovery after an illness will all take longer. The digestion will not be as good as it once was; sight and hearing may weaken; there is a tendency to kidney failure or heart disease.

The old Sheltie is more sensitive to extremes of temperature and must be kept warmer in winter and cooler in summer. He should be bathed as little as possible and then dried quickly to avoid chilling. Frequent grooming can help compensate for the lack of bathing, and dry or foam shampoos can be used if the coat gets oily or dirty. He will exercise less and sleep more, and you probably will have to encourage him to go for walks. Exercise is important so do not allow your Sheltie to become too sedentary when he first begins to slow down. However, overexertion can occur if the ten-year-old housepet is taken on a weekend hiking trip without prior gradual conditioning. In fact any abrupt change in his lifestyle can be stressful. Make changes gradually when possible and have your oldtimer cared for at home rather than in a boarding kennel when you are away from home. Older dogs seem to be more insecure and need contact with familiar people and places.

Abrupt changes in temperature are to be avoided, as is exposure to extreme wet or cold weather conditions. It is especially important that the older dog has a warm, draft-free sleeping place. A carpeted box with a raised wooden floor works nicely. Kennel heating units are available and should be kept on low heat levels. Plenty of bedding or a thick foam rubber cushion will make him more comfortable. Many of us know it isn't as much fun to sleep on the floor now as when we were youngsters. Those old boards get mighty hard as we age!

Shelties enjoy the security of their own crate.

Ch. September's Lulu In Lace at fourteen. Barbara Linden's lovely foundation bitch.

Ch. Kinni's Caprice shows the profuse coat exhibited by some veterans. Owner, Marta Pascuzzo.

Obesity in an old dog can be a real problem as it puts too much strain on his heart and system. If your dog gets fat consult your veterinarian about a low-fat prescription diet and a mild exercise program. On the other hand, some old dogs do not utilize their food well and become thin, developing a harsh, dry coat. A geriatric vitamin supplement may be helpful. Feeding two or three times a day instead of one is advisable because it makes digestion easier. Since old dogs are sensitive to dietary changes, make any change in ration very gradually. Canned food or soaked kibble are easier for the old dog to eat as his gums may be tender, or he may have missing teeth. Since his teeth will break easier than when he was young, do not give him bones. Rawhide chews are beneficial. You will probably have to clean his teeth more often. Doing this at home will mean less frequent cleaning under anesthesia at the veterinary clinic. The risks associated with anesthesia increase in an older dog.

There is evidence that Vitamin E and minerals benefit the aging dog and help alleviate arthiritis pain. Geriatric vitamin/mineral supplements are available from veterinary clinics or pet supply stores. Aspirin may be used to treat acute symptoms of arthritis, or your veterinarian can prescribe pain relievers for chronic conditions.

Ten-week-old tri male bred by Shelby Price. (Photo by Price)

If your old dog seems not to hear your command, he may be deaf. If his eyesight is still good, switch to hand signals, or tap the ground so he can feel the vibrations. An old dog in familiar surroundings may lose his sight without your ever noticing. However, if the furniture is moved or he is taken into unfamiliar surroundings he may become frightened or run into things. He will get along well once he becomes used to the new environment. If you pick him up, set him down near his bed or some other familiar scent. A film over the eyeballs may indicate cataracts which sometimes can be surgically removed. But blindness is often permanent.

No one is ever ready to give up a living companion. Nevertheless, the day may come when you see him not as the happy, carefree fellow who once bounced at your side, but as an old dog in pain and discomfort. You must decide whether to let him suffer until natural death takes its course or to end his misery by euthanasia. The idea of euthanasia is distasteful to most dog owners, but actually it is very humane, and something every breeder should witness at some point just to reassure himself. The veterinarian simply injects an overdose of anesthetic and the dog drifts gently into a peaceful, permanent sleep. There is no pain, no fear, and the process takes only a few seconds—so much better than prolonged suffering or painful "do it yourself" methods.

Sheltie Medicare

During the years that I have been raising Shelties I have experienced few serious illnesses among them. It is one of the qualities I appreciate about the breed.

But of course, no animal, nor human for that matter, is likely to go through life without a day of illness or an injury now and then. Once you get to know your Sheltie it should be easy to tell when he is not feeling well. He's not a complaining sort, but he is communicative if you watch him carefully.

He may be listless, tired, or whine a lot, or he may show actual signs of illness. Don't panic—he may just be having an "off" day or a case of indigestion. But if, perchance, he is coming down with something more serious you'll be glad you caught it in the earliest stages.

The first thing to do is try to determine what is causing the problem, and observe the dog for all symptoms. First, take his temperature. Check his eyes, nose, and mouth. Try to determine whether he is constipated or has diarrhea. Notice whether he is urinating more frequently than usual, or whether he is vomiting. Watch for signs of soreness or lameness. Check his quarters for signs of poisonous or harmful substances which he might have swallowed.

If you can rule out the possibility of poisoning, and if the condition doesn't seem to be serious, keep your Sheltie quiet and warm and just observe him for 12 to 24 hours. If he doesn't improve by the following day, call your veterinarian.

However, if high temperature, labored breathing, continuous vomiting, convulsions, or other acute symptoms appear, or the dog loses interest in everything and wants to hide, don't hesitate. Take him immediately to your veterinary hospital.

WHEN YOU HAVE TO PLAY DOCTOR

Every dog owner, like every mother, soon learns to give medical care and first aid. It always pays to be prepared, so I recommend that you set up a supply shelf near your Sheltie's quarters and stock it with a few basic items.

If you live in a remote area where emergency veterinary care is almost impossible to obtain, you may also want to keep an all purpose antibiotic and a bottle of injectible glucose. These could save a dog's life if a veterinarian isn't available. Talk to your veterinarian about obtaining and using such supplies if you are located some distance from a clinic.

Taking Your Dog's Temperature

Lubricate any ordinary rectal thermometer with petroleum jelly and insert half its length into the dog's rectum. Hold it there for three minutes. If you don't hold the end, the thermometer can be pushed out, or it can work completely into the rectum.

A Sheltie's average temperature is 101.5 degrees, but it can vary .5 degrees with no cause for concern.

Giving Medication

To give your Sheltie a pill, grasp his muzzle with your palm over his foreface, tilting his head back. Squeeze the lips over the teeth at the back of the mouth, thus forcing the mouth open with the lips between the teeth and your fingers. With your other hand, place the pill as far back on the dog's tongue as you can reach. Remove your hand and quickly close his mouth. Hold the dog's jaws shut and stroke his throat until he swallows. Greasing the pill with butter will help it go down easier.

If you have trouble getting a dog to swallow a tablet or capsule, try wrapping it with raw hamburger. Be sure he swallows the pill as well as the meat. Some dogs are adept at separating the two and spitting out the pill.

Checking Pulse

A dog's pulse can easily be determined by feeling for throbbing of the femoral artery. To locate this artery, place your index finger inside the hind leg as far up against the body as possible. In a healthy animal the pulsing artery is easily found.

Another method is to place the fingers over the heart itself. A dog's heart rate is determined by counting the number of beats per minute. The average is 90 to 100 beats per minute. They should be rhythmical and steady, although slight arythmia is not uncommon.

The Medicine Chest

Your Medicine chest should include the following items:

- A rectal thermometer. Same as for humans and obtainable at any drugstore or pet supply store.
- A good antiseptic liquid soap
- *Q-TIPS* cotton swabs
- Peroxide
- Cotton balls
- Gauze pads and bandage wrap
- Alcohol
- Antiseptic spray for minor wounds
- Clean towels
- A blunt-nosed scissors for cutting hair around wounds, cutting bandages, etc.
- Styptic powder or silver nitrate to control bleeding of minor cuts and bites. (Note: Silver nitrate is poisonous if swallowed and will stain anything it touches.)
- An old nylon stocking to use as a muzzle
- *Kaopectate*® for diarrhea
- An antibiotic, anti-inflammatory drug for severe diarrhea such as *Amforal*® or *Biosol M.*®
- *Milk of Magnesia*® tablets or rectal suppositories for a laxative
- Artificial Tears for washing out eyes. You may also want to keep a product from your veterinarian for mild eye inflammations
- A general purpose dip for fleas, ticks, mange, eczema
- Antiseptic surgical soap such as *Betadine*™
- *Panalog*® ointment for skin inflammation, mild skin infections, cuts, and scratches
- A medication for ear mites
- Something for motion sickness. *Dramamine*® for humans is fine, ¼ tablet for a Sheltie
- A product such as *Bitter Apple*® to prevent chewing
- Activated charcoal as universal antidote for poison

Liquid medications may be drawn into a plastic syringe (minus the needle) for easier measurement. The syringe measures in cubic centimeters (cc's) and you can convert measures as follows:

16 drops	= 1 cc or ¼ teaspoon
5 cc.	= 1 teaspoon
15 cc.	= 1 tablespoon
½ oz.	= 1 tablespoon or 15 cc.
1 oz.	= 30 cc. or 2 tablespoons
8 oz.	= 1 cup
1 liter	= 1 quart or 4 cups

To give liquid medication, place your Sheltie in a sitting position. Pull the corner of the lower lip outward and upward, forming a small pocket into which to pour the liquid, a little at a time. Raise the dog's head slightly, allowing the liquid to run through his teeth and down into the throat. Then hold the jaws closed until he swallows. If you are gentle but firm your Sheltie will learn to take medications without a fuss. A clean hypodermic syringe with the needle removed works very well for measuring and administering liquid medication.

It is important when giving medications to give only the exact amount specified at the time interval specified.

Artificial Respiration

An unconscious dog who is not breathing but whose heart is still beating may need only artificial respiration to revive him.

1. Place the dog on his right side with head and neck extended so that the windpipe is in a straight line.
2. Pull the tongue forward and out.
3. With the heels of your hands, press the chest moderately hard just behind the dog's shoulder blade, forcing air out of the lungs.
4. Relax the pressure, count to five, and repeat. *It is important that the rhythm be smooth and regular.*

Continue until the dog is breathing smoothly on his own. Then treat for shock. A normal respiration rate for dogs is 15 to 20 times per minute.

COMMON SHELTIE ILLS

Learning to recognize problems and administer temporary aid may save a lot of trouble, expense, and even save a dog's life. *Never try to diagnose and treat an infection yourself;* but knowing how to treat some common symptoms is helpful to both you and your vet.

Acute Moist Dermatitis (Hot Spots)

Caused by heat rash, fleas, scratching, or an allergy. The hair falls out and the exposed skin is raw, flakey, and

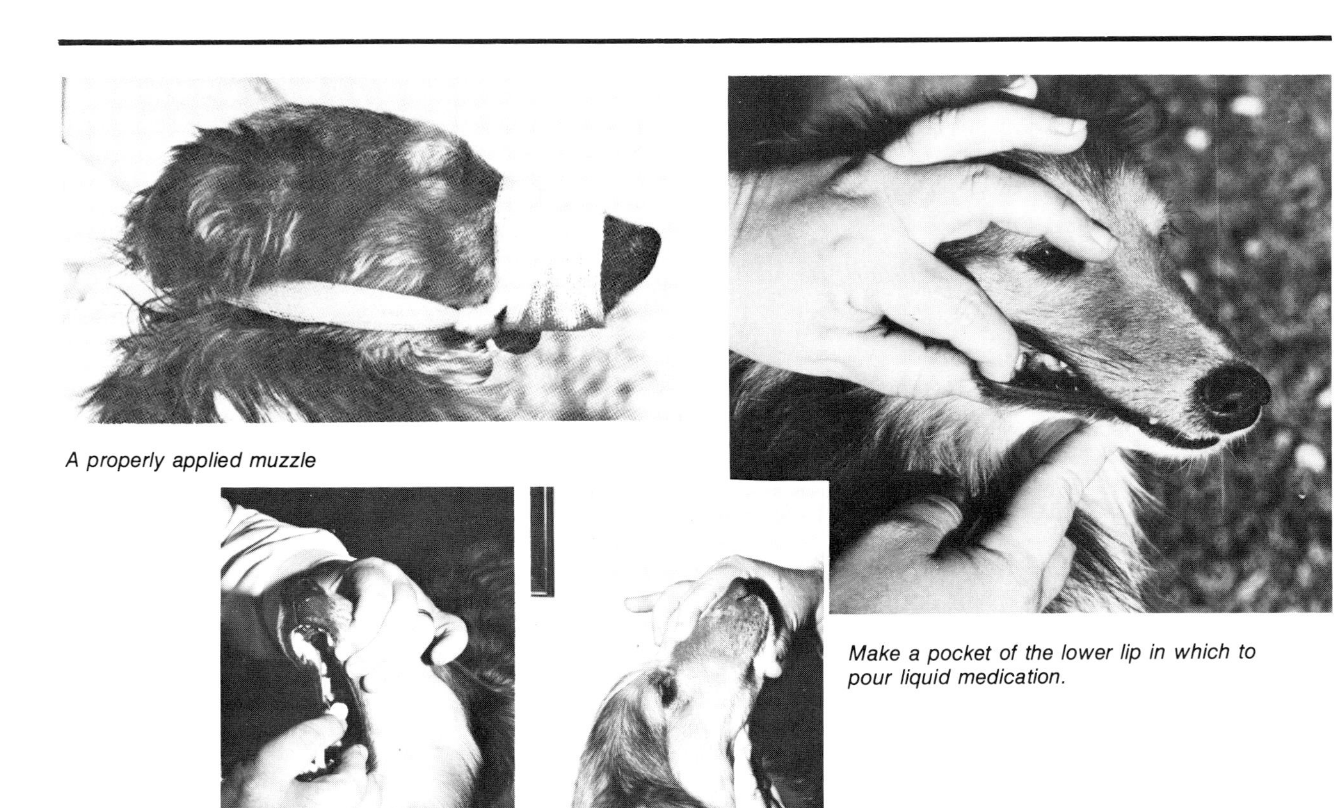

A properly applied muzzle

Make a pocket of the lower lip in which to pour liquid medication.

Place the pill or capsule as far into the throat as possible. Close the dog's mouth and massage the throat until he swallows.

Another method of artificial respiration is to cup your hands into a cone and breathe into the dog's mouth and nostrils.

Muzzling

When dogs are in pain they may bite at anyone who tries to handle them. To prevent being bitten, tie the mouth of the frightened animal shut with an old nylon stocking or strip of soft cloth. Make two wraps around the muzzle and tie under the chin in a hard knot; then bring the ends back of the ears and tie in a bow knot.

sometimes bleeds. Treat small spots with a soothing and drying ointment such as *Furaspor®*. Large areas must be treated by a veterinarian.

Arthritis and Rheumatism

Older dogs often become arthritic. Arthritis may be caused by an injury or by a congenital deformity such as hip dysplasia. Symptoms are stiffness in gait which often eases after the dog has warmed up, lameness, arched back, and pain or swelling of the joints.

Complete rest only makes the lameness or stiffness worse. Keep the dog in a warm, dry place and limit, but do not discontinue his exercise. Aspirin will relieve the pain temporarily, but *Tylenol®* is better because it won't upset the stomach. (Dogs are the animal most prone to nausea.) More advanced arthritic conditions may require veterinary treatment with cortisones.

Muscular rheumatism also occurs in older dogs. Affected Shelties exhibit obscure pain that cannot be attributed to arthritis which affects the joints. Brewer's yeast tablets may help.

Car Sickness

Sheltie puppies are easily prone to motion sickness, although they usually outgrow it with age. It is a good idea to take puppies on very short rides at first and try to make traveling fun for them. Take them to the park or the country for a romp, then back home for feeding. Some breeders train show puppies to eat in a crate in a motionless car.

Excitable Shelties may always get carsick. You can help prevent this by not feeding before a trip. Give only small amounts of water before leaving and scattered throughout the day if the trip is long. Wait until you have arrived at your destination or stopped for the night to feed and give all the water your dog wants.

Bonine® given 30 minutes before traveling will last all day and won't cause depression. *Dramamine®* tablets given at the rate of 0.5 mg. per pound (¼ to ½ tablet for a Sheltie) are also quite good. Don't use tranquilizers if you are going to a show or obedience trial and expect your dog to perform. Even if you give no medication at all to a motion sickness-prone dog, plan to arrive at least an hour prior to the time he is to show.

Constipation

Constipation can result from fecal impaction due to overly long confinement while traveling or in the kennel, from improper diet, tumors, internal parasites, abscessed anal sacs, or old age, among other things. A tablespoon of *Milk of Magnesia®* may relieve the condition. If not, try a human rectal suppository.

Dermatitis

In addition to hot spots, dermatitis can occur from numerous other causes, including food allergy, flea allergy, auto-immune problems, and mites, lice, or mange. If a small spot of hair-loss and itchy skin shows up, try washing it off and applying *Panolog®* ointment. If fleas or other insects are suspected, bathe the dog first with an insecticide shampoo.

If the area does not heal within a week or two, or if it spreads rapidly, the best procedure is to have your veterinarian do a skin scraping to determine the cause. If hair loss starts around the eye and spreads toward the ears, suspect one of the Sheltie skin diseases which may be hereditary. If the hair loss occurs on the muzzle and begins to spread rapidly over the head and body, the problem could be mange. Again, diagnosis is best left to a veterinarian.

Diarrhea

Diarrhea can indicate a disease or infection, but often it simply results from overeating, eating spoiled food, change of diet, too much excitement, parasites, or other upsets of the digestive system. It is most common in puppies. If no other symptoms are present to indicate a more serious problem, a simple dose of *Kaopectate®* may clear up the diarrhea—about two to three tablespoons every four hours for an adult Sheltie. Your vet may administer stronger medication for mild infectious cases.

Use the stronger diarrhea medications carefully as some can be dangerous if used improperly. With acute diarrhea, discontinue food for 12 to 24 hours, then bring the dog back on food slowly with a diet high in rice, meat, cottage cheese, or cooked eggs, and low in commercial meal. Change gradually to the regular ration. Milk can cause diarrhea.

Unchecked diarrhea will cause dehydration. Young puppies dehydrate in a surprisingly short time unless fluids are given subcutaneously. Always contact your vet if diarrhea persists.

Ear Mites and Other Ear Problems

Ear mites are common in some areas of the country. These parasites burrow into the dog's ear causing considerable discomfort. A dark brown to grey waxy discharge can be seen in the ear.

Cleanse the ear with a cotton swab dipped in alcohol, then apply an ear-mite insecticide such as *Mitox®*.

Occasionally a Sheltie will get weed seeds or other foreign material into the ear, causing him to scratch, tilt his head sideways, or shake his head continually. Look into the ear for matter that can be easily removed. If you can't see what's causing the problem, have your veterinarian check. There may be an infection, or a foreign body may have migrated to the inner ear where it can cause deafness. Heat at the base of the ear is indicative of an infection.

Eye Irritations and Inflammations

Dust, pollen, or foreign objects often cause a Sheltie's eyes to water. Wash the eye area with a cotton ball dipped in warm water or mild salt water solution (1 tsp. to 8 oz. water), or use Artificial Tears (made for contact lens wearers) or a mild eyewash as recommended by your veterinarian.

Sometimes conjunctivitis will develop. This is an inflammation of the thin, transparent mucous membrane lining the inner surface of the eyelids and the front of the eye, excluding the cornea. The eyes water and the membranes in the corner of the eye will be red. Conjunctivitis may be caused by irritation from dust, etc., or from a bacterial or viral infection. Treatment depends on the cause. The infectious form is often contagious and may spread through an entire kennel.

If reddened eyes fail to clear up in a few days with the application of eyewash, take your dog to the veterinarian for an examination and culture.

DISEASES OF DOGS

The following diseases are much more serious than the mild symtoms listed above. You should *never* attempt to treat these conditions yourself, but it is important to *recognize the symptoms*.

Vaccinate puppies at 7, 11, and 15 weeks, with annual boosters thereafter. (Photo by Price)

Distemper

An acute infectious, highly contagious disease that can be contacted through direct association with mucus, fecal matter or urine, or through airborne virus which can be carried for miles. Distemper virus, therefore, is literally everywhere. You can even carry it into the house on your clothing. Distemper germs linger on the premises of an infected area for at least 30 days.

The best cure for distemper is adequate prevention by immunization, starting when the dog is seven weeks of age, followed by two more shots at monthly intervals, with yearly boosters thereafter. Distemper has been known to occur even in immunized dogs, and old dogs are only slightly less vulnerable than puppies. *Do not neglect distemper immunizations.*

The symptoms are often at first unnoticed. The dog may chill, limp slightly, have a nasal discharge, vomit, or run a temperature. He may then appear to be completely normal for two or three days or longer before the second stage sets in. During this stage the temperature rises to 102.5 to 104 degrees; there is diarrhea, nasal discharge, coughing, loss of appetite and weight, watering of the eyes, and conjunctivitis. Eventually the nerves are affected, with damage to the brain, spinal cord, and nervous system. There is no vaccine or antibiotic that will kill the virus once it enters the dog's cells and treatment is merely symptomatic. Prognosis is always unfavorable.

Corona Virus

Corona is a highly contagious, infectious hermorrhagic gastroenteritis with very sudden onset. The usual symptoms are very foul-smelling orangish diarrhea, lethargy, and occasionally vomiting. Fever is not common. The disease is often fatal due to hemorrhaging, especially with puppies.

There is no prevention except cleanliness, avoiding exposure, and cleaning with Clorox diluted 1 part to 30 parts water. Prompt veterinary care is essential.

Enteritis

This is an acute hemorrhagic diarrhea caused by bacterial infection, systemic disease, poisoning, or an acute allergy to food or foreign material which the dog has eaten. The onset is sudden, characterized by acute bloody diarrhea, cramping of the stomach, gas, and sometimes vomiting. Give a dose of *Kaopectate®* to quiet the stomach and *get the dog to the vet fast.* Untreated cases have been known to die in a very few hours.

Infectious Canine Hepatitis

This is an acute, infectious disease affecting the dog's liver. As with distemper, there is no effective antiviral drug and treatment is merely symptomatic. The disease can be almost totally prevented by immunization, usually combined with the distemper vaccine. Yearly boosters are required.

Symptoms of hepatitis include high temperature, vomiting, diarrhea (often bloody), depression, flaming red mucous membranes and tonsils, abdominal pain, and occasionally corneal opacity (a white film over the cornea of the eye). The fatal damage done by the disease primarily affects the liver.

Kennel Cough

Tracheobronchitis, or kennel cough, is probably the most contagious disease seen in dogs. An airborne virus, it is easily picked up at clinics, boarding kennels, or shows, and within a week can infect every dog on your premises. It is characterized by a dry, hacking, persistent cough with no temperature elevation or other symptoms. The disease is not usually serious except in young puppies and will usually run its course in three to six weeks.

Kennel cough responds to treatment with broad spectrum antibiotics and to cough medications, but even then may have to run its course. However, a new vaccine is now available which provides immunization from tracheobronchitis. It can be given separately or in conjunction with DHL vaccines, and we strongly recommend it if you plan to show, travel with, or board your Sheltie.

Kidney Diseases

The most common forms are interstitial nephritis, which involves mild to acute kidney damage, and cystitis, an infection of the bladder. Both can be either acute or chronic.

Nephritis is a common problem of older Shelties and may simply accompany the aging process. It can also be caused by leptospirosis, other infectious diseases, or by injestion of chemicals, paint, or paint removers, etc. Dogs with acute nephritis will generally run a temperature. They may arch their back in pain, drink voluminous amounts of water, vomit, be depressed, or have a strong body or breath odor. A urinalysis is required for accurate diagnosis. Acute cases require prompt treatment with antibiotics to prevent kidney damage. Chronic cases may be controlled by medications and by placing the dog on a special diet.

Signs of cystitis include increased frequency of urination, pain when urinating, blood tinged or cloudy urine, wet hair around the vulva, and a very strong odor. Give the dog plenty of water and take him to the vet. Treatment with antibiotics is necessary, often for several weeks' duration.

Leptospirosis

This is an acute infectious disease carried by rodents. It affects older dogs more frequently than puppies, and it is contagious to man. Germs are spread primarily by rat or mouse urine contaminating foodstuffs and also from dog to dog by contact with the urine of an affected dog. The bacteria can enter the dog orally, through contact with the skin or mucous membranes, or through sexual intercourse.

Vaccination will protect your dog from Leptospirosis, but since the disease is uncommon in some areas of the country the vaccine (generally administered in combination with distemper and hepatitis vaccine) may not be routinely given. If you plan to show or breed your dog, or travel into areas where this disease is common, by all means request a DHL vaccine (distemper, hepatitis, leptospirosis) or have the lepto shot given separately. Immunity is relatively short, so, if you are shipping your dog into an area where you suspect he will be exposed, give a booster every six months.

Symptoms include depression, vomiting, constipation followed by diarrhea, soreness, stiffness accompanied by a reluctance to move, walking with short, choppy steps and with the back arched, hemorrhaging, bad breath, and darkening of the tongue. In some dogs the infection is so slight as to go unnoticed, or appear to be interstitial nephritis. Laboratory tests are required for accurate diagnosis. The disease can be anything from mild to fatal, and recovered animals may be carriers. The disease is contagious to humans.

Parvovirus

Another highly contagious viral enteritis, Parvo, can spread rapidly throughout a show ground, kennel, or even entire towns. Transmission is through direct exposure to infected feces and some researchers now feel that the disease may be airborne as well. At any rate, it is highly contagious and germs may be carried in on shoes, leashes, containers, or the hair or pads of the dogs. Disinfecting with Clorox solution will cut down on environmental exposure.

Ch. Wyndcliff the Successor, owned by Joan Surber. Drawing by M. Obermiller.

Parvo was rampant in the early 1980's, but both killed vaccines and modified live canine cell origin vaccines have since been developed. I consider Parvovirus immunization just as important as distemper vaccinations. My veterinarian presently recommends giving the killed vaccine to puppies at 5 to 6 weeks, followed by the modified live combination Parvo and DHLP vaccine at 11 and 14 weeks. Annual boosters are recommended thereafter, however,

I personally believe it is best to give the Parvo vaccine several months before a bitch comes in season, or within a day or two after whelping. There is some speculation that giving the vaccination just prior to breeding may cause a bitch to miss or to whelp weak puppies. There is to date no conclusive scientific evidence of this.

Parvovirus symptoms are generally a high fever, vomiting, and diarrhea. The stools are usually greyish in color and quite watery, with a foul odor. Both the vomit and diarrhea may contain blood. A laboratory test can make positive diagnosis.

Treatment is mainly supportive: drugs to control the vomiting and diarrhea, keep the dog quiet and warm, and administer fluids for dehydration. Infected dogs should be totally isolated for two to three weeks.

Tonsillitis

Dogs have tonsils too—open the mouth wide and you can probably see them. If the tonsils are red and swollen, or the dog refuses to eat, has trouble swallowing, gags or vomits, and is running a slight temperature, he probably has tonsillitis. It is fairly common in bad weather or when dogs are forced to adapt to rapidly changing temperatures.

Antibiotics are usually effective in clearing up the infection, but some dogs have recurrent problems and must have their tonsils removed.

Tumors

Lumps or growths on or below the skin are considered tumors. Benign (non-cancerous) tumors usually spread slowly or not at all. Malignant (cancerous) tumors usually grow and spread within a few weeks or months. Any kind of growth should be checked by your veterinarian. Most tumors, even cancerous ones, are not painful, so don't ignore them just because they do not cause the dog discomfort. They are fairly common in old dogs, and may need to be surgically removed.

Vomiting

Vomiting is associated with numerous diseases and conditions, both serious and not so serious. The most common causes are eating too much or too fast, motion sickness, or eating grass. If your Sheltie vomits once or twice and otherwise appears perfectly normal, no treatment is required and you should not be alarmed.

Vomiting blood, vomiting accompanied by diarrhea or a high fever, or frequently recurring vomiting indicates more serious disorders and should signal a medical checkup.

A dog will vomit forcefully and repeatedly when the upper intestinal tract is blocked or when he has a bone splinter or foreign object lodged in the digestive tract. Puppies with heavy roundworm infestations may vomit the adult worms.

FIRST AID

First aid is a temporary emergency treatment intended to maintain the life of your dog until professional medical help may be obtained. It is not intended to be a remedy. Applied quickly and correctly first aid may save your dog's life. Likewise, mistakes can make an otherwise curable case hopeless.

Transporting an Injured Dog

If no bones appear to be broken, carry the injured animal under one arm with your forearm supporting his weight and your hand under his chest. Use the other hand to steady his head. If the dog is badly injured or appears to have broken bones, back or neck injuries, place him gently on a stretcher made from a sheet, towel, or board. The bottom board from a crate also works well. Lacking any of these, place two sticks through the sleeves of a jacket to form a stretcher. Try to disturb his position as little as possible in order to avoid further damage.

External Heart Massage

If your dog's heart has stopped, combine artificial respiration with external cardiac massage.

1. With the animal on his back, legs in the air put the palms of your hands on the sternum with your fingers on one side of the chest and your thumb on the other.
2. Alternately compress and release the chest. Compress the chest strongly between thumb and fingers, pushing the ribs together, and at the same time press the sternum downward toward the spine. (Do not press hard enough to fracture the ribs of a puppy.) Release the pressure suddenly.
3. Repeat the compression at the rate of 70 times per minute until the heart starts beating again. A dog can only last about three minutes after the heart stops, so massaging for greater lengths of time in hopes of reviving the dog are probably futile.

Treating for Shock

Shock is an overresponse of the dog's system to trauma, injury, or stress. A dog in shock has pale mucous membranes and a weak, but rapid, pulse. He may shiver and feel cold to the touch. Breathing is slow and the eyes are glazed. Keep the dog warm by wrapping him in towels or blankets and get him to a veterinarian. It is generally best to withhold liquids, although a tablespoon or so of whiskey may help revive a dazed dog.

First Aid for Specific Conditions

Bee stings. Apply an ice cube to the area to reduce swelling and pain. Give the dog one human aspirin tablet.

If an allergic reaction to the sting sets in, see your veterinarian. *Dristan*® will stop most allergic reactions—1 tablet per adult; ⅓ tablet for a puppy.

Bleeding. Cover the wound with a sterile gauze and apply a pressure bandage by wrapping the injury tightly. Use a tourniquet between an arterial injury and the heart *only* if pressure bandages will not stop the bleeding. Tourniquets must be loosened every 10 minutes.

Superficial cuts and scratches should be washed with a germicidal soap and water and sprayed with antiseptic. You may need to clip the long hair around the wound to avoid irritation.

Panda, out of coat after weaning her litter, broke her leg while going down steps. Dogs usually handle a cast far better than we expect. (Photo courtesy Norene Meltvedt)

Broken nails. Apply a styptic powder, silver nitrate, or powdered alum to stop the bleeding. Smooth the nail with a coarse file after bleeding has stopped.

Bruises. If the injury is recent and swelling has not yet begun, apply a cold wet towel. If the injury is swollen, apply a hot compress.

Burns. Run cold water over the burned area. Do not apply butter, petroleum jelly, or ointments. A little *Bactine*® spray may be used. If the burn is serious get the dog to a veterinarian before shock sets in.

Cactus or porcupine quills. Remove with tweezers or small pliers. Treat with antiseptic spray.

Dog bites. Wash with water and antiseptic soap and treat with a topical antiseptic ointment. Deep puncture wounds or tears may need sutures.

Drowning. Hold the dog up by his hind legs to drain out the water, then administer artificial respiration. Keep him warm and rub vigorously. If he is unconscious, try to revive him with spirits of ammonia under the nose.

Frostbite or chilling. Warm the dog *slowly* by wrapping in warm towels. If he is a puppy, place him inside your coat and carry him around until he is warmed. Apply tepid water to frostbitten feet and gradually increase the temperature of the water to 100 degrees. Do *not* apply dry heat. Give a tablespoon of whiskey mixed with a tablespoon of water as a stimulant.

Fractures. If your dog has been hit by a car or has had an accident and is carrying or dragging a leg, one or more bones may be broken. Compound fractures, where the bones are penetrating the tissue, require *immediate* attention. Put the dog on a stretcher and take him to the nearest veterinarian. Other types of broken bones do not require immediate attention. Keep the dog quiet to avoid shock and get him to the vet as soon as you can. *Do not* apply a splint or bandage as this may complicate, rather than relieve, the injury.

Heat stroke. The most common cause of heat stroke is shutting a dog in a hot car or kenneling him in a hot, unventilated area. Cool the dog quickly by wetting him down or immersing him in cold water. Place ice cubes on his tongue and nose. *Do not* give stimulants.

Puncture wounds. Remove a small object carefully and apply a pressure bandage to stop bleeding. If the object is large or deeply embedded into the abdomen, or has punctured an eye, let your veterinarian remove it.

Skunk odor. Bathe in tomato juice, followed by soap and water. Wash eyes with mild salt solution and apply an eye ointment. If you cannot bathe the dog, you can make him more acceptable by rubbing him with a damp sponge sprinkled with baking soda.

Snake bites. Use a snake bite kit or make a sharp cut through the wound to induce bleeding. Keep the dog quiet and treat the wound with antiseptic. If he was bitten by a poisonous snake, get veterinary help.

Swallowing a foreign object. Feed bread or other soft food which will wrap itself around the object. Check with your vet.

IN CASE OF POISONING

Identifying the poison is of utmost importance. *Call a veterinarian.* If you *cannot* get a vet and you know what the poison material was, administer the antidote and then drive the dog to the clinic. *Do not treat for poisoning unless you are sure what material was ingested.* You can induce vomiting by giving one ounce peroxide in one ounce of water.

If the poison is a contact poison, always wash the contact area with large amounts of water. If the dog goes into convulsions try to keep him from injuring himself and hold him as still as possible until you get to the vet.

Some common poisons include the following:

Alkalis. Household drain cleaner is the most common of this type. It causes profuse salivation, nausea and sometimes vomiting. DO NOT induce vomiting. Give vegetable oil or 4 egg whites followed by vinegar (diluted 1:4) or lemon juice.

Analine dyes. Found in shoe polish, crayons, and other household dyes. The lip and oral membranes may turn brown, breathing is labored, and the dog is listless. Induce vomiting with peroxide and give coffee as a stimulant.

Aspirin. Too much aspirin will cause weakness, rapid breathing, stomach pain, and sometimes collapse. Induce vomiting, then give sodium bicarbonate (baking soda) in water. Activated charcoal can also be given.

Bleaches. Cause a general upset stomach. Induce vomiting. Then give the dog an egg white or a little olive oil.

Cleaning fluids. Either inhaling the fumes or ingesting the fluid may cause poisoning. For inhalation poisoning, give artificial respiration if needed and move the dog to a well ventilated area. Wash the eyes with water. If the fluid was swallowed, induce vomiting, then give *Milk of Magnesia®* as a laxative.

Cyanide or phosphorus. Found in some rat poisons. They are fast acting poisons and cause pain, convulsions, a deep coma, and an odor of bitter almonds. Treat with activated charcoal and hydrogen peroxide. Prognosis is poor. Get the dog to a veterinarian fast.

Ethylene glycol. Radiator antifreeze contains this poison and is readily ingested by dogs. Induce vomiting at once. Do not wait for signs to appear. Be sure that this dog is taken to the vet. He may recover from the acute poisoning only to die several days later from kidney failure.

Paint. Lead base paint can cause lead poisoning, either when the liquid paint is swallowed or when excessive amounts of dry flaked paint are chewed from a painted surface. Symptoms include rapid breathing, restlessness, collapse. Induce vomiting and give epsom salts or egg whites as an antidote.

Pyrophosphates (Malathion, Parathion, Pestox, etc.). These are absorbed through the skin. Symptoms include pinpoint pupils, salivation, cramps, watery eyes, muscular twitching. Bathe the dog with soap and water and get to a veterinarian quickly. If ingested, give *Milk of Magnesia®*.

Strychnine. The kind of poison people use to intentionally poison dogs and rodents. Violent convulsions with the head and legs extended are a good sign of ingested strychnine. DO induce vomiting if the dog is not in convulsions. Activated charcoal is a specific antidote and may be lifesaving. Give artificial respiration if the dog becomes rigid. They can die of suffocation. Contact your veterinarian at once.

Warfarin. A common ingredient in rat poison. It is not supposed to harm dogs, but it sometimes does. The drug acts as an anticoagulant, causing death by internal bleeding. If your dog has eaten warfarin, induce vomiting, then take him to your vet for a shot which will cause his blood to coagulate. If you wait until symptoms appear it may be too late.

EXTERNAL PARASITES

Fleas and Lice

Most dogs are bothered by fleas at one time or another. Dog fleas are small fly-like brownish insects which bite the dog and irritate his skin, often precipitating "hot spots," summer eczema, or other skin diseases. While the adult fleas live on the dog, they do not reproduce there, but rather breed in the debris, dust, hair or sand around kennel corners, fences, and floors. Any treatment for fleas, therefore, requires spraying of the dog's quarters as well as treatment of the dog. Lindane, chlordane, or malathion sprays used according to directions on the package will eradicate the pests from the kennel. While the quarters are drying, bathe the dog in a good commercial flea shampoo, or rinse him in a solution of one ounce pine oil to a quart of warm water, or use a lindane or malathion base dip. If you can't bathe him, use a good flea powder or *Sevin*® insecticide dust. Part the hair to the skin and dust thoroughly, brushing every inch of the body, especially belly, flanks, top of back, and behind ears. Place the dog on newspapers while dusting and burn them immediately. Most powders are less effective than shampoos or dips.

Lice are small bloodsucking bugs which infect dogs less frequently than fleas. Treatment is the same as for fleas except lice die quickly when they fall off the dog, so quarters need not be treated.

Ticks

There are many different species of "dog" or "wood" ticks, all of which attach themselves to the flesh and engorge themselves with the blood of their host. They carry disease, as well as weakening the dog by loss of blood. After the female tick has filled herself with blood she drops off the dog and deposits thousands of eggs in clumps of grass, cracks, or debris-filled corners. The larvae can survive for a full year without feeding and adult ticks can live up to two years if they fail to encounter a host on which to attach themselves.

The only sure way to rid a dog of ticks is with a good commercial dip. It will not only kill ticks hidden in the coat, but will repel further infestation. Spraying kennels and yards with 10 percent DDT solution or with malathion will kill most of the larvae. However, you may have to repeat the spraying several times in order to kill those ticks hidden out of reach of earlier sprays.

No Pest® strips hung in the kennel will kill newly hatched ticks, but do not use near dogs that have been dipped or that have been given *Task*® worm medication. The phenol in both products combined could constitute a lethal dose.

Flies and Mosquitoes

Mosquitoes present a real health problem for dogs in that they spread disease and act as hosts to heartworm larva. Spraying with malathion or a good dairy spray will deter mosquitoes as well as flies. Be sure to follow product directions implicitly. In southern areas where mosquito populations are extremely high it may be necessary to screen kennel buildings and runs and keep dogs inside at night.

INTERNAL PARASITES

There are several kinds of worms common to dogs throughout the United States, with the southern and coastal areas generally having the heaviest infestation. Some varieties of worms cause little serious harm, while others can be deadly.

The signs of worm infestation vary. Puppies may be pot bellied but thin or in poor general condition; poor hair coat, inability to gain or maintain weight, chronic coughing, diarrhea, or even behavior problems, can indicate worms. However, the same symptoms may come from other problems which unnecessary worming can aggravate. Do not worm a dog unless you *know* it has worms. The administration of some worm medicines to a weak or diseased animal could kill it.

To check for worms, collect a small sampling from fresh stool and take it to your vet for examination under a microscope. He can tell you which kind of worms, if any, are present and prescribe treatment. Puppies should be checked at three, six, nine weeks, and every six months thereafter, more often if worms are known to be a problem.

Worming is only the beginning. Kennel areas should be thoroughly cleaned and treated with salt (stock salt applied like fine snow and raked in) for roundworms or *Boraxo*® for hookworms (10 lb./100 sq. feet). Keep all droppings picked up and recheck the stool in two to three weeks.

Roundworms or Ascarids

Toxocara canis and *toxascaris leonina* are the most common varieties of worms, and may also be transmitted to humans. Puppies can acquire these while still a fetus or while nursing, or pick up the eggs from contaminated surfaces.

Roundworm infestations can seriously affect young puppies, even causing the death of entire litters. Infected puppies may vomit the worms or pass them in their stools. Fortunately treatment with *piperazine* is effective and safe, and can be administered even to three-week-old puppies in the form of a product called *Erliworm*®, or in liquid form. Wormers used to kill hookworms are also effective against ascarids.

Hookworms

Hookworms are found more commonly in the eastern and southern states, and in kennel situations anywhere. Infected areas are difficult to rid of larva, although *Boraxo*® (sodium borate) or malathion applied to the ground does considerable good. The hookworm sucks the blood of the dog through the walls of the intestine. Heavily infected dogs are severely weakened and even adult dogs can die. Infection occurs by ingestion of the eggs, skin penetration by the larva, or prenatal infection.

Symptoms vary from poor condition and loss of weight to persistent coughing and bloody or black, tarry stools. Hookworms must be treated quickly, and dogs in bad condition may require hospitalization and even blood transfusions. Treatment consists of giving disophenal shots subcutaneously or giving an oral medication such as *Task®* (dichlorvos) or *Nermex®*. These medications must be strong enough to kill the parasite, thus they should be *used with care under veterinary supervision.* Don't buy commercial over the counter preparations as they may be either ineffective or harmful. Excessive use of almost any hookworm medication may cause liver or kidney damage.

Classic's Gifted Geraldine, U.D. retrieves more than dumbbells! This talented lady belongs to Alane and Thomas Gomez.

Heartworm

Heartworm disease is a very serious problem. Because the infection is spread from dog to dog by mosquitoes, the disease was initially prevalent only in southern coastal areas, but today it has spread into almost every state.

The adult heartworm is 6 to 12 inches long. It lives on the right side of the dog's heart where it causes coughing, labored breathing, tiring, and weakness. In advanced stages the heart becomes badly damaged and many dogs die of circulation failure. Visible symptoms do not occur until damage has been done. If you live in an area where heartworm has been detected or where mosquitoes are especially bad, have your veterinarian take a blood test for heartworm. Preferably this should be done at night or in late evening when the microfilariae are more active.

If the test is positive, the dog must be treated with two separate medications, one to kill the microfilariae and one for the adult worms. Once free of these, or if the initial test is negative, medications can prevent maturation of infective larvae still in the bloodstream. If you live in an area where heartworm (or just mosquitos) are a problem, ask your veterinarian about using a heartworm preventative such as *Caricide* or *Filarbits®*. Tests must first be done to insure that no microfilaria are present in the bloodstream. Daily doses of medication given from one month before to one month after mosquito season effectively prevents heartworm infection. The residual effect lasts only 24 hours so effectiveness is lost if doses are skipped. Annual retesting is required.

Tapeworms and Whipworms

These worms are generally less common in dogs and cause less damage. Tapeworms are transmitted via fleas or rabbits, while whipworms are transmitted through ingestion of the eggs or larva. Both require a specific wormer.

Be sure any tapeworm medication is designed to get the head of the worm. These worms break into sections and the head may remain inside the intestine of the dog. Drugstore remedies again are generally ineffective, sloughing off only the segments and leaving the head intact.

Protozoa

Thin watery stools, dark loose stools, stools containing yellow gel, and a persistent diarrhea which does not respond to normal anti-diarrhea drugs and which is not accompanied by vomiting or depression may indicate a protozoan infection. Protozoa are easily missed as diagnosis requires *immediate* examination of fecal matter and thus the parasite is rarely seen if a stool sample is carried to the veterinarian.

Giardia reside in the small intestine rather than the colon as do most worms. The tiny one-celled parasites absorb nourishment in the form of carbohydrates directly from the host. *Flagyl®* is used in treatment.

Coccidia is more common in puppies than in adults, and occur most frequently in filthy conditions. However, once infected a bitch can carry the parasite encysted in her muscle tissue until hormonal changes of pregnancy activate them and they in turn infect her pups. Coccidia generally runs its course in a few days to a week and the dogs become resistant to reinfection. However, severe dehydration or recurrent cases can be serious. Treatment is generally with *nitrofurazone* or similar drugs. Fluid therapy may be needed.

Protozoa can be destroyed by careful steam or hot water cleaning of floors and kennel area.

"Sometimes, quite a few times of late, I think I should quit. Fifty years with a steady diet of dogs and horses is a long time. Perhaps I should go to live in an "old ladies home" and take up knitting or something of that sort.... I might be happy. No dogs or horses or people to worry about, no sitting up all night with a new litter.... No illnessness, no worming, no heartaches, no worries about selling dogs, no more frustrations in the show ring, no disappointments in people connected with dogs. At this point I have almost talked myself into it, but let me sit back a minute or so and think about it first.

What about my many friends whom I love so dearly? ...What about the dogs? Can I exist without their love and the entertainment they afford me? Never play with a group of pretty puppies or watch...my loved ones racing and playing in the snow.... How about the way they flock to me for love and attention? Their love and devotion demanding the same from me. I get tired, my feet hurt, and I get discouraged, but I still go on and on and on. When I weigh the pros and cons of each side of the matter, I feel that I cannot and will not give up. It will have to be my life until the end.... As long as a new litter of puppies can excite me with their beauty, charm, and potential, this is the only life I can live or want to live.

So, you fellow breeders out there, don't get discouraged and give up. Stick with it, and you will find the good things will far outweigh the bad...."

Betty Whelen, 1984
from *The New Mexican Sheltie*

The Challenge of Breeding

12

People breed dogs for many reasons. For many of us, the primary reason is the desire to create. As a potter molds the clay or the sculptor wields his knife to create a beautiful work of art, so the dog breeder creates with genes. There is tremendous satisfaction in having successfully chosen the breeding partners that produced a champion and a great deal of pride in exhibiting a dog that you have bred. The perfect dog always eludes, and the challenge of the dedicated breeder is to come ever closer to perfection, seeing improvement in every generation, and leaving for posterity a gene pool, a bloodline, that is better than what existed before. The desire to create drives us in the wake of failure after failure, stirs our hope of eventual success, and sometimes consumes our time and energy. Success as a Sheltie breeder does not come easily...it is the result of love, patience, study, and the development of an "eye for a dog." Over the years only a handful of breeders have made a lasting impact on our breed. But do not let this discourage you from trying; your efforts can be highly rewarding.

There are many other reasons for breeding; I think I have heard most of them. To make money, to educate the kids, because a litter of puppies is so much fun, because a bitch should be bred once before she is spayed, because your friends all love 'Tammy' and want a puppy from her, and so on. Before you breed for reasons such as these I encourage you to look at the other side of the picture. There is more to becoming a breeder than the obvious.

SOME CONSIDERATIONS

Bringing new life into the world requires responsibility, and the decision deserves serious consideration. Each and every hour more than two thousand dogs and cats are born in the United States. Every year approximately 18 million of these are impounded at a cost to taxpayers of about $200 million. Of those impounded, only one percent are adopted into permanent homes. The others are destroyed. Many of these are purebred; an increasing number of Shelties are being reported.

Contrary to popular opinion that this overpopulation is caused by pet owners who breed a litter of poor quality animals or people who allow their mixed breed to roam and get pregnant accidently, serious purebred breeders are also partially at fault. Producing too many puppies so that supply exceeds demand, failing to require neutering of pets, or selling to pet shops that encourage breeding contribute. Failure to screen buyers adequately or to educate them in responsible pet ownership multiplies the problem. When there are too many pups available or the price is too low, the "product" seems to have less value in the opinion of the owner and is generally less well cared for than the rarer or more expensive pet. If you breed, I encourage you: breed with restraint. Produce no more puppies than you can be sure to find homes for. And never make a breeding unless you have reason to believe that the new generation will be an improvement over the parents, will be sound in mind and temperament, and will include a puppy that you could use to carry on the line.

Now, let's examine some other fallacies regarding the breeding of dogs. Number one—"Puppies would be so much fun." Remember this when you are cleaning puppy papers or scooping poop, or when you are nursing that weak puppy every two hours around the clock for the fifth straight day. Remember it when your latest hopeful doesn't place or when your neighbors complain about the three noisy six-month-olds that you cannot sell.

"Of course it's work," you say, "but I can make some money." Have you considered that the price of dog food and veterinary care has been doubling every few years? Do you know about zoning requirements that restrict the breeding or keeping of too many dogs, and the tremendous expense required to meet some state requirements? Have you computed the investment required and the expected rate of return? In other words, do you know how much raising a litter can be expected to cost? Let's take a look at one example of the expenses of raising a litter:

Cost of bitch ($500) divided by number of litters produced in her lifetime (5)	$100.00
Pre-breeding veterinary exam	$ 60.00
Stud fee (average for champion)	$200.00
Shipping to & from stud	$150.00
Feed and vitamins for dam	$ 40.00
Feed for puppies during 8 weeks	$ 50.00
Puppies vaccinations ($12 ea. for 5 pups).	$ 72.00
Advertising	$100.00
TOTAL AVERAGE COST OF LITTER	$772.00

Some litters will cost more because of higher stud fees or initial investment, shipping expenses, or veterinary bills. A few will cost less—for example, if you use your own stud dog. Professional breeders who show and who consistently produce top quality litters will make a small profit. Lesser-known breeders may be able to break even, but for most hobby breeders raising a litter is just that...a very expensive hobby. The small profit you do occasionally make on a litter will barely support the adults during the remainder of the year, and if you add show expenses to the overhead, you can expect a loss.

More than anything else, raising a litter of puppies takes time. Feeding and attending a nursing litter requires at least thirty to sixty minutes a day. In addition, each pup should be handled individually, and by the third week should be receiving a minimum of ten minutes of individual attention at least three times a week. Multiplied by the average litter of five puppies, this equals two-and-one-half-hours per week just socializing a litter. Breeders are sometimes criticized for breeding only for looks without regard to temperament or intelligence. In most cases this is a false accusation, but there are a few people who breed litter after litter of kennel raised puppies seeking only that elusive champion and sending the rest into pet homes with little early socialization. Unless pups are given love, attention, and the opportunity to interact with humans, how can we expect them to become good family pets? *If you cannot or will not make this time allotment, please do not breed.*

Even if your Shelties are absolutely top quality, many of the puppies produced will be sold as pets for reasons of size, hereditary problems, or lack of quality. Unlike some breeds, Shetland Sheepdogs do not consistently produce puppies equal to or better than themselves in quality. Ours is a comparatively young breed, therefore throwbacks in type and size are common. Where will these pet puppies go? Will they contribute to the overwhelming dog population or will you find loving homes where they can spend their entire life? You face these questions with every puppy that you breed.

The responsible breeder screens buyers with care. Have they owned a dog before? Do they have a fenced yard? Do they have time to love, train, and take care of a dog? Have they given ample consideration to the breed and temperament that is right for their family? Is a Sheltie suited to their needs and lifestyle?

Can you tactfully talk a person out of buying the wrong dog even if you desperately need to sell the puppy? Are you willing to take the time and responsibility to find a good home for every puppy you breed? What will you do if the market is flooded or the economy tight and you still have unsold four-or five-month-olds underfoot? You cannot afford to keep them; you cannot sell them for the accepted pet price for your area. What do you do? As a responsible breeder you do not want to be identified with the pet shop market. You have a responsibility to other breeders to maintain a minimum price level or you will ruin the market for everyone else and make even cost recovery for expenses impossible. You could give the puppy to some deserving youngster who otherwise could not afford a dog, but a pet that costs nothing is often not valued or properly cared for. You can abdicate all responsiblity and give the puppies to the local shelter. Or you can humanely dispose of those you cannot place. Breeder, are you ready for that?

Even if you never have a pet you cannot place, you may whelp defective or mismarked puppies. And what about the pup that shows up with a heart defect at eight weeks or hip dysplasia after you have grown it out to six months as a show prospect? Is it ethical to sell these dogs? No. You must face facts. Are you ready to handle the responsibility for these animals just as you are for the promising show dogs?

Selling also requires time and patience. Ads must be prepared, phone calls taken, visitors received. Many will try your patience to the limit, but the responsible breeder teaches people about the breed, directs them to clubs and books, refers them to other breeders if necessary, and instructs on care, grooming, and health problems. A buyer's education often continues throughout the first year of ownership. Potential breeder/exhibitors need additional coaching. My buyers often bring puppies they have purchased back for ear correction. Follow-up on every puppy is required. If you want to know what your bitch or stud is producing you must look at each pup when it is mature. All of this takes time and energy.

A breeder must be able to accept criticism of his "product." There is much variation in our breed. Not everyone is going to admire your lovely homebred champion, that may be the nearest thing you've seen to perfection. I think a requirement for every breeder should be "thick skin" when it comes to criticism. And no breeder is infallable in judgement. Puppies you sincerely believe to be show quality will "go off," sometimes giving cause for hard feelings or misunderstanding. The runt you sold as a pet may blossom into the most beautiful show prospect...but the owner has it neutered. Write a sales contract; spell out everything you and the buyer expect; then honor it. It will prevent many misunderstandings. If you don't have enough confidence in your dogs to stand behind a written agreement, don't breed.

At three months, quality is obvious—but anything can happen. At 14 months and still immature, Ch. Spook Holler Winter Wind owned by Wendy Louring shows real promise for breeding and show. (Photos by Krook)

Sheltie clubs provide an opportunity to learn. See appendix for club in your area.

LAYING THE GROUND WORK

Having considered all the responsibilities, you are willing to accept them and eager to get started. Where do you begin? The basic and most valuable first step is: *develop a clear mental picture of your ideal Sheltie*. Start with that good ol' breeder's guide, the Standard. Memorize it. Examine Sheltie after Sheltie, rating them against the scale of points. Visit shows and kennels until you find a number of related dogs that closely approximate your interpretation of the ideal. Watch how they place. If your choice repeatedly disagrees with the judges, ask an experienced breeder to explain. Look at the overall dog, and learn to pick out the exceptional one, the dog strong in a particular quality or qualities. Watch puppies from various lines to see how they develop.

Study gait and structure. It amazes me how few breeders truly understand the mechanics of gait in this, a working breed. Study other breeds, too, looking for similarities and differences in structure and movement. Read everything you can about Shetland Sheepdogs, gait, and structure. Arrive at a visual understanding of how your ideal Sheltie would look, move, and act. *Unless you have an ideal firmly planted in your mind, you cannot make progress in breeding toward it.*

Always keep the total dog in mind. There are many champions with atrocious movement, miserable temperaments, common appearance...the list goes on and on. Strive for overall balance, moderation, and correctness. Don't be carried away by currently winning fads or the idea that breeding a *winning* Sheltie is synonymous with breeding a *better* Sheltie. I am thankful for the dedicated breeders who have been steadfast in their quest for the *totally* better Sheltie, regardless of current trends. They breed according to the Standard, keeping in mind temperament, personality, character, and the preservation of native ability, as well as beauty, elegance, moderation, balance and harmony in all parts. I challenge you to be uncompromising in your Standards. BREED FOR EXCELLENCE OR NOT AT ALL!

The study of genetics is important, too, but only if you learn to apply the principles to your dogs. Once you understand the basis of inheritance, begin to learn the dominant characteristics of each line, note frequently occurring faults, and determine which studs consistently produce certain virtues in their offspring. Take advantage of males that seem to consistently sire what you need. Never be afraid to go outside your own line to bring in a needed characteristic. If you are to breed dogs successfully, you must know where to go to get certain qualities. Established breeders and others who have been students of the breed for many years can be a big help to the novice in this area. Photographs in handbooks, individuals, photo collections, and old publications are helpful. For the most part, each person must learn this on his or her own, from one per-

Banchory Reflection, an inbred son of Ch. Banchory High Born, is the sire of more than 20 champions. He has probably been most influencial when outcrossed with bitches linebred on Ch. Halstor's Peter Pumpkin. Owners, Tom and Nioma Coen.

Ch. Shadow Hill's Sunrise, a Reflection daughter ex Macdega Under the Rainbow, owned by Jane Hammett.

Ch. Color Guard of Kinni, a Reflection son ex Ch. Canden Kinni Charisma (a Ch. Gerthstone's Jon Christopher daughter) owned by the author. (Photo by Jan.)

son to another. Be sure your sources are reliable, not gossip or hearsay. The more information you can find, the more rapidly your own breeding program will progress.

LAYING THE FOUNDATION

Now, with your visual picture of the ideal Sheltie firmly in mind and some idea of the line or lines you feel most closely approximates your ideal, begin your search for foundation stock. Most would-be breeders are encouraged to start with a bitch since the best stud dogs in the country are accessible for breeding. Remember to select on the basis of the total dog, looking at both her physical characteristics (quality) and her pedigree. Never select on pedigree alone. Remember that structural faults are the most difficult to correct, and that mental qualities are also hereditary. Don't be in a hurry. Take your time, look at many bitches, and be willing to *wait* for the one that most nearly fits your ideal.

A great deal of excellent published material is available on the subject of selecting foundation breeding stock

Backstop is dominant for white-factoring. Note the white stifle of all three dogs.

Ch. Banchory Backstop resulted from breeding Reflection to a granddaughter of High Born and Ch. Cherden Sock It To 'Em. He has 14 champion offspring. Note how a prepotent sire stamps his type on the offspring. Above, Backstop, head and full body; left, Am. Can. Ch. Akirene's Clasşic Image; top left, Kinni the Scotsman.

and we suggest that you read as much of it as possible (see bibliography). Here are a few very important points.

1. Start with a bitch. A dog will probably hinder your progress more than help it. No dog will suit every bitch you own and he may not produce well with even one of them.
2. Select the very best adult bitch you can get, one who is proven and has an excellent pedigree linebred on the greats in the breed.
3. Look for a bitch who has a number of top producing bitches in her pedigree, as well as top producing sires. A strong bitch line in a pedigree helps insure that your bitch has the genetic makeup to become a potential producer herself.
4. If you can't find an older, proven bitch, select the best older puppy bitch that you can find.
5. Decide which qualities you absolutely must have in your line and be sure your foundation bitch has these qualities. Be sure any faults she has are ones you can live with.

A good brood bitch must be capable of producing a high percentage of healthy, good quality puppies. She should be from a line of bitches who whelp easily and produce litters uniform in type, size, and quality. Be suspicious of a bitch, no matter how glamorous, who comes from a line prone to breeding difficulties, weakling puppies, oversize, or other serious problems. These qualities tend to be inherited, and even the most terrific bitch is rarely worth the trouble if she has a tendency toward such problems.

A "doggy" or masculine bitch may not be able to win in shows but often excels in the whelping box. A bitch known to control size (i.e., produce a majority of insize puppies even from studs close to 16 inches) can also be a valuable asset.

I do not believe that a good foundation bitch must necessarily be a champion, or even a show dog, although preferably she will be an exceptional specimen of the breed. In theory the show ring evaluates breeding stock; in practice the best producers are not always the big winners. In the ring too much emphasis may be placed on the "extras" such as showmanship, use of ears, coat, and condition, while the basics are too often overlooked. The "basics" are extremely important in breeding stock. They include such things as correct structure and angulation, sound movement, substance, correct temperament, correct type, and good health.

Certain hard-to-get qualities can also make an otherwise average brood bitch a valuable asset. Some qualities which I value and find hard to get are correct stop, correct eye, full muzzle and underjaw, extremely clean cheekbones, superb angulation, and correct, sweet expression combined with a look of elegance. I appreciate a bitch who can reproduce these qualities consistently even though she may be lacking in some other minor detail.

Of course, the ideal bitch is one who fulfills all the requirements of a good brood bitch and can also win in the conformation ring. She should be treasured and used wisely! Because beginning breeders may not recognize or appreciate the really superb animal, established breeders are often reluctant to trust her to a neophyte.

When I was looking for a foundation bitch, after a long and fruitless search, I finally located two equally well-bred bitches from a kennel whose overall type impressed me. Both were priced the same, with the same guarantee. In writing their owner I specified that the one thing I was most eager to obtain was a bitch who was absolutely sound and could move correctly. I was told that one bitch was sound and moved nicely but lacked elegance. The other was stylish and showy but not as sound.

Am. Can. Ch. Carmylie Elusive Dream, by Ch. Halstor's Peter Pumpkin, sire of 9 champions. Owned by Jean Simmonds, Carmylie. (Photo by Krook.)

Of course, I hoped to show and even finish the bitch I bought, but her primary purpose was the foundation of my kennel. I had to make a choice. The sound one would be harder to finish, but the elegant one might become a champion who would instill poor movement and unsoundness in my line. I chose the sound bitch, and I have not been sorry.

The best buy in a brood bitch is usually the older, proven bitch. Sometimes a five- or six-year-old may be available to a novice or small breeder if they agree to provide a retirement home for her. Other mature bitches are sold because their previous owner is keeping one or more daughters and no longer has space for the dam. If you cannot obtain a proven bitch, purchase the best unproven six- to eighteen-month-old you can afford. Expect to pay a good price—the right bitch will be well worth it!

TERMS

Arrangements on price and method of payment are part of the sales contract, which should be completed and signed before a puppy is shipped. The ideal terms for the seller, of course, are cash. However, some breeders will arrange for time payments or a charge card. The registration papers always remain the property of the seller until the dog is paid for in full.

SALES CONTRACT FOR SHOW OR BREEDING QUALITY DOGS

On ______ (date), ______ (name) kennels agrees to sell

to ______ (name) of ______ (address)

the following ______ (breed) for the sum of $______

Name: ______ Whelped ______

Sire: ______ Color: ______

Dam: ______ Sex: ______

Reg. #: ______

This animal is guaranteed to be free from all hereditary defects affecting its suitability for breeding, and is guaranteed to be free of disqualifying and serious faults of a structural or temperamental nature. Health is guaranteed for 48 hrs. and it is recommended that the buyer have the animal examined by a reputable veterinarian during that time.

A replacement or credit for the amount of purchase will be given for any animal sold for $______ or more if the dog matures at less than the represented quality at 18 mos. of age, unless it is mutually agreed to determine this at another date.

Special Provisions of sale:

Signed: ______ (buyer)

Signed: ______ (seller)

Address: ______

CONTRACT FOR CO-OWNERSHIP OF A DOG

On ______ (date), ______ (name) kennels agrees to sell

co-ownership in the following ______ (breed) to ______ (name)

of ______ (address) for the sum of $______

Name: ______ Color: ______

Sire: ______ Whelped: ______

Dam: ______ Sex: ______

Registration # ______

The buyer agrees to be responsible for adequate maintenance and promotion (i.e., training, showing, and advertising) of this animal except as specified below or when the dog is in the possession of ______ kennels.

Co-ownership entitles ______ kennels in the case of a male to ½ of all outside stud fees earned by the dog (both co-owners may use the dog free) and in the case of a bitch to use her for every other litter when she is not being shown.

Special Provisions:

In the event of sale of this dog, the remaining co-owner will have first chance to purchase the dog.

Signed: ______ (buyer)

Signed: ______ (seller)

Address: ______

Breeders Terms

Occasionally it is advantageous to buy a dog on co-ownership or "breeder's terms." Some very good dogs may be for sale only on such terms. This enables the breeder to use a stud dog or get a puppy back from a bitch without keeping the animal permanently. It also helps assure that a very high quality animal will get proper care, training, and promotion, and will be shown advantageously. If the terms are agreeable to both parties and the two owners can work together reasonably, this can be an advantageous arrangement for both. Be sure before entering into such an agreement, that you understand the terms perfectly, and that they are spelled out clearly in writing as well.

A bitch may be sold with a puppy or puppies (or even a litter) back as part of the purchase price. Or she may be sold on a permanent co-ownership where both parties co-own the bitch indefinitely (generally each owner takes every other litter). In both cases the buyer of the co-ownership is usually expected to keep the bitch at all times except when the breeder/seller is breeding or showing her. The particulars of such an agreement will vary with each individual case. A contract for co-ownership is shown.

Males are also sometimes offered on co-ownership. Other males will be sold outright but with the seller retaining *stud privileges.* This means that the seller has the right to breed the male to any of her personal bitches at any time in the future if he so desires. Allowance for this privilege may or may not be included in the price of the dog.

Leasing

When you lease a Sheltie you pay a fee for the use of that dog for a specified period of time, after which the dog is returned to the owner. Most breeders will not lease a dog to a novice, but occasionally they will lease to a small new breeder or a handler. If there is a specific quality which you need but do not have in your line and cannot afford a dog with this quality, the answer might be leasing. Leasing such a bitch to breed to a stud of your choice might give you a puppy or two with the desired quality with which to continue. You might also want to lease a bitch who complements a stud you wish to prove or to make a desirable breeding to your male which might otherwise never be made.

Bitches are generally leased for a period of six months. A lease card must be obtained from the American Kennel Club and signed by both the owner and the lessee in order for the litter to be registered with the lessee as breeder. If the bitch is leased for longer than six months a lease card must be filled out for each six month period. Lease fees start around $100 and go up, depending on the merits of the bitch. In addition, the lessee is responsible for shipping cost, stud fee and expenses on the litter.

Males are also leased occasionally, but this agreement is not recorded by AKC. It is usually in the form of a personal agreement between two breeders. Arrangements vary to suit individual needs. An example would be for the lessee to pay advertisement, show expenses if any, and routine care in return for free personal use (or reduced stud fee) and a percentage of any stud fees from bitches not owned by the lessee. The owner receives a percentage of the outside fees and the benefit of having his dog promoted in a new area. Obviously the success of this venture rests on the degree of responsibility and agreement between the two parties.

RESEARCH AND EVALUATION

Having selected the best quality individual available, one with a good linebred pedigree and meeting most of your requirements for your ideal Sheltie—a bitch of quality with no outstanding faults and hopefully at least one outstanding virtue—begin an indepth study of her background. Trace her pedigree back as far as you can through correspondence with her breeder and others who owned the dogs in her background. Learn everything you can about the line and accumulate pictures of the parents, grandparents, and any others possible. Each name on the pedigree should mean something to you. What was the dog like—color, size, head qualities, body type. What were its strengths and weaknesses? What are some of the other offspring like? With luck you can compile enough photos and information so that each name calls up an image of that Sheltie. If you continue searching you will eventually learn the background of the major stud dogs and bloodlines. *The more you know about the forebearers of your bitch, the more successful you will be in breeding her*.

If you have been fortunate to obtain a mature bitch, you will be ready to start looking for a mate immediately, but not before you have formulated a breeding plan. Plan early so that soon after purchasing a puppy you can begin evaluating potential mates. Your image of the ideal Sheltie, of course, becomes the basis for your plan. Begin with your chosen line, then evaluate your bitch to determine where she needs improvement and which strengths you especially want to keep. Each breeding should take you one step closer to your ideal. Look first within your basic line for a mate that compliments the bitch, brings in a needed quality, and does not double on any fault. If none is available, do not hesitate to go to another line to get the needed quality—but with the idea that you will breed the offspring right back into your basic bloodline. Always look at the total dog, and remember to take advantage of those dogs that are known producers of a characteristic your bitch needs. Include in your plan an idea of what you expect to get from the mating and where you will breed the offspring. Although it may change somewhat as you go along, your plan should include breedings for at least three generations.

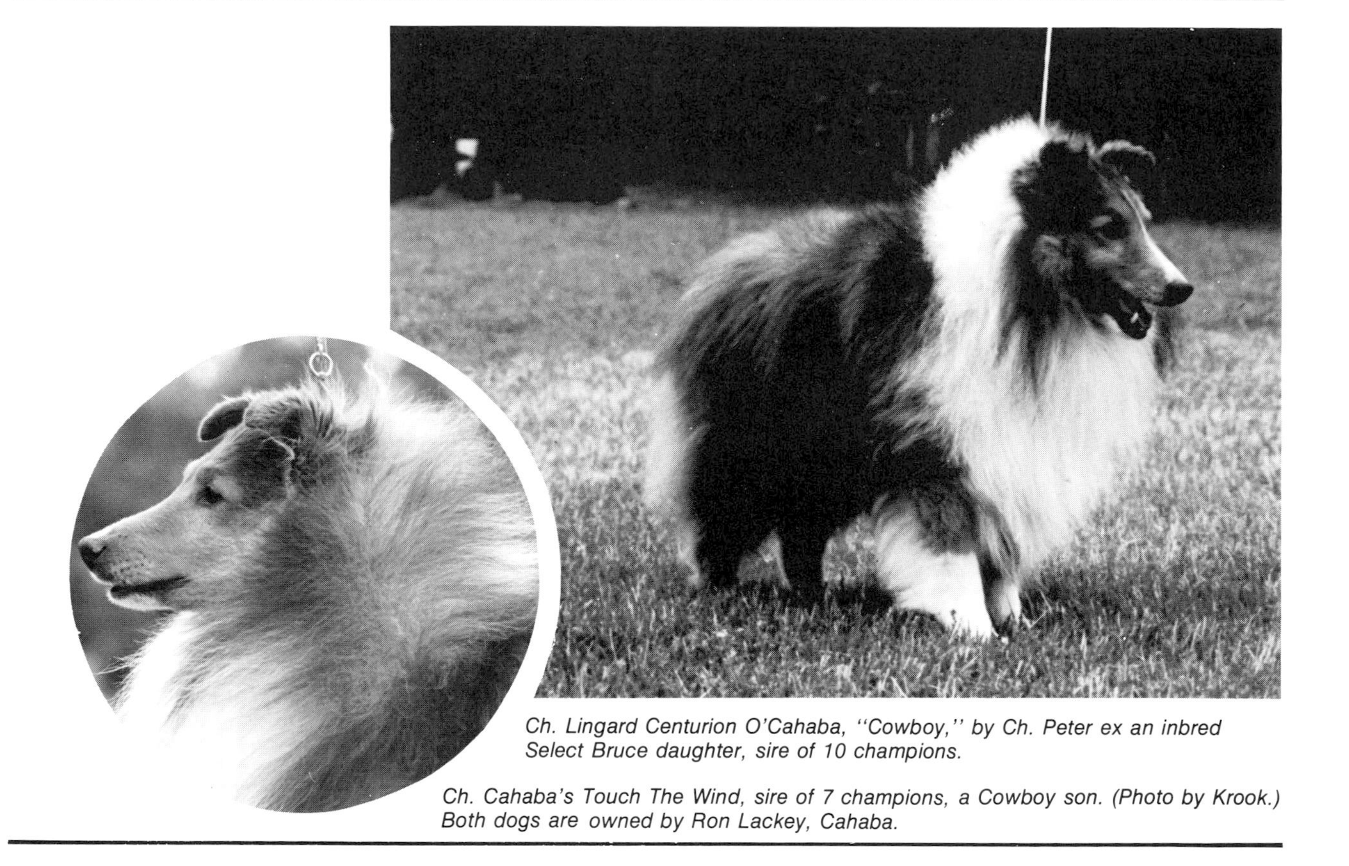

Ch. Lingard Centurion O'Cahaba, "Cowboy," by Ch. Peter ex an inbred Select Bruce daughter, sire of 10 champions.

Ch. Cahaba's Touch The Wind, sire of 7 champions, a Cowboy son. (Photo by Krook.) Both dogs are owned by Ron Lackey, Cahaba.

One of the most difficult aspects of breeding is the need to be ruthlessly objective in evaluating your progress. Keep only those offspring that are better than the parent and that are one step closer to your ideal Sheltie. If there is improvement, but the pup is not closer to your ideal, sell it. Be very selective in what you keep.

Every year, stand back and evaluate your dogs. Have you, indeed, come closer to your ideal? Have you eliminated a fault by breeding selectively? Is the worst puppy in your last litter better than the worst puppy in your first litter? If not, you are making no progress.

Every breeding animal should be evaluated on the quality of its offspring. If a bitch doesn't contribute her share to breed improvement, or a stud is not, when bred wisely, producing puppies better than himself, eliminate them from your breeding program. Are there serious faults in your dogs that you cannot breed out, or are you contributing to the betterment of the breed as a whole? If after two or three generations your litters are not consistently higher quality than when you first began, consider starting over with better stock. If your foundation bitch is a proven producer of high quality with a good linebred pedigree but you have not raised a quality litter from her, ask her breeder or another breeder successfully working with that bloodline to help you plan her next mating. Never be afraid to ask the more experienced person for advice, to go outside your own area, bloodline, or circle of acquaintances to find the right stud. Consider the total dog—body, mind, and personality. Evaluate all "get" by the contributions of both parents, and never settle for anything but the best.

THOSE IMPORTANT RECORDS

If you are like me, breeding is a challenge, puppies are fun, but keeping records is a drudgery likely to be neglected. Honest and thorough evaluation of your breeding program is impossible without good records. They are also required by the American Kennel Club.

I keep a file folder on every dog: registration papers, pedigree, certificates of vaccination, health records, breeding and show records. It should also include a photo and physical description of each dog, record of tattoo, if any, and a record of a bitch's heat cycle. Breeding records will include the date bred, day of heat cycle, name and details on the stud, how many puppies resulted, date whelped, their sex and color, the name, address and phone number of the new owners, date of sale, sale price, and any other pertinent information. The AKC supplies a litter record form which is convenient. To the back of it I attach sales contracts, growth records of the pups, and other information that I find helpful.

Good follow-up records on each litter are extremely valuable when evaluating litters and planning future breedings. I like to photograph each pup in the litter at three, four, six and eight weeks of age, and older if the puppy isn't sold. I then ask the new owners to bring the puppy by or send photos of it at six months, one year, and when fully mature. Sometimes these are difficult to obtain. I wish each buyer would realize the importance to the breeder of such records and be more helpful in supplying them. Jotting down height and other details on the back of the photo is also helpful. Such detailed record keeping is absolutely essential for the breeder who wants to attain success. If a promising litter does not mature out as hoped, go back to your records, examine pedigrees and pictures, study the sire and dam to try to determine why the mating did not click. Consider whether environment or lack of socialization played a part. Re-examine offspring by that sire, looking for pups with similar defects. If you find none, try to determine whether the lack of quality is coming from your bitch. In most cases, I would give a *quality* bitch a second or even a third chance to produce from different sires. If she still does not produce, find another bitch. Don't keep one of her mediocre daughters hoping for improvment in the second generation.

When it comes time to bring in new blood, go back to your records. Look at the sires and dams that most consistently produced the type of Sheltie you like. Don't get hung up on keeping only dogs you have bred. Look for other individuals related to your pool of top producers, selecting only those dogs that compliment what you already own. Fresh blood must continually be added if you want to stay on top.

Ch. Macdega the Piano Man, a bi-black owned by Macdega, is proving to be a dominant young sire (Photo by Krook.)

THE FINAL QUESTION

Why do you want to breed? Is it to produce that next group winner; or is it because there are people who want Sheltie puppies and you hope to provide healthy, well adjusted dogs that will bring joy and beauty into someone's life? Do you breed for conformation without proper regard for qualities that make a dog enjoyable to own? Will your stable, intelligent puppies grow up to be a constant pleasure to their owners; or are you breeding noisy, neurotic dogs that will become a constant source of agitation?

Will the Shelties you produce live long, healthy lives free of inherited eye, hip, skin, or other problems; or are you propagating a line prone to disease and weakness? Are there hidden recessives in the genes that may bring grief and heartbreak to some child or elderly person whose only companion is a dog? Is your "search for excellence" limited to only certain aspects; or is the total animal and its future held precious?

Note how inbreeding stamps type. Ch. Northcountry Westering Son "Blazer," a Ch. Halstor's Peter Pumpkin son, left, with his mother Ch. Malpsh Count Your Blessings, also by Peter. (Photo by Krook.)

Introduction To Genetics 13

How does a trait pass from one generation to another? This has been the subject of much scientific study and a multitude of old wives' tales. The modes of inheritance have become known to man through the study of genetics, but practical application of the basic principles as they pertain to breeding Shelties is largely unknown. Some traits can be easily predicted, but others, where the number and type of controlling factors has not been determined, still pose questions.

HOW INHERITANCE WORKS

In the nineteenth century Mendel conducted his famous experiments with pea plants and discovered that traits which were not *seen* in the parents could be passed on to the offspring if the parents carried factors for that trait. While this is generally accepted today, it was revolutionary in Mendel's time and is the basis for all genetic understanding.

Genes and DNA

A gene has been defined as the hereditary blueprint which determines what trait an animal will possess. It is like a program for a computer which controls what the computer turns out. A gene has never been seen but its location can be pin-pointed. It is believed to be made of a complicated chemical substance, deoxyribonucleic acid, abbreviated as DNA. The DNA molecule is shaped like a spiral ladder (fig. 1), and on each rung the atoms are in a slightly different order. The variations are infinite. Every living being is what it is because of the orders stamped in its DNA. People, horses, dogs, birds, snakes, plants, amoebas, and even viruses are programmed by DNA. A "gene" is nothing more than a location on one of these DNA chains with one or more molecules actually transmitting orders for one particular trait.

Chromosomes

Long strands of DNA molecules are found in nearly every cell in every animal. These strands are known as chromosomes and are aligned in pairs. Each chromosome has a mate which is called its "allele," and corresponding points (or "loci") on each strand represent genes for any given trait (i.e., one on each allele for eye color, tail length, coat color, or whatever). In other words, *each cell contains two genes for each trait represented.* As each gene locus can have more than one DNA molecule, some traits can be controlled by more than one pair of genes. If the locations of the multiple genes are close together on the chromosome, they will usually be linked and inherited together as if they were only one gene. If they are widely separated they may be recombined differently during reproduction.

The number of chromosomes varies from species to species and is not necessarily indicative of the complexity of the organism. A fruit fly has only two allelic pairs (four chromosomes), which makes it ideal for genetic research. Humans have 46 chromosomes and domestic dogs are believed to have 78 chromosomes with a slight variation sometimes noted between individual breeds.

Most cells resemble a fried egg—the nucleus being the yolk, the cytoplasm corresponding to the egg white, and the cell membrane holding the whole thing together. The nucleus contains the chromosomes, which are visible under a microscope when stained. Each cell in a body contains the allotted number of chromosomes for that species. Your big toe is made of cells whose nuclei contain chromosomes having genes for characteristics of that toe and every other trait including eye color!

The DNA keeps everything straight and dictates where and when each gene will manifest itself. The orders of the DNA are carried out by a related substance, ribonucleic acid, known as RNA, which travels throughout the cytoplasm as a messenger. The DNA never leaves the nucleus except during cell division. The RNA triggers each specialized cell to do its job at the appropriate time.

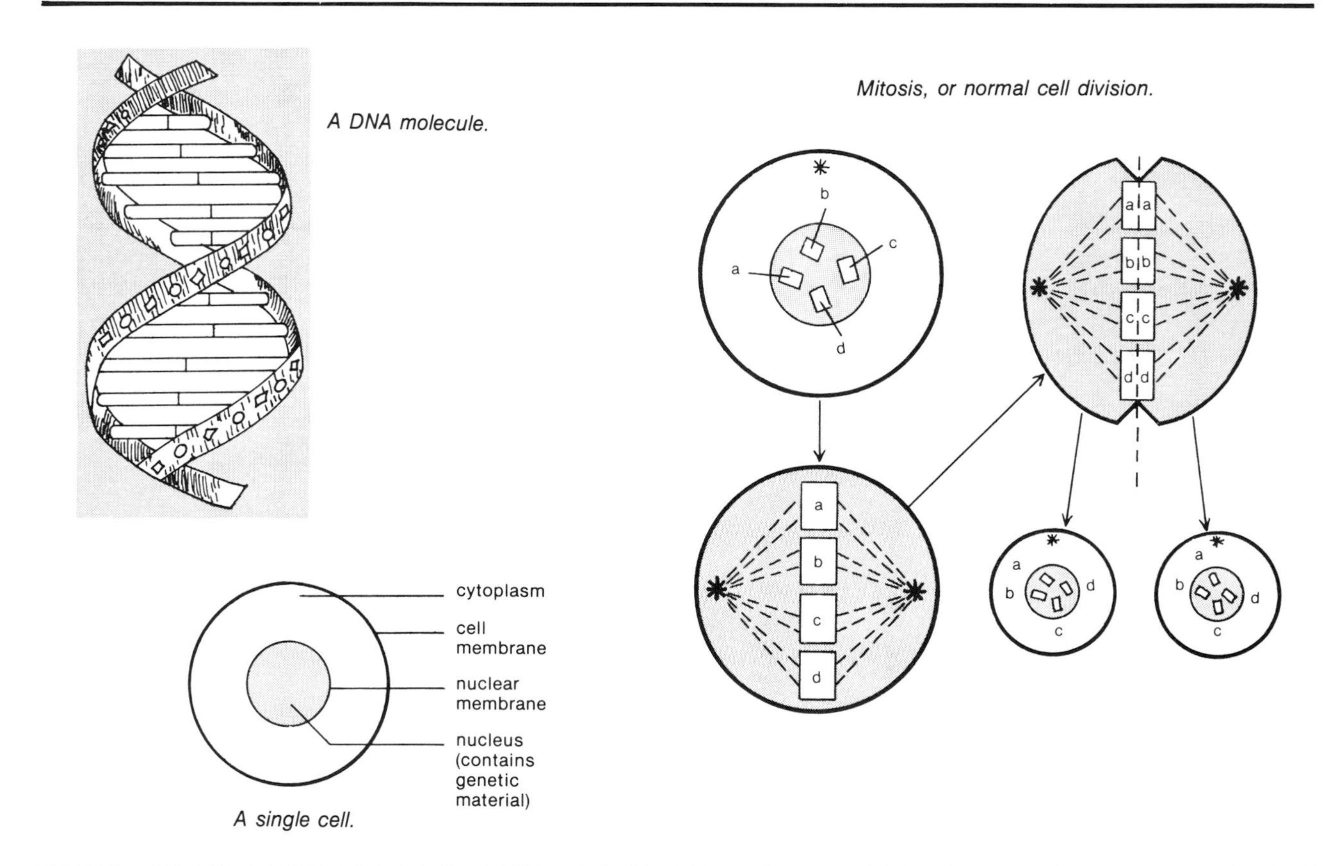

A DNA molecule.

A single cell.

Mitosis, or normal cell division.

Cell Division by Mitosis

In dogs, body cell growth occurs by cell division, known as mitosis. The chromosomes, which are normally in a tangled mass, neatly pair off, go through an intricate dance where they duplicate themselves, and the nucleus separates, forming two nuclei, each with 39 pairs of chromosomes. The cytoplasm pinches in two around each nucleus and two cells appear where only one was before. Nothing has changed in the genetic make-up of these cells. They are both identical to the original cell.

Reproductive Cell Division

The only cells in a dog which do not have 39 *pairs* of chromosomes are the reproductive cells. The formation of the sex cells (gametes) in preparation for reproduction is known as meiosis. As in mitosis, the chromosomes in the gametes during meiosis pair off with corresponding alleles. They go through a similar dance but do not duplicate. Therefore, when the nucleus divides, only one allele from each pair goes to each side, and the resulting cell has only 39 chromosomes (*not pairs*), half the original number. Meiosis insures that the recipient will not inherit four genes for hair color but none for eyes.

Each trait is governed by at least two genes, one on each allele. However, the *reproductive cell carries only one gene for every trait*. When this cell combines with a reproductive cell from the other parent animal, the offspring receives a new genetic combination having one allele for each set of traits from each parent. These alleles may be either identical (homozygous) or different (heterozygous).

Genetic characteristics usually express themselves as either dominant or recessive. If a dog is homozygous for a certain trait he has only one type of gene for that trait and that is all he can give his offspring. However, a dog heterozygous for a certain trait carries both a dominant and a recessive gene for that characteristic, and either can be passed to his offspring. For example, a tri-factored sable (see chapter 15) will produce 50 percent gametes with just a tri gene and 50 percent with just a sable gene, but none with both. His offspring will inherit only one color factor from him and one from the other parent, which recombine to form a new entity. This principle is true for genes governing every trait.

Meiosis, division of the reproductive cells.

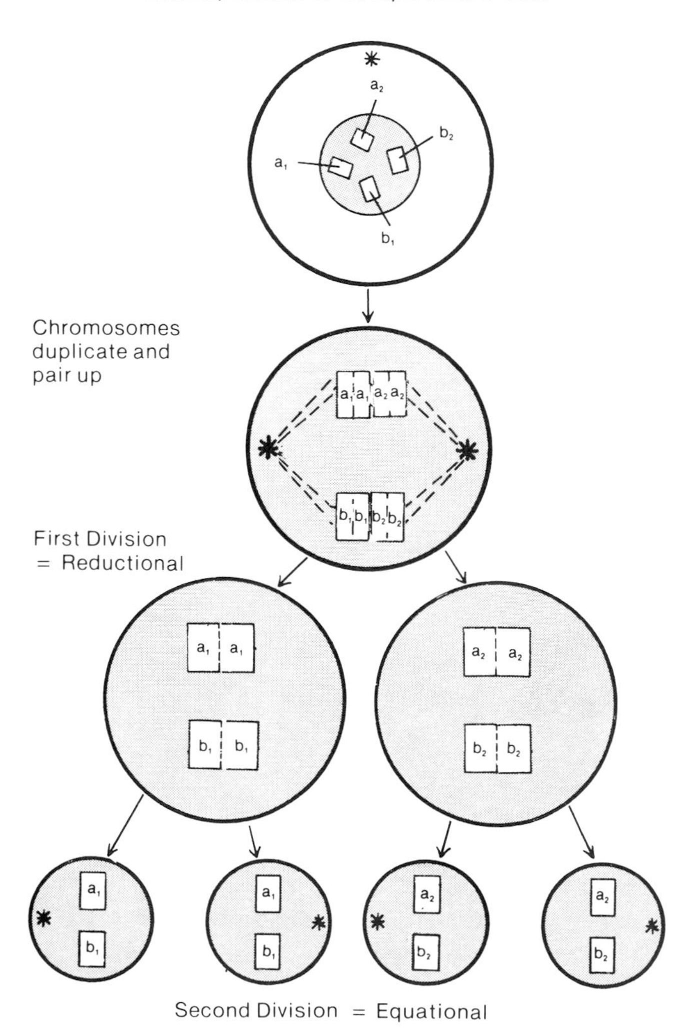

Banchory Bi Jingo of Carmylie, the first influential bi-black. Owner, Jean Simmonds. (Photo by Krook)

HOW GENES AFFECT APPEARANCE

The factors controlling inheritance, which we now call genes, exhibit various degrees of expression. Every dog has two facets to consider before breeding. One is his *phenotype*, or what the dog looks like. Phenotype is determined by the genes which are *fully expressed*. Full expression comes when the genes are in the pure form (i.e., homozygous; both genes for the trait are the same), or when a dominant gene masks the expression of a recessive gene. In the latter case the alleles are different but only the dominant one is seen.

The other consideration is the *genotype*, which cannot be seen. The genotype describes the genetic makeup of the dog and is equally important from a breeding standpoint. For example, when a known dominant characteristic appears in the phenotype, it is impossible to tell without test breeding whether the dog carries two dominant genes for that characteristic or whether the dominant gene is simply masking the expression of a recessive. Recessive characteristics are sometimes carried in the genetic makeup for generations without being seen.

Genetics would still be easy, however, if all traits fell into the simple dominant-recessive category (i.e., controlled by only one set of alleles in which one trait is completely dominant over the other). But in nine out of 10 cases the answer is much more complicated, making lists of dominant and recessive traits not worth the paper they're written on.

Not all dominant traits are *completely* dominant. Some are only partially expressed, producing an actual blending of the two genes. An example is a Manx cat (tailless) bred to a normal, long-tailed cat producing a short-tailed offspring. The Manx has no stump at all, but most mixed-breed Manx kittens have a tail, usually not as long as that of the other parent.

Also, many traits are controlled by *multiple gene combinations*. If more than two pairs of genes influence any trait, the possible combinations mushroom in number. Add to this the possibility of variable expressivity where genes may express themselves, but not necessarily to the same degree each time—the overall scope is staggering!

One obvious error in assuming all traits are either simple dominant or recessive can be illustrated: Straight front angulation has been argued heatedly. One group says it is dominant because it is common and hard to breed out. The other faction argues that it is recessive and therefore will be in a pure form whenever seen. Both arguments are ridiculous! Straight shoulders are created by a combination of shoulder lay-back, length of shoulder blade, length of upper arm, angle of upper arm, point of attachment of shoulder blade to spine, distance between shoulder blades at the withers, tension of ligaments which bind the muscles to the front assembly, length and condition of every individual muscle involved, and shape of each bone. Obviously straight shoulders involve more than a simple dominant or recessive. Obviously too, they are controlled by more than one set of alleles; they are a combination of many different parts.

Mutation

During meiosis a mistake occasionally occurs. When the chromosomes divide, one may break or go to the wrong place. This produces a gamete with different genetic makeup than the original. If the alteration is drastic, the cell will probably not reproduce. If, however, the change is slight, the recipient may turn out in an unexpected way. This phenomena is called *mutation*. A genetic mutant will continue to produce his newly acquired trait in his progeny. If cultivated and isolated, a new strain of animals can be created from one such mutant. Mutation is relatively rare and accounts for far less instances of unexpected inheritance than it is credited with.

GENETICS APPLIED TO BREEDING SHELTIES

As you have deduced by now, the world of genetics is both complex and fascinating; full of surprises, frustration, and revelation. So how can this be applied to breeding Shelties?

At our present state of knowledge much of it cannot. Until we know more about inheritance particular to Shelties, there are a few sensible guidelines you can follow. First, learn which traits seem to be more dominant. Second, determine which problems are most persistent, particularly problems not exhibited by either parent but evident in the offspring. These are probably recessive and therefore can skip generations only to reappear further down the line. Dominants can be seen, so are more easily controlled. Third, determine which traits have a tendency to inherit in unison and decide if they can be separated or whether they must be accepted in the natural order. Fourth (and most important), know what faults and strong points each dog in a pedigree has. Try to concentrate the virtues as much as possible and follow some pattern in eliminating the weaknesses in a long-term breeding program. The need for accurate records and analysis of statistics becomes obvious.

DOMINANT AND RECESSIVE TRAITS IN THE SHETLAND SHEEPDOG

Few traits except color have been accurately determined to be simple dominants or recessives. Most traits will involve more than one set of genes, and some of the examples, which are taken from a few breedings only, may be incorrect. *Anyone who wants to become a serious breeder ought to keep accurate records of his own litters to determine what traits in his particular line seem to follow which patterns of inheritance*.

Refer to chapter 15 for information on expected ratios in the offspring once the dominant and recessive have been isolated. Remember that when two individuals who are homozygous recessive for a trait are bred together, the offspring will all exhibit that trait in the pure recessive form.

THE NEED FOR RESEARCH

Since theoretical genetics is now understood, the problem becomes one of determining which traits are governed by which laws of inheritance. Until now, research has been limited to rapidly multiplying, cheaply raised laboratory animals such as rodents and to economically important animals such as cattle and sheep.

DOMINANT AND RECESSIVE CHARACTERISTICS IN SHELTIES

Traits Tending To Appear More Dominant (Those which are bred in most easily)		**Traits Appearing More Recessive** (Those which can skip a generation)
Harsh Coat	...dominant over...	Soft Coat
Full Coat		Sparse Coat
Sable Color		Tricolor
Gay Tails		Natural Carriage of Tails
Round Eyes		Almond Shaped Eye
Blue Merle Color		Tricolor
Straight Angulation (actually complex)		Good Angulation
Long Tails		Short Tails
Correct Bite		Overshot or Undershot Mouth
Slow Development		Fast Maturation
Straight Coat		Wavy Coat
Long Heads		Short Heads
Correct Medium Sized Eye		Large or Small Eye
Broad Skulls		Lean Skulls
Poor Stops		Good Profiles
Correct Rears		Crooked Rears
Dark Eye		Light Eye
Prominent Cheekbones		Smooth Skull
Good Temperament		Shyness
Terrier Temperament		Correct Temperament
Slab Sides		Correct Rib Spring
Snipy Muzzles		Rounded Foreface
Barrel Ribs		Correct Rib Spring
Long Back		Short Back
Correct Number of Teeth		Missing or Crooked Teeth

Traits Which Tend To Inherit Together (These can be separated but more concentrated effort is required)		
Too-Lean Skulls	inherits with	Domed Skull
Broad Skulls		Flat Skulls
Straight Shoulders		Short Neck
Excessive Rear Angulation		Cow Hocks
High-Set Hocks		Straight Stifles
Too-Short Back		Straight Angulation
Long Neck		Long Back
Too-High Ear Set		Domed Skull
Too-Long Head		Sliding Stops and Two-Angled Head Planes
Small Ears		Thick or Prick Ears
Wavy Coat		Soft Coat
Correct Shoulders		Correct Pasterns

Ch. Cahaba's Magic O' Marion, a grandson of Ch. Halstor's Peter Pumpkin owned by Ginny Cavallaro. (Photo by Krook)

Culprits in the Genes 14

About 100 separate diseases or defects in the dog are known or believed to be hereditary. Some, such as heart, eye, and hip abnormalities, affect the health and usefulness of the dog. Others, such as dewclaws on all four feet, blue eyes, and so forth, are simply undesirable.

Raising an otherwise promising Sheltie only to find that he has a hereditary defect is one of the most devastating experiences a breeder has to face. It is always a difficult problem to cope with. When a serious genetic defect occurs with a high degree of frequency in a line its economic impact can be serious, and if uncontrolled the defect can ruin a breed. Once a defect becomes widespread it may take generations of carefully selective breeding to breed it out, if indeed it can ever be eradicated. Also, many hereditary problems are not easily discernible, especially to the novice, and therefore go unnoticed and are perpetuated.

Sheltie breeders have been extremely lucky, for hereditary problems are not widespread in the breed. It is not unusual for a person to breed Shelties for several years without encountering a genetic defect. Compare this with other breeds, such as collie eye anomaly in Collies or dysplasia in Shepherds, and our breed looks good indeed!

But the fact that we have a sound breed must not invite complacency. Defects crop up in any breed no matter how carefully the matings are planned. Perhaps Sheltie breeders have been a bit too complacent, as hereditary defects do appear to be on the increase in our breed; or at least we are discovering them now where in the past they may have gone unnoticed.

If you breed a dog with a genetic abnormality, hiding your head in the sand and pretending it doesn't exist will not help the breed. It would be far more beneficial to the breed if breeders would help one another in determining where the defective genes are coming from and how they are being inherited.

WHAT IS A HEREDITARY DEFECT?

A congenital defect is present at birth. It may be either genetic or be the result of intrauterine factors such as nutritional deficiency, toxicity, or the effect of a drug administered to the bitch during pregnancy. An *inherited* defect is *transmitted on the genes*. It is possible for a defect to be *both* hereditary and congenital. Unfortunately, not all inherited defects are visible at birth. A dog with progressive retinal atrophy may be normal at weaning and develop clinical blindness by six months of age, while another dog may not develop signs of diminished vision until he is six or more years old.

Gene combinations which produce defects take many forms. They may be dominant, recessive, or incompletely dominant. They may or may not be sex linked (i.e., affecting or perpetuated only by one sex because the gene for the defect is on the sex chromosome). If only one pair of genes is responsible for the defective characteristic it is said to be "autosomal." This is the ideal genetic situation and most easily bred out. However, if more than one pair of genes are involved, as is often the case, the defect will be much harder to breed out. This occurrence is referred to as polygenic inheritance.

To further complicate the problem, enough is not known about many defects to enable researchers to accurately determine which type of inheritance pattern is involved. In addition, a breed may be "predisposed" to a problem even though direct inheritance cannot be demonstrated, as in the case of "Collie nose" in Shelties.

A discussion of some of the hereditary defects more commonly seen in Shelties follows. There are, of course, numerous others.

EYE DEFECTS

Eye defects, which have plagued Collie breeders for years, are also present in Shetland Sheepdogs. Although veterinarians report that the incidence of eye anomalies in Shelties affects only a small percent of the total Sheltie population, there is adequate cause for concern.

The Eye Structure

The portion of the eye which we see as the colored portion is called the iris. In the center of the iris is the pupil (the dark area), through which light enters the eye.

The posterior portion of the eye is constructed in three layers. The outer layer, the sclera, coats and protects the entire eyeball. A middle layer, the choroid, lies between the retina and the sclera and is a highly vascular structure. The inner lining of the eye, the retina, is a neural, light sensitive layer.

Light enters the eye through the pupil, then reaches the retina, where it is converted to nervous impulses which are transmitted to the brain by the optic nerve to produce sight. The area on which the image is projected is called the fundus. The fundus consists of the tapetal, or reflective, part, and the non-tapetal, or non-reflective, area. The tapetal, or reflective, portion of the fundus has the texture of the fine granulated beading, literally a projection screen. In the center of this area is the optic disc where the optic nerve and the blood vessels enter the eyeball.

Sheltie Eye Syndrome

This defect is similar to Collie eye anomaly. SES describes a condition in which there is no reflective material on the fundus, or where the material that is there is only partially formed or is damaged, or where the optic nerve is underdeveloped. The optic disc may be pitted or deteriorated, or it may appear to be from two to five times normal size. The blood vessels are sometimes tortuous and the tapetal area may appear an orange-red color. Minor defects of this sort produce little or no loss of vision, but major defects result in total blindness.

SES can usually be detected in a five to six week old puppy. Veterinarians grade the defect from I to V in order of severity. There is very little sight loss in a dog with grade I to III Sheltie Eye Syndrome. The danger with breeding these dogs is that a dog exhibiting *any* degree of the defect, if bred to a dog carrying genes for SES, is capable of producing a Grade V or blind puppy. Therefore, Shelties with any degree of SES should not be bred. *An exception would be a merle graded II with a notation "OK to breed." This simply means that there is a lack of pigmentation, which is caused by the influence of the merle color gene on the eye and is not a genetic defect.* No symptoms are associated with the milder grades of this defect. Unless you have your dog's eyes examined, you may never know he has it. While the average veterinarian can pick up severe grades of SES, an examination by a certified veterinary ophthalmologist is essential for Shelties you plan to breed. SES is not progressive, so a dog certified normal at eight weeks can be expected to remain free of this defect.

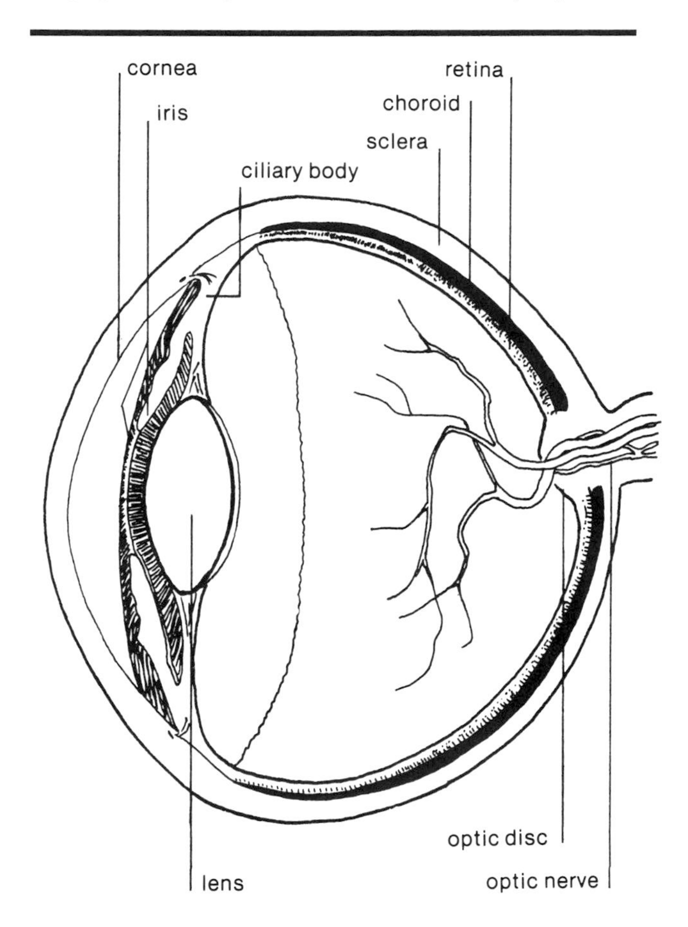

Structure of the eye.

Inheritance and Possible Causes. Sheltie Eye Syndrome is generally believed to be controlled by a single recessive gene with variable expressivity. However, Frede-

[1]Frederick B. Hutt. *Genetics for Dog Breeders,* San Francisco, W.H. Freeman and Co., 1979.

rick Hutt of Cornell University[1] suggests that the defect is polygenic and linked to selection for some characteristic which dictates a high chance for the defect to occur. SES can obviously be carried by normal eyed dogs for many generations without surfacing until the right combination of genes occurs to produce the defect.

It has been recognized that the incidence of Collie eye syndrome increased in Collies with the tendency to breed for smaller eyes. Hutt and many other veterinarians contend that the same thing is happening to Shelties. As breeders select for a narrower head with eyes set more obliquely, the lesions seen in SES—abnormally tortuous vessels in the retina, excavation of the optic disc, and dysplasia of the choroid and retinal layers—may be caused by unusual pressure on the eyeball and constriction of the optic nerve.

The Standard calls for the head to be "a long, blunt wedge, tapering slightly from ears to nose," and for "eyes medium size with dark, almond-shaped rims, set *somewhat* obliquely in the skull" (italics mine). Nothing was said about the head being lean or narrow, or the eye needing to be small, although both are definitely in vogue. We may, in short, be propagating a head type that many breeders feel not only is un-Sheltie-like, but is doing away with both brain capacity and normal eyes. The truly wedge-shaped head with a correct, definite stop gives the eyes a ready-made place to set. But narrow heads, usually accompanied by lack of stop, force the eye to set more obliquely in less space. The optic nerve enters the eye at a more acute angle than normal, thus the flow of blood to the eye may be restricted. So, Sheltie breeders are encouraged to take a hard look at the implications of the choices they are making while there is still time.

Progressive Retinal Atrophy

Two hereditary retinal atrophies have been identified and they affect many breeds. One is generalized progressive atrophy, referred to as PRA, and the other is central progressive retinal atrophy or CPRA. Both diseases are progressive and eventually result in blindness. Retinal atrophy is a special problem to the breeder because of its late onset, usually when the dog is three to six years of age.

Central progressive retinal atrophy is the more common form seen in the Shetland Sheepdog. The first clinical sign is that the dog has difficulty picking out objects directly in front of him but still has good peripheral vision. The central portion of the retina is affected initially, with the outer portions gradually becoming involved. Total blindness may or may not result as the condition progresses over several years.

CPRA is thought to be inherited as a genetic dominant, thus at least one parent would have to be affected. The danger, of course, is that a Sheltie at five or six years of age may have produced many puppies by the time the disease is diagnosed.

PRA is seen less frequently in Shelties; more frequently in Collies. Initially the pupils are semi-dilated and respond sluggishly to light. There is increased tapetal reflectivity and the small blood vessels are diminished in size. The first warning that the owner may observe is night blindness. Later he will become day blind as well. Many owners note a personality change and wonder why their dog reacts differently in low light situations.

Diagnosis. There is only one positive diagnostic method capable of detecting PRA in puppies and it is not widely available—that is the electroretinograph or ERG. The puppy must be anesthetized and a special contact lens fitted over each eye is connected to an electrical recording device. The reaction to a strong source of light is then recorded and evaluated. This test is certainly recommended if you know that CPRA or PRA has occurred in the ancestors of your puppy, or if either parent has produced an affected Sheltie.

Microphthalmia

Microphthalmia is congenital smallness of the eye which varies from eyes that appear normal in structure and function, with smallness as the only defect, to eyes complicated by multiple defects such as cataracts, retinal dysplasia, and coloboma. It is frequently seen in color-dilute Shelties such as double merle whites or maltese. In some other breeds microphthalmia is inherited as a dominant, unrelated to color.

Distichiasis

Congenital eyelash disease affects many breeds, including some Shelties. The eyelashes grow around the tear duct or on the inside of the eyelid where they touch and irritate the cornea, sometimes causing ulceration. If they present too much of a problem, they can be surgically removed. The disease should be supsected of hereditary origin if it repeatedly appears within a line.

Persistent Pupillary Membrane

While the puppy is in utero, a membrane covers the pupil of the eyes. By the time the eyes open, the membranes have usually degenerated, or if not, all traces are gone by the time the puppy is five to six weeks of age. However, sometimes small particles remain as tiny white spots on the pupil, and these will be noted on the eye certification form as PPMs. Most ophthalmologists feel that they are of little significance unless strands of the membrane remain attached to the cornea or lens. The disease is hereditary in Beagles, and more persistent cases are suspected of being inherited in the Sheltie.

Corneal Opacity

In 1982 some West Coast veterinarians reported frequent cases of a form of corneal opacity in Shelties that was due to the complex of the tear itself (not the tear duct). It is similar to a condition known as "dry eye" that occurs in other breeds, except that dry eye does not cause significant corneal problems. In the case of the Shelties, opacity was picked up during eye checks or because the dog was brought in for squinting or pain in the eye. The opacity showed up under ophthalmic lighting as ten to thirty or more round or oval spots within the cornea. The opaque spots sometimes caused ulcers and the surface of the cornea would then erode, causing pain.

The disease can be treated with artificial tears, and ulcers treated with antibiotics or steroids. It can be controlled, but not cured. No cases of blindness had been reported, however.

Some veterinarians suspected that the problem might be hereditary since it was seen in Shelties and not in other breeds, but no data is available to date to prove or disprove this theory.

Eye Problems and CERF Registration

The Canine Eye Registration Foundation, Inc. (CERF) was founded to provide a central registry with the purpose of certifying dogs that have been found upon examination by a certified veterinary ophthalmologist to be free of hereditary eye diseases. Exams for the purpose of registering dogs with the organization can be done only by a member of the American College of Veterinary Ophthalmology (ACVO), a specialty board approved by the American Veterinary Medical Association. The organization was discontinued for a time between 1979 and 1982, but has since reopened and provides a valuable service to breeders.

In order to qualify for certification, a written report signed by a certified examiner must be sent to CERF along with a registration fee. The report must indicate that the dog was at least 12 months old at the time of examination and was free of major hereditary disease at the time, and must be on a form approved by CERF. Exams must be repeated annually.

For further information write to Canine Eye Registration Foundation Inc., P.O. Box 15095, Station A, San Francisco, CA 94115.

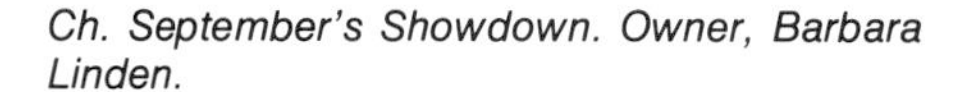

Ch. September's Showdown. Owner, Barbara Linden.

Ch. Rock N' Seawood The Townsman, at age 9, owned by Marjorie Tuff, and Ch. Rockwoods Talk to Me, age 11, dam of 5 champions, owned by Barbara Kenealy.

Ch. Tantera Merri Lon's Destiny, owned by Beverly and Vernon Peterson.

What If My Sheltie Has An Eye Defect?

Puppies with any degree of SES should be neutered and sold as pets. It is recommended that entire litters be examined by a certified veterinary ophthalmologist before they are sold. If this is not possible, eyes should be checked by your local veterinary clinician and any puppies suspected of having SES should either be re-examined by a specialist or sold with a contract specifying that they be neutered.

Puppies sold for breeding and show should be checked for eye defects by a certified ophthalmologist, and the new owners encouraged to have the Sheltie rechecked annually, especially at one year of age before breeding.

If you own a pet Sheltie with a mild grade of SES, be aware that this in no way harms the usefulness of your Sheltie as a pet. The danger is that if these mildly affected dogs were bred, they might produce puppies with a more severe form of the disease, which could include blind puppies.

If your Sheltie develops CPRA at a later age, always inform the breeder of the development. If you own a dog that has produced a puppy with either of these defects, the wisest thing to do would be to remove him or her from the breeding pool and follow your conscience regarding the notification of other breeders. Don't panic, and don't spread rumors on the basis of hearsay or suspected problems. It is always a good idea to get a second opinion from another ophthalmologist. I know of at least one case where a dog's reputation was severely damaged by the overreaction of his owner and other breeders to what turned out to be a mis-diagnosis.

HIP DYSPLASIA

Hip dysplasia is a polygenic, hereditary, and developmental condition. It occasionally shows up in puppies as early as eight weeks, but more commonly cannot be detected until somewhere between four months and two years. It is apparently related in some way to the amount of inherited muscle mass around the hip joint as well as the actual bone formation, and it is also influenced by environmental factors such as too rapid growth rate, excess weight, and poor diet.

The hip joint is a ball and socket joint. The thigh bone of the dog has an offset protrusion at the top in the shape of a ball. Normally this ball fits into a socket in the pelvis and is held firmly in place by muscles and ligaments. Occasionally, however, the socket is not deep enough, or is improperly formed, thus allowing the thigh bone to slip. Other times the ball is not properly formed and does not fit well into the socket. This is hip dysplasia.

A Sheltie may go through life with a very mild degree of hip dysplasia that is noticeable only as a sort of hitch in his rear gait, or he may occasionally suffer a great deal of pain. If your Sheltie falls easily, sways from side to side when walking, or has noticeable difficulty getting up, suspect dysplasia. There is no cure, although an operation can sometimes relieve the symptoms.

Diagnosis and the OFA

The only positive method of diagnosing hip dysplasia is by x-ray. This must be carefully done with the dog anesthetised and in an exact position. Even then, mild dysplasia can be difficult to diagnose. For this reason an organization called the Orthopedic Foundation for Animals (OFA) was established for the purpose of checking and certifying dogs of all breeds for hip dysplasia.

HD is another defect which cannot always be picked up in a young dog. If you want your dog certified, wait until he is two years old or over to have him x-rayed. Your veterinarian will forward the x-ray films, along with an application form and fee, to OFA. There the x-ray will be identified, given an application number, inspected for quality, and sent to three different veterinary radiologists for diagnosis. A report based on their findings will be sent to the owner and to the veterinarian who took the x-rays.

In 1974 OFA adopted the following method of classifying hip dysplasia:

1. Excellent conformation.
2. Good conformation.
3. Fair conformation.
4. Borderline conformation/Intermediate.
5. Mild degree of dysplasia.
6. Moderate degree of dysplasia.
7. Severe degree of dysplasia.

More information about OFA may be obtained by writing them at University of Missouri, Columbia, MO 65201.

Inheritance

Being polygenic in mode of inheritance, hip dysplasia is difficult to breed out of a line or a breed of dogs. Many genes are involved, and all must occur in a dog before the condition is expressed. Non-dysplastic Shelties may not have any of the genes for dysplasia, or the genes for the defect may be present but not in the right combination to allow the defect to be expressed. The latter may produce dysplastic puppies if mated with another carrier. In order to consistently produce dysplasia-free Shelties, you must know that the defect was not present in the ancestors of a dog (or the littermates of those ancestors) for at least three to six generations. This, of course, is a tremendous undertaking, and without the cooperation of breeders in obtaining certification and making this information available, it is impossible.

HEART DEFECTS

Twenty-five distinct forms of congenital heart disease have been found in dogs; some rare, others fairly common.[2] Together they form one of the more common types of hereditary defect.

[2] Donald F. Patterson, DVM, D.SC., and R.L. Pyle, VMD., "Genetic Aspects of Congenital Heart Disease in the Dog," in *The New Knowledge About Dogs,* papers presented at the twenty-first Gaines Veterinary Symposium, October 20, 1971, Ames, Iowa.

One form, *patent ductus arteriosus*, has been found to be fairly common in the Sheltie. It is believed to be hereditary and of a polygenic nature. Test matings conducted with mixed breeds show that when a normal dog is mated with a known carrier of PDA, nearly 59 percent of the puppies were affected; when two defective dogs were mated, the ratio increased to 68 percent.[3]

Prior to birth, a blood vessel in the whelp called the ductus arteriosus allows blood pumped from the right side of the heart to bypass the nonfunctioning lungs. At birth, as soon as the puppy starts using his lungs, the ductus normally closes and blood circulates through the lungs for proper oxygenation. The term patent ductus arteriosus refers to a condition in which the ductus fails to close after birth, allowing blood to recirculate through the lungs. This overworks and enlarges the heart. If the patent ductus arteriosus is large, the volume of blood shunted to the pulmonary circulation will be correspondingly great, and may result in congestion of the lungs and heart failure. This can be evidenced by shortness of breath, rapid, labored breathing, coughing, and occasionally collection of fluid in the abdominal cavity. If the ductus is small the dog may appear normal for years.

PDA is generally accompanied by a heart murmur which can usually be detected by a veterinarian when a puppy is two or three weeks old. Severe cases develop signs of heart failure before weaning, and it is often possible to feel the throbbing heart vibrating in the chest. Most affected dogs will present signs of cardiac insufficiency before maturity. Chest x-rays and an electrocardiogram are beneficial in establishing a positive diagnosis. The condition can be corrected surgically by tying off the ductus, thus eliminating the abnormal pattern of blood flow, and the dog usually can then lead a normal life. If a corrected dog is bred, however, *all* the puppies would be carriers for the defect.

MONORCHIDISM OR CRYPTORCHIDISM

When a male Sheltie is born the testes should already be in position, although they are not easily felt. As the puppy grows the testes descend into the scrotum. Sometimes this does not happen, and either one or both testicles remain in the abdominal cavity, or incompletely descended. A dog with one testicle descended is called a monorchid; one with neither testicle descended is referred to as a cryptorchid. The condition is hereditary, probably a simple recessive. Although monorchids are usually fertile, they should never be used at stud.

AKC regulations for conformation showing state that testicles must be normally descended. Therefore, it is unethical for a veterinarian to do surgery or give medications to a show dog which might cause the testicle to come down. When testicles do not descend properly they are held at a higher body temperature, which has been related to an increased incidence of testicular tumors.[4] Therefore, the best procedure is to have the dog castrated.

Shelties are notorious for slow or late descending testicles. Sometimes the testicles come into position but the puppy may be able to pull them up into the abdomen so tightly they cannot be palpated. Only when the testicles grow large enough that they cannot be pulled out of reach can you be sure whether they are both descended properly. Since Shelties are slower to reach this stage of development than many breeds, it is not uncommon for a veterinarian to advise that a Sheltie male two months old without both testicles in position be discarded as a show or breeding prospect. I find this a bit harsh, but a male whose testicles are not down by six months of age is a questionable risk. There is some evidence to support the fact that dogs whose testicles descend late tend to produce a higher percentage monorchid or cryptorchid puppies.

EPILEPSY

One of the oldest brain diseases affecting man, epilepsy also occurs in dogs. There are many kinds of epilepsy and many causes, including tumors, post-traumatic scars, inflammation, lesions due to infectious agents such as viruses, mycotic agents, and bacteria. The distemper virus is a very common cause. Only when all the other causes have been ruled out should a dog be considered to have "idiopathic" (cause unknown or possibly hereditary) epilepsy. Most cases have specific acquired causes. The idiopathic form has been suspected by breeders to affect Shetland Sheepdogs, as it seems to reappear in certain lines. However, there is no clinical evidence to support this. It is also possible that a predisposition is inherited which makes certain lines more susceptible to outside influences.

The inherited form of grand mal epilepsy is characterized by recurring seizures during which the dog may be unconscious. There are alternating muscular contractions and relaxation, followed by running movements. Profuse salivation, urination, and defecation often occur. Sometimes the dog will howl, become restless, or show marked behavioral changes just before a seizure. After a seizure the dog usually is physically exhausted for varying periods of time and may be blind.

Typically, in the inherited form of grand mal epilepsy, seizures begin when the dog is in its second year of life, although they may occur earlier. The convulsions are recurrent, with few, if any, other physical signs. The seizure pattern becomes progressively more severe, as characterized by increased frequency and severity of the seizures. Single seizures are not life threatening, however if several seizures occur in a series with a minimal or no time interval between them (status epilepticus) the dog could die from hyperthermia and electrolyte imbalances.

---

[3] "Congenital Heart Disease in the Dog," in *Circulation Research,* XX, August 1968.

[4] Leon F. Whitney, *How to Breed Dogs,* New York: Howell Book House, 1971, p.33

Seizures can generally be partially controlled by the use of anticonvulsant drugs.

If a Sheltie is known to have epilepsy and all physical causes have been ruled out, the inherited form of the disease should be suspected. Since the cause is difficult to determine, dogs with epilepsy (or ones producing it frequently) should not be bred.

HEREDITARY BLEEDING DISORDERS

Von Willebrand's disease (VWD) was first recognized in the Shetland Sheepdog in 1980, and studies since that time have determined it to be fairly widespread in the breed. The disease affects the ability of the blood to clot normally. Symptoms include fatal bleeding after surgery or neutering, bloody diarrhea frequently misdiagnosed as parvo or corona virus, excessive bleeding after whelping or even after toenails are cut, and early puppy deaths.

The disease inherits as a polygenic trait with incomplete dominance. VWD and hemophilia A are expressed in the blood by a deficiency or abnormality of one or more coagulation proteins. Therefore, a test was easily developed to determine carriers and affected individuals. It is important that breeders avail themselves of opportunities to determine the soundness of their breeding stock. For information write to W. Jean Dodds, DVM, Research Director, Laboratories for Veterinary Science, Division of Laboratories and Research, New York State Department of Health, Albany, New York. Blood samples drawn by your local veterinarian are easily frozen for shipment to this laboratory. At the time of this revision no charge is being made for the test, and the results are confidential, although information is requested for use in the research project on the mode of inheritance.

SOLAR NASAL DERMATITIS

Solar nasal dermatitis is referred to as "Collie nose" because it is most commonly seen in Collies and related breeds. Essentially it is an inflammatory reaction of the skin of the nose, and occasionally the eyes, to sunlight. Studies have been unable to pinpoint the cause. Shelties are predisposed, but inheritance studies have been inconclusive.

The first sign of Collie nose is loss of pigment at the junction of the haired and non-haired tissue of the nose, and sometimes around the eyelids. The hair will drop off, the lesion forms, crusts, and scales; and when rubbed off the area will bleed. The lesions may spread up the nose to the eyes, into the nares, and possibly the upper lip. If the eyes are affected, conjuctivitis may develop. Untreated Collie nose can result in cancer of the nose. *Lesions similar to Collie nose can result from infections or neoplasia.* Therefore a positive diagnosis should be made before any treatment is started.

Shelties with Collie nose should be bred judiciously and careful records kept. Although the infection attacks Shelties of all colors, it seems more prevalent in tricolors.

Keeping the affected Sheltie out of sunlight, and sometimes out of all light, is beneficial but impractical. Topical application of sunscreen preparations or medicated ointments may help some. Corticosteroids may be prescribed orally. Tattooing the affected area works in many cases but is expensive and usually must be repeated. The condition tends to become more severe in summer or at high altitudes.

A mild case of solar nasal dermatitis (Collie nose).

LUPUS AND OTHER SKIN DISEASES

A number of skin diseases characterized by severe itching, loss of hair, and skin irritation, have been reported in Shelties. Some are believed to be hereditary. Many cases are difficult to diagnose and treat. Most published information has been sketchy and inconclusive, so I choose not to comment further on the problem. A research project on skin problems in the Sheltie is being conducted by Dr. William Miller at the University of Pennsylvania School of Veterinary Medicine. If you have a problem that you suspect is hereditary, you may wish to contact the school.

Lupus, an autoimmune response in which the animal or person builds up antibodies to itself (the body tries to reject itself), has been diagnosed in Shelties. There are two kinds of lupus. One form expresses itself only as a skin problem, for which there is no cure. Another form involves not only the skin but the liver, kidneys, and joints as well. Lupus is thought to be genetic in origin, but research is limited and inconclusive.

CONTROLLING GENETIC DEFECTS

The sensible approach to genetic defects is to be aware that they exist in our breed and to strive to eliminate from breeding all known or suspected defectives. If a Sheltie develops *any* serious structural or physical defect which your veterinarian cannot attribute to injury, illness, or other environmental condition, suspect the defect to be genetic in nature.

Telling someone not to breed their defective dog is easy. Observing that rule when the defective dog is your own champion or prospective champion is something else again. And there's an old saying among dog breeders that it is always the pick of the litter that has the defect. The only real answer, then, is to weigh the contributions this dog can give to the breed, with the disadvantages of breeding him.

Shamont Ghost of a Chance, a double dilution merle owned by Linda Sanders. (Photo by Krook)

Color Inheritance 15

The Shetland Sheepdog has only two basic coat colors, sable and black, with sable being genetically dominant. (This is an interesting point because in most other breeds the black coat is dominant.) Superimposed on those two basic colors are the pattern and dilution factors which produce the many color variations seen in the breed.

Colors accepted by the Standard include sable, black (with tan being a tricolor, without tan being a bicolor or bi black), and blue merle (with or without tan). All of these can occur with or without white markings as long as the dog is not over fifty percent white.

Contrary to what many pet owners think, markings are one of the least important characteristics of a show dog. Many people have a preference for plain faces or faces marked by a pencil blaze, but this depends on the individual. Flashy markings are definitely attractive and face blazes are one of the characteristics which make the Sheltie distinctively different from the Collie. Some large or asymmetrical blazes detract from the correct Sheltie expression.

THE BASIC COLORS

Keep in mind that there are genetically only *TWO basic colors—sable and black*. All other coat colors are the result of other factors influencing these two basic coat colors.

Sable

Sable ranges from golden through red to deep mahogany with an overlay of black. Genetically, sables may be pure for sable (carrying two sable genes and therefore able to produce only sable colored offspring), or tri- or bi-factored sables (those carrying one gene for sable and one recessive gene for black). Generally the pure for sable dogs are lighter and clearer in color, while the black factored dogs will be heavily shaded with black. But, in color genetics, especially, there seems to be an exception to every rule. The only test of whether a dog is carrying a recessive factor for bi or tri-color is what he produces when bred to a black dog. Sables may be mated with other sables or with tricolors.

Tricolor

The tricolor dog is basically black, with tan points over the eyes, on the cheeks, and usually on the legs. Tricolors also have varying amounts of the traditional white markings on face, collar, legs and tail tip. *Tricolors are NOT (as many pet owners commonly believe) a sable with an overlay of black shading.* The basic coat should be rich black color with no rustiness. Genetically, tricolors may carry two genes for tricolor, or one for tricolor and one for bicolor. bicolor.

The value of a tricolor is that it can safely be bred with any other color.

Bi Blacks

The bi-black Sheltie is black with white markings (no tan). It is believed by most breeders that the bi-color gene is recessive to tricolor and therefore must be inherited from both parents in order to be expressed.

Like the tricolor, the bi-black can safely be mated to sable, tricolor, blue merle, bi-black, or double merle white.

The Blue Merle

Merling is created by a dilution factor acting on the basic coat color to produce a mottled effect. Each hair is shaded differently, creating variations in the blue merle from silver to steel-blue with varying amounts of black patches throughout.

Genetically, merling is not a color but a pattern; therefore a blue merle must have two genes for tricolor plus one for merling, or one gene for tricolor, one for bi-black, and one for merling. Merling is dominant, so it is expressed when only one gene for merle is present. Blue merles have the characteristic tan markings on the face and legs.

The novice who is unfamiliar with color genetics is avised to mate a blue merle only to a tricolor.

Barwoods Formal Attire, a tricolor dog owned by Barbara Thompson.

Ch. Windhover Sweet Music Man, a bright sable dog owned by Anne and Tom Power. (Photo by Jan)

The Bi-Blue

As with the bi-black, the bi-blue merle displays only white markings, no tan. Genetically they are believed to have two genes for bi-black and one for merling.

Bi-blue merles should be bred the same as the blue merle.

The Sable Merle

Sable merle results from the merling gene acting on the sable coat, the result of breeding a tri- or bi-factored sable or pure sable to a blue merle, or breeding a sable merle to any color, Sable merles are generally considered sables for purposes of showing and are accepted as such under the Standard. There is a danger, however, in using them for breeding. As puppies, the sable merles have the characteristic mottled appearance of a merle. Pure for sable merles may have a silvery, peach, or pinkish cast. Tri-factored sables generally have a lighter sable coat with patches of darker mottling. However, as these puppies mature the merling often becomes so indistinct as to be barely recognizeable, if indeed you can see it at all. If a sable merle is registered as a sable and later bred, a myriad of colors can result—quite a shock to the unsuspecting owner. The American Shetland Sheepdog Association, therefore, suggests that all sable merles be registered as such by writing "sable merle" in the "Other" category under color on the application for registration with AKC.

Sable merles may have brown, merled, or blue eyes. Blue-eyed sables are not acceptable in the show ring. When mature, some sable merles will still have a pinkish, orange, or coral coat color.

The color-headed white is genetically a sable, black, or merle dog on which the white factoring has created a white or spotted body coloration. They are produced by mating two Shelties carrying the white factor.

When bred to a non-white-factored dog they will produce like any other white factored dog, so even though they cannot be shown, a good white may be used in a breeding program by the knowledgeable student of genetics.

Color headed whites are genetically unrelated to the homozygous or double merle whites and are NOT defective, nor do they produce defective puppies. They are defined as those Shelties which have over fifty percent white. The head is always normally colored and marked. Bodies may be entirely white, solid colored with white spots, or white with colored spots.

Am. Can. Ch. Wyndcliff the Successor, a golden sable dog owned by J. Surber.

Ch. Northcountry Westering Son, formerly owned by Tom Coen and now in Japan, is a shaded sable. (Photo by Carter)

Ch. September the Provider, a mahogany sable or dark shaded sable dog owned by Barbara Linden. (Photo by Krook)

Sable merles, if bred at all, should be used for breeding only in the hands of the breeder who has a thorough understanding of color genetics.

White Factor Whites

Although once accepted for show competition, the current Standard penalizes any dog that is more than fifty percent white. Prior to 1952, white factor whites (also known as color-headed whites) were allowed to compete, and white Collies have always been exhibited.

Double Merle or Homozygous Whites

Homozygous whites result from breeding two merles (either blue or sable), thus transmitting to the offspring two merle genes. These homozygous merles, often called "double merles", appear white with a few spots of diluted color. They are not genetically white, but a dilute created by the doubling of the merling gene. Many of these individuals are defective in sight or hearing or both. A few have been born without eyes, and many have very small or undeveloped eyes. *The defects are color linked, and have NO effect on normal colored offspring produced by a double merle.*

Homozygous whites can be extremely valuable in a blue breeding program. When bred to a tri or bi-black, they will produce almost 100% blue offspring, often with an exceptionally clear blue color that is most attractive.

OTHER FACTORS

Tan Pattern Factor

Among the most common factors modifying the basic sable or black coat are the tan face and leg markings which, when found on a black dog, produce the characteristic black and tan (tricolor) pattern. The absence of tan markings allows for the bicolor and probably also is responsible for the unmasked sable.

The presence of tan seems to be incompletely dominant over the absence of it. This means that *in some cases*

Shadow Hills Double Trouble, a homozygous white Sheltie owned by Jane Hammett. Note pink eyerims.

Top left: Ch. Marwal Struttin' the Blues at three months. Note the blue eyes and the pink nose pigment which had not yet filled in.
Below: As an adult, a clear silver blue. Owner, Margaret Huening. (Photos by Carillon).

a tricolor dog that carries the bicolor gene will have a smaller area of tan on the face and can thereby be distinguished from the dog that carries two genes for tan.

Homozygous whites occur in approximately a twenty-five percent ratio in merle to merle breedings. Defective double merle whites in a litter will have no effect on the normal colored littermates, *nor will they carry* any defects. The difficulty in breeding merle to merle lies in what to do with the homozygous whites produced. It is generally impossible to determine whether the puppies will be blind or deaf until they are walking. So, do you destroy them at birth or wait it out? Deaf puppies may live a reasonably normal life, but blind ones are severely handicapped. A defective dog should never be sold. Occasionally you will find a person willing to give a deaf dog a home.

Merling

Merling is a dilution factor which works randomly on a solid coat color to produce a mottling effect. Merling works on either a black or sable coat. The merling gene also affects eye pigment. A blue merle may have brown, blue, or merle (partially brown and partially blue) eyes.

Most breeders prefer a dark eye for expression, but all colors are acceptable in a blue merle. A sable merle with blue or speckled eyes will be severely faulted in the show ring. Regardless of the color of the pupil, the retina of a merle Sheltie's eyes will show a lack of pigment and characteristic orange flecks when examined with an ophthalmoscope.

Merling is dominant. A dog that is not a merle cannot produce it or pass on the merling gene. *The merle gene has no influence on a non merle, no matter how many merles are in its pedigree. Neither can the blue or merle eye be passed on to any non-merle dog.*

White Face Blazes

The white face blaze seems to inherit separately from any other pattern. Blazes can cover the muzzle, foreface, topskull, or in a few cases extend between the ears into the ruff. The presence of a face blaze does NOT indicate white factoring. (Some white factored dogs have plain faces.) Multiple gene control is suspected, with white blazes tending to be recessive.

Cryptic blues are blues merles with a large amount of black which often produce as though they were a tricolor.

Ch. Cameo Love in the Afternoon, a top-winning bi-blue bitch owned by Marilyn Marlow. (Cott-Francis photo)

Ch. Macdega Canden Coming Home exhibits what was once considered a classic Sheltie blaze. This BIS winner is owned by Tom and Nioma Coen.

Ch. Cameo Bi Way of Shal-Dan, a bi-black owned by Ann Ratajik. (Photo by Whitefield)

Harlequin blues are born looking like whites with black patches of merling over the entire body, much like the harlequin Great Danes. They become more normal-looking merles as they mature, but the black splotches remain, and there are few blue spots. This pattern appears to be recessive and is unrelated to the white factor or the double merle.

Maltese

The maltese gene is another form of dilution factor which *dilutes hair pigment evenly throughout the body, and also dilutes pigment of the nose, eyes, eyerims, and pads.* Maltese acting on a black coat produces a solid grey dog. Maltese sables are a straw or champagne color, with self-colored noses. Maltese blues are a self-colored silver with various shades of grey but no black.

All indications are that maltese coloring inherits as a recessive. Although sometimes attractive, this is an unacceptable color which should be severely faulted and which should never be bred.

Lethal Silvers

Lethal silvers occur fairly frequently in Collies, but rarely in Shelties. Puppies are an even silver dollar color at birth. The color is unmistakable even if you have never seen it before, and appears in litters of any color. Both parents must carry the lethal recessive. It in no way relates to the merle pattern, but rather *is associated with a genetic defect causing leukemia.* The dogs rarely live to maturity, so research in breeding them is extremely difficult. If you have such a puppy in one of your litters it should be euthanized.

Blue Eyes in Non-Merles

One color factor which is rarely talked about is the blue eye in the sable, tricolor or bi-black. This blue eye is in no way related to the blue eye in the merle, and is not associated with a blue-sable breeding. *Affected individuals are always seen with one solid brown eye and one solid blue eye which is very light in color*, similar to the "glass eye" in horses.

This factor is carried as a recessive, probably polygenic. It has been traced in all lines, and can generally be related back to one male.

The Irish Pattern

This factor controls the lovely white collars, chest, legs, and tail tip. It is NOT connected with the white factor, although there may be some tendency to inherit both to-

Above left: Note unusual coloring of this "domino" patterned merle.

Above: Ch. Shadypines the Elizabethian, a cryptic blue, sires like a tricolor. One side of this dog is nearly black, the other is normally-marked blue (Photo by Krook)

Left: Collie puppies from a blue to sable breeding. Note the two sable merles, (From **Collie Concept.** *Used with permission.*

gether. The Irish Pattern seems to inherit as a recessive, and in varying degrees of expression.

The White Factor

The white factor controls the amount of white on the body from the neck back, excluding the collar. White body marking can be superimposed upon any basic coat color. Most commonly, presence of the white factor is indicated by a white stifle (or sometimes only a tiny line of white extending up the stifle). If the white on the stifle connects with the white on the belly, you can generally be sure that the dog is white factored. However, the absence of white on the stifle does not necessarily indicate that a dog is non-white factored.

A non-white-factored dog will never produce a predominantly white puppy, whereas two white-factored parents have a twenty-five percent chance of producing a color-headed white dog. Non-white factoring is believed to be incompletely dominant over white factor. Full white collars and white face blazes do *not* indicate white factoring.

"Mismarks" or puppies with white spots are fairly common. *They are not defective, and make suitable pets if they are neutered.*

Probably, multiple genes control the white factor pattern because white factor whites or mismarked dogs sometimes produce spotted or white puppies when bred to known non-white-factored dogs. White spots are penalized in the show ring, and dogs with more than fifty percent white are severely penalized. A good white factored white is sometimes kept for breeding by an experienced breeder who knows the genetic background of his or her dogs.

Homozygous whites from a blue to blue breeding are sometimes deaf or blind. Silver Songbird of Karelane at 15 years has normal sight. Note the black nose and eye pigment. (Photo courtesy Elaine Samuels)

Ch. Marwal Steppin Out, owned by Diane Bostwick, a clear sable.

A color-headed white puppy from a breeding of two white-factored sables is perfectly normal in every way.

UNUSUAL VARIATIONS

There have been cases reported of recessive sables (actually browns) and dominant blacks. These probably are throwbacks to early crosses with other breeds such as the spaniel. Occasionally a dog which appears to be a tricolor will be determined by breeding to be either a blue or sable excessively marked with black.

Blue eyed sables or tris have normal eyesight. Other puppies in the litter will not be affected, although they may carry the genes. Non-merle Shelties with a blue eye should be neutered and sold as pets as this defect is unacceptable by the breed Standard.

UNDERSTANDING COLOR GENETICS

Every dog carries two genes for a given trait—one inherited from his dam and the other from his sire. Each parent also had two genes, and these were either homozygous (both identical) or heterozygous (one dominant and one recessive). If one or both parents were heterozygous for a certain color, the offspring inherit varying color patterns more or less at random. Geneticists use the "Punnet square" to determine the various possibilities a mating could produce. For example, let the symbol "b" indicate black coat color. The "b" is lower case because black is recessive in the Sheltie. Let "B" represent the sable coat (capital letter because sable is dominant). "M" would represent the dominant merle gene.

CHART OF EXPECTED RESULTS FROM VARIOUS COLOR BREEDINGS

SABLES

Pure for sable + Pure for sable = All pure for sable
Pure for sable + tri-factored sable = 50% pure for sable, 50% tri-factored sable
Pure for sable + tricolor = all tri-factored sables
Pure for sable + bicolor = all bi-factored sables
Pure for sable + blue merle = 50% tri-factored sables, 50% tri-factored sable merle
Pure for sable + tri-factored sable merle = 25% each pure for sable, tri-factored sable, pure for sable merle, tri-factored sable merle
Tri-factored sable + tri-factored sable = 25% pure for sable; 50% tri-factored sable, 25% tricolor
Tri-factored sable + tricolor = 50% tri-factored sable, 50% tricolor
Tri-factored sable + blue merle = 25% each tri-factored sable, tricolor, sable merle, blue merle
Tri-factored sable + tri-factored sable merle = all colors except bi-colors or whites (unless dogs were also bi- or white-factored)

TRICOLORS

Tricolor + tricolor = all tricolors
Tricolor + bicolor = all bi-factored tricolors
Tricolor + blue merle = 50% tricolor, 50% blue merle
Tricolor + bi-factored blue merle = 25% each tricolor, bi-factored tri, blue merle, bi-factored blue merle
Bi-factored tri + bi-factored tri = 25% tricolor, 50% bi-factored tri, 25% bicolor
Bi-factored tri + bi-blue = 25% each bi-factored tri, bi-black, bi-factored blue, bi-blue
Bi-black + bi-black = all bi-black

BLUES

Blue merle + blue merle = 50% blue merle, 25% tricolor, 25% double merle
Blue merle + tri-factored sable merle = tri-factored sable, tricolor, tri-factored sable merle, blue merle, double merle
Bi-blue + bi-blue = 50% bi-blue, 25% bi-black, 25% double merle
Bi-factored blue merle + tri-factored sable merle = almost all colors possible
Bi-blue + bi-factored sable merle = 25% each bi-factored sable, bi-black, bi-factored sable merle, bi-blue

WHITE FACTORED DOGS

White-factored + white-factored = 50% white-factored, 25% non-white-factored, 25% color-headed-white
White-factored + non-white-factored = 50% white-factored; 50% non-white-factored
Non-white-factored + color-headed-white = all white-factored
Color-headed-white + color-headed-white = all color-headed-whites

A homozygous sable (pure for sable) would be BB
A heterozygous (tri-factored sable) would be Bb
A tricolor (black, tan, and white) would be bb
A blue merle would be bbM

The expected ratios are just that—expected. They are based on hundreds of puppies, and will not average out in one (or even in two or three) litters. They simply indicate the percentage of chance for a certain color to result.

A sable with one blue eye. This is a hereditary defect and the dog should not be used for breeding.

Using the Punnet square we see that a pure for sable dog can produce nothing but sable, regardless of the color he is bred to:

Parent #2 \ Parent #1	B	B
B	BB	BB
b	Bb	Bb

1 pure for sable parent plus 1 tri-factored sable parent = all sables, ½ of which are tri-factored.

Parent #2 \ Parent #1	B	B
B	BB	BB
B	BB	BB

2 pure for sable parents = all pure for sable pups.

Ch. Karelane Royal Flush O' Kismet, top winning Sheltie with 37 all-breed Best in Shows, a beautiful blue merle owned by Guy and Thelma Mauldin.

However, the tri-factored sable, bred to various colors, can produce many variations.

Parent #2 \ Parent #1	B	b
B	BB	Bb
b	Bb	bb

2 tri-factored sable parents = ¼ pure for sable pups; ½ tri-factored sables; ¼ tri pups.

Parent #2 \ Parent #1	B	B
b	Bb	Bb
b	Bb	Bb

1 pure for sable parent plus 1 tri parent = all tri-factored sables.

Parent #2 \ Parent #1	B	b
b	Bb	bb
b	Bb	bb

1 tri-factored sable parent plus 1 tri parent = ½ tri-factored sables; ½ tri pups.

Parent #2 \ Parent #1	b	b
b	bb	bb
b	bb	bb

2 tricolor parents = all tri pups.

Using this method you can estimate the percentage of nearly any breeding where dominants and recessives are known.

Daveza Chardia Royal exhibits the beautiful clear, deep red that is rarely seen in American Shelties.

Only recently have dogs been studied at all, and even now work is primarily limited to human medical research. Many records still need to be kept and data covering a vast number of breedings collected before all our questions are answered. It is slow, tedious work, but it must be started sometime. Even after such data is collected, it must be interpreted by a trained statistician and geneticist in order to become useful.

Collection of data in this field was started by Sheltie enthusiast Rev. Clinton Neyman, but his death slowed the progress considerably. From time to time others have attempted to collect data, but most of these people have been unqualified for the task. We as breeders need someone knowledgeable in genetics who is also interested in Shelties. We also need breeders to be honest and open concerning results of their breedings. Self-appointed experts and those "researching" for selfish motives (such as discrediting a competitor's stud dog) do more harm than good and give all researchers a bad name.

Ch. Macdega Canden Casablanca, WB, ASSA 1983, by Banchory Reflection ex Ch. Macdega Fantasy World. Owned by Tom and Nioma Coen, Macdega. (Photo by Krook.)

Practical Breeding 16

In order to improve the breed and achieve a certain uniformity and quality in your Shelties, you, the breeder, need a long-term breeding program. Your aim is to retain the virtues of your foundation stock, while at the same time improving the faults. In order to make any great impact on the breed, you must establish a line that *consistently produces a great virtue that is needed in the breed*, not simply a line free of any gross faults.

This is a difficult task. As mentioned before, you must begin with high quality foundation stock and a vivid picture of the perfect Sheltie. Start with Shelties as nearly correct in type as you can find, certainly with individuals possessing no more than one or two major faults. Keep your standards high; never keep more than two generations with a bad fault. It is useless to try to breed up from poor stock, and it is easier to start over than to keep on trying to breed out persistent faults. At the same time remember that perfection is an ideal, not a physical reality. Time and experience are sometimes necessary, and it takes several generations before the results of a planned breeding program can be achieved.

You will find it advantageous to cultivate a working relationship with breeders experienced in the bloodlines you have chosen. Their advice can save you years of frustration and expense. On the other hand, don't expect them to make decisions for you.

To offer anything unique to the world of Shelties, you must *think* for yourself. Ask advice. Examine as many Shelties from as many different lines as possible. Then form your own opinions and modify them as your knowledge increases. Don't consider the show ring to be the only authority for quality, nor the opinions of popular breeders to be accepted as gospel. Be open to constructive advice; be objective about the quality of your dogs and those of others; and, most of all, have a genuine affection for each individual dog.

DECIDING ON AN APPROACH

There are several ways to approach the breeding of dogs. One is to breed strictly for a certain type or for certain qualities regardless of pedigree. This is commonly known as "breeding type to type." Another method is to breed on paper, considering only genetic factors, with a plan to concentrate the blood of certain dogs that you admire. The third, and most successful approach is to combine both of these methods and breed for a specific type within the bounds of a genetically sound program. Selecting for type irrespective of pedigree is often successful for one generation, but the results of further breedings are often inconsistent and unpredictable. On the other hand, pedigree breeding of dogs who concentrate the blood of one or a few individuals will result in retention of the faults as well as the virtues of those individuals. Without careful selection for type and quality these faults will become just as set in the offspring as are the good qualities. Whatever the method, only a carefully thought out plan encompassing several generations will produce the desired results with any consistency.

Most breedings fit into one of three categories: inbreeding, linebreeding, or outcrossing. The aspects of these three theories must be clearly understood before you can formulate a successful breeding plan.

INBREEDING

Inbreeding, by definition, is the mating of two closely related individuals—father to daughter, brother to sister,

Ch. Banchory the Cornerstone, a shaded mahogany brown.

mother to son, or half-brother to half-sister. Inbreeding is the fastest method of establishing uniformity because it concentrates the gene pool and, if continued, all individuals produced will have similar genetic makeup. Type can sometimes be set in one generation of inbreedings. Breeding brother to sister is sometimes employed when the combination of a sire and a particular dam have been extremely successful. Breeding a daughter to her sire concentrates the blood of the sire. When it is the dam's pedigree one desires to preserve, breed the dam to a son or a half-brother to half-sister by the same dam.

Although every conceivable defect has at sometime been blamed unjustly on inbreeding, if it is carefully done inbreeding does not create problems. It simply concentrates qualities already existing and brings hidden recessives to the surface. These can be either desirable or undesirable in nature. Inbreeding, therefore, is successful only if outstanding representatives of the breed with few or no recessive genes for serious defects are used. Properly used, it becomes the way in which the blood of an exceptional dog can be preserved and used to influence an entire line. A really good inbred individual can have great influence. He will be reasonably pure for the qualities he exhibits, and therefore should be fairly consistent in producing them. This is even more true of a Sheltie produced by two generations of inbreeding or by inbreeding individuals who have behind them linebred dogs of the same line with a minimum of outcrossing in the background of either.

An example of an influential inbred Sheltie was Ch. Sea Isle Serenade. He was sired by American Canadian Champion Nashcrest Golden Note. His dam, Ch. Sea Isle Serenata, was a Golden Note daughter. Serenade consistently produced a "look" which is very much in evidence in many winning sables today.

Limitations of Inbreeding

Since inbreeding simply concentrates qualities already existing in a line, it has potential to "set" defects as well as virtue. This system should never be used with less than top quality animals, and is not recommended when insufficient knowledge exists concerning dogs in the background for at least three generations. A poor quality inbred specimen is abhorred in a breeding program more than an inferior dog of more diverse lineage. After a certain number of related inbreedings are made, some faults may become prevalent. With each inbred generation they become more difficult to eliminate, and the poor quality inbred dog will become dominant for producing his faults.

When evaluating inbred puppies, the breeder must be adamant about keeping only the exceptional and eliminating all the others from a breeding program. The thing to remember is that inbreeding does not, as old wive's tales lead us to believe, create any problem. It simply concentrates what was already present genetically until it begins to show up consistently. ANY characteristic can be bred up or down, strengthened or weakened by inbreeding. Therefore, while it is always tempting to use a dog with a fabulous pedigree regardless of individual quality, be forever conscious of the pitfalls, especially with an inbred animal.

When to Quit Inbreeding

With exceptional individuals that do not double on any faults, inbreeding can be continued for several generations without harm. An occasional outcross or linebreeding may need to be made to bring in needed improvements. If the results are not up to expectations you may be dealing with too many recessive faults and you should not continue inbreeding. In addition to physical qualities, the breeder using this method must be critically selective for mental qualities as well. Some people prefer to use inbreeding only one or two generations, just long enough to set one or two virtues in the line. Others continue the practice until improvement is no longer seen with each succeeding generation, or until there are no longer inbred individuals available that cross-fault well.

LINEBREEDING

Linebreeding involves breeding two individuals with common ancestors on both sides of the pedigree, but not as closely related as inbreeding. The individuals being linebred upon should be dogs whose type you desire to retain. Lloyd Brackett, in his excellent book "Planned Breeding," states that when one mentions a dog is linebred, our immediate question should be "Linebred to what?" A pedigree that simply doubles one or more dogs is not of value unless those dogs were of an exceptional type which we desire to preserve. Linebreeding on mediocre quality is almost as dangerous as inbreeding two animals with the same defect.

Linebreeding is the safest long-term program because both desirable and undesirable traits are concentrated

Linebreeding for the sake of pedigree alone, however, is absurd. The dogs must also complement each other as individuals. The line must be worthy of concentrating or a breeder can multiply his problems. As with inbreeding, outcrosses must sometimes be used to bring in needed improvement.

My personal feeling is that the most valuable dog for breeding is one with a linebred pedigree. This dog will be more consistent as a producer than a dog with unrelated parents. He can be used to continue an established strain

- **CH. HALSTOR'S PETER PUMPKIN, (D)**
  - Fair Play Of Sea Isle
    - **Ch. Malpsh The Duke Of Erle**
      - **Ch. Sea Isle Serenade**
        - **Ch. Nashcrest Golden Note**
          - **Ch. Prince George O'Page's Hill**
          - Nashcrest Rhythm
        - **Ch. Sea Isle Serenata**
          - **Ch. Nashcrest Golden Note**
          - **Ch. Sea Isle Sandra**
      - Sea Isle Dusky Belle
        - **Ch. Pixie Dell Bright Vision**
          - **Ch. Brandell's Break-A-Way II**
          - **Ch. Va Gore's Bright Promise**
        - Bagaduce Hannah Of Sea Isle
          - **Ch. Sheltieland Kiltie O'Sea Isle**
          - Bagaduce Dinah
    - **Ch. Kawartha's Fair Game**
      - **Ch. Sheltieland Kiltie O'Sea Isle**
        - **Ch. Bogota Blaze**
          - **Ch. Victory Of Pocono, CDX**
          - Bravo Of Tavistock
        - **Ch. Sheltieland Peg O'The Picts**
          - **Ch. Mountaineer O'Page's Hill**
          - **Ch. Pinafore O'The Picts**
      - **Ch. Kawartha's Sabrina Fair**
        - **Ch. Teaberry Lane's Little Pecos**
          - **Ch. Grayson's Range Rider**
          - Oak-Lawn's Autumn Leaf
        - Miss Ruffles Of Oak Lawn
          - **Ch. Oak Lawn's Crusader, C.D.**
          - Oak-Lawn's Little Miss Muffet, C.D.X.
  - **Ch. Sea Isle Rhapsody Of Halstor**
    - **Ch. Sea Isle Serenade**
      - **Ch. Nashcrest Golden Note**
        - **Ch. Prince George O'Page's Hill**
          - **Ch. Kalandar Prince O'Page's Hill**
          - **Ch. Timberidge Temptress**
        - Nashcrest Rhythm
          - Shelt-E-Ain Little Sir Echo
          - Shelt-E-Ain-Pirouette
      - **Ch. Sea Isle Serenata**
        - **Ch. Nashcrest Golden Note**
          - **Ch. Prince George O'Pages's Hill**
          - Nashcrest Rhythm
        - **Ch. Sea Isle Sandra**
          - **Sheltieland Kiltie O'Sea Isle**
          - **Ch. Sea Isle Summer Breeze**
    - **Ch. Colvidale Soliloquy**
      - **Ch. Sheltieland Kiltie O'Sea Isle**
        - **Ch. Bogota Blaze**
          - **Ch. Victory Of Pocono, C.D.X.**
          - Bravo Of Tavistock
        - **Ch. Sheltieland Peg O'The Picts**
          - **Ch. Mountaineer O'Page's Hill**
          - **Ch. Pinafore O'The Picts**
      - **Ch. Lochelven's Reverie**
        - **Ch. Grayson's Range Rider**
          - Grayson's Runaway Chum
          - Cindy Lou Of Windy Oaks
        - **Ch. Lochelven's Caprice, C.D.**
          - **Ch. Rocket Of Exford**
          - Oak-Lawn's Little Katy

Pedigree of Ch. Halstor's Peter Pumpkin, the breed's top sire, illustrates a linebred pedigree.

gradually over several generations. Since all the faults in the line rarely surface at once, they can be dealt with in stages. Linebreeding can be continued indefinitely if the line has individuals who offer correction for the particular faults encountered.

Although slower than inbreeding, linebreeding eventually results in a uniform, dominant strain, usually by the second or third generation. When inbreeding and linebreeding are combined in a program, the result can be a very strong pedigree.

or linebred on a particular dog to form a new line. He may be inbred or outcrossed as needed and should still produce somewhat predictably. The breeding of either an outcross or an inbred dog is much more limited.

OUTCROSSING

Outcrossing technically refers to breeding two unrelated individuals. Since nearly all Shelties in this country are related if one traces the pedigrees back to their origin, we will consider any dog having few or no names appearing more than once in a four generation pedigree to be essentially an outcross. Two inbred individuals from different lines can be bred together to produce what is known as a "first generation outcross." A resultant offspring bred back into either line would produce linebred puppies. Outcrossing as a general practice for several generations cannot be considered a planned breeding progam unless strict selection is made on the basis of type. When both the genetic background and the phenotype of the dogs vary, the program has no direction.

PERCENTAGE OF LINEBREEDING

You can determine which percentage of a dog's pedigree consists of a certain ancestor by using the following chart:

Pedigree Percentages

Sire or dam	=	**50% of the pedigree**
Grandsire or granddam	=	**25%**
Great grandparent	=	**12.5%**
Ancestor in the 5th generation	=	**6.25%**
Ancestor in the 6th generation	=	**3.13%**
Ancestor in the 7th generation	=	**1.56%**
Ancestor in the 8th generation	=	**.78%**

Count the number of times that the same ancestor's name appears in each generation, then add the total together. (For example, Ch. Halstor's Peter Pumpkin appears twice in the fourth generation and once in the seventh, the formula is 12.5 + 12.5 + 1.56 = 26.56. The dog has approximately 27% Peter in its pedigree.)

The Sheltie...a bit of a snob, yet he melts your heart. Ch. Myvale Recollection, owned by Marna Obermiller. (Photo by Obermiller.)

When to Outcross

Outcrossing is the only method by which a trait that does not exist in a line may be introduced, and therein lies its value to a breeding program. Lloyd Brackett succinctly stated: "If even through careful selection during the building of his strain, a breeder finds he has some shortcoming he cannot eliminate or improve without using outside blood, then it is time to outcross." He further defines a "strain as being a 'variety within a variety' having a distinct type, the members of which are recognizeable as being that of a family." Because these separate families often go back to the same ancestors, there is less risk when outcrosses are made than when there are no common ancestors.

Outcrossing is not a simple method to use because faults are introduced right along with the sought-after virtues. The only way to eliminate these is to continue inbreeding or linebreeding the offspring from an outcross mating back into your original line. Therefore, when an outcross is made, it should be carefully planned and should utilize only the best possible specimen from a line relatively free of faults and dominant for the characteristic(s) you want to introduce. Try not to introduce too many faults for just a few virtues. More to the point, don't mess up your pedigrees for no gain. The possible benefit must be greater than the risk involved.

PRACTICAL APPLICATIONS

In summary, you must first know what you want to achieve before you make a breeding. There is no substitute for a thorough understanding of what constitutes a good Sheltie. Then you should conceive a plan utilizing closely related dogs whenever possible; going outside the basic line only when necessary to bring in traits that are not available within the line.

Balance is important. A breeder who is a fanatic for one trait, i.e. good eyes, head, expression, may develop a line with faults in areas on which he places less emphasis, i.e., fronts. This breeder may not particularly want poor fronts, but the trend develops because he ignores the total dog. In order to correct this tendency, his Sheltie bitches should be mated only with dogs extremely correct in front, even if they are not particularly good in eye. Then he should keep only puppies that are good in both eye and front, with concern for the total dog.

Carrying the above example one step further, suppose that one of the bitch puppies has larger eyes, but good shoulders, neck, profile, and a moderate coat. The male, in addition to his excellent head and eye, has good shoulders, a long neck, and as a bonus, superb coat and earset. Both are adequate in rear angulation and in temperament. If the pedigrees suit well and the four grandparents did not possess any major faults in common, this should be an excellent mating. The virtues are concentrated, no serious fault is doubled, and the male should correct the bitch's most outstanding problem.

Too often in reality the breeder selects as a mate for this bitch a dog strong in eye with only a slightly better front and no dominant genes for good front in the pedigree.

Ch. Calcurt Luke, a Peter son, sire of 21 champions. Owned by Tom Coen, (Photo by Krook)

In the original edition of **Sheltie Talk**, *we pictured Ch. Macdega All In The Family (above left), and Ch. Calcurt Luke (above), top producing son of Ch. Halstor's Peter Pumpkin, as an example of a close linebreeding that appeared to crossfault well. We thought you would like to see what has resulted. (Photos by Krook)*

The offspring, Ch. Macdega Fantasy World at 8 months and as an adult. A petite fourteen inches, "Mandy" became a specialty winner, dam of three champions to date, and winner of the ASSA Brood Bitch Class 1983. Owners, Jessie and Glennis Carroll. (Photos by Krook)

He is not willing to compromise temporarily on eye shape in order to bring in the other quality. Because the overall dog is neglected, extremes tend to evolve, and thus lines develop which are strong in one particular virtue while the balance needed to produce an overall outstanding Sheltie is lost. The successful breeder is ever aware of such tendencies and tenaciously keeps the overall Sheltie in mind.

Keep your bitch puppies, not your males. In fact, it is advisable to grow out two bitch puppies, if there are two good ones, in case one should go off while maturing or in case one is lost. Take that puppy, when she matures, back into the line. There are numerous theories, such as breeding the daughter back to the sire or to her half brother by the same sire, assuming they cross-fault well. Another possibility is breeding the bitch to her grandsire on either side. And still another theory, one of Mr. Brackett's favorites, is to "Let the sire of the sire be the grandsire of the dam on the dam's side."

Cross-faulting must always be a part of planning. A good match doubles the outstanding traits as well as compensates for each fault. Any time a fault is doubled (i.e., both dogs exhibit an identical fault) the chances are extremely high that all the offspring will also exhibit this fault.

Cross faulting does not mean breeding one extreme to the other. It refers instead to breeding a dog with a fault in any particular trait to a dog that is as nearly correct as possible in that same trait. For example, your bitch's head is too long. You may think that breeding her to a short-headed dog will enable you to come up with head length that is in between. Not so. Mating one extreme to the other will give you some short heads and some long heads, but few or none in between. The same principle applies to almost any other characteristic. Like produces like—it does not oblige you by meeting halfway. Instead, mate your long-headed bitch to a dog with a correct, nearly perfect head, and keep only those puppies which inherit the correct head plus the virtues in other areas which your bitch exhibited.

Puppies

- Banchory Reflection
  - **Ch. Banchory High Born**
    - **Ch. Philidove Heir Presumptive**
      - **Ch. Heir Apparent Of Karelane**
        - **Ch. Blue Heritage Of Pocono**
        - Karelane Fair Lady Of Pocono
      - Wansor's Flashy Flame
        - **Ch. Magnet's Royalty Of Astolat**
        - Astolat Emblem's Radiance
    - Tiree Hall Solo's High-Lite
      - **Ch. Baderton Wit O'Meadow Ridge**
        - **Ch. Katie-J's Ronny**
        - **Ch. Badgerton Pantomine Patsy**
      - **Ch. Lochindaal Solo Of Tiree Hall**
        - Flying Kilt O'Lochindaal
        - Alnphyll Ginger Gumdrop
  - Banchory High Glow
    - **Ch. Banchory High Born**
      - **Ch. Philidove Heir Presumptive**
        - **Ch. Heir Apparent Of Karelane**
        - Wansor's Flashy Flame
      - Tiree Hall Solo's High-Lite
        - **Ch. Badgerton Wit O'Meadow Ridge**
        - **Ch. Lochindaal Solor Of Tiree Hall**
    - Banchory All-A-Glow
      - **Ch. Banchory Royal Heiritage**
        - **Ch. Thistlerose Arcwood Aladdin**
        - Banchory Bit Of Gold
      - Briarwood Bells-A-Ringing
        - **Ch. Malpsh Great Scott**
        - Sea Isle Dusky Belle
- **Ch. Macdega Fantasy World**
  - **Ch. Calcurt Luke**
    - **Ch. Halstor's Peter Pumpkin**
      - Fair Play Of Sea Isle
        - **Ch. Malpsh The Duke Of Erle**
        - **Ch. Kawartha's Fair Game**
      - **Ch. Sea Isle Rhapsody Of Halstor**
        - **Ch. Sea Isle Serenade**
        - **Ch. Colvidale Soliloquy**
    - Calcurt Black Angie
      - Black Laird Of Calcurt
        - Silver Talisman Of Pocono
        - **Ch. Lingard Blue Heather**
      - Calcurt Molly Fitchett
        - **Am. & Can. Ch. Topo Gigio**
        - Jomar's Happy Miss Tam
  - **Ch. Macdega All In The Family**
    - **Ch. Halstor's Peter Pumpkin**
      - Fair Play Of Sea Isle
        - **Ch. Malpsh The Duke Of Erle**
        - **Ch. Kawartha's Fair Game**
      - **Ch. Sea Isle Rhapsody Of Halstor**
        - **Ch. Sea Isle Serenade**
        - **Ch. Colvidale Soliloquy**
    - Habilu Macdega Marni
      - **Ch. Halstor's Peter Pumpkin**
        - Fair Play Of Sea Isle
        - **Ch. Sea Isle Rhapsody Of Halstor**
      - Habilu Granada
        - Habilu Trailblazer
        - Habilu Fair Missy

Pedigree of Acclaim, Casablanca, and others. An **inbred** *sire to an* **inbred** *bitch of a different line, producing in the puppies a* **first generation outcross***.*

ESTABLISHING A NEW STRAIN

Building your own strain or "line" is a tempting goal, but generally unwise until you have had several generations worth of experience working with established lines. When you are ready to embark on building a unique line of your own, be prepared to spend many years working at it and possibly experiencing many setbacks.

Study what other breeders have done, and how they have achieved success. Some have bred hundreds of puppies in order to select those few near-perfect ones on which to establish their bloodline. Others, the breeders that I most admire, achieved a unique bloodline with limited breedings, keeping only a handful (five to ten) of the best Shelties at any one time. This requires the strictest

Dogs with a high percentage of only one ancestor tend to exhibit to extreme the faults, as well as the virtues, possessed by that dog. Over-concentrating on any one individual is generally unwise because no Sheltie, no matter how great, has been perfect in every aspect.

Sometimes the blood of two dogs is maintained in a fifty-fifty ratio; other breeders have used combinations of seventy-five and twenty-five percent ratios. Working with cross-breeding is much more difficult than working with two linebred or inbred individuals.

Ch. Canden Fantasia, by CH. Chenterra Thunderation ex Ch. Macdega Fantasy World (at 4 months and adult) was Best of Opposite Sex at the ASSA National Specialty for two consecutive years, 1978 and 1979.

Above, Ch. Macdega Canden Acclaim, by Banchory Reflection, owned by Christine and Jerry Machado. (Dear photo)

Left, Canden Kinni Fascination, a Fantasy World daughter by Banchory Reflection. (Cott/Francis photo)

culling and selection, but to me represents a greater accomplishment.

Some of the most successful bloodlines have been established by keeping an even blend of two or more dogs. An example is the winning cross which was so successful for Sea Isle kennels. *Ch. Sheltieland Kiltie O'Sea Isle* and *Ch. Nashcrest Golden Note* were combined to produce individuals consistently exhibiting the better traits of both dogs. The best representatives seem to have about fifty percent Kiltie and fifty percent Note in their pedigrees.

Part of the challenge and difficulty of establishing a successful new line is in assessing the results and determining just how to achieve and maintain them. Even the best planned breeding programs involve an element of chance. Not all pups will receive the best attributes from both parents; the breeder must hope they will not inherit the worst. Often the results of a particular mating cannot be seen until the puppies are grown, and the value of a mating to the overall breeding program may not be apparent for two or three further generations.

Ch. Lakehill Portrait in Blue, bred by Ginny Cavallaro and owned by Steven Barger, was one of those "once in a lifetime" bitches whose memory lingers in the minds of many Sheltie breeders. (Photo by Krook)

The Brood Bitch 17

The term "brood bitch" means more than a bitch that is not neutered. The brood bitch is the backbone of our breeding program, and her worth cannot be overestimated. She may not have been shown, but she should be of show quality. The idea that a second rate bitch is good enough to use as the foundation of your kennel is absurd.

Genetically both the sire and dam influence the puppies, but we often fail to realize that it is the behavior of the dam that most influences the temperament and personality of the puppies. Yet in many kennels the bitches take a definite back seat to the males. They may be carelessly handled, overbred, and treated as puppy factories whose sole purpose is the production of puppies for monetary gain.

Value your Sheltie bitch. Select her wisely, considering pedigree, conformation and type, soundness, producing history of the bitch line, temperament and intelligence. Give her the best of care, manage her breedings prudently, always with concern for her welfare, and she will reward you richly.

AGE TO BREED

A Sheltie bitch reaches puberty between eight and 14 months and begins her heat cycle. She will repeat the cycle every six to ten months, with the average being eight months. I never breed a Sheltie on her first heat because she is just too immature and is still growing herself.

Ideally, it is preferable for the bitch to whelp her first litter before she is three years old. Older maiden bitches sometimes do not conceive or are prone to whelping complications. If your Sheltie bitch comes in season only every 10 or 12 months she can be mated every season provided she is in good condition. If, however, her cycles come every six or eight months, most breeders will breed two seasons in a row at most and then skip one.

Bitches are generally bred through their seventh or eighth year and then retired, but some have produced litters, even champions, in their tenth year. As the bitch ages, though, the heat cycles come less often and with less regularity. Litter size generally gets smaller and conception and whelping problems tend to increase. An older bitch in whelp requires more veterinary and owner attention, and it is often an uneconomical choice to continue to breed her. After a bitch has raised her last litter, spaying her will avoid the possibility of uterine infection or cancer, as well as eliminate the problem of protecting her while she is in heat.

CONDITIONING THE BITCH

Your future mother cannot be put away in a kennel, fed a simple maintenance diet, and then taken out when she comes in heat and expected to produce a vigorous, top quality litter. Only a bitch in prime condition through careful management will produce at peak ability. There is plenty to do before your bitch comes in season.

About three months in advance of pregnancy, start your bitch on a conditioning program involving diet and exercise. She should be in good hard condition through road work or free running. If your girl is too thin start her on a high protein, high calorie diet until she reaches the stage where there is a *thin* covering of fat on her ribs and the backbone is not prominent. If you can pinch a half-inch or more of fat around the shoulders your bitch is overweight. An overweight bitch may not conceive and frequently has difficulty whelping. Put her on a strict low-calorie diet until she reaches an acceptable weight.

A good quality, moderately high protein, diet is important for every brood bitch. In addition, eggs, cottage cheese, lean ground beef, or liver may be added as supplements. Brewer's yeast is often recommended, and, if your bitch is older or has been in poor condition, a balanced vitamin mineral supplement may be advised.

THE PRE-BREEDING PHYSICAL EXAM

Three months before the planned breeding, take your bitch to the clinic for a checkup and administer any booster

THE TOP PRODUCING DAMS

Shelties are not a breed likely to produce several champions in one litter. Top producing dams with large numbers of champion offspring are rare to the breed, as illustrated below, and these very special bitches are a once-in-a-lifetime occurrence. Statistics prove that Sheltie breeders have not progressed in this regard in recent years.

DAMS OF SIX OR MORE CHAMPIONS

No. Chs.	Name	Yr. of Birth
16	Ch. Larkspur of Pocono	1939
13	Kismet's Rubaiyyat	1967
8	Ch. Larkspur's Replica of Pocono	1955
7	Ch. Gra-John's Little Tim Tam	1958
7	Ch. Stylish Miss of Hatfield	1957
7	Ch. Westwood's Suzy Q	1962
6	Annie Laurie of Cross Acres	1946
6	Banchory Mist O'Brigadoon, C.D.	1967
6	Ch. Barwood's Scotchguard Sonata	1968
6	Ch. Kerianne Sweetquean	1960
6	Lady Diana of Rowcliffe	1933
6	Ch. Sheltieland Shasta Geronimo	1944
6	Ch. Shu-La-Le's Sweet Charity	1966
6	Tull-E-Ho's Love Token	1975
6	Ch. Willow Want Touch O'Gold	1965

*These statistics were compiled by Barbara Curry including data through June 1983. Taken from the *Sheltie Pacesetter*.

Kismet's Rubaiyyat, by Ch. Ken-Rob's Bobbie ex Ch. Kismet's Coquette, dam of 13 champions. Owners, Guy and Thelma Mauldin, Kismet.

Ch. Larkspur of Pocono, 1939, owned by Betty Whelen, the breed's top producing dam.

Ch. Larkspur's Replica, also owned by Betty Whelen, dam of 8 champions.

shots needed. I prefer to give parvovirus boosters at this time. If the bitch will be due for rabies, DHLP or other boosters within the next five months, give them at this time to insure a high titer in the puppies. Take a fecal sample to be checked for internal parasites. Worm and recheck in a month if necessary. A heartworm test and brucella canis tube titer should be done at this time.

In addition, some veterinarians suggest doing a complete blood count, urinalysis, and serum chemistry profile. In any event, the clinician should do a complete physical exam plus a digital examination of the vagina to assess vulvar conformation, size, and presence of strictures. The latter is especially important for maiden bitches, but even an older, proven bitch may develop a stricture and she should also be checked. If a stricture is present it may be surgically corrected in advance of breeding. A bitch that is unusually tight may need an episiotomy, or your veterinarian may suggest that she be brought in for dilation when she comes in season. This is preferable to risking an injury during mating or failing to accomplish a tie.

Ch. Barwood's Scotchguard Sonata, owned by Barbara Thompson, produced 6 champions.

Ch. Stylish Miss of Hatfield, dam of 7 champions.

Ch. Nashcrest Rhythm, dam of Ch. Nashcrest Golden Note.

Ch. Willow Wand Touch O' Gold, by Ch. Halstor's Peter Pumpkin ex Willow Wand Lil Liza Jane, dam of 7 champions, pictured during her prime and in a head study at age 14. Owner, Helen Hurlbert.

If your bitch has a history of infection or reproductive failure, vaginal cultures should be taken and a treatment program outlined at this time. Any obvious problems or infection should be cleared up now. Even an abscessed tooth can cause acid milk or other problems for the lactating bitch.

BIRTH CONTROL METHODS

The safest method of birth control for your bitch is simply to confine her to a crate and chain link fenced run during the entire duration of her heat cycle. Various sprays and tablets are available to control odor and make the bitch less attractive to males. Most of them contain chlorophyl and are probably harmless. I cannot say whether or not they are of value.

Recently the Food and Drug administration approved a hormone marketed under the name *Cheque®*, that blocks the secretion of the pituitary gonad-stimulating hormones. *Cheque®* is given daily beginning the first day of heat. While some of the symptoms of heat may remain, the drug is effective as a contraceptive, and few side effects are reported.

Another drug, *Ovaban®*, has been widely promoted. *Ovaban®* pills are given for short periods of time to block an expected heat or prevent ovulation once proestrus has begun. *Ovaban®* has reportedly caused breast enlargement, vomiting, hives, and weight gain.

Several additional hormones have been used, but all of them carry risks both from side effects and from disruption of future estrus cycles. If you have a top quality female that you plan on breeding in the future, the best advice is to avoid any and all hormone treatments, either to prevent pregnancy, abort a litter, or induce estrus. Following the use of hormone injections, some bitches never return to normal, regular heat cycles. Pyometra infections have also been reported following hormone treatments.

RECORD KEEPING IMPORTANT TO BREEDING MANAGEMENT

In the event that your bitch ever experiences reproductive failure, a serious infection, or other reproductive problems, it is important that you keep accurate, detailed records. Knowledge of previous cycles is the foundation for evaluation and treatment. Therefore, each heat season record the following information:

1. Date of first sign of vaginal bleeding.
2. Date bitch would first stand and accept a male.
3. Vaginal cytology if available (see Ch. 23).
4. Breeding dates, if bred.
5. Date of first refusal of male.
6. Any abnormal behavior or symptoms, vaginal discharge, etc.
7. Whelping date or date of false pregnancy if one occurred.
8. Any problems, infections, abortion, etc.

Take this record to the clinic with the bitch when she comes in season. If you have had difficulty getting a litter, any veterinary examinations, diagnoses, and treatment should also be carefully recorded.

Ch. September's Sasha In Satin, by Ch. Halstor's Peter Pumpkin ex Ch. September's Lulu In Lace, stamped her expression on September Shelties.

Banchory High Glow, owned by Donna Harden, is behind numerous Banchory champions, and typical of the Banchory type.

Left: Am. Can. Ch. Brown Acres Butterscotch, owned by Dave and Joan Howard of Jubilee, is behind many Val Dawn and Rockwood champions.

Right: Ch. Syncopating Sue of Anahassitt, by Ch. Dancing Master of Anahassitt, dam of 4 champions—an early producer for Pocono.

THE FEMALE REPRODUCTIVE SYSTEM

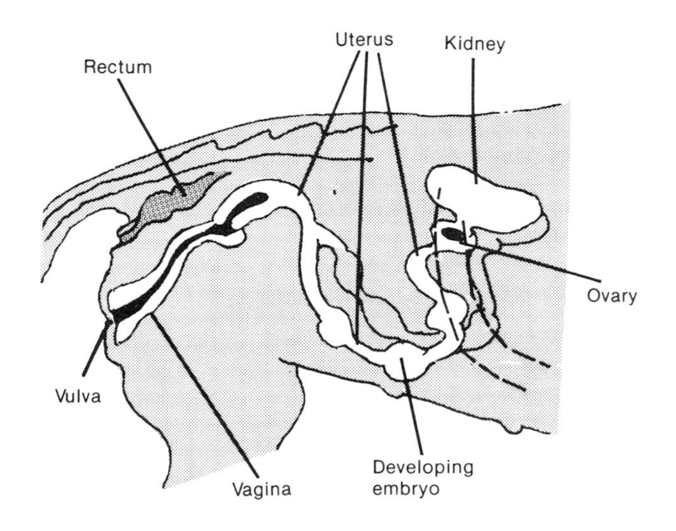

The female reproductive system consists of the ovaries, uterine tubes, uterus, vagina, and vulva, as illustrated.

The ovaries are responsible for egg production, and are also the source of certain hormones. The ovaries of the newborn bitch contain her lifetime supply of eggs—hundreds of thousands.

After ovulation the eggs pass through the tubes into the uterus. Each tube is about the size of a two-inch section of spaghetti. Unlike most mammals, in the dog fertilization takes place in the uterine tubes, and the fertilized eggs remain there for about six days before moving to the uterine horn.

The uterus is "Y" shaped, and during pregnancy the developing fetuses are distributed between the two horns. The uterus is divided into three areas: the horns, the body, and the cervix. The horns lead to the body of the uterus, which is the passageway to the vagina. The cervix, lying at the base of the uterus, is the doorway. On one side of it lies the uterus, the ideal environment for the incubation of the fertilized eggs. On the other side lies the vagina, the opening to the outside.

The vulva is the external genitalia of the female. The lips of the vulva swell and become puffy during estrus.

Ch. Peabody Silver Phantasy, imported foundation bitch for Betty Whelen's blue merles.

Ch. Halstor's Peter Pumpkin, the breed's top producing sire with 159 champion offspring. Peter also excelled in the show ring, winning the National Specialty twice, three Best in Show awards, 105 Best of Breed and 16 Group firsts. Peter was owned and handled by Tom Coen, Macdega. (Photo by Krook)

The Stud Dog 18

A "stud dog" is more than a male that is occasionally used to breed a bitch. He is, or should be, an excellent specimen of his breed *and* an experienced, eager worker trained to mate with bitches of every size and personality. A stud dog is a luxury—expensive to promote, usually unappreciated by other breeders, and possibly annoying to live around. He rarely pays his own way, and if not used judiciously he can be a detriment to your breeding program.

If you want a male Sheltie to show, purchase the best youngster you can find; if he grows into a dog worthy of the designation "stud dog" consider yourself lucky. Only a small percentage of males are used at stud, and fewer still excell as producers.

Obtaining a male for the convenience of breeding your own bitch is unwise and not a sound financial investment. If the dog is worthy of use at all, his purchase price will be several times the amount of the stud fee for a top producer. Just keeping a male all year—the feed, care, and training—will probably cost more than the breeding and shipping expenses for several bitches. Furthermore, a really top male is rarely available to a novice; he will instead be sold to the experienced exhibitor/breeder who has the time, resources and expertise to promote him properly. Not even the best stud will suit every bitch, and more than one stud is essential in a successful breeding program. After the first generation of offspring, the male will be of minimal value. Still another consideration is that an unknown sire does not draw overwhelming interest from buyers, while there is usually a ready market for good puppies sired by a well-known, top-producing stud.

As a somewhat more experienced breeder, however, you may find that a good show/breeding home for your top male show prospect is difficult to find, so you may benefit by keeping him to insure he is promoted and used. Many kennels have built a reputation on the quality of their stud dogs, but not without considerable effort and expense. Keeping the dog allows the breeder to seek out and use suitable bitches, promote the puppies, and have a wider influence on the breed than he might have with only bitches in the kennel. As the owner of a stud dog, the breeder will be expected to show and promote the dog, have the expertise and ability to handle difficult matings, help evaluate puppies, and even provide referrals of puppy buyers. For that reason, a good stud dog is best utilized in the hands of an experienced fancier.

WHAT MAKES A GOOD STUD?

First and foremost, a stud dog must have some outstanding virtue or virtues to offer the breed. Good temperament is absolutely essential. He need not be a champion, but he should be of championship quality. He may lack the little extras so necessary in a show winner such as showmanship, exceptional coat, or perfect earset, however, he must excell in the basics—gait, structure and angulation, eye, expression, substance, balance, and fine points of head. Many prepotent studs did not finish their championship due to injury or other extraneous conditions; however, a dog that simply is not good enough to win should rarely be considered.

In addition to being of superior type and conformation, the stud must have a well-bred pedigree. If quality is found in depth, that is, three or four generations back, the dog will be more likely to consistently produce his strong points.

Of course, the ultimate measure of a stud dog, and the only one that is really meaningful, is the quality of the puppies he sires. Some dogs are very prepotent for their good qualities; others are not. Some well-bred dogs produce better than themselves. A show record has absolutely nothing to do with a producing record, and some of the most highly promoted, top winning dogs do not produce well at all, while a lesser known dog may produce champion after champion. If you happen across one of those rare individuals that can both win in the show ring and become a top producer, you indeed have a prize Sheltie.

Finally, a stud dog must be a reliable breeder that can be counted upon to breed a bitch if she is shipped across the country to him. He must stay in good, hard condition, have no fertility problems and produce vigorous, uniform puppies when bred to healthy, suitable bitches. He should be clear of any known hereditary disease; neither should he be a known carrier of any hereditary problem.

RAISING THE YOUNG STUD

The psychological and mental conditioning of a young male to be used at stud is as important as his physical conditioning. From an early age he should be made to feel special and his libido encouraged. Never discourage play mounting or other sexual behavior. He may be taught with careful handling that there is a place for such behavior, but he should never be made to feel that sexual behavior is bad.

Keep the your stud with *subordinates*, at least until he reaches late puberty. A male that is dominated by an older, more aggressive dog—male or female—will often refuse to mate.

Socialization—both with people and with other dogs and bitches—is important. The young stud should be conditioned early to car rides, obedience or show classes, matches, and fun trips. Accustom him to meeting the public and teach him to accept other dogs and their owners without shying or becoming aggressive. As he approaches puberty, he is apt to become a nuisance by trying to ride other dogs (sex and age are immaterial to many adolescent males). Do not punish him. Separate him if necessary, but be careful not to give him the idea that mounting a

TOP-PRODUCING SIRES

No. Chs.	Name	Yr. of Birth
158	Ch. Halstor's Peter Pumpkin	1965
77	Ch. Banchory High Born	1968
46	Ch. Lingard Sealect Bruce	1960
35	Ch. Cherdon Sock It To 'Em C.D.	1968
35	Ch. Kismet's Conquistador	1973
32	Ch. Timberidge Temptation	1942
29	Ch. Romayne's Sportin' Life	1974
29	Ch. Sea Isle Serenade	1956
26	Ch. Nashcrest Golden Note	1951
25	Ch. Kawartha's Match Maker	1956
25	Ch. Merrymaker of Pocono	1935
22	Ch. Diamond's Robert Bruce	1964
22	Ch. Malpsh Great Scott	1963
22	Ch. Mountaineer O' Page's Hill	1941
22	Ch. Dorlane's Kings Ransome	1973
21	Ch. Calcurt Luke	1972
21	Ch. Merry Meddler Of Pocono	1937
20	Banchory Reflection	1972
20	Ch. Musket O' Page's Hill	1945
19	Ch. Mowgli	1931
19	Ch. Sundowner Mr. Bojangles C.D.	1971
18	Ch. Banchory Deep Purple	1975
18	Ch. Chenterra Thunderation	1973
18	Ch. Elf Dale Viking	1958
18	Ch. Pixie Dell Bright Vision	1957
17	Ch. Chisterling Florian	1960
15	Ch. Barwoods Bold Venture C.D.	1965
15	Ch. September's Rainmaker	1972

bitch is forbidden. More than one male has been ruined for breeding because he was discouraged at a young age. When the time comes for him to breed, you will want him to do it without fear of chastisement.

Expose the young stud to bitches in season, even to the point of kenneling him next to one. He should learn to behave and accept their presence without making a disturbance, but he will also learn to recognize the stages of the heat cycle.

Most stud owners accustom the young male to having the genital area handled, either for examination or in case it is necessary to breed a bitch by artificial insemination. Do not tolerate snapping or aggressive behavior from your male when you touch his sheath or testicles. I personally feel that it is better not to collect a male artificially until after he has had one or two natural matings.

A stud that has experienced a wide variety of situations—traveling, being handled by different people—and that has been trained to concentrate on his handler in distracting situations around other people is easier to handle when it comes time to breed him. Don't start your male out wrong by letting him be too "private." It is often necessary to have two or more people assist with a breeding, and the male should accept this from the beginning.

PHYSICAL CONDITIONING

It is absolutely vital that a stud dog be in optimum condition and excellent health. Proper diet, parasite control, and routine care and exercise are extremely important to even the young stud prospect. He should have plenty of exercise and sunshine and be maintained in a hard, lean condition. Since temperatures over 82° F. can lower sperm count and fertility, the stud should be kenneled in cool or air conditioned quarters during the summer. Trimming the hair around the scrotum also helps.

A high quality, high protein food is essential. Diet can affect fertility. The heavily used stud, the dog in less than optimum health or condition, or the male who is being campaigned or worked while at stud should receive additional vitamin-mineral supplements. Since vitamins A, D, and K are retained in the system, do not oversupplement with these. Vitamin E is known to affect the thyroid and pituitary, both important to reproductive functions. Vitamin A is easi-

Ch. Banchory High Born (by Ch. Philidove Heir Presumptive ex Tiree Hall Solo's High-Lite, sire of 77 champions. Owned by Kismet. (Photo by Carter)

ly supplied by feeding eggs, liver, or alfalfa. Other dietary supplements considered important by many breeders include zinc, B-complex vitamins (often supplied in the form of Brewer's Yeast), Sea Kelp, and Pantothentic Acid. If you feed an oil supplement such as wheat germ or vegetable oil, be sure to refrigerate it to avoid rancidity. Rancid oil destroys the B-vitamins.

Water supplies have been known to affect fertility in dogs. High nitrate levels can interfere with the utilization of vitamin A and thyroid production. High levels of minerals in well water have been thought to have an adverse effect on reproduction.

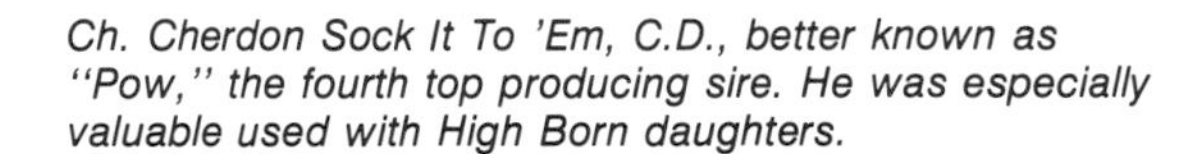

Ch. Cherdon Sock It To 'Em, C.D., better known as "Pow," the fourth top producing sire. He was especially valuable used with High Born daughters.

Ch. Lingard Select Bruce, third on the top sire list with 46 champions, was owned by Jean Cunningham Jeu, Lingard.

HEALTH CONSIDERATIONS

Check your male regularly for any discharge or swelling which would indicate a sheath infection. These are relatively easy to treat but should not be left unattended. Treatment consists of trimming the hair around the sheath and keeping the area clean, plus application of a topical antibiotic. Never breed a male while he has any type of infection because it may transmit to the bitch.

Chronic infections may contribute to sterility, as can fever, prolonged use of antibiotics, stroke, or any illness. Sterility from temporary health conditions usually clears up when health is restored. A dog in run down physical condition from malnutrition, overwork, illness, or parasite infestation will generally have a microscopically reduced sperm count. Semen quality and amount should be examined periodically by a qualifed veterinarian, or you can learn to do your own.

Brucella Canis

Of special importance to the owner of the stud dog is the infectious venereal disease *brucella canis*. Symptoms of this highly contagious and devastating disease include abortion (usually between 45 and 55 days) reproductive failure in males and females, enlargement of the lymph nodes, abnormal sperm or reduced motility of sperm, stillbirths, AND poor condition. The disease is transmitted from the infected dog through all mucous membranes (nose, mouth, genitals). There is no cure and no vaccination. The disease can spread rapidly through a kennel or from an infected stud. Infected animals are generally destroyed, or neutered and removed to a pet home where they cannot contact other breeding animals.

It is essential that bitches being presented to a stud be tested and clear of the infection. One infected bitch could spread the disease to your stud and he, in turn, might infect numerous females that would then spread the disease into their respective kennels. Males should also be routinely checked (annually or more often if heavily used). New dogs brought into a kennel should also be tested, and all females with a history of abortion or infertility, all males with painful or enlarged testes or poor semen quality should be checked.

Ch. Kismet's Conquistador, a High Born son, is currently tied with Pow with 35 champion get. Owned by Kismet. (Photo by Carter)

A simple blood test which any veterinary clinic can provide will protect your dog or bitch from Brucella canis and prevent the spread of this dreaded infection. It is not common, but that is no reason for laxity. Brucellosis has destroyed entire breeding colonies at research facilities.

THE FIRST BITCH

Before a male is advertised at public stud he should be "proven," which means that he has sired at least one living puppy. The fact that he has successfully consumated a tie does not "prove" him.

Most breeders use a male for the first time when he is around one year of age. Some Shelties will not show interest in a bitch until later, while others are ready and willing at eight months. He should not be overused at this tender age, as this can contribute to fertility problems later. If possible, wait until the dog is eighteen to twenty-four months before using him regularly at stud. A bitch at twelve months and another at eighteen months would be considered ideal. It should be noted that while some older, unproven males will breed willingly, many Shelties three years or older who have not been used at stud will simply refuse to mate naturally when given the chance.

A male is ready to use when he shows interest in mounting a bitch in heat, when both testicles are normally descended and of mature size, and when he produces viable sperm. Although a monorchid dog (having one testicle descended) can sire a litter, the condition is heriditary and he should not be used at stud.

Make sure the bitch is ready before presenting her to a young male. The vulva should be quite swollen and the discharge should have turned from red to straw-colored. When the bitch is ready to accept she will "flag," that is, hold her tail to one side, plant her feet and stand for the male to mount. She may "flag" when touched or scratched on the rump. Although she will flirt and play, if she is ready and her season is normal, she will not snap at this point. However, she may cry out, growl, or attempt to bite as the male penetrates, so be prepared to control her.

Most dogs are capable of breeding unassisted. However, should they try to pull apart during the tie, or should a bitch be snappy, there is considerable chance of injury to either or both dogs. Since valuable animals are involved, careful breeders never allow unsupervised contact between a male and a bitch in season. Your stud, therefore, should learn from the beginning to work with your assistance. Every stud will sooner or later have a difficult bitch sent to him. She may snap, scream, throw herself on the ground, and generally be impossible to breed unless restrained. A male who is unaccustomed to having his bitches held will probably refuse to breed her. Therefore, train your stud to work the way *you* want him to under *any* conditions.

Whenever possible, the first bitch should be an amiable, experienced breeder that can teach the dog what it is all about and can be depended upon not to snap or growl. If a proven bitch is not available, your dog's first exeprience may of necessity be with a maiden bitch. If this is the case, she should be muzzled and restrained.

Opinions are somewhat divided as to how the dog is taught to breed his first bitch. Many breeders refuse to allow the male to breed unassisted. If he learns to accept help, the stud can be depended upon to cooperate with the most difficult bitch. So, many breeders insist on at least holding the bitch during the first mating. A dog that refuses to accept this is simply not used at stud until he will mate with the handler assisting.

Other breeders feel it is better to let the dog tie the bitch on his own the first time and then step in to hold and assist the male to turn. The pair should be confined to an exercise pen or small area with the handler present but not actively interfering. It is not a good idea to play hide and wait—at the very least the male should accept your watching from the sidelines. By the second mating he should allow you to hold the bitch, and eventually he must be trained to accept more direct assistance.

A young Sheltie may require considerable patience and assistance on your part. Do not hurry him, for a correct attitude is mandatory to his future success. Give him lots of praise. Never, lose your temper, regardless of how irritated you become. Most breeders feel that fifteen to thirty minutes at a time with the bitch is sufficient. If a mating is not accomplished, put the two away in separate areas and try again twelve hours later. Repeated attempts to penetrate without accomplishing a tie may bruise the male.

Ch. Romayne Sportin' Life, a half-brother to Peter through their sire Fair Play of Sea Isle, has sired 29 champions to date. Owner, George and Tatsuko Danforth, (Photo by Krook)

Ch. Sea Isle Serenade, an early sire whose 29 champion offspring made a great impact on our breed. Owned by Sea Isle.

Ch. Kawartha's Match Maker, dominant sire from the '60s that stamped his get with bone, coat, and substance. Owned by Marlin Roll.

You are training your Sheltie for this just as you would for any other activity. Communication is foremost, and he must be confident of your approval. While you may need to vary your approach slightly for each dog, try to establish a routine which works for you. Some breeders always mate their dogs in the same place, or on the same rug, or give a word of command to the dog. Be reasonable, be consistent, and above all, be patient. This initial care will pay off later. After two or three bitches, you should be able to work smoothly with him.

THE PHYSICAL ASPECTS OF MATING

Dogs are unique among domestic animals when it comes to mating. The male dog, unlike most other animals, lacks a mechanism for spontaneously ejaculating semen. When the penis penetrates the vagina of the bitch, pressure from the vaginal muscles stimulates a swelling of the penis which locks the organ in place until the seminal fluid is deposited. This is called the "tie."

Once the tie is accomplished the male will generally turn and stand tail to tail with the bitch until the tie breaks. While a tie is not necessary for conception to occur, it is considered the surest sign of a successful breeding. The tie may last from a few minutes to an hour or more, the average being 15 to 20 minutes. Only the first three or four minutes are necessary. Some dogs never tie, yet sire consistently. The length of the tie is determined by the size of the swelling of the penis and by the muscle tone of the bitch. The primary advantage of a tie is that the penis remains in place until all semen is deposited far into the vaginal tract and is prevented from draining out. However, sperm reaches the ova in a matter of a few seconds, so a long tie is totally unnecessary.

Breaking a Tie

Occasionally a tie will last excessively long, usually due to pressure on the penis which prevents blood in the erectile tissue from escaping. This only tires both dogs needlessly and does not affect the possibility of pregnancy. To break a tie, turn the male very gently back onto the bitch and press his rump against the bitch. This will push the penis slightly further in, thus allowing pressure to lessen. Hold him in position for a minute or two and then release him. The tie should break within a few seconds if this is done properly.

Frequency of Breeding

It takes about 36 hours for the amount of mature sperm to rebuild in a male after ejaculation. Research suggests that a dog used daily over a period of time will decrease his supply of viable sperm until eventually he is no longer fertile. However, a stud can remain fertile indefinitely if bred every two days. It is a waste of the stud's energy and sperm to breed every day, and it does nothing at all to improve the chance of conception.

Refer to chapter 19 on the estrus cycle in bitches, and you will see that the optimum time to breed is on the day of first acceptance and two to five days later, the optimum being four days later. This will insure that sperm has been deposited within the bitch's fertile period. If smears have been taken on the bitch, the time can be narrowed even more to pinpoint the time of ovulation. It is recommended therefore, that any owner of a popular stud dog obtain a microscope and learn to take vaginal smears on all bitches which come in for breeding. This will help improve the producing record of the sire and enable the breeder to use him only at the correct time, thereby avoiding overuse and depletion of viable sperm during peak breeding seasons. It will also help the breeder spot an infected bitch before she is mated with and infects his stud dog.

Most stud owners breed the dogs twice, although one properly timed breeding is sufficient. More than two breedings should be unnecessary, but may be called for in cases where a bitch has been difficult to get pregnant, when the date she came in season is uncertain, or where smears have not been taken. Proper management should alleviate the necessity of repeated breedings for every bitch. Eventually a heavily used male may go off feed and lose weight or lose interest in the bitches. This indicates a rest is needed before he resumes his activities.

Most stud dogs remain fertile and active through the tenth year of age, and many go on siring until they are 12 or 13. This is controlled to a great extent by the health and condition of the dog throughout his life and to some degree by his heredity. The fertility of older dogs may come and go, so sperm counts should be made periodically. Aging sperm is known to have some effect on causing unthrifty or defective puppies, but many old dogs have also sired champions. When possible it is desirable to mate older dogs with young, vigorous bitches, and older females with young males.

THE MALE REPRODUCTIVE SYSTEM

The male reproductive system of the dog is unique in that the bulbis glandis enlarges after intromission. The swelling of this gland locks the dog and bitch together until ejaculation has taken place. This "tie" may last anywhere from five to thirty minutes or more.

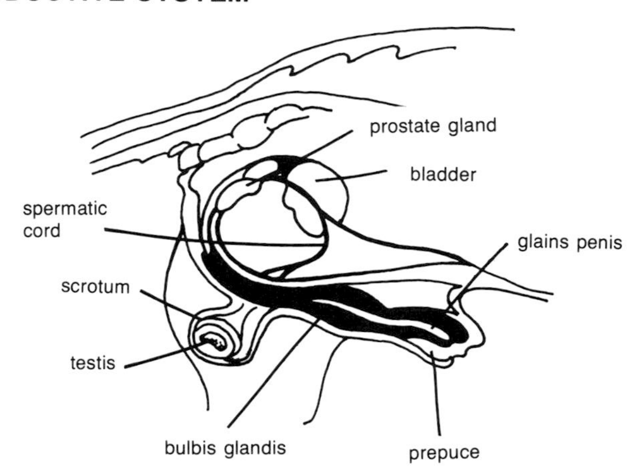

HANDLING THE MATING

Many breeders prefer to have two people handle a breeding—one holding the bitch and another assisting the stud. Shelties are reasonably small, however, and from necessity over the years, Barbara Rieseberg developed a successful method of handling even the toughest bitch single-handed with safety and efficiency. Her method can be adapted to suit your own situation.

1. The bitch should arrive a day or two before she is ready to accept. This allows her to become accustomed to you and to settle down from traveling. She should be left at the stud owner's kennel until the mating is completed. (The stud is rarely taken to the bitch because it is he who has to perform and who

to do vaginal smears, this should be done before attempting a mating. Look for the presence of white blood cells which might indicate infection as well as observing the epithelial cells as outlined in chapter 19. If the hair of the "pants" (hair on the thighs) interferes, tape losely with masking tape wrapped around the thigh.

Even the nicest bitches may become frightened and snap. To be safe, muzzle every bitch. A nylon stocking wrapped about the muzzle and head or a cotton sock pulled over the head will suffice.

Ch. Dorlane's Kings Ransome, sire of 22 champions. Owner, Dorothy Kerwood. (Photo by Jan)

Ch. Chosen Jubilation, owned by Barbara B. Thompson, Chosen Shelties, sire of 10 champions. Jubilation is by Int. Mex. Am. Ch. Macdega the Chosen C.D. ex September's Highly Likely.

might be intimidated by strange surroundings.) Allow the pair to become acquainted from opposite sides of a fence or pen until the bitch appears to be ready.

2. Prepare the bitch for mating by trimming the long hairs around the vulva if this hasn't been done. It is not necessary to trim the long skirt hair, and in fact this would be taboo if the bitch is being shown. Check to see if the discharge looks normal, has changed to straw colored, and if the vulva appears to be dilated. (The experienced breeder may wish to check with a sterile gloved index finger.) If you have the equipment

3. Shelties generally prefer to get acquainted, play, and flirt before proceeding with the actual mating. This is particularly important for a young dog or bitch. Keep the bitch on leash but allow her to romp for a few minutes before being held for mounting.

4. Sit on the floor, preferably with a back support since you may be there for awhile. Stand the bitch over your left leg with her front feet on the floor between your legs. This way you can lift your knee to support her if she tries to lie down. Hold her head in a manner which gives you absolute control if she jumps. You

may prefer to place your palm under the bitch's jaw and clasp the muzzle. Since my hands are small, I find it easier to hook my left thumb through her collar and my forefinger under a layer of the muzzle. If she becomes unmanageable I twist my hand counter-clockwise about 90 degrees to tighten the muzzle and exert control. I can release it immediately when she quiets down.

5. With your left hand, grasp the tip of the tail and hold it taut against her side. I find it best to hold the tail on the right stifle so the bitch can be held against the dog with the same hand while he ties. If the bitch is willing and flags her tail out of the way your left hand can be free. Some dogs will lose interest if you obviously interfere with the bitch's hindquarters, but they should be taught to tolerate your hand on the side in front of her hind leg.

6. If the dog is uninterested in breeding, stay in position but release the bitch to flirt with him for a few minutes. Hold the end of the leash so you can reel her back into position when he shows interest in mounting.

7. Be sure the male has sure footing. An old piece of carpeting or a rubber mat works well. Be prepared for a few spots on whatever you use and protect household carpet accordingly.

8. As the male mounts you can slip your left hand off the tail and between the bitch's hind legs. Press two fingers under the vulva on either side and guide the bitch against the dog's penis. This way he will not be discouraged by feeling your hand, but you will still be able to feel if he is reaching her, and he won't spend himself between her legs because he is lined up improperly.

   If he tries to mount her head or side, gently turn her hindquarters toward him until he gets the idea. Push him off gently if necessary, but don't say "no." The less obvious you are, the better. Ignore him if he comes to you for petting, but encourage him quietly if he does the right thing. You want him to focus his attention on the bitch.

Am. Can. Ch. Banchory Deep Purple, sire of 18 champions. Owners, Dr. and Mrs. Dale B. Gouger, Cedarhope. (Photo by Krook)

9. As soon as the male penetrates he will take control of the situation. Your concern is to make sure the bitch stands and doesn't throw him off balance. Push her back against him and hold her still until he stops thrusting. It takes a few seconds for a tie to form, so don't let him turn too quickly. Check to make sure he has tied properly with the bulb inside the vagina. If all is OK, turn him gently to the side and help his hind leg over her hip. If he cries out turn him back *immediately*. Normally dogs will be most comfortable standing tail to tail until the tie breaks. If you have someone to assist, you can lay them on their sides, making sure no pressure is exerted on the penis.

10. The tie will break naturally when the time comes, and the bitch should be crated and kept quiet for a few hours before being let out. Keep the dog and bitch apart between breedings unless you are trying to excite a reluctant stud by letting him see the bitch through a fence.

PROBLEMS WITH THE MATING

Occasionally a bitch will be so tight that breeding is difficult if not impossible. If both dogs are willing but cannot tie, a veterinarian may be able to dilate the bitch. He should check for any strictures. (Her owner pays the fee.)

If the male penetrates but a tie does not occur, the bitch can conceive and should not be bred to another male during the same heat cycle. The dog ejaculates in three separate fractions: the first fraction is a clear fluid which acts as a lubricant; the second fraction contains the sperm; and the third fraction, which is released over a period of up to fifteen minutes, contains prostatic fluid. The sperm-rich portion is ejaculated quickly, often before the tie is completed.

Occasionally a male will penetrate but the bulbis glandis will swell outside the vagina. This is called an "outside tie." Holding the dog and bitch together for a few minutes is all that is required to successfully complete the breeding.

If a mating cannot be accomplished, either because the male refuses or because the bitch has an obstruction, artificial insemination can be used. Most veterinarians are knowledgeable concerning this process and will be willing to teach you how to do it at home. AI is also the method of choice if the bitch has a bacterial infection which might not prevent conception but which could transmit to the male, or if a bitch has a snappy, nasty disposition.

Breeders always feel they have to "make everything work," but often failure to mate naturally is a clue to some physiological abnormality on the part of one or both animals and conception will not take place no matter what you do.

KENNEL STUD SERVICE CONTRACT

The ______________________ stud dog, ______________________
BREED NAME

Registration # ______________ owned by ______________________ kennels

was bred on ______________ to the bitch ______________________

owned by ______________________ of ______________________.

______________________ kennels guarantees two living puppies to the age of eight weeks.

If less than that number result the owners of the bitch are entitled to a free return service to a male owned by ________

______________________ kennels subject to the availability of the dog requested. Stud fees are payable at the time of service and will not be refunded. A culture may be required at the owner's expense to protect both dogs if an infection is suspected.

The owner of the bitch agrees that no puppies from the resultant litter will be sold to pet shops or other wholesale outlets.

Stud fee for this animal: $______________. Paid in full ☐ yes ☐ no

Special Provisions:

Signed ______________________
owner of bitch

Signed ______________________
owner of stud

Address ______________________

STUD FEES AND CONTRACTS

Payment of the stud fee is expected to accompany the bitch, although it should be refunded if no mating takes place. Sometimes a breeder will accept partial payment at the time of breeding and the remainder when the litter application is signed, or will take a pick puppy in lieu of a stud fee. Again, such arrangements should be spelled out in the contract.

The owner of a stud assumes a great deal of responsibility, not the least of which is caring for the visiting bitches. He or she has the right to refuse any bitch for breeding that is incompatible in type with the stud, is of inferior quality, or has not been tested for venereal or inheritable disease. A concerned breeder will want to know something about the reputation of the owner of the bitch and his or her kennel. My breeding agreement spells out that no puppies sired by my stud dog will be sold to pet shops or wholesalers. I would not hesitate to turn down a bitch that might belong to an irresponsible or puppy mill breeder, or to a breeder with a reputation for taking poor care of puppies.

can offer advice or assistance. The owner of a popular stud frequently gets requests for his puppies. On the other hand, don't let this become an incentive for an inexperienced or pet breeder to use your stud. The improvement of the breed should always be foremost in your mind, and it is your responsiblity as a stud owner to protect the integrity of the breed. Money can talk. Showing and promoting a dog can be very costly. You may face some unpopular decisions. If you cannot put the welfare of the breed above the welfare of your pocketbook, let someone else bear the responsiblity of offering a male at stud.

Ch. Cahaba Som'n Special, a multiple Best in Show winner owned by Cahaba Kennels.

Ch. Willow Wand Gold Rush II, a Peter son, was a pillar sire at Willow Wand for Helen Hurlbert.

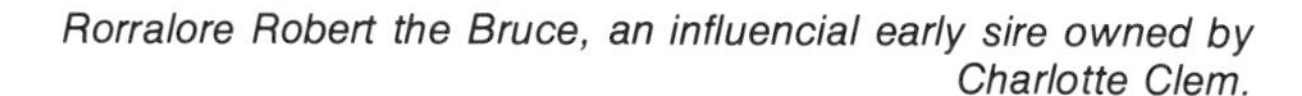

Rorralore Robert the Bruce, an influencial early sire owned by Charlotte Clem.

Ch. Gerthstone's Jon Christopher, sire of eleven champions to date. Owner, Dot Gerth.

It takes time to screen breeders to the point that you are able to determine this, and even then you may make mistakes. Follow up—checking on all puppies produced by your male before they are weaned and sold—is the best way to evaluate how your stud is producing and to avoid problems with irresponsible breeders. If the breeder is having difficulty caring for or selling the puppies, perhaps you

The owner of the stud must also take responsibility for care of the visiting bitches. Frequently, trips to the airport will be required. At the very least, a clean, securely fenced run must be provided. Large wire kenneling crates and an area isolated from your own Shelties are beneficial. Careful sanitary measures must be taken at all times. Should a bitch become ill while in your care, it is up to you to notify the owner and obtain veterinary care.

A beautiful head study of Ch. Macdega Mainstay, by Ch. Chenterra Thunderation out of Macdega Leave It To Beaver, owned by Tetsuo Miyama and Stephen W. Barger. (Photo by Krook)

The Mating Game 19

The mating game is always a gamble—the genes are the cards; and your success in combining them is the factor that increases the odds in your favor. As the owner of a good foundation bitch, undoubtedly the most crucial job you will have is the selection of the right stud. Since new dogs with new combinations of bloodlines appear every year, your search will be a continuing one—supported by much trial and error. There are some basic steps along the way, however, that will help stack the odds in your favor.

FINDING MR. RIGHT

1. **Set a goal.** Decide what you want to achieve with a particular breeding.
2. **Evaluate the bitch.** Every good mating starts with a thorough and honest evaluation of the bitch, for from her will come 50 percent of the genes of all her offspring. Decide what quality she most needs improved. Consider which of her good and bad qualities are prominent in her bloodline or pedigree. Prominent faults will be difficult to overcome. Uncommon strengths may be easily lost.
3. **Find a male who complements her.** Naturally, then, your search for the sire of your bitch's litter begins with a search for a male who is strong in the virtue she is lacking. He should not double any prominent fault which she exhibits, and he should have as many of her virtues as possible while introducing few new faults.
4. **Evaluate the male.** It is extremely difficult to accurately assess a dog you have not seen, especially if you're a novice and the male is a famous, top winning or producing stud that is heavily promoted. You must *see* the dog in the flesh if at all possible, and *feel* the structure underneath that coat. Learn to look at every male with an eye for what your bitch needs, as well as for his overall physical appearance.

   The best way to see a lot of males is travel to specialty shows or go on "kennel hopping" tours. If you cannot see a dog, but are interested in him, the next best alternative is to ask if home movies are available. These will show gait and temperament as well as overall appearance. Also, it is harder to camouflage faults in movies than it is in still pictures.

   If movies are not available, ask for pictures from all angles, including whole body and head shots. Action shots are invaluable, and pictures of a soaking wet dog will tell volumes—if you can get them.
5. **Ask the opinions of others.** You can learn a great deal about dogs you have been unable to see by talking with more experienced and well-traveled breeders and handlers. Choose a long-time breeder whose line and type of Shelties are similar to yours and whose judgement you respect.
6. **Compare grandparents.** Once you've located a number of males who seem to cross-fault well with

your bitch, you can begin to delve deeper into the genetic aspects. Ask to see the dog's parents. They, too, should be evaluated in terms of your bitch's qualities and those of her parents. If three of the potential grandparents have the same virtue, or for that matter the same fault, it will quite likely show up in the puppies. Beware of a stud who is either inferior to outstanding parents or outstandingly better than either parent.

7. **Evaluate progeny.** Unless the male is quite young he should have offspring. Seeing entire litters, even in photographs, is infinitely better than assessing only the pick puppy. Be wary of a dog who has produced well from one bitch but poorly from several other good bitches. A good, prepotent stud should produce a majority of nice puppies from a variety of bitches of equal quality but varied backgrounds.

Remember...the sire is only half the pedigree. Ch. Rosmoor Robert of Migadala, owned by Rose and Jennie Tomlin. (Photo by Krook.)

Ch. Lynnlea's Rhinestone Cowboy, C.D., owned by Ray & Dorothy Christiansen, Lynnlea.

8. **Study pedigrees.** Some breeders devise a system of codes to represent the various traits, then indicate on a pedigree the codes for the particular strengths or weaknesses each dog possesses. This makes it easy to calculate how many times a certain vice or virtue appears.

   Remember, it's the names on the left side of the pedigree that matter. All those champions and influential forefathers in the fifth generation won't carry an ounce of influence if the blood has been watered down by too many outcrosses or too many "Laddies" and "Lassies." One sixty-fifth part of "Champion Perfection's" blood will not do the pups much good if the remaining parts are rubbish.

9. **Make sure the mating would not double faults.** Before making the final selection, fault your bitch to the owner of the stud, and ask if the breeding would double on any of these characteristics. While some stud owners are reluctant to fault their dogs outright, they will generally be willing to cross-fault in this manner.

10. **Discover an unknown.** Not all winning puppies come from champion sires. If the owner of "Mr. Wellknown" does not think the dog is suitable for your bitch, ask him to recommend another dog. If you cannot find a suitable male among those advertised and promoted, contact an established breeder knowledgeable in your line and ask for the names of three or four dogs that might meet your requirements. There may be a young, unproven male somewhere with exactly the qualities and pedigree you are seeking.

THE ESTROUS CYCLE[1]

When your bitch comes in heat, a complex series of events is taking place within her reproductive organs. The sequence of events leading to heat, ovulation, and possibly pregnancy is governed by four hormones—estrogen and progesterone from the ovaries, follicular stimulation hormone (FSH), and luteinizing hormone from the pituitary. Depending on the influence of these hormones, the sex-

[1]Information on the estrus cycle in the bitch was supplied by Phyllis A. Holst, M.S., D.V.M., from research collected during eight years of studies on reproduction in beagle bitches. This was done at the Collaborative Radiological Health Laboratory, Department of Pathology, Colorado State University. She has published numerous articles on this subject in technical journals.

ual cycle of the dog can be divided into four stages: proestrus, estrus, diestrus, and anestrus.[2]

Anestrus is the period of rest between reproductive cycles which lasts an average of four to nine months. Hormonal activity in the bitch's system during this time is low and quite steady.

During *proestrus*, or the *first stage of the heat cycle*, the ovaries are stimulated by FSH. Follicles containing the eggs grow and as they grow they produce estrogen. The estrogen stimulates the discharge, sexual interest of the bitch, and other outward signs of heat.

duces progesterone. The rise in progesterone and corresponding lowering of the levels of the other hormones stimulate the beginning of the third part of the heat cycle, *diestrus*. During this stage the bitch is going out of heat and her reproductive tract is preparing itself for pregnancy. Progesterone maintains a high level in the bitch for about two months, whether or not she is pregnant. However, should she become pregnant and a hormonal deficiency cause the level of progesterone to drop, she will either abort or resorb the whelps.

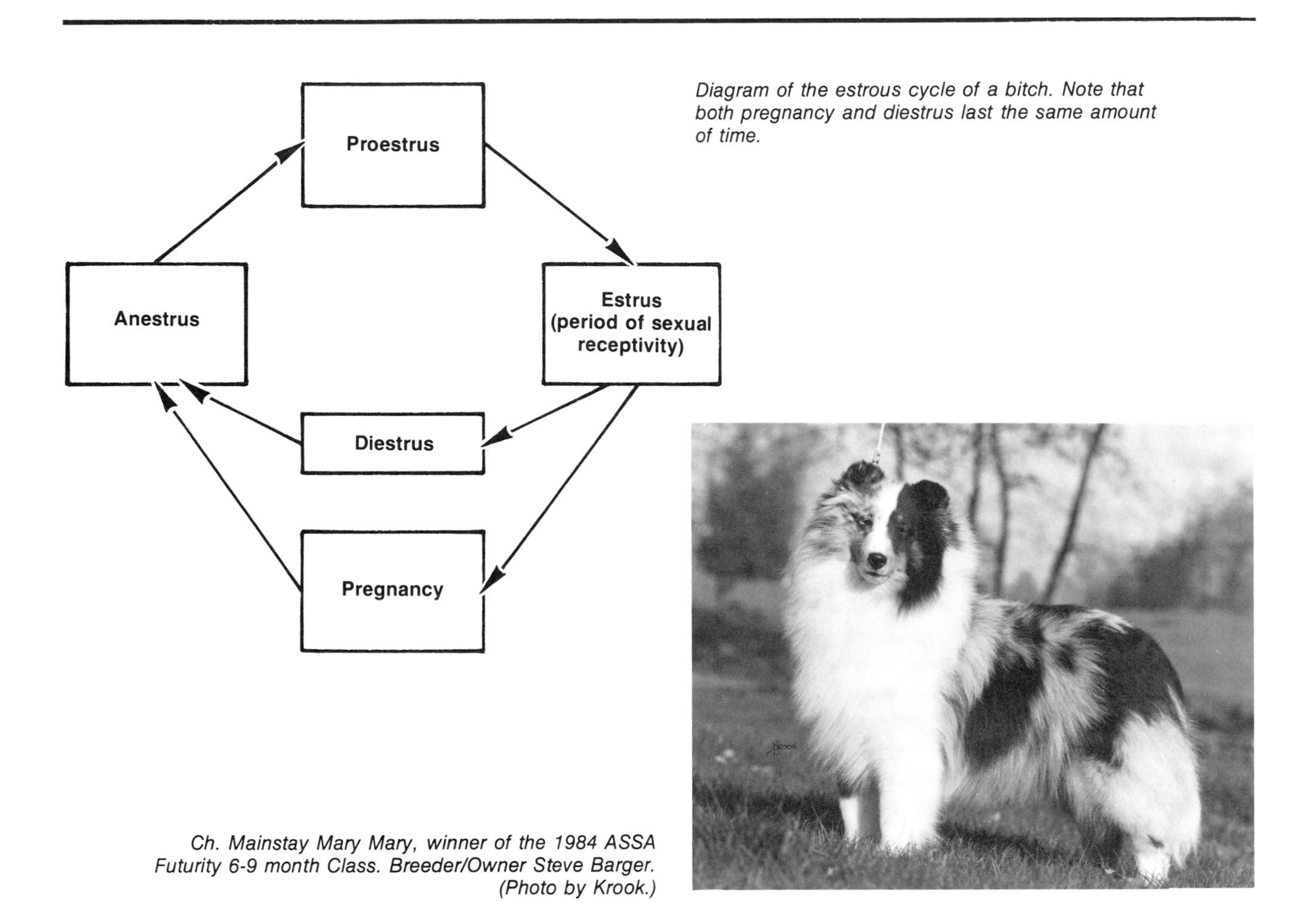

Diagram of the estrous cycle of a bitch. Note that both pregnancy and diestrus last the same amount of time.

Ch. Mainstay Mary Mary, winner of the 1984 ASSA Futurity 6-9 month Class. Breeder/Owner Steve Barger. (Photo by Krook.)

Estrogen reaches a peak about the tenth day of heat, at which point the bitch will usually stand for a male dog. This marks the beginning of *estrus*. After the estrogen peak, the luteinizing hormone level reaches a peak, and it is believed that this triggers ovulation two days later.

The follicles, which formerly contained the eggs, now become a new gland, the corpus luteum, which in turn pro-

[2]Phyllis A. Holst, M.S., and R. D. Phemister, D.V.M. March 1974. "Onset of Diestrus in the Beagle Bitch: Definition and Significance." *Am. J. Vet. Res.* 35(3).

Recognizing the Various Stages

During *proestrus*, or stage one of heat, the vulva will become firm and swollen and a bright red discharge can be seen. Usually the bitch will urinate frequently; she may be restless, anxious to get outside, and flirty with other dogs, male or female. However, she normally will not flag (flip her tail to the side) or stand for a male dog. This stage usually lasts for six to nine days, although individual bitches may vary considerably from the norm. During this time within her ovaries the follicles, each containing one egg, are developing; the horns of the uterus are thickening in preparation for nourishing the fertilized eggs.

The second part of the cycle, *estrus*, is marked by the bitch standing for breeding. Her flirtations turn to eagerness as she flags her tail and stands to be mounted. The vaginal discharge has become clear or straw colored. Most Sheltie bitches remain in estrus for about eight days, and under normal circumstances can be bred during this entire period with good success.

Ovulation usually has not occurred the first day the bitch will stand. On the average, ovulation occurs about the third day of estrus, and all the follicles discharge their eggs within a short time. The eggs are not mature at ovulation and cannot be fertilized until they are mature, about three days later.

The final stage of heat, *diestrus*, begins about six days after ovulation. The bitch refuses to stand, the discharge becomes brownish and then decreases, and the swelling goes out of the vulva. By the 18th to 21st day, she is normally out of heat. Whether she is pregnant or not is impossible to detect at this stage and has no bearing on the termination of the season.

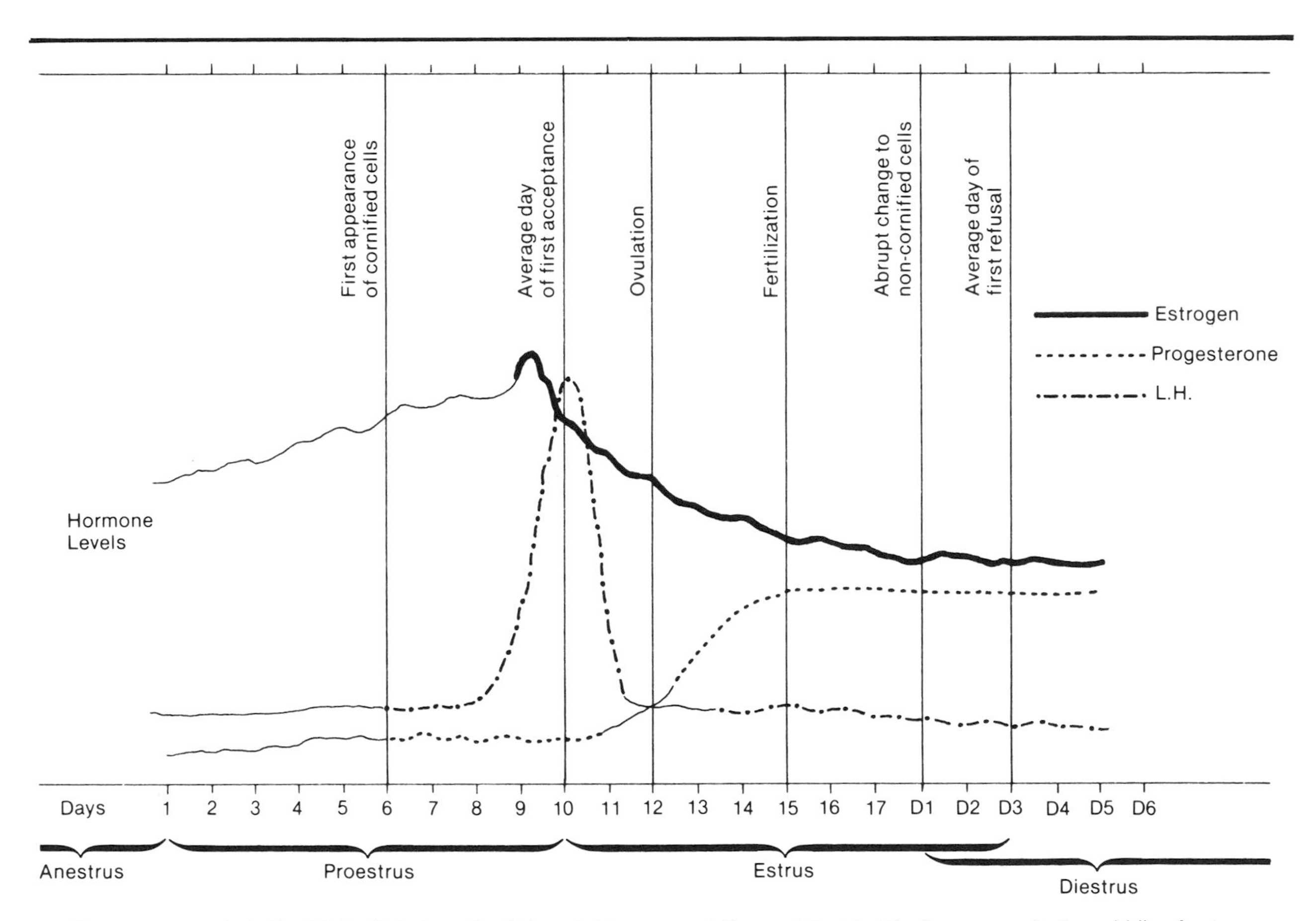

The estrous cycle in the bitch. Note how the LH peak triggers ovulation and that fertilization occurs in the middle of estrus, approximately five days after a bitch will first accept.

WHEN TO BREED

Since the bitch will stand for the dog on the first day of estrus, some 5 to 9 days before the eggs are mature and ready to be fertilized, we have a unique situation. Luckily, the spermatozoa of the dog are remarkably long lived and can remain fertile for as long as eight days. A high rate of conception occurs from breedings made from four days before to three days after ovulation. Litter size falls off sharply from breedings made more than four days before or three days after ovulation. *The optimum breeding time, of course, would be at or about the time of ovulation, normally about three days after the day the bitch will first stand (beginning of estrus) or about 12 days after the initial signs of heat (proestrus).* There seems to be slightly larger litter size from experimental breedings made even later, about two days after ovulation, or about the 14th day of heat.

In order to insure that a bitch is bred close to the time of ovulation, two breedings are generally made. A good rule of thumb is to breed on the first day of acceptance and again four days later. Some breeders prefer to service the bitch every two days for three breedings, but this is normally not necessary.

USING VAGINAL SMEARS TO PINPOINT OPTIMUM BREEDING TIME

Most bitches have a fairly normal season in which the outward signs of heat and acceptance correspond with what is going on inside their reproductive tract, hence the success of breeding when nature says "breed." However, it is not unusual to find a bitch who will accept a male on the first or second day of heat and throughout her season. Conversely, some will never want to accept at all and may have to be restrained, even muzzled and forcibly held for breeding. Still others have "silent" heats and show almost no visible swelling or other outward signs. For these bitches, and for estimating the time of ovulation and fertilization within the cycle, vaginal smears are invaluable.

As estrogen levels rise, the vaginal epithelium (lining) increases in thickness. Cells are sloughed off the surface of this lining and carried away by the discharge. Variation of the appearance of these epithelial cells under the influence of estrogen gives an accurate reading on the estrogen influence the bitch is undergoing.

In order to read these cells, you will need at least a moderately good microscope, one that gives good resolution at 100 power, and a lab kit containing slides, stain, cotton swabs, pipettes, and small bottles. You may use either a pipette or a cotton swab, inserted about 1½ inches into the vagina, to collect the material. Transfer this onto a slide and let it set for several minutes before staining.

Ch. Flair Peg O' My Heart, owned by Shirley Valo, Flair, was a lovely favorite among Sheltie breeders.

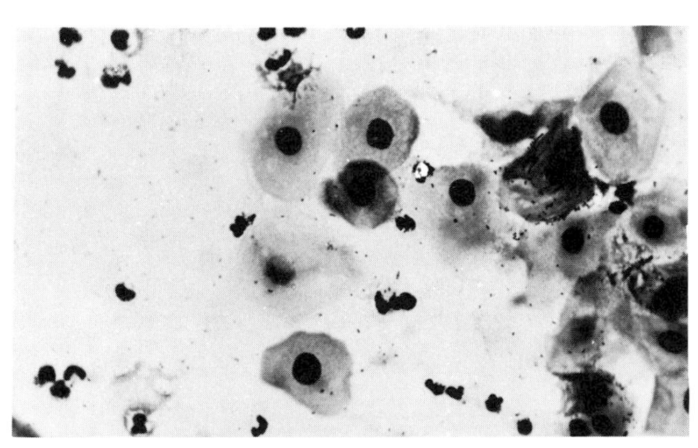

Non-cornified epithelial cells and some white blood cells.

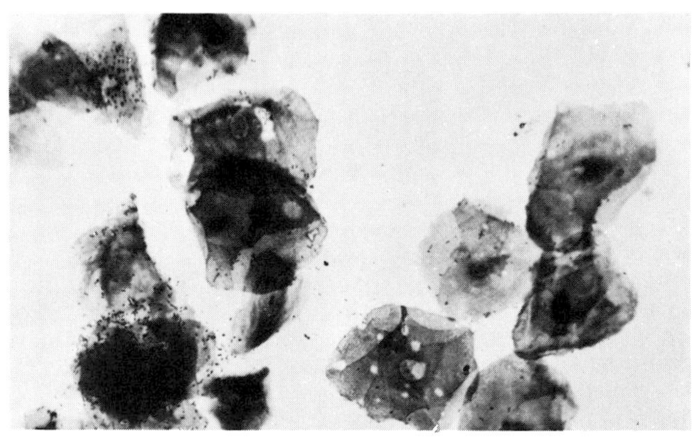

Fully cornified cells.

Fill one bottle with Wright's stain or a substitute, and two bottles with distilled water. You will need to dip the slide into the stain for several seconds (following the instructions on the stain bottle), then into the first water bath for several more seconds. Finally, rinse in the second container of water. Prop the slide on end to dry.

Reading the Slides

Three kinds of cells are present in the vagina: red blood cells, white blood cells, and epithelial cells. During the early stages of a normal season the microscope will reveal numerous red blood cells.

You will also see white blood cells, which are larger than the red ones and stain dark blue. (If an infection is present the white blood cells will completely obliterate the other types. However, any time you see a large number of white cells it would be a good idea to have your veterinarian culture the bitch before breeding.)

The third type of cell, the epithelial, is still larger and resembles a fried egg in appearance. These cells have a nucleus (the yolk of the egg) which the stain will have turned a deep blue, surrounded by a wide translucent rim.

Harvest Hill's Tom Jones C.D., a Deep Purple son owned by Mr. and Mrs. Gene Dickinson.(Centeno photo)

As the season progresses the slides will show fewer and fewer red and white blood cells, and a gradual progression in the changing shape of the epithelial cells from the more regular egg shape to an irregular shape closely resembling a potato chip or a taco. The edges begin to turn up so that the cell looks like a deep "U" and the nucleus is almost, if not completely, invisible. Such cells are referred to as cornified.

Pinpointing Ovulation

The appearance of nearly 100 percent of these "cornified" cells in the smear marks the beginning of true estrus, even though the bitch may or may not stand for the dog at this point. The cells will remain fully cornified for between 10 and 14 days.

Approximately six days after the epithelial cells are all cornified, ovulation occurs. The cells will remain cornified for five more days, but on the sixth day following ovulation there will be an *abrupt change* in the appearance of the slide as the epithelial cells return to their former fried-egg, noncornified state. *This marks the onset of diestrus*[3] and is an important date to keep on your calendar, as you will see later. The bitch may continue to stand for the male for one or two additional days but eggs can no longer be fertilized.

Smears and Irregular Heats

Occasionally bitches will ovulate only one or two days after the onset of any visible signs of heat, or conversely, very late in their season. If the epithelial cells are cornified, breed regardless of the outward signs. If you know the day that cornified cells first predominate, you will also know that ovulation will occur about six days later, and that is the time to breed. Counting backward from the first day of diestrus, you can calculate that fertilization took place in the bitch three days previously and if she was bred within seven days before this date the chances of fertilization are good. (Remember, the spermatozoa survive eight days.)

If you do not know whether a bitch is in the early or late stage of her season, vaginal smears taken over a period of three days should tell you. If she is in proestrus you will see a progression toward the cornified cells. If she is in diestrus the progression will be in the other direction. If a bitch comes in heat but no cornified cells appear at any stage of the season you can be sure that no ovulation has occurred; therefore, the bitch cannot conceive.

HOW CONCEPTION OCCURS

A bitch will ovulate about 1¼ times as many eggs as she actually produces puppies. Providing that live sperm are present in the oviduct, fertilization takes place as soon as the eggs mature. Research has proven that all eggs mature and are fertilized at the same time; therefore, all the puppies in a litter are the same age. Size differences in puppies are due to genetic makeup, positioning, and the nutrition each receives, not to age difference as is commonly imagined. Blood comes up the uterine horn from the bottom; therefore, puppies lower in the uterus get blood first and tend to be better nourished and sometimes larger.

It takes only a few seconds for ejaculated sperm to find its way up the reproductive tract to the oviduct. If the ova are mature they will be fertilized immediately. If they are immature the sperm will surround them and remain motile (alive and able to move) for several days. The eggs are then fertilized as soon as maturation allows.

[3]Ibid.

It is possible for a *litter* to have two or more sires from matings several days apart, providing all matings occurred prior to the time the eggs were mature. However, no *individual* puppy can have two sires. Once a sperm has fertilized an egg, that egg becomes impervious to other sperm, even though surrounded by them.

CARING FOR THE BITCH IN HEAT

A bitch in season is anything but modest and unless you choose to take the risk of a promiscuous mating, you had better keep her confined during her heat period. Clever breed that they are, many Sheltie bitches are extremely flirtatious and will go to great lengths to get out and find a mate. Also, the urine odor of a bitch in heat is quite strong, attracting males from a mile or more radius. Males, too, are quite ingenious about the matter and will scale high fences, open doors, break windows, or even copulate with the female through a fence.

Not all bitches follow the book; some breed as early as the second or third day after what appears to be the onset of their season. Since sperm can remain alive for about a week, a mismating early in heat may still allow fertilization of eggs released during the normal time in the season. *For safety, keep your bitch confined from the onset of bleeding until all signs of estrus are gone, usually at least three weeks.*

If a mismating should occur, it is best to let the bitch whelp the litter and dispose of most or all of the puppies if necessary. An estrogen injection given immediately after the mismating will prevent conception, but it can also cause allergic reaction, upset to the reproductive cycle, or other problems. Such instances are rare, but if the female is a valuable brood bitch and the male was not overly large (so as to create danger in whelping oversize puppies), the risk of giving the shot probably will outweigh the convenience of preventing a mismated litter.

Litter sisters (above) Ch. Rosmoor Fancy That and (below) Ch. Rosmoor Katy-Did, from a three champion litter bred by Rose Tomlin. By Ch. Romayne Sportin' Life ex Ch. Rosmoor Honey-Do. Katy is now the dam of 2 champions. (Photos by Krook and Maynard.)

The ability to produce carries down through many generations in the tail-female line. Also, look for a sire whose dam is from a strong bitch line.

MAKING THE FINAL ARRANGEMENTS

On the first day of the bitch's season, contact the owner of the stud of your choice to make sure he will be available. Firm up shipping or delivery arrangements and how the stud fee will be paid.

Many stud owners require a vaginal culture before they will accept the bitch. If this is the case, you must take your female to the veterinary clinic immediately to have this done. Growing the culture takes four days to a week. If bacteria are present and the clinician requests a sensitivity test as well, the results will take ten days or more.

The necessity and value of vaginal cultures are a controversial subject. Many types of bacteria are normally present in the vagina, and infections are easily picked up on the vaginal smear by the presence of an abnormally large number of white blood cells. Nevertheless, obtain a culture if the owner of the male requires it or if your female has a history of misses or infection.

The vaginal culture must be done during proestrus. The vaginal fluid to be cultured should be collected using a guarded swab. Veterinarians who are not accustomed to working with purebred dog breeders may use a cotton swab much as when collecting a sample for the vaginal smear. This inevitably results in contamination from the outside. The guarded swab is contained in a sterile tube. The tube is inserted several inches into the vagina, the swab is extended to collect the fluid and then withdrawn into the tube again. The tube is removed, sealed, and sent to the laboratory where the culture is grown.

The normal vagina is *not* sterile. E-coli, Staphylococcus sp., Streptococcus sp., Proteus mirabilis and pseudomonas aeruginosa are commonly cultured from a normal female. However, these bacteria have also been indicated as contributing to infertility, especially when cultured persistently in a colony of dogs or when other predisposing conditions are present.

One of the most often recommended treatments is douching with 4 cc. Furacin for three to five days during proestrus. Treatment should be discontinued at least forty-eight hours before mating. If an infection is present the

Ch. Timberidge Temptress, dam of Ch. Timberidge Temptation.

Ch. Willow Wand Lil Liza Jane, dam of four champions, all by Ch. Peter Pumpkin. Pictured at age 14, she was owned by Helen Hurlbert.

veterinarian will prescribe antibiotics and in most cases recommend that you do not breed. If bacteria are present, the laboratory and the veterinary clinic will make judgements as to whether the particular type and amount of bacteria have any clinical significance and make recommendations accordingly. You should discuss this with the owner of the stud to determine if he or she will accept your female. Some breeders will accept on the condition that the breeding is done by artificial insemination. If you are unwilling to risk the slightly lower conception rate, wait until her next heat.

If you are lucky enough to find a suitable stud within driving distance you can deliver the bitch on the day she is ready to mate. If you must ship her, plan for her to arrive about two days early so she can settle down from the trip. Usually this would mean shipping on about the ninth day. If you are taking smears, wait until the cells become cornified before shipping. If you are unsure about when to breed, take her early and let the stud decide. Be prepared to leave the female for several days or a week. If possible, ask that she not make the return flight until twenty-four hours after the last breeding.

Ch. Sea Isle Rhapsody of Halstor, dam of Ch. Halstor's Peter Pumpkin.

Ch. Kismet's Cee Dee Pollyanna, left, and her sire, Ch. Philidove Kismet Heir Borne. Pollyanna is the dam of Karelane Royal Flush O' Kismet, a top winner. (Photo by Rockwell.)

Ch. Sea Isle Serenata, dam of Ch. Sea Isle Serenade.

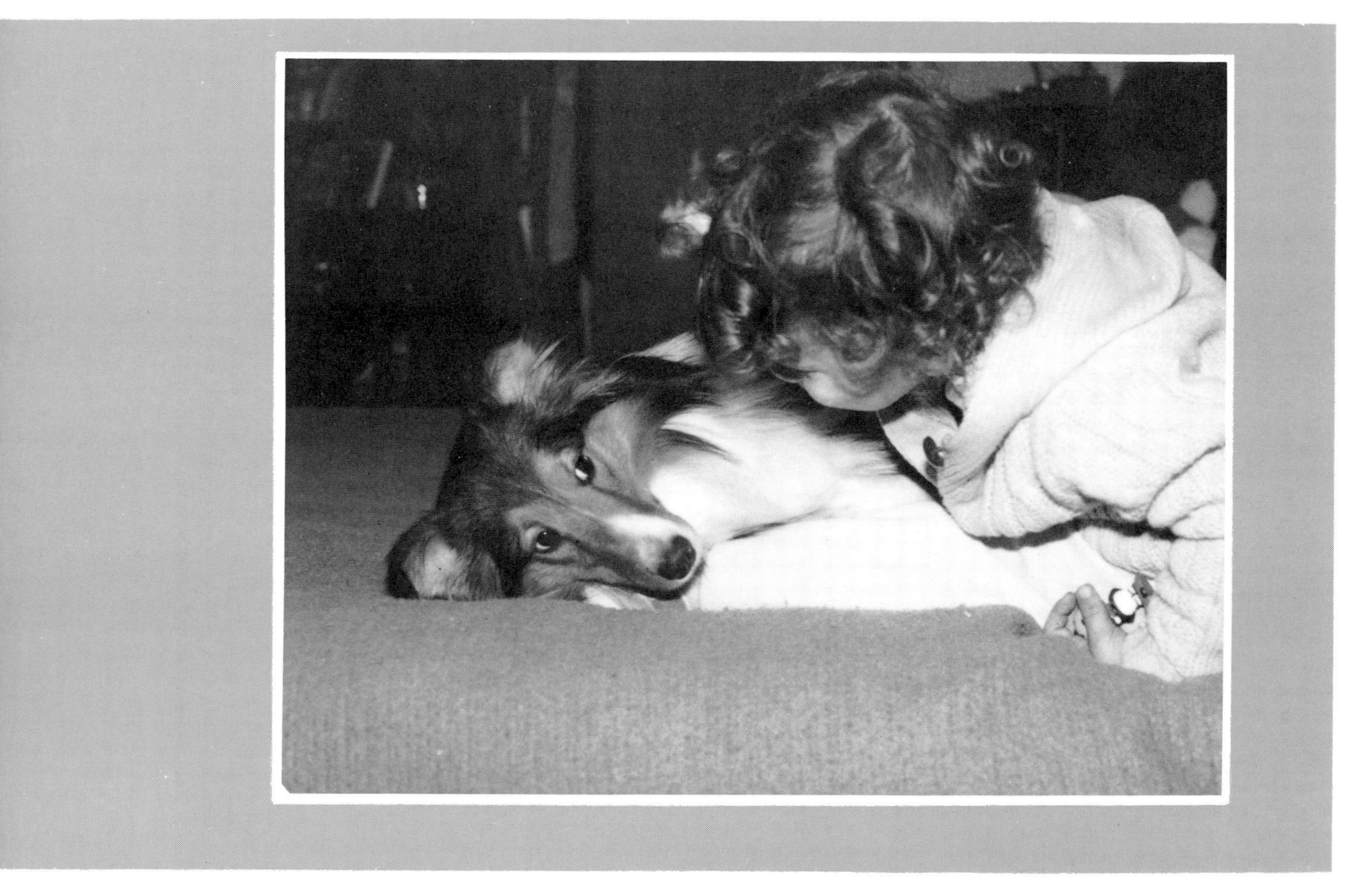

Hyalti Whispering Heather consults with a friend. Photo by owner, Sharon Uzarewicz, Larkspur.

Waiting and Watching 20

There are *no* dependable signs of pregnancy during the first few weeks after breeding. The fertilized egg, however, is gradually moving from the oviduct into the uterus where it implants itself in the uterine wall about twelve days after the onset of diestrus.

Traditionally, the gestation period of the bitch is 63 days from the date of the first breeding, with 58 to 65 days being within normal range. A whelping chart indicates the 63rd day (see illus.).

According to recent research by Holst and Phemister,[1] a more accurate prediction is based on the number of days from the onset of diestrus, the day that the cornified epithelial cells return to a noncornified shape. (In order to accurately pinpoint this date you must take vaginal smears every day during the middle and latter part of estrus.)

In their study, average date of whelping calculated from day of breeding ranged from 59.4 to 64.8 days. When calculated from the onset of diestrus, however, a sharp increase in the number of bitches whelping occurred on the 57th day, with most bitches whelping between the 56th and 58th day of diestrus. Since fertilization occurs three days before diestrus, the true average gestation period becomes an average of 60 days. It's interesting to note that bitches whelping earlier than the 56th day of diestrus had larger than average litters, while those whelping after the 58th day tended to have smaller than average litters.

FIRST SIGNS OF PREGNANCY

About the 28th to the 35th day of pregnancy it may be possible to palpate the uterine swellings containing the fetuses. Some veterinarians are experts at this; others have had little or no training and may not be any more adept than you are. Take the bitch's abdomen between your thumb and forefinger and gently palpate from the rear toward the rib cage. Be gentle, and don't palpate too hard or too often. The fetuses will feel like hard lumps about the size of a walnut. Although you may be able to feel several puppies, it is virtually impossible to do more than guess at the litter size since some of the puppies are likely to be carried high under the rib cage. After the 35th day the sacs begin to fill with fluid and become too soft to palpate easily.

About the fourth week of pregnancy the bitch's appetite usually begins to increase and she will begin to fill out in the loin. Before you can actually see the gain, put your hands around her flank and feel the increasing width. At about five weeks the nipples become pink and sometimes a bit swollen. By the sixth week pregnancy is generally obvious from the distended tummy, and soon the mammary glands begin to fill with milk.

Young bitches are slower to show signs of pregnancy than old brood bitches because their muscles are tighter

[1]Phylis A. Holst, M.S., and R. D. Phemister, D.V.M., March 1974. "Onset of Diestrus in the Beagle Bitch: Definition and Significance." *Am. J. Vet. Res.* 35(3).

WHELPING CHART

Date bred	Date due to whelp	Date bred	Date due to whelp	Date bred	Date due to whelp	Date bred	Date due to whelp	Date bred	Date due to whelp	Date bred	Date due to whelp	Date bred	Date due to whelp	Date bred	Date due to whelp	Date bred	Date due to whelp	Date bred	Date due to whelp	Date bred	Date due to whelp	Date bred	Date due to whelp
January	March	February	April	March	May	April	June	May	July	June	August	July	September	August	October	September	November	October	December	November	January	December	February
1	5	1	5	1	3	1	3	1	3	1	3	1	2	1	3	1	3	1	3	1	3	1	2
2	6	2	6	2	4	2	4	2	4	2	4	2	3	2	4	2	4	2	4	2	4	2	3
3	7	3	7	3	5	3	5	3	5	3	5	3	4	3	5	3	5	3	5	3	5	3	4
4	8	4	8	4	6	4	6	4	6	4	6	4	5	4	6	4	6	4	6	4	6	4	5
5	9	5	9	5	7	5	7	5	7	5	7	5	6	5	7	5	7	5	7	5	7	5	6
6	10	6	10	6	8	6	8	6	8	6	8	6	7	6	8	6	8	6	8	6	8	6	7
7	11	7	11	7	9	7	9	7	9	7	9	7	8	7	9	7	9	7	9	7	9	7	8
8	12	8	12	8	10	8	10	8	10	8	10	8	9	8	10	8	10	8	10	8	10	8	9
9	13	9	13	9	11	9	11	9	11	9	11	9	10	9	11	9	11	9	11	9	11	9	10
10	14	10	14	10	12	10	12	10	12	10	12	10	11	10	12	10	12	10	12	10	12	10	11
11	15	11	15	11	13	11	13	11	13	11	13	11	12	11	13	11	13	11	13	11	13	11	12
12	16	12	16	12	14	12	14	12	14	12	14	12	13	12	14	12	14	12	14	12	14	12	13
13	17	13	17	13	15	13	15	13	15	13	15	13	14	13	15	13	15	13	15	13	15	13	14
14	18	14	18	14	16	14	16	14	16	14	16	14	15	14	16	14	16	14	16	14	16	14	15
15	19	15	19	15	17	15	17	15	17	15	17	15	16	15	17	15	17	15	17	15	17	15	16
16	20	16	20	16	18	16	18	16	18	16	18	16	17	16	18	16	18	16	18	16	18	16	17
17	21	17	21	17	19	17	19	17	19	17	19	17	18	17	19	17	19	17	19	17	19	17	18
18	22	18	22	18	20	18	20	18	20	18	20	18	19	18	20	18	20	18	20	18	20	18	19
19	23	19	23	19	21	19	21	19	21	19	21	19	20	19	21	19	21	19	21	19	21	19	20
20	24	20	24	20	22	20	22	20	22	20	22	20	21	20	22	20	22	20	22	20	22	20	21
21	25	21	25	21	23	21	23	21	23	21	23	21	22	21	23	21	23	21	23	21	23	21	22
22	26	22	26	22	24	22	24	22	24	22	24	22	23	22	24	22	24	22	24	22	24	22	23
23	27	23	27	23	25	23	25	23	25	23	25	23	24	23	25	23	25	23	25	23	25	23	24
24	28	24	28	24	26	24	26	24	26	24	26	24	25	24	26	24	26	24	26	24	26	24	25
25	29	25	29	25	27	25	27	25	27	25	27	25	26	25	27	25	27	25	27	25	27	25	26
26	30	26	30	26	28	26	28	26	28	26	28	26	27	26	28	26	28	26	28	26	28	26	27
27	31	27	May 1	27	29	27	29	27	29	27	29	27	28	27	29	27	29	27	29	27	29	27	28
28	Apr. 1	28	2	28	30	28	30	28	30	28	30	28	29	28	30	28	30	28	30	28	30	28	Mar. 1
29	2			29	31	29	July 1	29	31	29	31	29	30	29	31	29	Dec. 1	29	31	29	31	29	2
30	3			30	June 1	30	2	30	Aug. 1	30	Sep. 1	30	Oct. 1	30	Nov. 1	30	2	30	Jan. 1	30	Feb. 1	30	3
31	4			31	2			31	2			31	2	31	2			31	2			31	4

Courtesy of Gaines.

and their puppies are carried higher. A young bitch may have a smaller litter the first time and she may not develop milk until just before or during whelping. It is sometimes impossible to detect pregnancy if a bitch is carrying only one puppy. Do not give up and neglect the bitch who shows no obvious signs unless you are very experienced or have had her x-rayed.

EXERCISE AND HANDLING

More than at any other time, the pregnant bitch must be kept fit and healthy. Daily exercise is very important. During the first five weeks romping, running, and road work will help build up internal as well as structural muscles, thus making whelping easier. During the last two or three weeks, however, the bitch should be prevented from jumping or strenuous exercise, but at the same time encouraged to do plenty of walking and running. She should have at least one hour of exercise and sunlight daily. Do not let her jump or fall from your arms or high porches or furniture. When you pick her up support her tummy by placing one hand under her rump and supporting her chest and forelegs on your other arm.

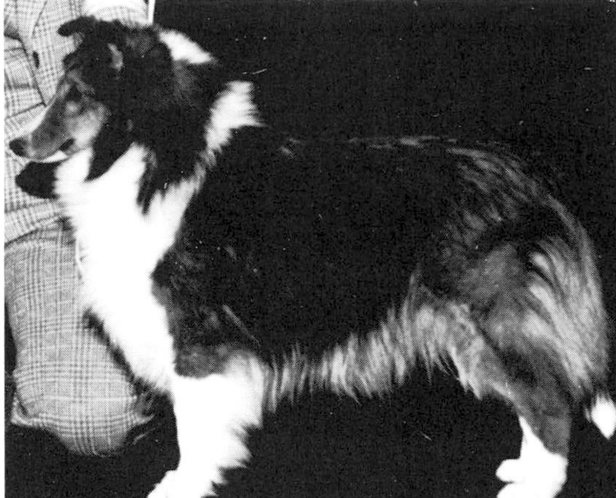

Ch. Barwoods Symphony, a specialty winner bred by Barbara Thompson, and now in Japan.

Am. Can. Ch. Banchory Orange Chiffon, a daughter of Am. Can. Ch. Wyndcliff the Successor (Photo by Yuhl.)

Ch. Mountainlair Sandmere Margo, another specialty winner owned by the Griffiths.

FEEDING AND CARE

During the first five weeks of pregnancy your bitch's diet should be the same as before she was bred—a nutritionally complete ration containing at least twenty-five percent protein on a dry matter basis. She should have access to fresh, clean drinking water at all times.

A high quality ration for the latter stages of pregnancy will include thirty percent protein and should list meat as one of the first three ingredients. Additional protein in the form of eggs, liver, cottage cheese or an all-meat canned ration may be helpful. Do not overfeed, and don't oversupplement with calcium, vitamin D, or fat. Excess fat in the diet of a pregnant bitch has been shown to decrease vigor and increase the death rate of puppies. Likewise, too much calcium or vitamin D can cause congenital abnormalities.

Liver is an excellent source of vitamins and minerals. Calf liver is recommended because the liver of an animal absorbs all the impurities in the system, and may become contaminated by the steroids and growth hormones in cattle feed. One-half ounce liver per day is maximum for a

Sheltie. If you cannot obtain fresh liver, liver extract is available at health food stores.

Bone meal is considered a safe and inexpensive calcium/phosphorus supplement, but I rarely use it unless a bitch appears to be carrying an unusually large litter or has a history of eclampsia while nursing.

As she grows larger and her stomach becomes crowded, the expectant mother will appreciate two or three small meals daily instead of her usual one. Gradually increase the ration until just prior to whelping when she is consuming about twenty to thirty percent more than her normal amount.

Except for adequate exercise and proper diet, a pregnant Sheltie needs little special attention and can go about her daily routine of training, showing (except for jumping in obedience), and other work. Protect her from drafts and dampness, and check regularly for any abnormal vaginal discharge. A clear, sticky discharge is normal during the latter half or one-third of the pregnancy. No medication, immunizations, or worming preparations should be given during pregnancy unless absolutely necessary and then only under the direction and supervision of your veterinarian.

BREEDING DIFFICULTIES

It would be impossible to cover here all the reasons for a bitch failing to conceive or carry a litter to term. Every breeder, at some time or another, will be confronted with a problem of this kind. About half are one time occurrences that happen for no determinable reason. Others fall into one of the following categories.

Failure to Conceive

Poor breeding management or the stress of shipping bitches long distances by air accounts for about half of all reproductive failures. Poor nutrition, overweight or underweight condition, breeding at the wrong time, and failure of the stud manager to be present and insure that a tie occurs fall under the category of poor management. Once these causes have been ruled out, consider the history of previous estrous cycles. If the bitch has had normal cycles at regular, normal intervals, suspect an infection or an obstruction in the genital tract. Abnormal or irregular cycles often indicate hormonal imbalance, tumor, or other more complex problems.

The first time a bitch misses I review the dates bred, environmental conditions such as shipping or unusual stress, and length of season. Consider whether a culture was done prior to breeding and the results. Also note whether a pregnancy check was done by a veterinarian at the fourth week. Write this information down and file it so that it will be available at her next season. Next season, have a culture and brucella canis test done, review the notes and try to correct any potential mismanagement problems, treat for any bacteria or infection, and if possible, repeat the breeding. This bitch should be bred on the first day she will accept and repeated every day until she will no longer stand. This time be sure to have a pregnancy check done at the vet clinic about four or four-and-a-half weeks post breeding.

Usually a bitch handled in this manner will conceive. If she does not, and her physical exam reveals nothing abnormal, you have the choice of trying again, spending a considerable sum to have various tests done, asking your veterinarian to experiment with drug treatment if he or she has any ideas, or putting the bitch in a pet home. Your decision should be determined by the value of the bitch, her past producing record, and the availability of a bitch of similar lineage and quality to replace her in your breeding program. Many novices make the mistake of spending far too much trying to get a litter from a bitch that could be replaced by a Sheltie of far better quality at less cost than the veterinary bills. On the other hand, don't give up too easily on a bitch of exquisite quality whose bloodline would be difficult to replace.

Ch. Rorralore Rejoice, WB at the 1981 National, owned by Charlotte Clem McGowan. (Photo by Krook.)

If you decide to pursue further veterinary assistance, the first step is usually a complete blood workup, urinalysis, serum chemistry and possibly tests for various hormone levels. If the tests are normal, you may find that breeding locally or to your own male will get her settled. Then ship on the following heat instead of skipping a cycle between breedings.

Occasionally a bitch will not conceive when bred to a certain male but will whelp a normal litter by another male—call it "Sheltie incompatibility." Science cannot explain why this happens, but breeders know occasionally it does occur.

In my experience the system that insures the best breeding results is to breed a bitch between her first and second birthday, usually at her second heat, and again on the third or fourth heat. Then, if you want to skip her a year or so for showing, do so, but realize that if you wait too long between litters you may have difficulty getting her to settle. Showing a bitch while she is young may mean you end up with a champion with few or no offspring, as the female that is not bred until four or five years of age is often difficult to settle and a poor producer. However, breeding some bitches early may ruin them for a show career. Carrying a litter tends to spring the rib cage, drop the chest, weaken a soft back, and accentuate any tendency to go out at elbows. Sometimes we can't have it all; a choice may need to be made. Always keep a replacement daugher from the first litter if possible, and consider any later ones a bonus. You can always cull the older daughter when a better one comes along.

Ch. Berridale Alnphyll Brigette, by Ch. Calcurt Luke. (Photo by Krook)

False Pregnancy

Occasionally bitches, bred or not, will have all the symptoms of pregnancy. The uterus enlarges under the influence of progesterone; mammary glands fill with milk. At about the time they would be due to whelp, some of these bitches actually go through the process of nesting, and in rare cases even labor. It is difficult at first to determine whether such a bitch is really pregnant, the only difference being that the whelps cannot be felt.

False pregnancy ends at about the time a normal pregnancy would terminate. It does not harm the bitch and little is really known about what causes the condition. Some bitches with a history of false pregnancy never conceive. Others conceive normally when bred.

Resorption of Whelps

If a bitch conceives and something goes wrong—hormone imbalance, injury, toxicity from medication or poison—before the sixth week of pregnancy, she will simply resorb the puppies which are dead or which her body cannot sustain. Resorption sometimes occurs so early in the pregnancy that one may never know if the bitch was actually pregnant.

One problem I have experienced in Shelties is the inability of a bitch to maintain a pregnancy due to a deficiency of progesterone. The bitch shows all the early signs of pregnancy, whelps can definitely be felt at 28 days, but then the abdomen ceases growing larger and she either never whelps or has only one puppy, the rest having been resorbed. This condition occurs in young bitches, but is even more common as bitches age. It can be easily corrected by the administration of repositol progesterone given after breeding and repeated at two week intervals through about the sixth week. The injections will have to be repeated with each breeding since the deficiency does not correct itself.

Thyroid Imbalance

Another common hormonal malfunction in Shelties, especially older bitches, is an over- or under-active thyroid. If unadequate thyroid is produced a bitch will not ovulate. The affected Sheltie is often overweight, lazy, and has a greasy-looking coat. Other symptoms include infrequent heat cycles, reduced intensity of estrus, prolonged bleeding, and abortion.

Thyroid malfunction can be easily detected through blood tests and corrected by the administration of the hormone, but it is one conception problem few veterinarians consider. If you suspect thyroid deficiency, request a T3 *and* T4 thyroid test. However, if there is a history of thyroid deficiency in her pedigree you are probably dealing with a hereditary condition in which case the bitch should not be bred.

Abortion

Until the emergence of canine brucellosis, abortion was considered to be rare in bitches. The death of one fetus will not cause a bitch to abort. Rather she will resorb or partially resorb the fetus. If something goes wrong very early in pregnancy she will probably resorb the entire litter. Fetuses dying in the last week of pregnancy will probably be delivered along with the rest of the puppies. Abortion, therefore, is only recognized during the fifth to eighth week.

Beginning around 1962, an infectious disease characterized by abortion and by infertility in males and females occurred in epidemic form in all regions of the U.S. By 1968 the disease had been diagnosed in over 800 bitches in 38 states. The most striking characteristic of Brucellosis *B. Canis* is that abortion usually occurs between the 45th and 55th day of gestation, without any forewarning and without fever or illness in the bitch. Most aborted litters are stillborn or die shortly after birth.

Bitches commonly exhibit a vaginal discharge for several weeks. Once they have aborted, most bitches fail to conceive thereafter, although a few may deliver normal litters a year or so later.

Genital infection in males may be accompanied by scrotal dermatitis and painful swelling of the scrotal sac, followed by testical atrophy and sterility.

At present no known cure or immunization exists. The disease is detected by testing elevated serum antibody titers with a standardized tube agglutination test. Suspect brucellosis when a bitch aborts late in pregnancy or fails to conceive twice in a row. (See chapter 22 for more information.)

Uterine Infections

While the uterus of a nonpregnant bitch is remarkably resistant to infection, the pregnant or pseudopregnant uterus is quite susceptible to infection from a variety of bacteria. Therefore, the period between breeding and whelping, and immediately after birth of a litter are key times to check your bitch for vaginal discharge, odor, or other signs of infection.

There is a host of potential low-grade uterine infections. Most are characterized by some type of discharge and may be treated with antibiotics. In addition, there are several more serious types.

Pyometra. By far the most serious uterine infection is pyometra. Caused by a retained placenta, infection entering the uterus while it is open during estrus or whelping, or hormone level imbalance, the disease is characterized by a high temperature and an extremely odorous, pus-colored discharge. The bitch may be mildly depressed and drink unusually large amounts of water. If not treated immediately she will become very ill and go into shock.

Pyometra commonly occurs one or two months after estrus or after whelping, usually in bitches six years or older. The cervix closes under the influence of progesterone at this time and the infected uterus fills with pus. There are two forms of pyometra—open, where the uterus is open and draining, and closed, where the cervix is so tightly closed that the infection has no way to drain and clean out. Open pyometra can sometimes be treated successfully with *prostaglandin* F_2 and oral *cloramphenical.* Closed pyometra cannot be treated and the only hope of saving the bitch is immediate removal of the uterus.

Ch. Birch Hollow the Choir Boy, owned by Mildred Nicoll. (Photo by Krook)

Acute Metritis. This infections occurs from bacteria introduced during whelping, or less commonly, during breeding. The chances of metritis are increased in cases of abortion, retained whelp or placenta, or lacerations of the uterine wall. Bacteria isolated from infected bitches includes staph, strep, and E. Coli. The bitch appears depressed and has a foul smelling, dark reddish discharge. She may become feverish and not want to care for her litter. Immediate treatment with antibiotics is required and spaying is sometimes necessary.

CULTURING AND TREATING AN INFECTION

Any time a colored or foul smelling discharge is noticed, a bitch aborts, or fails to conceive, or other indications of uterine infection are present, a culture should be taken. If symptoms indicate infection, treatment with antibiotics should be started even before the culture results are obtained. Treatment for staph, strep, E. coli and similar organisms is a combination of antibiotics administered both orally and as a vaginal douche. Breeders who have experienced chronic low grade infections have reported good results from routine douching with *Furacin®* prior to breeding. Antibiotics also may be infused directly into the uterus under anesthesia in severe cases.

Prevention is the Cure

Care and cleanliness in handling your own and other's Shelties will help immensely in protecting valuable breeding animals. If you have or suspect an infection, have cultures taken, treat immediately, and repeat the culturing until the infection is positively cleared up. Never mate an animal that has or is suspected of having an infection and thus run the risk of spreading it. Viral infections have become so rampant that some breeders service all outside bitches by artificial insemination. Even this may not protect your kennel from contacting someone else's problem.

Ch. Hatfield's Stardust with Tom Coen in the 1960's. Stardust was influencial in the breeding program at Rorralore.

Am. Can. Ch. Banchory Arabesque, dam of Banchory Formal Notice, owned by Banchory. (Photo by Lindemaier.)

Ch. Liz Bi Sonewall, a bi-blue, multiple specialty winner and dam of Ch. Shadypines The Elizabethian, a foundation bitch for Lynn Broussard, Shadypines. (Photo by Jan.)

Ch. Nadia, dam of Macdega the Piano Man, owned by Nioma Coen. Note the lovely expression of this bi-black. (Photo by Krook.)

The Maternity Ward 21

We are all a little shaky the first time we whelp a pure-bred litter—all potential champions, of course! Your Sheltie bitch may be shaky too, especially if it's her first. Some bitches are quite calm about the whole thing, but as a rule Shelties aren't too adept at whelping by themselves. One of mine whelped her first puppy quite effortlessly and then, with a terribly guilty look, ran off to hide. She had no idea that the mass lying on the floor was really her baby.

For this reason, and many others, it is a good idea for you to be there at the critical time to watch over and help if needed. Some bitches insist that you stay with them—otherwise they will follow you around and whelp at your feet. Remain cool and collected and watch without interfering any more than is necessary.

ADVANCE PREPARATIONS

Whelping will go much smoother if both you and the bitch are prepared. Therefore, a full week in advance of the expected whelping date, gather your equipment and your wits and make ready for the big event.

You will need a whelping box: a large appliance box cut off on one side to about eight inches high; the bottom half of a large fiberglass crate; or a wooden box made especially for whelping. Place the box in a quiet, draft-free corner. It should be located where you can view it easily from your work or living area, but out of the mainstream of family activities. If possible, place it within reach of the telephone and near a cot or easy chair in case you spend a sleepless night or two sitting up with the bitch.

Thoroughly clean and disinfect wooden boxes or crates with a 30% Clorox solution. Wooden boxes must be coated previously with polyurethane to prevent contamination. Place a thick layer of newspapers in the bottom. These are removed and replaced many times during whelping, so keep a large garbage bag handy. Warm the area around the whelping box to 80° F. or warmer, preferably with a small space heater placed well out of the way. If the floor is cold, elevate the whelping box on cement blocks or a wooden platform, or place several layers of rugs between it and the floor. Some people use a heat lamp over the box, but I do not like this method. The bitch suffers needlessly from the heat and the temperature is difficult to regulate. If a heat lamp is used, be sure it is protected by a metal guard or screen.

You will need a small box for the newborns while mom is still in the process of whelping. A shoe box or small grocery box is ideal. Place a heating pad or hot water bottle wrapped in towels on the bottom and use a small hand towel to cover most of the top, providing an incubator-like atmosphere.

The entire area where your bitch will whelp should be tediously cleaned and disinfected. This includes floors, walls, heat vents, humidifier and furnace filters, and other objects. Since roaches and water bugs can carry strep and staph from one room to another, be sure the area has been "bug-proofed" some time earlier.

Since I use a "Lectro-Kennel" heating pad in the bottom of the one end of the whelping box after the litter is born, this is also disinfected with Clorox solution, dried, and during whelping it is set on end and turned on so that it warms gradually. After bitch and puppies have settled down and most of the bleeding has stopped, I remove the bitch and puppies and all the papers from the whelping box and re-clean it with 30% Clorox. Let the bitch out to exercise and leave the newborns in their "incubator box." When the whelping box has dried (quickly due to the heater or heat lamp), I replace a layer of papers in the bottom of the box, then cover the Lectro-Kennel Pad with a soft flannel baby crib sheet, terry towel, or disposable diapers. Some breeders cover the entire crate bottom with a towel or indoor-outdoor carpeting. Carpeting must be washed often or it can cause burns from accumulated urine. Covering the entire bottom of the box is essential if there are weak puppies that have difficulty getting to the dam. But if the litter is strong and healthy, I have found that using paper on part of the floor encourages the puppies to urinate and defecate on the paper, keeping their sleeping area clean. Newspaper also provides a cool surface for the bitch. Puppies raised to four weeks on carpet or toweling have proven more difficult to housebreak.

Things To Do

Bathe the bitch a few days in advance of whelping. Call your veterinarian and let him know the date your bitch is due and make sure he will be available. If he will be out of town, ask him to recommend another vet. Keep in touch throughout the days before whelping so that you know he will be available if you need him and can get him in a moment's notice. Looking for a vet when you need one during whelping just doesn't work, so be sure to take this extra precaution. The difference of even a few minutes can be critical when a puppy is delayed in the birth canal. If your bitch has had problems previously you may want to have her examined a few days before her due date.

A week prior to whelping is the time to start keeping a temperature chart on your bitch. At this time her temperature, normally about 101.5° or 102° F., will be hovering around 100.5° or as low as 100°F. As whelping

Supplies

On the other side of the delivery box place a stand or table for supplies. Prepare the tools and materials you will need and place them on the table. Your supplies might include:

- Disinfectant surgical soap such as *Betadine®*
- Washcloths
- Disposable plastic or rubber gloves
- KY lubricating jelly
- Tincture of iodine for disinfecting navels
- Dental floss for tying cords
- Hemostat for clamping cords
- Cotton balls
- Several small hand towels
- A large pile of clean newspapers
- Plastic garbage bags
- Clock
- Notebook for keeping records
- Baby scale for weighing puppies

Also keep on hand a can of *Esbilac®* bitch's milk substitute, a feeding tube or a bottle with premature baby nipple, and some liquid glucose. If you are experienced enough at whelping, your vet may also give you some oxytocin to keep on hand.

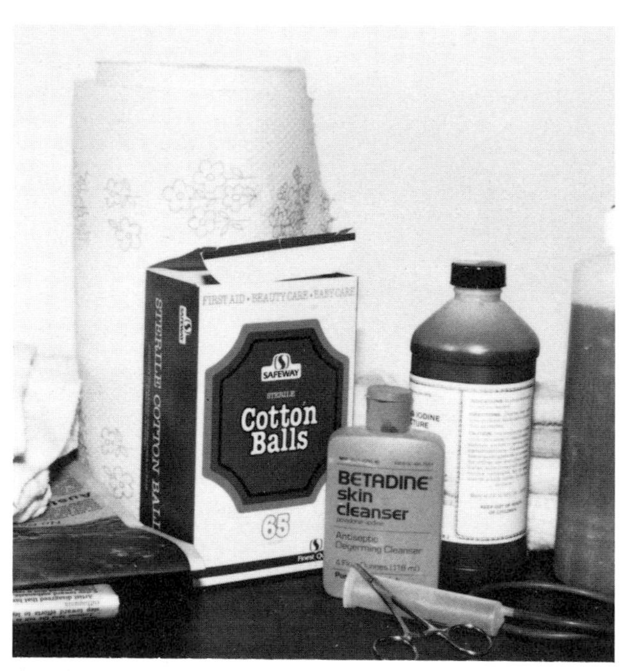

Supplies for whelping: towels, hemostats, dental floss for tying cords, KY lubricating jelly, and tincture of iodine are essentials.

approaches, the temperature gradually drops to between 100° and 99.5°. It may fluctuate as much as a degree during the course of the day, usually being higher at night.

Taking the bitch's temperature once in the morning and once before bedtime will give you a good feeling for what is taking place. Between eight and twelve hours before she goes into labor the temperature will drop abruptly to between 98° and 99° F. It may rise again slightly just before she whelps. When you see an abrupt drop in the temperature, whelping is imminent—twelve to twenty-four hours. If no signs of labor occur within twenty-four hours of this drop, consult your veterinarian; there may be trouble.

THE FIRST SIGNS

If anything definite can be said about Sheltie bitches in whelp it is that they are all individuals—no two behave alike. Some happily announce the approaching event days in advance with much nesting, scratching, pacing, and complaining. Others are perfectly normal and nonchalant right up to the time they go into labor. Some retreat to their whelping box where you are sure they are beginning to show signs of prelabor three days before the actual event. Others go through prelabor and hard labor in the course of an afternoon with no fuss or bother, giving birth to the first whelp only a few hours after you first suspected delivery time was approaching.

Often the first hint is that the bitch refuses to eat or eats very little. Again, however, some bitches stop eating three or four days in advance of whelping, while others eat a hearty meal the same day. The refusal to eat, however, generally comes before the abrupt drop in temperature.

If the litter is large, you can see that the puppies have dropped by the caved-in appearance in the bitch's loin. This will be less obvious in a young bitch than in an old brood bitch or one carrying a very large litter. The bitch will probably want lots of attention and sympathy and will stay close to you if possible. She may seem uncomfortable and just a little restless as the whelping day grows nearer.

FINAL PREPARATIONS

Make your final preparations after the bitch's temperature has dropped. Clipping the inner layers of the feathering from the bitch's hindquarters will keep the area cleaner and prevent a puppy from getting entangled in the long hairs. Also clip the feathering from the sides of the belly and the hair around the breasts. Wash her hindquarters and tummy with surgical soap, then dry her gently with a large towel.

Check the supplies you set up earlier. Is everything in order? Sterilize the scissors and hemostat by boiling for twenty minutes, then keep them covered or wrapped in a towel until they are needed.

PRELABOR

According to a recent article in *Dog World*[1] the mortality rate in unattended whelpings is as high as thirty-seven percent, so it pays to be on hand when your bitch whelps. I have heard of Sheltie bitches that were unattended scattering their whelps throughout the house, leaving them to suffocate in the sack or die from chilling. Carefully managed pregnancies and being in attendance when your bitch goes in labor should reduce the death rate of newborns to less than five percent.

The bottom half of a fiberglass shipping crate makes an accessible, easily disinfected whelping box. Note the cord to the heating pad which is under the towel. Toweling is tucked under the floor board.

The early stage of labor is sometimes difficult to detect. It will last from two or three to 36 hours. During this time the cervix and birth canal are dilating to make room for the puppies to pass through. The bitch may become increasingly restless or nervous. She may vomit, seem sick at her stomach, or pant. She may scratch feverishly at her newspaper padded box, turn, twist, lie down, and then get up to scratch some more. On the other hand, she may lie quietly in the box and sleep, with only occasional periods of pacing the floor, groaning, stretching as

[1]How to Save Newborn Pups. Elizabeth Hall. *Dog World Magazine*, April, 1983.

though uncomfortable, or nesting. She may even get out of the box between these sessions and go about her business as though everything is perfectly normal.

As the time of birth draws nearer, the vulva enlarges and softens and extrudes a clear, thick, sticky discharge. The bitch will begin to seem quite uncomfortable and will lick her rear parts or watch her sides curiously. She may whine or groan periodically and may occasionally quiver like an aspen leaf.

Watch the bitch carefully during this stage, and keep your eye on the clock, but don't fuss over or excite her. If possible watch from another room or sit quietly in a corner so that she doesn't get more nervous from your watching. If she wants out to relieve her bladder, let her out, but keep an eye on her just in case she should have a contraction from the exercise and whelp a puppy in the yard.

Wooden whelping boxes have a rail around the edge to prevent the bitch from crushing the puppies against the wall. Boxes such as this one are easily constructed. They should be painted inside and out to facilitate cleaning.

A small box with a heating pad in the bottom keeps puppies warm and dry while the bitch is busy whelping the next in line. If left in the box with their dam while another pup is being delivered they may be wet, chilled, or accidently injuried.

A little exercise periodically during prelabor is actually beneficial and can speed up the progress. It will also help tell you if the bitch is proceeding without problems. A bitch in trouble will not want to go outside and may seem stiff or have difficulty walking. Before she goes back into the whelping box her feet should be disinfected.

Danger Signs

A bitch that stays in prelabor more than twenty-four hours without going into hard labor or one that fails to show any signs of prelabor within twenty-four hours after the temperature has dropped abruptly to its lowest point may be in trouble. Excessive nervousness or pain; bleeding from the vagina, even one drop; a greenish discharge from the vulva; or lying listlessly in the whelping box for several hours without wanting to move or get up can all signal problems. If in doubt call your veterinarian or take the bitch in for an examination.

If a puppy is too large or there is an obstruction, a bitch may not go into labor at all. If you think whelping is progressing abnormally or that it has been too long since the onset of prelabor or the temperature drop, insist on a veterinary examination. Many veterinarians will advise clients to wait until the bitch goes into actual labor before being concerned. However, you may never actually see a contraction, yet other signs all point to a problem whelping.

If a bitch has gone past the sixty-third day from the first breeding without showing any sign of going into labor, contact your vet clinic. At no time should she be allowed to go past the sixty-fifth day without a checkup. If you feel something is wrong, *insist* on a veterinary examination. The assurance that everything is all right is well worth the expense of an office call. And, you might save the life of your litter. Waiting four hours too long, or in some cases even one hour, can mean death to the puppies and danger to the bitch.

ON THEIR WAY

Most Sheltie bitches progress from prelabor to hard labor in two to twelve hours. The first contractions may be hardly noticeable, just a mere tensing of the abdominal muscles. The bitch may shiver and shake violently; her teeth may chatter. Between contractions she may lie quietly, pant heavily, or scratch frantically at her nest.

As contractions grow stronger you can see side and abdominal muscles contract, and soon the bitch will strain as though she were having a bowel movement. She may cry out in pain. This is "hard" labor. The bitch may have a number of contractions spaced ten or fifteen minutes apart or longer, or two or three close together, resulting in a puppy almost immediately. The majority of my Shelties whelp effortlessly and quickly, sometimes with only one or two hard contractions before a puppy is born.

When the water bag bursts the first puppy is in the birth canal. The water bag serves the purpose of dilating the passage and when it finally breaks during a contraction the fluid lubricates the passage, making the way easier for the whelp. Generally contractions subside for a few minutes after the water bag ruptures to allow the bitch to rest in preparation for the harder contractions needed to expell the first whelp. A puppy generally appears within fifteen minutes.

Problems

More than two hours in hard labor without results may mean trouble, as does a Sheltie bitch experiencing excessive pain during labor without producing a puppy. If a bitch goes into hard labor and suddenly stops having contractions, this is a sign of complications. You may be able to insert a sterile, gloved finger into the vagina (which should be dilated and open), and feel if a puppy is close. This may tell you if the puppy is too large to get through the pelvic opening. If no puppy can be felt, suspect a problem further back in the birth canal.

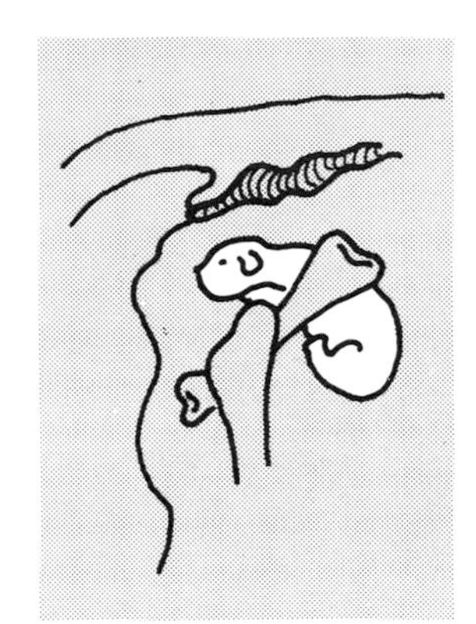

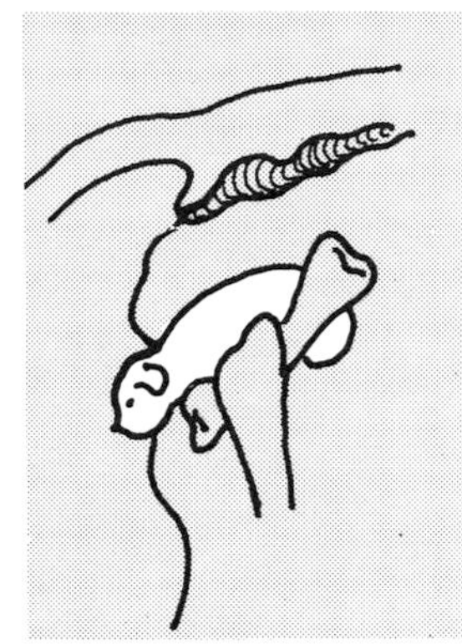

A normal birth; the puppy is head first. Note the way the birth canal curves over the pelvic bone. If you need to assist, always pull down, towards the bitch's stomach.

A breech birth. The puppy's rear is first. Breech births are sometimes more difficult. If possible, keep the bitch from breaking the sac until the puppy's head is out.

Sometimes a puppy can get jammed at the junction of the horns of the uterus and the birth canal. If the puppy is blocked at the pelvis, you may be able to feel if it is in correct position or to free it if a foot is hanging up. However, you will probably want to seek veterinary assistance.

It is not advisable to give an injection of oxytocin until at least one puppy has been born. If there is an obstruction, the contractions stimulated by the shot could cause the uterus to rupture.

THE MIRACLE OF BIRTH

Puppies arrive either head first, which is preferable, or hind feet first, called "breech birth." Considerable

First signs of labor are panting and shivering.

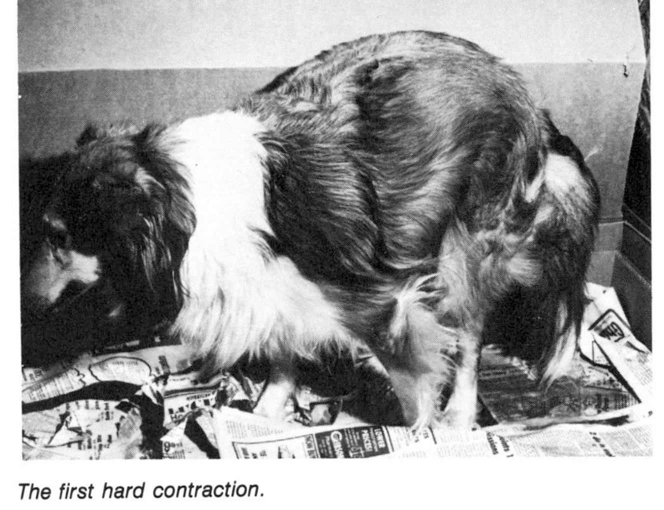

The first hard contraction.

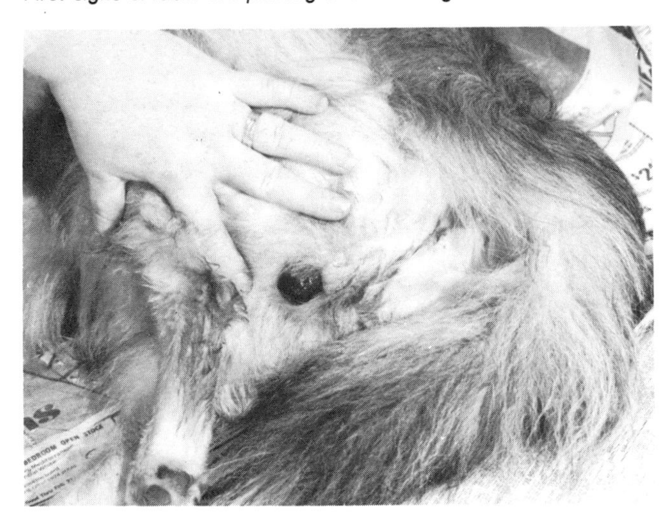

A dark-colored sac protrudes.

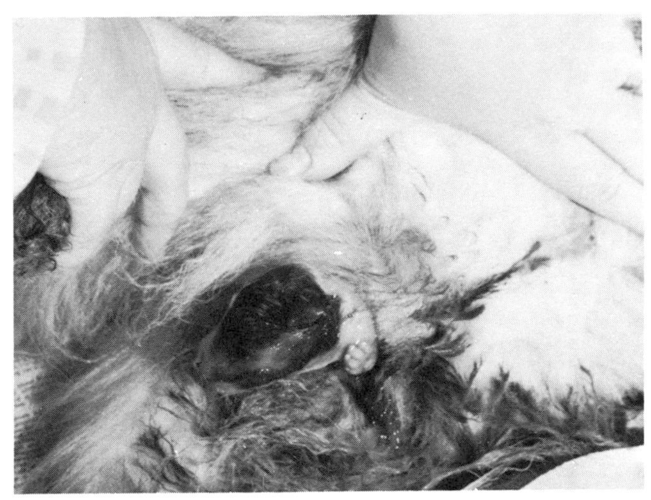

The puppy's head is out.

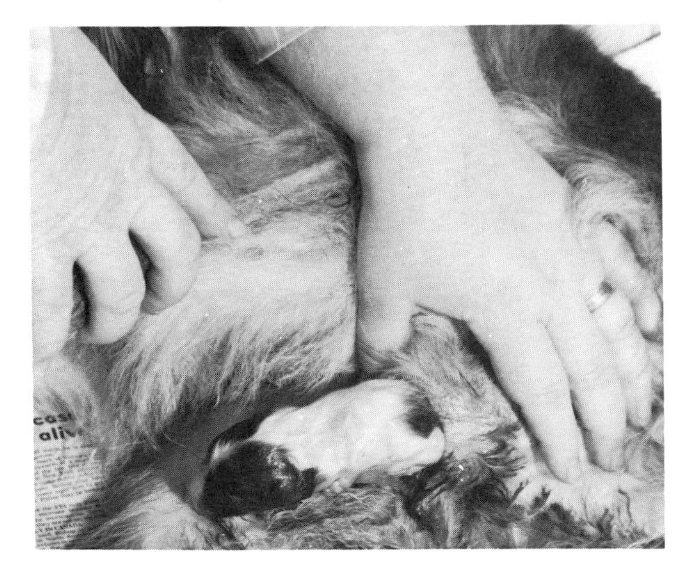

Another contraction forces the shoulders out.

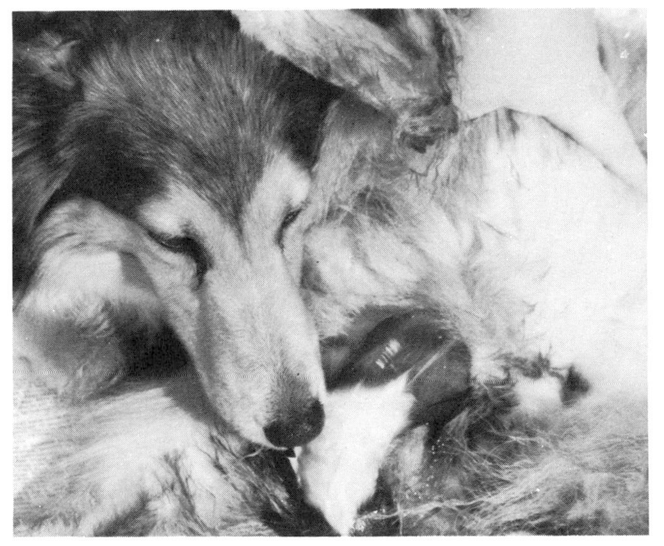

The bitch begins to remove the sac.

The puppy is out, still partially encased in the sac.

The dam cleans and stimulates the pup.

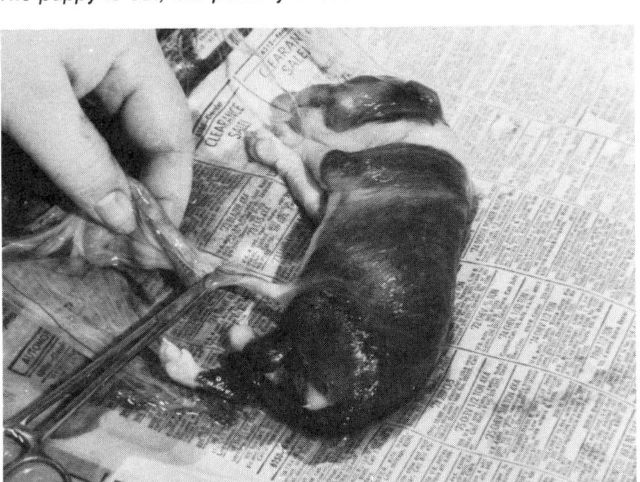

Clamp the cord with a hemostat.

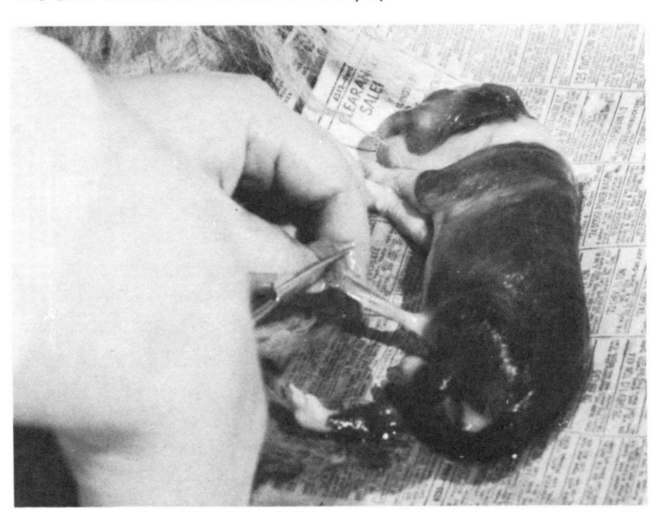

Cut or tear the cord about an inch from the puppy's abdomen if the bitch doesn't cut it. (Hemostat was removed for photograph.)

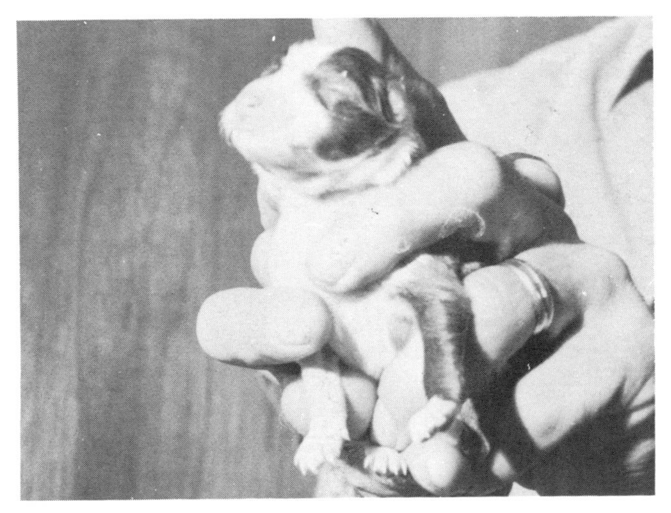

Hold the puppy firmly between both hands, forefingers bracing the head. Do not let his head snap back as you shake him.

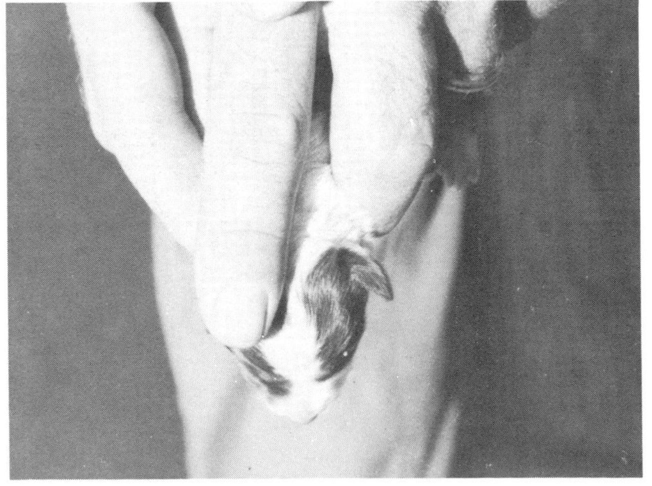

Starting with arms outstretched, bring the puppy downward, stopping abruptly when his head is straight down. This clears the lungs and nostrils of fluid.

(Photos in above series by Freedo Rieseberg.)

pressure is required to force the shoulders of the puppy through the pelvic opening and this may take a while.

In the head first position the sac filled with dark fluid is seen first. Keep the bitch from breaking this. Soon the head, followed by forelegs and shoulders, should appear. As soon as the shoulders come free the entire puppy will be quickly forced out.

Generally the puppy is still enclosed in the sac. It is important that his head be freed as soon as possible for he will have been stimulated by the pressure of birth to start breathing, and if left in the sac too long he may suffocate. A good bitch will take care of this instinctively, pulling off the sac and eating it.

However, if the bitch does not get the puppy out, you will have to take over for her. Take the sac between your fingers and tear it apart over the puppy's nose, rapidly pulling the membrane back away from the head. If you have trouble holding the slippery membrane with your fingers, grasp it between folds of a dry terrycloth towel and pull forward away from the nostrils. The sac will break easily. Use the cloth to wipe the fluid from the nostrils, mouth, and head.

Providing that the placenta, or afterbirth, came free with the puppy, the bitch will likely turn her attentions to eating it and to severing the umbilical cord which is attached to the placenta. The placenta contains an abundance of hormones which help the bitch's uterus to contract after whelping and stimulate her to produce milk. The material also acts as a laxative. Too many placentas, however, can cause diarrhea and upset stomach, so I allow the bitch to eat only one or two and dispose of any additional ones.

It is important to notice that a placenta arrives with each puppy. Sometimes it will not come free immediately, but will be forced out by the birth of the next whelp. A retained placenta can cause uterine infection. Again, if the bitch does not sever the umbilical cord, or if the placenta does not come free, you must help out. If the placenta is still inside the bitch, take hold of the cord and pull *gently* downward, toward the bitch's stomach and toward the puppy, in an effort to free the membrane. If it does not come free easily, clamp a hemostat on the cord just outside the vagina to prevent the placenta from going back in the birth canal, and proceed to cut the cord.

Take the cord between your thumb and forefinger and milk the blood in it toward the puppy. Then, holding the cord firmly near the puppy so there is no pressure to cause an umbilical hernia, take the cord between the thumb and forefinger of your other hand. Pull and tear the cord about an inch from the puppy's tummy. Leave the hemostat clamped on the cord for several minutes until all bleeding has stopped and the cord naturally begins to seal itself off.

If hemostats are not available, or if the cord continues to ooze blood after a few minutes, make a small loop with dental floss or white sewing thread and tie it about one-half inch from the puppy's abdomen. Knot twice; then cut off the excess string so the bitch can't pull on it. Dab tincture of iodine on the cord.

Shake the Puppy

It is easy for a puppy to swallow or inhale fluid during birth and this can cause strangulation or pneumonia; therefore, it is good practice to shake each puppy in the following manner several times to force any fluid out of the respiratory system.

Hold him between the flat palms of your hands, being careful to support his head. Raise your arms and bring them sharply downward, stopping abruptly when the puppy is straight down. Take a good hold and don't be afraid of shaking too hard. Repeat several times if necessary. If the puppy is still breathing noisily from fluid in the nostrils, put your mouth over his nose and gently suck the fluid out, or use a human breast pump over the nostrils.

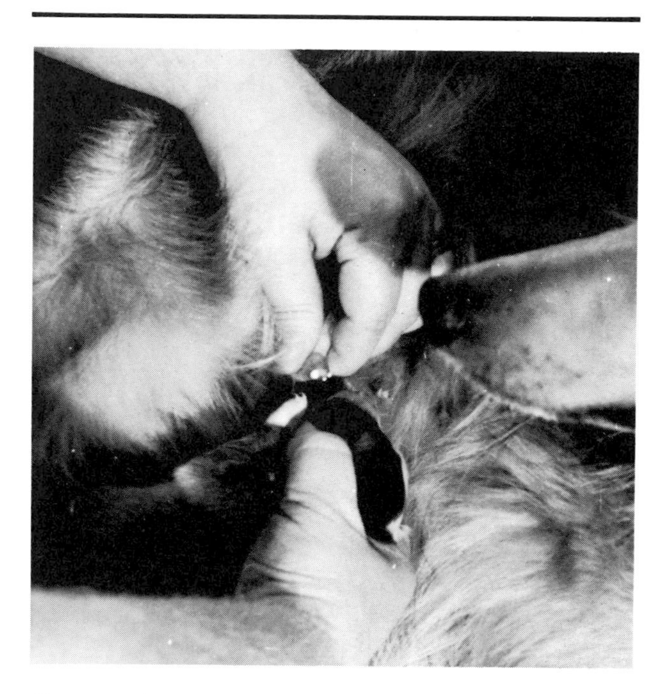

If a puppy has trouble nursing, express a drop of milk and press the sides of the puppy's mouth to force it open. Hold him on the teat for a few minutes or until he gains strength.

THE FIRST MEAL

As soon as the puppy is breathing evenly and the cord has been attended to, put him with his mother, providing she is not giving birth to another puppy. Her licking and nudging will stimulate the newborn, and soon he will be searching for something to eat. He will generally have no trouble locating the source of nourishment and getting his first meal.

If he does have trouble, give him a little time. It may take an hour for a puppy to gain strength after birth. If he seems weak or unable to suckle, hold him with your thumb and forefinger pressed on each side of his mouth, forcing it open. With the other hand express a drop of milk from a teat and place his mouth over it. Hold him there for a few minutes until he is nursing stongly enough to hold on by himself. Some puppies will fight and scream when you do this; never mind, they are just hungry and frustrated. Repeat the process until they can find and hold the nipples by themselves.

If the puppy will not suck even when placed on the teat, you can wrap your forefinger under his chin, the thumb on top of his nose, and work his mouth for him until he gets the idea. Persistence and patience with a weak puppy will pay off soon in a contented, fat one.

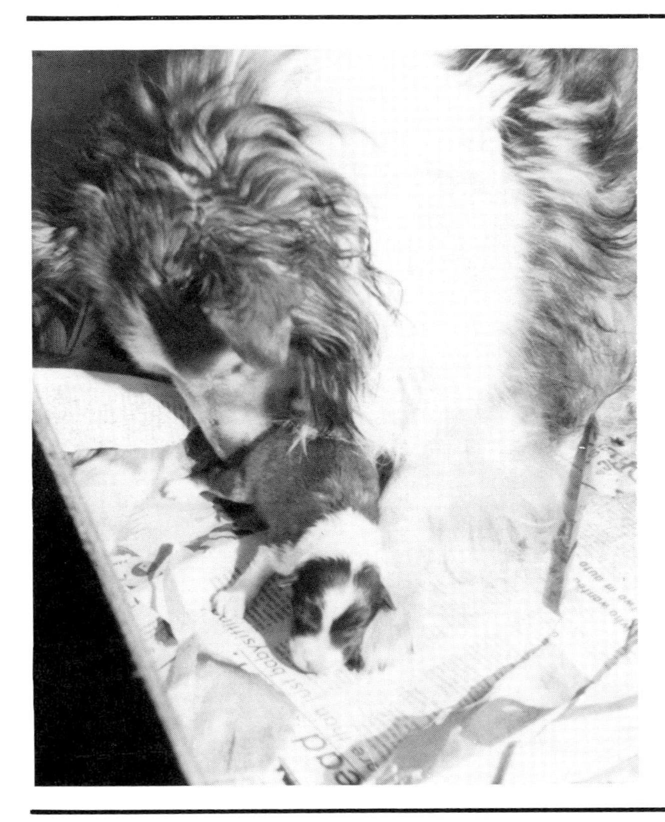

Bitch and puppy rest momentarily. Be sure she is licking the puppy to stimulate elimination of the meconium.

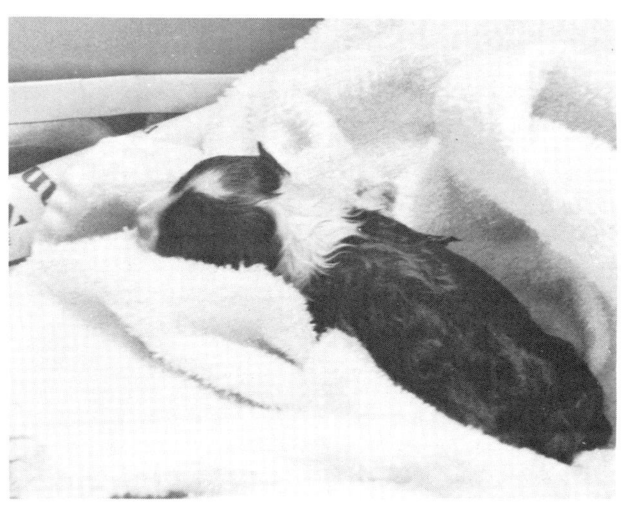

The second puppy is on its way. Place the first one in the separate box to dry off.

ADDITIONS TO THE FAMILY

Unless the second puppy comes within a few minutes, I leave the first puppy with the bitch until she starts having contractions again. At this point, move the puppy to the small box with the heating pad set on low. Cover the box with a towel and the newborn will soon contentedly drift off to sleep.

The placenta, if retained during the delivery of the first pup, should have come free by now. You may just have time to add some fresh newspaper to the box before the second puppy arrives and you have to repeat the delivery process. Some bitches whelp rapidly. A young one of mine gave birth to seven puppies in just over an hour. More commonly, however, a bitch will whelp two puppies fifteen to thirty minutes apart, and then rest for an hour or so before whelping another one or two.

More than two hours between puppies, more than one hour since the onset of hard contractions, or complete cessation of labor when more puppies are obviously inside the bitch signal a call to your veterinarian. Use your common sense too. If your vet says wait but you feel something is really wrong, insist on taking her in immediately. If she looks fine but is just slow, wait unless advised otherwise, but be alert and keep track of time.

WHELPING COMPLICATIONS

Difficult Delivery—Stuck Puppy

Sometimes if a puppy is large the head will come out but the shoulders will stick at the pelvic opening. If this happens a little assistance will usually release the pup. Wash your hands thoroughly with disinfectant soap and use a clean terrycloth washcloth to get a better grip on the puppy. Take the puppy (still in the sac) by the skin on on the neck and pull gently *down* and forward toward the bitch's stomach. *Never pull straight out.* If the pup doesn't come loose, pull him gently to one side, then the other, in an effort to free the shoulders.

If the feet are protruding you can pull first one, then the other until the shoulders come free. Do not attempt to draw the whelp out by the legs—you may dislocate or break them. Just pull them out enough to free the shoulders. Once the shoulders have cleared, turning the puppy in a corkscrew motion will help.

If the head is just visible but not out and the puppy seems stuck, insert a rubber gloved finger into the vagina and try to hook it around the back or neck of the puppy, pulling downward. A little KY lubricating jelly inserted into the vagina may ease delivery. If you have not succeeded in freeing the puppy within fifteen minutes and the bitch is having contractions to no avail, seek veterinary assistance. The life of this puppy and the others coming behind it are at stake.

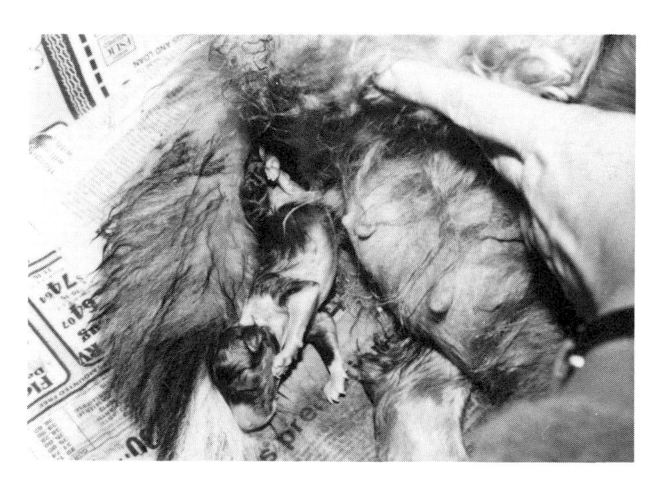

The placenta is still inside and will not come free. This can be a frightening experience for a young bitch or an inexperienced mid-wife. Steady the bitch and wait. Don't pull on the puppy.

Momma removes the sac as the puppy emerges.

Breech Births

Puppies born hind feet first are not at all uncommon. Sometimes they do need help, however, since the head and shoulders, which are the widest part, come last and tend to stick. If the hind legs are out and the rest of the puppy seems to be slow in coming, grasp the legs with your washcloth and hold on to prevent them from slipping back into the bitch. Try not to break the sac if it is still intact because once the sac is broken the puppy will try to breathe and can easily swallow fluid and choke to death. If the sac is already broken, every second counts.

Keep steady traction on the legs, again pulling downward toward the bitch's belly. Pull steadily, slowly, gently but firmly whether the bitch is having a contraction or not. If the shoulders stick, pull from side to side or in a corkscrew motion until they are freed. Once the puppy is out, quickly remove the sac from his head, cut the cord, and shake the puppy to free the air passages of fluid. Breech puppies always have more trouble with fluid.

Abnormal Presentations

Sometimes a puppy will come upside down or neck first with his head turned under. About all you can do is inject a little KY jelly into the vagina and, with a rubber gloved finger, try to turn the puppy to a more correct position.

Never try to pull a puppy that is upside down; you may break its back or neck. Instead, try to push it back or turn it until it is positioned correctly. If the puppy is breech and upside down, you should be aware that in turning him you can easily get the cord wrapped around his neck, thus strangling him. If you can't free the puppy easily, rush the bitch to the nearest vet.

Uterine Inertia

The most common problem bitches encounter while whelping is uterine inertia. They simply wear out and stop having contractions in the midst of delivery. Sometimes a short rest and a couple teaspoons of brandy in a bowl of milk will revive the bitch and she will resume contractions on her own.

Whelping completed, the new family settles down to eat as mom tries to get some rest. A piece of paneling keeps out drafts. In winter I cover the doorway with a towel hung from the top. When the pups are walking, remove the paneling and place an exercise pen around the crate.

Injections of oxytocin (pituitary hormone), intramuscularly, will start the contractions again. This should not be given *unless* the bitch has already delivered one puppy and you are sure there are more to come, but contractions have ceased with no puppy in sight. When the injection is given, the bitch should start contracting again in fifteen minutes or less.

If a puppy is not whelped within forty-five minutes, contact your vet. If the puppies are in position and not too large, he may want to try another injection. If the next pup is far enough back and is just not being pushed out, or is twisted, he may be able to remove it with forceps, thus avoiding a caesarian. If contractions do not begin and the puppies cannot be removed with forceps, a caesarian section must be performed in order to save the bitch and any remaining whelps.

Impossible Deliveries

If a puppy is too large to go through the pelvic opening, delivery will be impossible. The bitch will go into prelabor, but may or may not go into hard labor. She may lie quietly, quivering in pain, or seem extremely restless. Impossible delivery because of a large puppy is more common with the first puppy of a litter, or when there is only one puppy. However, the too-large whelp may also come in the middle or at the end of a normally delivered litter.

Sometimes two puppies will become jammed at the top of the birth canal, or entangled while passing down the canal, so that neither can be delivered. Again, this can occur at the beginning, middle, or end of whelping a litter. A caesarian section must be performed. Too long a delay before the operation will endanger all the remaining puppies.

Modern veterinary practices are almost as sophisticated as human medicine and it is generally possible for the vet to go in and remove all the puppies while still alive and have them nursing on the bitch within a few hours. While the bitch will be groggy for twelve hours or so, she will generally accept the puppies and be quite gentle with them. For a while you may have to help them nurse and stimulate them to defecate. Twenty-four hours after the operation, the bitch will be able to walk around and care for the puppies. She would be able to conceive and whelp a litter normally in the future. As many as two or three caesarians may be performed on a bitch before there is any danger to her health while carrying a litter. Any *Sheltie* who has to have caesarians as a matter of practice would definitely not be considered a good brood bitch, but the practice is quite routine in some pug-nosed breeds.

REVIVING WEAK PUPPIES

Never give up hope too easily with a newborn puppy. If a puppy is born limp and blue and does not immediately start breathing, there is still a chance. Shake him as previously illustrated to free the air passages of fluid. Get him warm by rubbing briskly with a towel while holding him close to your body. If he still does not breathe at all, a drop of ammonia on a cotton ball held under his nose for a second may cause him to gasp.

You can give artificial respiration by holding the head in one hand, hind legs in the other with the tummy downward. Bring your knuckles together, making the back concave, then go the other way, making it convex. Repeat twenty times per minute.

If all else fails, hold the puppy up and blow *gently* into its mouth and nose until the tiny lungs fill with air. Remove your lips, inhale, and repeat at one minute intervals until the pup begins to breathe. Do not blow with too much force as this could rupture the lungs. You can feel the air filling the lungs. Let your hands tell you when to stop and how much pressure to exert. Strangely enough, the first time I did this I could tell exactly how much pressure to use, and I saved the puppy.

Chilled pups should not be fed or allowed to nurse. Warm them *slowly* on a low heat pad, by carrying them next to your body, or by placing them in a box in an open oven, set at it's lowest temperature for fifteen or twenty minutes. Too much heat too fast causes shock and dyhydration. Keep a humidity in the whelping room between 50 and 60 percent if possible.

Limp, lifeless puppies can often be saved if you persevere. Pale, white pads are a worse sign than blue or red ones, and there should always be hope for the ones that are still pink. Often after these puppies have been revived the pads and membranes will turn fiery red, an indication of hyperventilation. They will return to normal in a few hours.

Ch. Rojean's A Classic Gem and litter, owned by Jean DeSmit. Healthy puppies are fat and sleek and able to nurse strongly. (Photo by Joan Smith.)

POSTWHELPING CARE OF THE BITCH

It is advisable to take the bitch into the veterinarian within twelve hours after the last puppy was delivered. He will check for retained placentas, abnormal discharge, tearing of the vagina, and signs of infection, eclampsia, or mastitis.

For the first two or three days the bitch should be fed lightly and often, gradually building up to her regular ration by the third or fourth day. Broth, cottage cheese, *Esbilic®*, and a little raw liver are good in the interim. Mix her dry food into a soft gruel with broth or milk and feed only small portions at a time, although her appetite may be voracious. She will be thirsty and drink lots of water, which should be available at all times.

For the first week after whelping the bitch should be observed carefully and her temperature recorded twice daily. Some discharge and bleeding from the vulva is to be expected, but excessive bleeding is cause for concern. So is a greenish or pus-filled discharge. If a whelp or placenta has been retained and infection has set it, the bitch's temperature will rise to 103°F or more and she will probably be quite ill. Immediate treatment is required.

A common problem, eclampsia, or "nursing fits," is caused by calcium deficiency. The bitch will appear staring, wobbly, or may go into convulsions. She may walk stiff legged or limp. Injections of calcium must be given immediately or she will go into convulsions and possibly die. Recovery is generally quite rapid when calcium is administered in time.

The Nursery 22

The first hour after whelping is an exciting time! Stay with the bitch and litter and enjoy speculating which puppy will be the future champion, which the top producer, which looks like its sire, and which like the dam. More constructively, during this time complete your records of the whelping, noting any complications or unusual happenings, identify each puppy, and record its weight.

It is important that each puppy get a good meal during the two hours after birth. The first milk, colostrum, contains antibodies which pass the bitch's immunity to infection and disease (such as distemper) to the puppies. Even a puppy which later must be hand fed should have one or two meals of colostrum if at all possible.

A puppy that is sucking strongly will be plump and sleek. His tongue will be almost still and wrapped tightly around the nipple. He will not be noisy while he is eating. The weak puppy will fall off the teat easily, make loud munching noises as he sucks, and his tongue will move in and out. This puppy must be helped to suck and held up to the teat until he becomes strong enough to hold on by himself.

In addition to checking to see if the puppies are nursing, you should also make sure the bitch is licking them enough to stimulate urination and defecation. The first bowel movement, called meconium, is very dark brown, and it too should occur during that first hour after whelping.

In a young puppy the reflexes to urinate and defecate come strictly as the result of outside stimulation. If the bitch does not lick the pups you can stimulate them yourself by rubbing the tummy with a damp cotton ball or warm washcloth. Rubbing a little butter on the pup's abdomen and anus may encourage the bitch to lick him more often.

Occasionally a navel cord will ooze blood for some time after birth. Blood loss should be prevented by tying off the cord with dental floss. If a navel hernia is present cut a small gauze pad and tape it firmly over the hernia. In a week the hernia will usually recede. Large ones may need surgical correction later.

Don't fuss over the litter unnecessarily, however. Sheltie mothers catch on easily to the fact that if they get lazy someone else will do the work for them. Maiden bitches, like first-time mothers, may think the whole "diaper routine" is rather distasteful and would just as soon leave it to someone else. They must be encouraged to accept the duties of motherhood so that, with experience, they can manage on their own.

EXAMINING THE PUPPIES

Each puppy must be checked for abnormalities. Examine the head first—eyes, nose, lips. Open the mouth and check for cleft-palate an opening in the roof of the mouth that allows air and food to enter the nasal passage. Puppies with this deformity will have difficulty sucking and often milk will bubble out of the nostrils. The opening is sometimes hard to see. It can range from a wide gap to a narrow slit extending over only a part of the roof of the mouth. Puppies with cleft palate should be "put down" immediately.

Next check for club feet, and count to see if the puppy has the correct number of toes. Club feet will usually correct themselves by the time the puppy is walking.

Look at nose and lip pigment (most will be pink at birth) and check for color dilution, excessive white, or other color deviation.

Are there puppies which really should be put down? It is easiest to do it now by having your veterinarian administer an overdose of anesthetic. Neither the bitch nor you will miss the newborn after a few hours.

Cheek bones on a potentially good head will feel very smooth and flat. The lean head is usually easy to spot as it will be very lean even at birth. Underjaw should be very deep at this age, and should come right out to the end of the upper jaw, nice and square.

You can tell a lot about *bone* on a newborn too, especially if he is fat and healthy. A Sheltie puppy should look substantial, not like it has toothpicks for legs. If you hold the puppy up with one hand under the chest and the other under his flanks and let him relax, you can sometimes feel the angulation. Short hocks and long stifles, a "plus" in the rear structure, should also be obvious at birth; so should arc of neck. A truly elegant puppy will have a long, arched neck which he will hold up proudly as he takes his first meal.

Holding a puppy to evaluate angulation and body length. Place your fingers under his chin and between the hind legs and hold until he relaxes.

The head of a young puppy should be a short rectangle, muzzle nearly as wide as backskull. Cheeks should be smooth and flat. Note squared-off foreface. From the side the underjaw should be deep clear to the end, planes parallel. I'd like to see a more definite stop than this puppy has. Many pups are domy on topskull at birth.

EVALUATING THE PUPS

How exciting to really look at these newborn, squirming creatures and find a truly promising Sheltie. I like to look at puppies critically at birth, and again in about three days. With experience you can begin to pick the promising ones even at this early age.

Heads are easy to evaluate in a newborn Sheltie. The muzzle should be full—almost as wide as the backskull, giving the head a very square look. A narrow, pointy muzzle will usually turn out snipey. The head will look short and squished, but the proportion should be there—equal length from occiput to stop, and from stop to tip of nose.

Color and markings can also be evaluated. White markings, especially on the face, tend to diminish as the Sheltie grows. What appears to be a superwide blaze will narrow, and the tiny white snip will probably disappear altogether. The merling pattern is apparent on a newborn merle and so is the shading on a heavily shaded sable. Sables tend to become about the color you see on the top of the head and ears just after they are dried off. But, when undercoat and guard hairs come in on a growing sable puppy, the color may appear washed out and drab for several months.

It is difficult to predict *size* by looking at a newborn, although if all puppies appear healthy and one stands out as being overly large or extremely tiny, this may be an indication of later size problems.

THE HEALTHY PUPPY

During the first two weeks of life, puppies can neither see nor hear, although they are responsive to heat, cold, vibrations, or touch. They just snuggle next to their dam, eat, sleep, and grow. One of the most pleasant sights a Sheltie breeder enjoys is a litter of tiny puppies contentedly nursing away, tails in the air, lips smacking hungrily.

The healthy puppy sleeps most of the day, waking only when his mother or littermates arouse him to eat. When he's full he will usually urinate and defecate in response to stimulation from his mother's tongue and promptly fall asleep again. He will twitch, jerk, or move his legs in a running motion while sleeping. This is perfectly normal activated sleep and is the way in which a puppy exercises his muscles.

Usually puppies will have no trouble nursing after their first awkward attempts. In fact, their suction may be so strong that it is difficult to pull them off a teat. Ideally, puppies make very steady weight gains, and therefore, a weight chart provides a very good indicator as to how they are developing. I weigh my puppies at birth and two or three times weekly thereafter. Newborn Sheltie puppies average about five to eight oz., but they may vary from three to 14 ounces. Birth weight has no correlation with adult size, by the way. During the first week they should gain about a half ounce to one ounce per day. In the second week most double in weight, and by the third week daily gains begin to slow slightly.

Most puppies will do well with only their mother's attention. The first week they should be handled only to check and clean. Their box should be kept draft free and warm, about 85°F. at first, then gradually reduced to 75°F. over a two-week period.

After a bitch has been bathed after whelping, replace the newspaper bedding with an old terrycloth bath mat, towels, or diapers. This gives the puppies far better footing and is easier for them to crawl around on than newspaper. If you use indoor-outdoor carpet, buy several pieces so one can be washed and hung in the sun to dry during the day, and change it twice a day.

When picked up, the healthy pup will wiggle and squirm in your hand. If instead it feels limp and weak, something is wrong and you must immediately locate the problem.

WEAK PUPPIES

Some puppies get off to a bad start. Either they are smaller and get pushed away easily, or they are thin and weak and just can't seem to snap out of it quickly. If a weak puppy is getting pushed away from the dam, hold the larger puppies back so the small ones can nurse unobstructed every few hours.

Occasionally a weak puppy will not have the strength to hold on to a teat but can still nurse if held to the dam. Hold this puppy to the bitch and keep him awake and nursing at least 15 minutes every two hours until he becomes stronger. Making a cupped bed out of a bathtowel and propping the puppy against the bitch may suffice if the other pups are removed so they don't push him off.

Weak pups also benefit from an extra feeding of liquid glucose and water immediately after birth and two or three times a day thereafter until they gain strength. *Mix one teaspoon of glucose in one ounce of water* and feed one cc. at a time by dropper or tube. *Gatorade®* is also reccommended because it contains electrolytes and glucose.

SUPPLEMENTAL FEEDING

Weak, sick, or orphaned puppies must be fed by hand. There are many ways of doing this. I prefer supplementing by bottle feeding as it develops the sucking reflex in the puppy and also bonds the puppy to me because of the extra handling. Bottle fed puppies respond to the touch of the human hand much more quickly than those that are not supplemented in this way.

Often, all it takes to get a weak puppy started is two or three feedings of glucose in water or *Gatorade®*. These are easier to digest and supply more quick energy than milk supplements, so I usually use them for the first two feedings, two hours apart. Some puppies continue to have trouble nursing. These are held to the bitch as much as I have time for, and supplemented as necessary, two or four times daily by bottle feeding either *Esbilac®* or *Meyerberg Canned Goats Milk* diluted half and half with distilled water. Goats milk is easily digested, very rich, and can be obtained at the local grocery store. Many breeders prefer it to commercial bitch's milk supplements since at least one brand of these supplements has been reported to cause juvenile cataracts when used over a period of several weeks.

Obtain a small baby bottle with a premature baby nipple. Fill it one-third full of formula which should be warmed to about 100°F., or so that a drop feels warm but not hot on your wrist. Hold the bottle upside down to check milk flow. Milk should ooze slowly from the openings. If it doesn't, enlarge the holes with a red hot needle.

Place the nipple in the pup's mouth and hold the bottle at an angle such that the flow is not too fast and yet air cannot get into the nipple. After each feeding you *must* burp the puppy as you would a baby. Place him over your shoulder and pat or rub his back until all the air is out. This is the disadvantage of bottle feeding—air in the stomach quickly causes colic.

If the puppy is too weak to nurse, even on a bottle, but appears healthy and vigorous otherwise, I will tube feed, again using the same formula. Personally, I prefer diluted bitch's milk substitute in this case, as even the straight formula may be too rich at first. If a puppy is healthy, he should be ready to go to bottle feeding within seventy-two hours. I have rarely been able to raise a puppy that had to be tube fed longer than this.

Tube Feeding

If you must feed an entire litter or feed a sick puppy over a long period of time, learn to tube feed. At first it is a bit unnerving, but done properly it is better for the puppy and easier on you.

You will need a 10 cc. plastic or glass syringe and a No. 5 rubber catheter. You can obtain these from a vet supply house or from your local hospital. These tubes are used on premature human babies.

Hold the puppy with its head stretched forward. Put the tip of the tube at the puppy's last (rear) rib and, following the curve of the neck, measure to the end of his nose. Mark this point on the tube with a piece of white adhesive or a bit of nail polish. Now boil the tube and syringe to sterilize.

Below: Measure tube from last rib to tip of muzzle with puppy's head extended and mark tube with tape.
Right: Hold the puppy and slowly insert tube. Do not force. If you feel resistance, remove tube and try again. Dipping the tip of the tube in formula encourages the pup to swallow it.

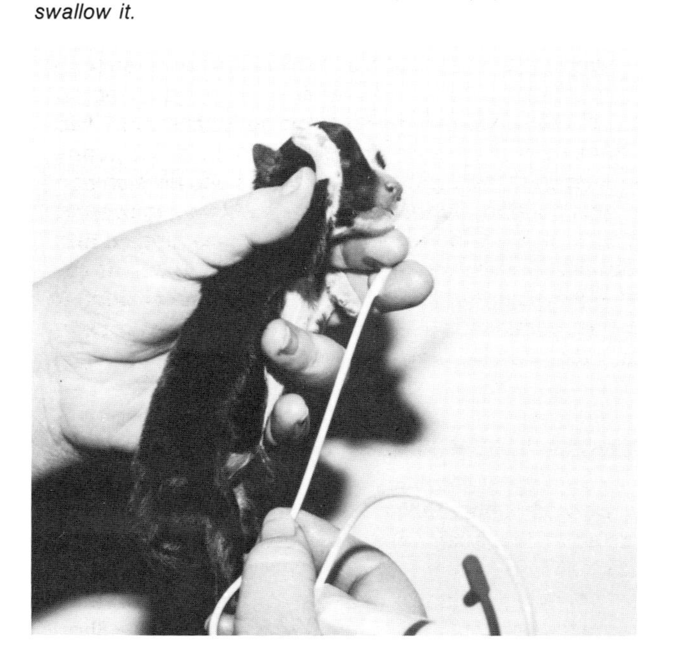

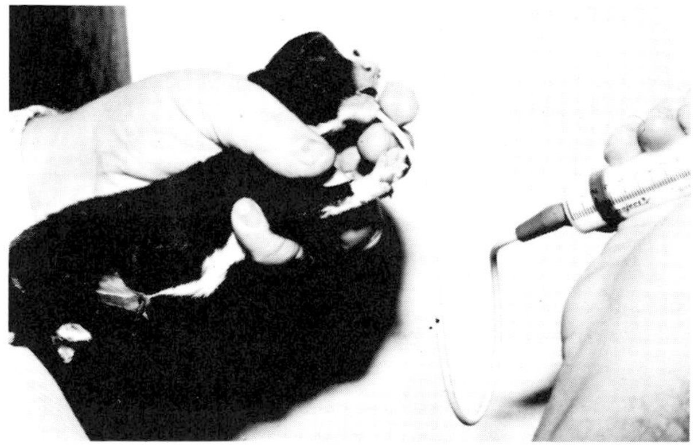

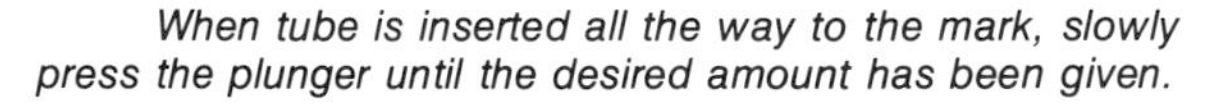

When tube is inserted all the way to the mark, slowly press the plunger until the desired amount has been given.

To feed, attach the tube to the syringe and draw up about one cc. more milk than the puppy will need. A tiny puppy should receive about one cc. at one hour intervals. The amount is increased slowly over the first few days and the intervals lengthened. Within a couple of days feedings should be two to three cc.'s every two to three hours.

Place the pup on its tummy, propped in a towel on a flat surface. Open the mouth and insert the tube. Since it probably is still dripping with milk, most puppies will start to swallow it on their own. It is important to keep the puppy's head downward and forward while inserting the tube. The tube will slide in easily if it is in the esophagus. If it hits an obstruction do not force it. Instead, withdraw the tube slowly and start over. It should slide in easily all the way to the mark which you made earlier. If it doesn't, it may be in the lungs.

There are two ways to check this if you are not sure. Remove the syringe from the tube and listen. If the tube is in the lungs instead of the stomach the pup's breathing should be quite audible when the tube end is held to your ear. You may also place the end of the tube in a glass of water. If bubbles appear the tube is in the lungs. The puppy can cry if the tube is in the esophagus, but he cannot cry if it is in the trachea. With a little experience you will be able to insert the tube into the stomach easily every time. Care is always necessary, however, for should you inject the liquid into the lungs by accident the puppy will take pneumonia and die. Luckily it is very rare that the tube does not enter the stomach as desired.

When you are sure the tube is all the way into the stomach, press the plunger of the syringe *very slowly* until about half the desired feeding is in. Check the stomach. It will begin to fill out. If it looks full and stretched, the puppy has had enough. If not, rest a second, then continue slowly forcing the liquid into the stomach until the full amount has been given. Wait a second more, then withdraw the tube quickly.

Check occasionally to make sure the dam is nursing and licking all the pups.

With practice you will be able to feed an entire litter in just a few minutes. The puppy exerts no energy in getting his food and strong puppies can soon go six hours between feedings. Be sure to carefully wash the tube and syringe between each meal.

How Much, When, and What to Feed

The easiest formula to feed is a bitch's milk supplement. These are readily available in either dry or liquid form at any pet supply store or from your veterinarian. If you use the dry form, mix only enough for one feeding at a time. Follow directions on the can for mixing and storing.

If you absolutely cannot obtain another supplement, mix one egg yolk with one-half cup of whole homogenized milk. Heat all formula to about 100° and test it on your wrist to make sure it does not feel either too hot or too cold.

Newborn puppies, very small, weak, or sick puppies should be fed every two hours. Larger, stronger puppies can get by with feedings every four hours. It is important to establish a schedule and try to stick with it. Irregular feedings cause colicky puppies. If the puppies cry between feedings they are probably hungry and either you are not feeding enough or you need to feed more often. No matter how hungry a puppy is, he should be fed slowly. A puppy that guzzles milk from a bottle will almost surely get colic.

Each puppy's need is an individual amount, and it depends on the weight and health of the pup. Sick puppies should not be overfed. In fact, it is always better to underfeed than to overfeed.

As a general rule, a twelve-ounce Sheltie puppy should get about 1½ oz. of formula a day. Divide this by the number of feedings per day to arrive at the amount per feeding. Six feedings, one every four hours, would mean that this puppy would receive ¼ oz. at each feeding.

If the puppy is small or ill, feed more often and not over one cc. each time at first. While a puppy on supplemental formula will not gain as fast as a pup raised on bitch's milk, he should gain at least an ounce every two or three days. If he is getting enough formula, the puppy will sleep contentedly between feedings and his stomach will look full and round. The puppy that is being overfed will look bloated and his stools will become curdled and yellowish. Cut the strength of the formula in half at the first sign of diarrhea and also cut back on the amount. If diarrhea continues you may want to switch to glucose in water for a few feedings.

DEWCLAW REMOVAL

Dewclaws are the fifth toe found high on the pastern of an adult dog. They are virtually useless and can easily be torn off or caught in weeds, wire, etc. Show dogs must have the rear dewclaws removed, and most breeders also remove the front ones for neatness and safety. Some Shelties are born with dewclaws only on the front, but others have dewclaws on all four legs; some even have double dewclaws.

Your veterinarian can remove the dewclaws for you when the pups are three to five days old, but this requires exposing the pups to the vets office at a tender age and extra stress to both puppies and dam. Removal is easily done at home.

The traditional method is to have someone assist in holding the puppies and removing the dewclaws when the pups are about three days old by the following method. Use a small curved mosquito hemostat. Good quality stainless steel ones are available from your vet clinic or a veterinary or hospital supply. Cheap hemostats won't clamp tightly enough—you must have professional quality.

Boil the hemostats for twenty minutes to sterilize them both before and after use. Wipe the dewclaw with alcohol or a cotton ball dipped in alcohol. Have someone hold the puppy on his back, pressing forefinger and thumb around the leg just above the dewclaw to be removed. (The dam should be out of the room.) Clamp the hemostat around the dewclaw as close to the leg as possible. Give it a quick twist, then flick the claw off with your fingernail. If it hangs on by a piece of skin, cut it with a sterilized surgical knife or cuticle scissors. Press a silver nitrate stick into the wound to stop any bleeding. If bleeding continues after a few minutes, apply a pressure bandage with gauze and adhesive tape.

Recently, however, I learned of a new and easier method from Barbara Thompson of Barwood. She comments that it is very easy to remove dewclaws by yourself, but cautions that you not try doing it unassisted unless you're already acquainted with the process.

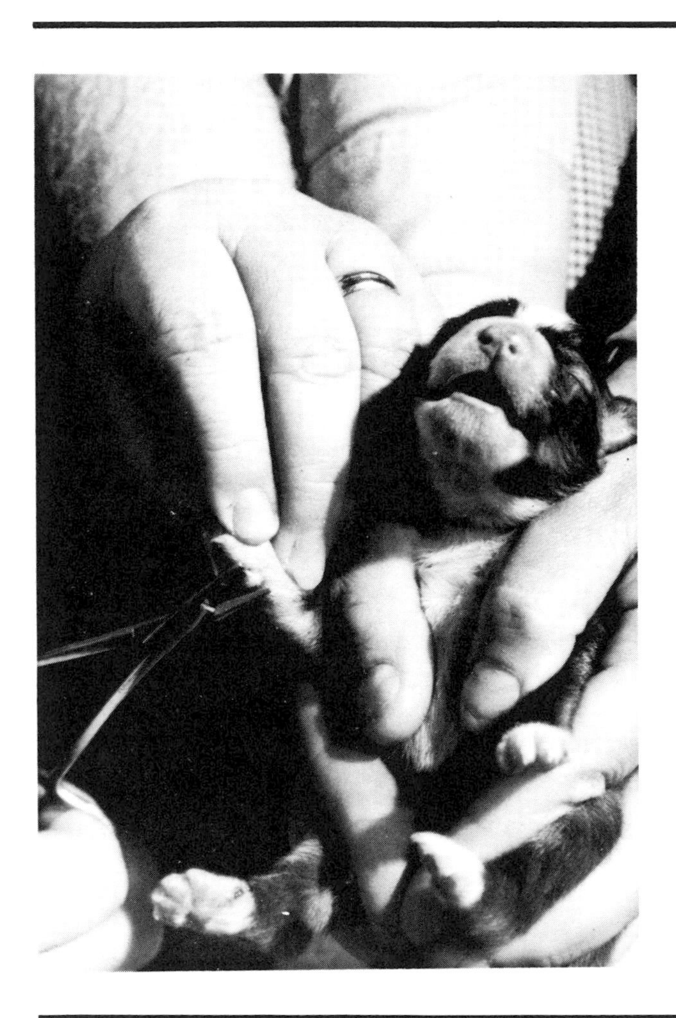

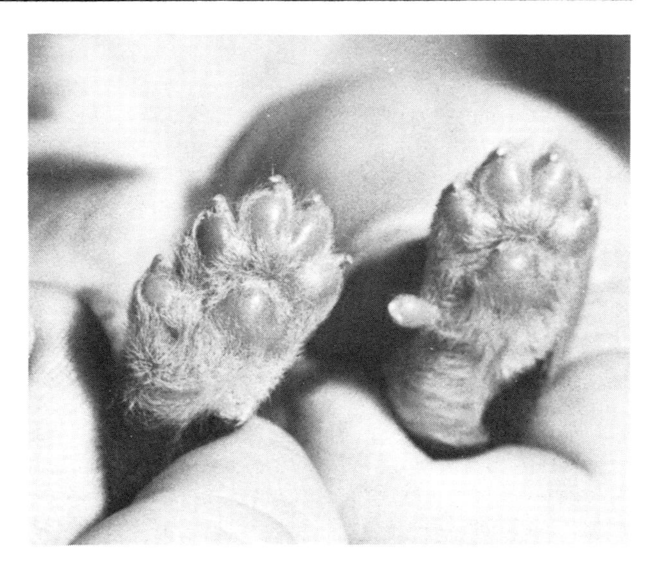

Dewclaws may be small and thin, fat and thick, or even double.

Have someone hold the puppy while you clamp the hemostat clear to the base of the dewclaw. Twist and flick off the dewclaw.

Dewclaw Removal At Birth

Mrs. Thompson's method follows:

"I've always had to wait until someone could come over to hold the pups for me. So one day when I had a litter due I prepared all the items for whelping plus all the necessary items for removing dew claws. At first I was nervous, but things worked out so beautifully that I've really enjoyed my new method.

The bitch whelps her first pup. I immediately grab the pup, put a hemostat on the cord and with a sharp scissors cut the after birth. I tear the sac away from the pup's head. Then I quickly put another hemostat on the first dew claw, flick if off, and repeat for the other dew claws on that pup. If there is bleeding I quickly stop it with the silver nitrate stick.

Next I tie the cord between the hemostat and the pup. I remove that hemostat and quickly pick the pup up and wrap it in a towel for a secure grip and then sling it a couple of times to remove any mucus. Rub the pup vigorously to get it breathing.

I know what you are thinking—the pup must be dead by now! The whole process is so swift and bloodless because the pup just lies there. You don't need anyone to hold it. If you time a dam from the time she whelps a pup until *she* gets it cleaned up and breathing, you will soon realize how easy it is for a skilled hand to safely do all that is necessary in a shorter period of time. I've never lost a pup doing this and have been thrilled at the results. The pups have *no* stress—they don't fuss that night and the wonderful part is that very few dewclaws bleed. Also, you can do it all yourself.

I place all hemostats and scissors in alcohol between puppies, and thoroughly boil them before and after every litter. I do not wipe each dewclaw with alcohol as is done at the five-day removal.

When the normal time comes for dewclaw removal, I breathe a sigh of relief."

TOENAILS

Nails should be clipped at three days and then twice a week thereafter to prevent them from scratching and injuring the mother's breasts. They are clipped just beyond the quick, the same as an adult Sheltie's nails, but using human fingernail clippers instead of large dog nail clippers.

DANGER SIGNS IN YOUNG PUPPIES

If you pick up a puppy and it feels limp, cold clammy or lifeless, you must act quickly to find and treat the cause. Common causes can be starvation, constipation (causing toxemia), overheating, or chilling.

Sick puppies are usually chilled, hypoglycemic, and dehydrated. Your immediate concern is to counteract these conditions. Chilled puppies may be warmed slowly. You can take the temperature of a newborn by inserting an infant's rectal thermometer one-half inch into the rectum. Environmental temperature should be monitored with an indoor thermometer placed on the floor of the whelping box. Humidity should be kept at 55 to 60 percent.

Giving the puppy a 5 to 15% glucose solution orally, 1 to 2 cc. every half hour aids in correcting both the hypoglycemia and dehydration. Very sick or chilled puppies should not be given formula as it will not be absorbed and may cause intestinal blockage.

If the puppies are placed on antibiotics, or if there are problems with diarrhea, most breeders give lactobacillus acidophilus or *Lactinex*™ to help restore normal intestinal flora. Giving a few drops of very fresh liver juice every few hours as soon as a puppy has started to recover may provide extra strength.

Chilling. First check the temperature of the box and adjust accordingly. A chilled puppy should be warmed gradually by rubbing briskly to stimulate circulation and then carried around under your shirt or coat. He can also be placed under a heat lamp or on a heating pad, but be careful not to cause shock by raising the temperature too quickly. Heating pads should be set on low or medium—never high—heat. Do not feed a chilled puppy until he has been thoroughly warmed as he will be unable to properly digest the formula or milk.

Constipation. If the pup's tummy is full and he appears normal colored and healthy, but he will not rouse and nurse, he may be toxic from constipation. Stimulate him by rubbing the tummy with cotton balls. If this does not bring relief and the puppy strains or whimpers or cries, give one cc. of warm water enema. You must inject the solution slowly so you do not cause too much pressure. If this does not give relief, get the puppy to a veterinarian right away as the bowel or rectum may be blocked, twisted, or ruptured and further stimulation could cause complications.

Overheating. An overheated puppy will cry and scream and may pant or hyperventilate. Remove him from the heat immediately and keep him quiet until his body has returned to normal temperature. He is usually red, limp, and exhausted.

Sore eyes. Occasionally a puppy's eye becomes puffy and pus accumulates under the lids. This must be removed by *gently* pressing around the eye socket to force the matter out of the lids, just as you would squeeze pus from a pimple. Clean the eye area with a cotton ball dipped in warm water. If the eyes are not yet open, the eyelid may have to be slit. Have your vet do this.

Diarrhea. This is common in puppies and may be caused by defective milk in the bitch, colic, overeating, incorrect formula mixtures when hand fed or any number of infections. Curdled, extremely foul-smelling or bright yellow feces are serious indications signaling a call to your veterinarian.

Ordinary diarrhea may be treated first with four drops of *Kaopectate*® every four hours. If the puppy is being hand fed, dilute the formula ½ strength, or feed only weak glucose water for 12 hours. If the diarrhea has not been curtailed in 12 hours, it is time to call your veterinarian. The puppy will probably require a course of antibiotics such as neomycin.

Be careful not to overdose antibiotics. A tiny Sheltie pup requires only one drop of neomycin every 12 hours. Overdose may cause fecal masses to accumulate so quickly that they block the intestine. Some antibiotics must be administered in liquid. Others may be dropped on the puppy's tongue. Follow exactly the directions given with the medication.

Prolonged diarrhea causes dehydration. To check for dehydration, pull up the skin on the pup's back between your thumb and forefinger and release. If the skin stays up in a ridge the puppy is dehydrated and will need injections of fluid in order to maintain life.

If you can't get to a vet, give subcutaneous injections of saline dextrose solution. For a three ounce puppy, six cc. saline dextrose should be sufficient. In a larger puppy, eight to 10 cc. should be administered. Inject just under the skin of the back and neck. You may have to put fluid in several locations, stopping when a puffy lump tightens the skin. A humidifier in the room with the puppies will help prevent dehydration. Lacking that, you can simply boil water and let the steam circulate about the room.

PUPPY DISEASES

Colic and Enteritis

A puppy that cries when it is touched and doubles up is probably colicky. This is common in puppies, as in babies, and generally is not cause for alarm. Usually colic is caused by gas in the stomach and intestines which is precipitated by the puppy swallowing air, either while bottle feeding, tube feeding, or nursing. Colic can also be caused by overeating or acid milk. Give the puppy four drops of *Kaopectate* and rub the tummy with cotton to stimulate the release of gas. If the puppy develops diarrhea, treat it accordingly. If the entire litter becomes colicky the cause is probably in the bitch's milk. Alkaline milk is common and necessitates hand feeding the litter.

Enteritis is a more serious stomach and intestinal inflammation. The puppy will scream and show obvious signs of intense abdominal pain, often occurring rather suddenly. Get the puppy to a veterinarian right away.

Pneumonia

Caused by a puppy getting chilled, getting milk or other fluid in the lungs or by a virus. Mechanical pneumonia caused from fluid going down the windpipe is probably most common. You will at first notice labored breathing followed by a rattling noise in the chest. The puppy will cry at first, then become limp and pale, later turning blue. Your vet can put the puppy on antibiotics, but the death rate is very high. Keep the puppy warm and tube feed if necessary.

Septicemia

Septicemia covers numerous conditions, usually caused by staphylococcus, strep, or other viruses transmitted to the puppy at birth from infection in the vagina of the bitch. An unclean environment can also contribute. Using unclean tools during whelping or when hand feeding is another cause.

Regardless, at the first sign of septicemia the puppy's feet, nose, lips, and tummy turn a bright purplish red. The puppy will cry incessantly, mew like a kitten, seem weak and refuse to nurse. The abdomen becomes bloated and the puppy rolls about aimlessly. Unless the infection is caught early and antibiotic treatment started, the puppies will die within twelve hours.

Occasionally a bitch regularly produces septicemic puppies. These bitches should be cultured while in season and again prior to whelping, and treated accordingly. In some cases the bitch must be placed on an antibiotic such as chlormycetin about a week before and two weeks after whelping. The antibiotic therapy will cause the puppies' teeth to be stained yellowish brown, and may contribute to monorchidism in males.

Canine Herpes Virus

Herpes is another virus that is apparently contracted through the vagina of a recently infected bitch. The virus attacks the liver where it causes severe damage and a high fatality rate in puppies under three weeks of age.

The first symptom is a profuse greenish yellow diarrhea. The puppies may be a week or more old, fat, and healthy. Suddenly they stop eating and scream endlessly, followed by shallow, labored breathing, vomiting or retching, gasping, and death. An autopsy will reveal liver damage, hemorrhaging from liver, kidneys, and lungs. The virus can usually be isolated.

If symptoms are caught early before the puppy starts to cry, you may be able to save it by raising the environmental temperature to 100° F. for 24 hours. Take the puppy off the dam and construct an incubator-like environment. High humidity must be maintained and fluids administered both by tube feeding and subcutaneously to prevent dehydration. If the puppy begins to snap back, give ½ cc. strained fresh liver blood twice daily in addition to the formula. Vitamin K_1 has also been suggested. Affected puppies may succumb to kidney failure at a later date.

Canine herpes is not associated with Herpes Simplex in humans, and the two viruses cannot be transmitted cross-species. However, humans can transmit the disease if they have been in contact with affected or carrier dogs and then handle puppies. If you have a recurrent problem with herpes in your kennel a preventative measure is giving gamma globulin serum to pregnant bitches and neonatal puppies. Feeding alfalfa, which contains vitamin K, may also help. Stringent cleanliness should be maintained.

Hypoglycemia

Hypoglycemia can strike newborn puppies for no apparent reason. It most commonly affects puppies under six ounces during the first three days of their life. A previously fat, healthy puppy may be found off in the corner of the box, weak, breathing irregularly, with a small bubbly froth around its lips. It may arch its neck backward and/or move in a circular motion. It may go into a seizure and become temporarily paralyzed. Afterward it will become very flaccid.

Treatment must be immediate. Subcutaneous injections of sterile glucose solution may be given, ½ cc. on each side of the shoulder or loin. Tube feed a mixture of 1 T. Karo syrup with 1 cup of canned goats milk diluted with 1 cup of distilled water.

Often entire litters will be affected, so it may be wise to treat the whole litter if one appears hypoglycemic.

Lymphocytic Myocarditis

This disease occurs in puppies three to ten weeks of age. Most of the puppies will appear robust and healthy until a few minutes or hours before they die. They may cry, try to vomit, and rapidly progress to prostration and death. Other pups have a more prolonged illness, developing respiratory failure, a heart murmur, and finally congestive heart failure.

Although no virus has yet been isolated, the disease is believed to be viral in nature. It affects all breeds and has been reported in all areas of the country.

Toxic Milk Syndrome

Bacterial toxins in the bitch's milk resulting from uterine infection or a retained afterbirth can produce very toxic effects in puppies up to two weeks of age. Sick puppies cry, bloat, have red protruding rectums, and diarrhea.

Take the puppies from the bitch and place them in an incubator. Give 5 to 15% glucose solution orally until the bloating subsides, then put them back on formula or give them to another lactating bitch if one is available and will take them.

The dam will need antibiotic treatment.

Check the bitch's temperature and watch for signs of vaginal discharge or infection. Be sure that the puppies are protected from draft, have adequate humidity, and are neither too hot or too cold.

If another puppy begins to exhibit symptoms similar to the puppy that died, take him to your veterinarian immediately or administer preventative medication as directed.

WHAT TO LOOK FOR:

The Healthy Puppy	The Sick Puppy
gains weight	doesn't gain weight
sleek, smooth coat	rough, dull coat
cries infrequently	cries frequently
good muscle and skin tone	limp, wrinkled skin
round, plump, firm body	flat, tucked up appearance
pink mucous membranes	pot-bellied
activated sleep	reddish-purple or blue mucous membranes
yawns frequently	scattered around the nest
nurses strongly	cries or mews
	diarrhea
	can't or won't suck

Careful observation will warn you of any complication. If your bitch seems abnormally depressed, anxious, or upset, it would be wise to have her checked. It is in whelping and caring for puppies and their mother, more than at any other time, that you and your vet will need to work as a team. Be sure to have a veterinarian you can trust and work with; then consult him regularly.

IF A PUPPY DIES

When one puppy in a litter dies but the remaining pups appear healthy, many breeders simply discard the dead puppy and make no further attempt to identify the cause of death. This is a mistake. If a puppy dies, whether from illness or for no apparent cause, you should have a post mortem examination done by a veterinary clinic or diagnostic laboratory. If an infection is suspected, ask that tissue be cultured to isolate the virus or bacteria. The sooner the cause of death can be determined, the better chance you have of protecting the health of the remaining pups. If you cannot get the body to the clinic immediately, place it in a plastic bag and freeze it for a few hours or a day.

After you have removed the dead puppy, bathe the bitch and let her out to exercise. Clean and disinfect the whelping box with 30% Clorox solution. Replace all newspapers and bedding with fresh, clean papers and towels. Wash any towels, cloth bedding or carpeting with detergent and Clorox, and disinfect the walls and floors in the whelping room.

Sources of Information:

Bulletin. Michigan State University, College of Veterinary Medicine, 1982.

Carlson and Griffon. *The Dog Owner's Home Veterinary Guide*. New York: Howell Book House, 1983.

The Fading Syndrome, Septicemia, and other puppy diseases. *Gaines Progress*, Summer, 1980.

Notes from a *Seminar on Canine Reproduction*. Colorado State University, 1981.

Please...Aren't they ready to be weaned? (Photo by Price)

Growing Pains 23

For the first three weeks the dam does most of the work of raising the puppies; you can just sit back and watch them grow. At this time the puppies' primary needs are warmth, food, sleep, and the security of their mother. They urinate and defecate only when stimulated by her licking, and seek her warmth as their own body temperature is not yet internally regulated. Their response to human touch is minimal, *unless* that human also provides food by supplemental feeding. Puppies that are supplemented by bottle feeding are the first to respond to human touch and voice. For that reason some breeders routinely offer a bottle to all the puppies once or twice daily as a means of early bonding.

During the first three weeks the breeder's primary responsibility is to observe. Continue to monitor growth rate, attend to any sick or uncomfortable puppies, and clean the box twice daily. Cleaning gives you an opportunity to pick up each puppy and examine it for normal color and activity. Hold the puppy securely, supporting the feet. To accustom the puppy to movement and restraint, turn it first to the left, then to the right. The next day, try holding it on its back. Cuddle it and provide security.

If the puppies are similarly marked they can be more easily identified if you place a different colored ribbon around each little neck. Yarn also makes a good identification collar, or you can paint nails or tails with nail polish for identification. Write down which puppy is wearing which color.

Nails should be trimmed every three days using a scissors type trimmer made for toy dogs or a human nail clipper. Be careful not to cut the nail too short—even puppy nails will bleed if you cut into the quick.

Somewhere between ten and fifteen days of age the puppies eyes open, followed by the opening of their previously sealed ears, and they begin to see, hear, and react. There's an old saying, "Last guy, smallest eye," which I believe often holds true. The puppy with eyes wide open at ten days may be the one with large, round eyes as an adult.

The day that a puppy begins to react to noise marks the beginning of the "socialization period," a critical development stage which lasts until he is twelve weeks of age. Almost overnight the puppy becomes a sensitive, responsive individual. He startles at loud noises, skitters into the corner when frightened, gurrs at threatening objects, and attempts to wage attacks on his brothers and sisters. Quiet around the puppy pen begins to wane. This is your cue to start handling the pups as much as possible and exposing them to a variety of stimuli.

THE THREE-WEEK-OLD

Suddenly the furry blobs crawling around the puppy pen become independent beings with personalities all their own. Signs of dominant or fearful behavior become evident. The dominant puppy will lie with his head on top of the other pups or his dam. He will shove and push the weaker brothers and sisters. Note this behavior on your records. Also note the effect it is having on the littermates.

"Perfection is attained by slow degrees; it requires the hand of time."

Voltaire

If there is a definite "underdog," that puppy should receive extra time and attention away from the others. He needs more reassurance, holding and cuddling, and also more opportunity to explore and build confidence without having to contend with the "bully." Don't baby fearful puppies. Reassure them; give them confidence; encourage them to experience new situations at their own pace.

Time passes quickly during this extremely critical week and there is much you can do. Your responsibilities become more important and more intense over the next several weeks until the time the puppies leave for new homes. *Lack of socialization and handling now can never be compensated for* by the new owner.

Short periods of cuddling away from dam and littermates are important. Pups can be introduced to various smells, sights, sounds, and tactile objects. A soft baby's ball with a bell inside is a favorite object of pups this age. Mobiles hung overhead provide objects to pull on and encourage the puppies to look up and become accustomed to overhead motion.

Depending on the maturity of the puppies, which will vary from one bloodline to another and also between the puppies in a litter, they may begin to lap milk from a bowl as early as three weeks of age. Shallow microwave containers in which some frozen dinners are packaged make excellent feed pans for Sheltie babies. The first few days the diet consists of warmed goats milk or *Esbilac*®. Start with two feedings daily, then increase to four feedings. When they are lapping milk easily, fill your blender with a high protein puppy chow and grind it finely. Store it in a closed container. For one or two meals, mix about 1 tablespoon of ground food with the goats milk to form a soupy gruel. After a few days, add more dog food until the mixture resembles the consistency of oatmeal. This is fed throughout the weaning period.

When the puppies begin walking, the whelping box or crate becomes too confining. Surround it with a portable exercise pen or homemade panels of wire mesh, or move the puppies to a raised floor pen such as the *Puppy-Aire*™. Puppies confined to dark areas or within solid walled boxes fail to develop stable personalities. The playpen should be located near your family's center of activity. From the twenty-first through twenty-eight day of age the puppies should not be overstressed, but should be exposed to voices, slamming doors, TV and radio, vacuum cleaners, children, doorbells, etc. Many breeders find the laundry room, family room, or kitchen to be a good location for the bitch and puppies during the next two weeks.

Don't overprotect puppies of this age, but due to the widespread incidence of parvo and corona viruses, do be careful not to allow visitors to come from kennels, shows, or public areas into the puppy room without disinfecting shoes and washing their hands. Avoid exposure to other dogs; and please, if at all possible, *don't* take puppies of this age with you to a dog show. Wait until they have been vaccinated.

Puppies should be handled individually at least twice daily. Begin placing them on various kinds of flooring—cement, carpet, papers, rubber mats, linoleum that is not so slick they cannot walk on it. Sit on the floor with the pup, allowing him to explore or seek the security of your body as he wishes.

Place a radio near the puppy pen and vary both volume and station. As you introduce new sights, sounds, and environment, encourage the puppies to become confident. Reassure them when they are frightened; do not allow them to hide or run away. Take care, however, not to deliberately frighten them, and never correct or punish a puppy of this age. A puppy that hangs back at three weeks is one to be concerned about. Give him a little extra time and attention; it may prevent shyness later. Pay attention also to the puppy that is afraid of loud noises.

Never too young to start if you're into obedience! Classic's Gifted Geraldine U.D. at six weeks. (Photo courtesy Alane Gomez.)

Submission to human restraint is also learned at this age. If, when you pick a puppy up he begins struggling and screaming, do not immediately put him down. Instead, hold him securely, supporting tummy and feet. Talk to him, calming him. Touching a puppy in the groin area is calming. You may have noticed his mother licking and nuzzling him in the groin.

Teach the puppy to submit to being held in an upright position, as well as to lying on his back and then on either side. Hold him in position for only a few seconds.

Begin now to teach a positive "baiting" response to food. Use a special noise or word to get the pup's attention each time you bring food—a sqeeker, jingle of your keychain, tap on the food bowl or side of the crate. The response quickly becomes ingrained and the sound can be transferred to get the pup to "bait" during show training.

FOUR WEEKS

Four-week-olds are much more nimble and coordinated. Their curiosity knows no bounds and they need as much stimulation as possible without introducing too much stress.

Puppies learn from playing; encourage them to play with your hands, as well as with toys. Anything they can roll, chew, pull, or climb over or into is fun. Be sure to choose toys made for dogs or those made of materials which are not harmful or will not break or splinter. Squeaky children's toys are easily torn and the rattle or squeaker can be accidently swallowed. Stuffed toys may be filled with harmful material. However, toys need not be expensive. Rubber balls and squeaky toys are standard, but discarded stuffed children's toys with eyes and buttons removed also make great playthings. Cut the bottom out of empty milk cartons or oatmeal boxes to provide small tunnels. Small cardboard boxes, wooden platforms with a ramp, empty bleach bottles with a few pebbles inside for noisemaking all provide cheap entertainment. Enjoyable toys can be created by braiding old nylon stockings, tieing a knot in both ends of a short piece of cotton rope, or tieing a rubber ball in the toe of an old sock. Fuzzy nylon pile stuffed with old nylon stockings can be fashioned into interesting playthings. Pieces of sheepskin and rawhide chewies are always welcomed.

During the next two weeks, continue taking the puppies one at a time into different areas of the house and encouraging them to explore. Teach them to follow your hand tapping on the floor or to follow a toy. Personalities are becoming more obvious, so begin making notes on each puppy's reaction to new situations and his overall behavior patterns. This will help you later in placing the right pup with the right family.

Keynote Cartoon, bred by Shelby Price, at eight weeks.

Puppies need a variety of playthings. (Photo courtesy Evelyn Peterson)

Socialization and human bonding begins in the fourth week. (Photo by Obermiller)

As soon as they are able to eat solid food, hand feeding or "baiting" may be introduced. Offer tidbits of meat or cheese so the puppy learns to accept from your hand. Do this individually, to teach attention, and also to the group so that they learn to compete. Discourage grabbing and biting by gently telling the pup "No Bite" and holding him back until the food is offered.

Most puppies have worms, and now is the time to check. If you don't want to go to the trouble of having stool samples examined, many breeders routinely worm with *Evict®* or *Erliworm®*, both of which are safe and effective against roundworm. Repeat in two weeks, with a stool check just prior to selling the puppies. If other types of worms are suspected, stool checks must be done and worming medication should be given according to veterinary supervision. This medication is stronger and the worms more difficult to eradicate.

By now the pups are receiving four meals daily of the ground-up puppy chow and goats milk. Mother, who is probably tired of the confinement, can be allowed to leave them for two hour intervals several times a day.

FIVE TO SEVEN WEEKS

These are perhaps the most critical weeks in your litter's development. The puppy's nervous system is growing rapidly and attention and time spent during this short period will reap the greatest rewards.

In good weather the pups can go outside during the day to explore a wider environment. Mild stress is important. Introduce the puppies to grass, dirt and gravel. Flashlights and colored lights can be used to provide visual stimulus. Place them in a hot or cold area for a few minutes. If possible, introduce them to young children—aha, automatic stress!

More challenging play areas can be created out of doors. Lawn chairs, tree limbs and rocks provide natural objects to explore. Plastic or ceramic drain pipes large enough in diameter that there is no danger of a puppy getting stuck in them make great tunnels to run through, sleep in, or jump over. A platform with two or three short steps is almost essential.

The bitch can be away from the pups for increasingly long periods now, but should be with them at night until they are six weeks old. The amount of food they are receiving is gradually increased, and cottage cheese, cooked eggs or hamburger will provide additional protein and vitamins. I do not believe in supplementing with calcium. Too much calcium is known to create bone deformities and other problems. Most puppy chow has adequate amounts of calcium, phosphorus, minerals and vitamins to meet the needs of growing Shelties. If a particular puppy has been sick or is slow to gain, add a vitamin-mineral tablet such as *Visorbits®* to his daily ration. In addition to the four meals of moistened gruel, six-week-old puppies can be allowed free access to dry puppy chow. Puppies raised on free feeding rarely overeat or become too fat.

Breeders and veterinarians alike are somewhat divided on the best routine for immunizations. If there is danger of exposure, puppies may be immunized with temporary vaccine as early as five weeks of age. My choice, and that of most other breeders, is to give killed canine parvovirus vaccine at 5 to 5½ weeks, followed by Distemper Measles vaccine at 5½ to 6 weeks. This provides safe temporary immunity and prepares for higher level of exposure when they leave home at seven weeks. Followup with permanent vaccinations is essential. We give combination modified live parvo at 10 weeks, followed by distemper, hepatitis and parainfluenza a week later, then a combination of DHLP and parvo at about 16 weeks. Some breeders vaccinate more frequently. Follow your veterinarian's advice, but DO NOT give the modified live combination shots prior to ten weeks. These vaccinations are not effective unless all maternal antibodies retained from nursing have cleared out of the puppy's system. Distemper measles vaccine and killed parvovirus, on the other hand, provide temporary immunity regardless of the titer level in the puppies. There is a period of overlap in which additional immunity is needed, but the titer level from the maternal antibodies is still high enough to prevent permanent adult vaccines from "taking." I know of an entire litter that died because the breeder gave the adult combination vaccine too early.

At six weeks the puppies are ready to be introduced to collar and lead. Leave a small buckled collar on each pup for an hour at a time. When he has become accustomed to wearing it, tie a foot long piece of clothesline cord to the collar and let the puppy drag it around during playtime. If you supervise, you can even leave it on or a few minutes while he is with his littermates—their tugging and pulling will get him used to resistance on the lead.

The puppy can also learn to stand and bait, both on the ground and on a table with a rubber surface. Expect him to stand still for only a few seconds. At this age, puppies are rapidly bored. Don't push them too hard. Make baiting and grooming fun times when they can count on your undivided attention.

I leash-train my puppies by sitting on the floor in front of the TV with the puppy on four-foot-long cord. Let him roam about and play as he wishes until he reaches the end of the cord. Coax him back to you with a piece of liver or cheese, reeling the leash in as he comes. Praise lavishly and give him a tidbit. Then repeat several times.

If the pup fights the lead when he hits the end of it, let him struggle for a few seconds to see if he will learn that the pressure releases when he comes towards you. If he does, coax him in and praise, But if he stubbornly pulls and struggles, just reach out and move him toward you with a hand under his tummy. Never drag him by the collar.

Keep the lessons short—one or two minutes daily. Never tire the puppy. Try to quit after he has performed successfully. Always give praise and a food reward. Soon, when you give a tug on the leash and a coaxing word, he will move toward you.

The next step is to walk away and have him follow the food for a few steps. Some puppies follow without a hassle. With another you can only progress a step or two at a time. Don't allow him to fight the leash. If he does, either walk in the direction he wants to go for a few steps or pick him up and start over. Hold the bait at his level. Over the next few days, gradually lengthen the distance you ask him to follow—but never more than two or three feet without a reward.

At this age the puppy can learn the meaning of the words "No," as well as "Off," (to command him to get off furniture or people). Hold the puppy by the scruff of his neck and give a firm shake as you tell him "No." He should also become acquainted with a praise word, such as "Good," and a calming word such as "Steady." These will be repeated many times during the next few months. Whatever word commands you use, share them with the puppy's new owner when he is sold.

The basics for housebreaking are easily begun when the puppies are still in puppy pen. By 28 days, puppies begin to use one area of their pen in which to urinate and defecate. Take advantage of their natural cleanliness by putting papers only in this area, not in the sleeping area. Gradually begin reducing the newspapers so that a smaller area is covered. Finally you will have only one fully opened paper left. The puppies are naturally training themselves to use a smaller and smaller area. They should be allowed free in the house *only* while someone is there to supervise them every second, and then they should always have access to an area with a newspaper—perhaps in front of the back door. As they grow older and have more control, you can substitute going outside for going on the papers.

Short car rides with the puppy on your lap are helpful and make the ride to a new home or to the veterinary clinic less traumatic. Take them to the park, around the block, or to the drive-in for ice cream. Crate training begins by feeding the puppies individually in a small airline crate. Before they are sold, they should be crated all night a few times. Lacking enough crates for all the pups in a litter? Let them take turns eating and sleeping in a crate for an hour or two during the day. If you don't have a crate, use a tall cardboard box or small wood-sided pen.

Show quality puppies should be introduced to baiting on a grooming table. If you don't have one, place a rubber bath mat on the washer or dryer. Get the puppy to accept food from your hand while on the table. Praise him and tell him how great he is. You instill confidence in a puppy by the way you speak to and about him and the way you handle him. Don't let him become overly dependent or a shrinking violet that clings to you for security. Develop a positive, confident attitude. Make him feel special.

This training and socialization requires only a few minutes each day, but is extremely important in determining the temperament, personality, and trainability of the adult Sheltie. *You can never go back and make up what you should have done during these few weeks.*

A nicely balanced 8-week-old, but I'd prefer cleaner cheekbones.

Even after weaning, puppies benefit from limited association with the dam, who provides reassurance and motherly discipline.

Puppies and kids are a natural. All pups should be exposed to handling by children by the time they are seven weeks of age. Puppies raised in a family with small children usually are well socialized.

SEVEN TO NINE WEEKS

The most critical period for puppies to relate to humans emotionally is their eighth week, or between 49 and 56 days of age. For this reason it is *not* the optimum time for weaning, shots, and sending the puppy to a new home. All this should be done before the 49th day. If the puppy has not been sold by then, wait a week or ten days. (Some Shelties seem to enter this critical period a bit later—perhaps 52 to 60 days of age.) Some puppies go through a frightened, traumatic stage. Others show few outward signs. Nevertheless, research has proven that stress or trauma during this one-week period may affect a dog's behavior for the rest of his life. So let your puppies play and assume a normal routine, but do not add new experiences or purposely stress them at this time. In other words, don't change the food, the environment, or the training routine—maintain a status quo.

A Puppy Aire pen with a Lectro Kennel heating pad makes for easy care of older puppies before and after weaning.

Ten-week old tri bitch bred by Yvonne DeFreitas. (Photo by Dear)

Lynnlea's Fortune Hunter, eight weeks, enjoys a romp in the leaves.

NINE TO TWELVE WEEKS

This is the key time for training. Housetraining, leash training, and association of words and commands are established now. In fact, dogs that are not trained during this time period show a marked reduction in responsiveness and ability to learn.

The puppy is ready for longer walks on lead. Carry him away from home at first and walk him back. Gradually take him to more distracting areas for his walk. Take him to a park or field and turn him loose. Walk away and encourage him to follow you for a short distance. He will soon learn to depend upon you to provide security and encouragement and will follow eagerly. Do not use a choke collar on a puppy under three months, and never tie a puppy for any length of time. He might panic and strangle.

As he approaches three months of age the puppy becomes more highly motivated to respond to praise and reward. He can begin learning basic obedience and even attend a kindergarten puppy training class if there is one in your area. He will enjoy short training sessions of about ten minutes each, followed by periods of romping and play.

If the puppy is still at home he should be totally separated from any remaining littermates and from his dam and should sleep and eat by himself.

It is easy to continue housebreaking. Take him out first thing in the morning before he has a chance to go in the house. Leave him out until he has finished his duties, then praise him and let him come inside to play. In a couple of hours, take him to the same spot outside, wait for him to go, praise, and bring him inside again. If he makes a mistake, tell him "Shame," and take him outside to the usual spot. A three-month-old should be dependable overnight and for one or two hours at a stretch during the day. He should *not* have the run of the house except under supervision. It is easier to establish good habits than to break old ones—especially after your carpet has retained the smell of urine.

THREE TO SIX MONTHS

During this next developmental period it is important that the owner establish himself as the "pack leader." This means that you must be in charge of the puppy—you set rules and he must obey them. Dogs are pack animals. If you will not be their leader, they will lead you. A dog will respect you if he knows you have set limits and are consistent in what you expect from him. "Sit" and "Come" are two commands that are especially important in establishing control.

The puppy begins to develop a sense of territory at this age. A few Shelties become somewhat aggressive. You must decide whether this will be allowed and discourge any unwanted behavior. This is also the time that

DEVELOPMENTAL STAGES OF A PUPPY

Age	Basic Needs	Behavior and Training
1-14 days (1st & 2nd week)	Warmth • Food Sleep • Mother	Not responsive to humans • Sleeps 90% of time Needs stimulation for urination & defecation
15-21 days (3rd & 4th week)	Warmth • Food Sleep • Mother	Eyes open • Begins to walk Should be handled carefully • Needs mother and littermates • First worming
22-35 days (4th & 5th week)	Socialization with canines and humans • Rest • Play	Begins to eat, bark, and play • Begins to respond to human voice Needs play and socialization outside the puppy pen
36-49 days (6th & 7th week)	Weaning • Separation from littermates • Human socialization	Strong dominant/subordinate relationships are developing • Motor skills improved • Temporary immunizations given • Capable of learning simple commands and being leash broken • May go to new home during seventh week
49-56 days (8th week)	Security • Love	Often termed the "fear period" • Puppy should not be frightened or unnecessarily stressed during this period
50-63 days (9-12 weeks)	Bonds to human • Learns to accept human as pack leader Socialization	Totally removed from dam and littermates • Capable of learning Come-Sit-Stay Needs confidence instilled • Begin housebreaking • Exposure to variety of environments important
64-112 days (12-16 weeks)	Security • Discipline Socialization • Attention	Learns by association • Goes through "avoidance period" Needs continued low-key socialization and exposure
113-168 days (16-24 weeks)	Socialization • Love • Consistent Discipline • Basic Training	Fully developed mentally; needs experience • Will attempt to establish dominance • Adapts a negative or positive attitude toward training at this time Praise lavishly for correct behavior
25-32 weeks (6-8 months)	Basic Training • Consistent discipline • Continued attention and socialization	Ready for beginning show or obedience classes • Attention span is lengthening • Needs continuing exposure to new situations • Males begin to assert dominance
33-56 weeks (8-12 months)	Continued socialization, reassurance and training • Affection and reassurance necessary	Show pups often in "puppy bloom" but should not be pushed too fast • Teething period ends • Puberty (period of sexual maturation) begins • May go through a second avoidance period • Neutering can be performed.
12-18 months (1-1½ years)	More disciplined and structured training • Love	Most Shelties out of coat at this age • First mating may take place • Training can be more intense, but most Shelties not ready for the stress of continuous showing.

puppies learn to bark. If you want to allow warning barks, let him bark one or two times when someone approaches and then distract him. If you are consistent he will learn the limits you set on barking. If he cannot be easily distracted, throw a pop can filled with pennies on the floor near him. Give him a sharp command, "No Bark."

Teething begins, and with it intense chewing. The puppy must learn what is and what is not acceptable for him to chew. Make sure that the baby teeth come out as the adult teeth come in. Retained puppy canines must be pulled so the adult ones can come in straight.

SIX TO TWELVE MONTHS

Between six and twelve months the Sheltie puppy goes from a happy-go-lucky, pretty ball of fluff and fun to a stately prince or princess, and then to a naked, ugly duckling. A great deal of change is taking place, and the puppy needs love, attention, and security as much as any other time.

Some puppies are ready for formal obedience and conformation training at six months; others are just too silly and immature. You must look at each pup as an individual and decide when to start formal training on the

Ch. Barwoods Dominator as a young puppy. Note exquisite almond eye and sweet expression. (Courtesy Barbara Thompson)

Holiday puppies? Try to get them into new homes before or after the holiday. Traumatic experiences are best handled during non-stressful days

Keynote Sugar 'N' Spice, a typical, leggy six-month-old just coating up. Owner, Shelby Price.

Somewhere around four months, the pup goes through an "avoidance period." He will become fearful and unsure of himself, difficult to catch, and suspicious of new people and environments. He will probably be rebellious and stubborn. The shy puppy can become a real problem during this stage.

Ease off on training and discipline of quiet, reserved puppies. Just reassure and enjoy your puppy. Don't neglect socialization—it is very important that the Sheltie puppy continue to be exposed to many different people and situations. But don't push him. In another month he will have more confidence and feel more cooperative.

basis of his maturity. Forcing an immature puppy to perform may totally ruin his attitude and cooperation later.

Show puppies should be kept in lean, hard condition by regulating their food and play. They are not ready for road work or long training sessions. Neither are most individuals ready to be sent out with a handler. If you show your puppy, take him yourself. Give him reassurance and time. If he has an off day leave him in the exercise pen and just play with him.

Somewhere between eight and ten months the Sheltie puppy reaches the age of puberty. The male pup suddenly is interested in every girl dog around. The bitch pup will come in heat the first time at around ten months. Puberty is usually accompanied by another period of fear, lack of confidence, and sometimes erratic behavior. Be patient. Don't overstress a puppy during this time. This is not the time for a major trip to a show, a big push in the obedience class, or a major change of environment. Once again the puppy must be given consistent discipline, a steadying hand, and time. And once again I must remind you that avoiding stress does not mean that you put your puppy in the closet—although about now you may feel like it. If you want him or her to become a friendly, outgoing adult, you must continue to socialize. Take the pup along to classes, matches, or shows and just let him sit it out on the sidelines. Go for walks at the park or the shopping center. Let him meet people and continue to have new and varied experiences; just don't ask more of him than he seems able to handle.

Some puppies snap out of this second avoidance stage quickly. Others go through a lengthy period of shying, not wanting to show, sulking in training, or generally acting like freaks until they are about fourteen months. Whatever they do, this is not the time to give up and put them in the kennel until they grow out of it.

The goal! Twenty-month-old Ch. Happy Glen Royal Dream just coming into mature show condition. Later he went Best in Show from the classes. Owners, Marvin and Barbara Ross. (Photo by Jan)

At around a year of age, sooner or later depending on the season of the year, your beautiful baby will lose the bouyant puppy coat and will spend the better part of the next year in rags and tatters. Ears go up. Faults hang out. The puppy may be overactive and not want to eat; He looks narrow and gangly. Or he may stay fat and sleek with a moderate coat, looking as if he is mature but just didn't quite pan out to be the beautiful animal you had hoped. Don't panic. I call it "the yearling yuks." If he was a promising youngster, don't scrap him now. In another year, nature may just work a miracle and the ugly duckling will turn into cinderella (or cinderfella)! Keep up the training and socialization and let your puppy enjoy his youth. The Sheltie that is perfectly mature and solidly stable at a year often ends up too overdone or as a deadheaded, lazy adult. The immature, awkward, undeveloped skatterbrain may become the perfectly mannered, enthusiastic worker or the show dog that holds into old age. Our breed is not noted for early maturation—but there are many beautiful, energetic old Shelties still bringing joy to their owners years after puppy-mates from faster maturing breeds are gone. Your silly, awkward, gangling one-year-old may be a blessing in disguise.

Robrovin Oh Susanna and her three-week-old son, future Am. Can. Ch. Robrovin Johnny Appleseed. Owners, Lorraine and Robert Still.

Pick of the Litter 24

When word got out that *Sheltie Talk* was being revised, the requests flooded in—"we want more on puppy development and picking puppies." Everyone in this breed wishes they had the magic formula—the method for selecting their next champion at eight weeks of age. No more growing out three pups to have every one go off at six or eight months of age. No more selling the less promising puppy at eight weeks because we can't keep them all and having the owner bring him by at two years old looking every bit a champion...but he's been neutered. The truth is, Shelties are not an easy breed to pick, and nature has a way of fooling the most experienced.

There are some guidelines, however, which we will attempt to share with you. It is especially important to know the line you are working with, since different lines mature quite differently. If you are a new Sheltie breeder, ask other more experienced breeders working with the same basic bloodlines to help pick your puppies. Listen carefully; get more than one opinion if there are qualified breeders available; then make your own decision. Careful notes and photo records are the most helpful methods of learning to make good judgements. After a few litters you will begin to recognize the outstanding pup and the ones that don't stand a chance of making it to the show ring. Judging the others—those good, sound but not outstanding pups—takes an experienced eye, a bit of luck, and a lifetime of learning. But that is what makes our breed such a challenge.

BIRTH TO THREE WEEKS

Between one and three weeks puppies are difficult to assess. I like to evaluate puppies at birth and at three days of age. If the litter is weak, tiny, or premature, evaluations at this age are almost useless, but if the puppies are fat, healthy (five-ounces or more pups at birth) some judgements may be made. Look for bone, square head with full muzzle, clean cheeks, and length of neck. Birth weight and size is not an indication of adult size except in the case of the tiny runt in a litter of average size puppies that does not rapidly catch up, or the huge puppy with tremendous bone and head size appearing in a litter of average size pups. Usually, unless these pups level out to the size of their littermates in the first three weeks, you can expect them to remain the runt or the moose of the litter as the case may be.

Evaluation at this age is based primarily on heads. Look for a blocky head with a very definite stop and full rounded foreface. If the underjaw is not apparent at this age, it rarely develops later. Instead, heavy underjaws tend to lessen or recede at four weeks, but if present at an early age, should come back later. Cheeks should be flat. Domey skulls may flatten later, but bumpy cheekbones rarely smooth out. Stops are deeper than they will appear later. Overfilled stops sometimes correct, but basic head planes, depth of backskull, and proportion of foreface to backskull are evident now.

THREE TO FOUR WEEKS

Eye shape and size is often apparent by three weeks, and the really melting expression can be picked out at this age. However, eyes may become rounder and larger as the puppy grows. The way the eye sets into the skull will tell you a great deal. Eyes set too far to the front tend to become round and large. Eyes that are set too obliquely will never have the correct Sheltie expression. Eye rims should be dark. White haws will be evident as soon as the eyes open, but generally recede and become barely noticeable by the eighth or twelfth week, although I have had some puppies with white eye haws that did not recede until the dog was nearly a year old. And, or course, some never recede and may detract from the expression.

Note the squared off wedge, definite stop, and full round muzzle on this three week old.

Pet puppies at about three weeks. Note especially the eye shape, proportion of muzzle to backskull, and lack of foreface on the pup in front. (Photo by E. Wishnow.)

Structure is more difficult to evaluate. Look for the puppy that stands foursquare and solid. Bodies at this age should appear compact and short. A long-bodied puppy at three weeks may look like a freight train at seven months. Balance and elegance become evident when the puppies are moving about well. A balanced puppy can rarely exhibit too much bone at this age, although out of proportion head, feet, or bone warns of oversize.

The best puppies look as if they have it all together most of the time. They are quite stocky compared to the adult, but at the same time have a look of elegance. The proud, confident ones who like to show off, have a real desire to please and an affinity for you, provided they are also sound and well balanced, should be your choice for showing.

Puppy coats come in all different types—some thick and furry, others long and fluffy like powder puffs, and still others flat and sleek like first cousin to a chihuahua. Puppy coat is not an indication of the amount of adult coat, but the presence of long guard hairs will indicate length, and the fluffy, double coated puppies generally carry a very full puppy coat throughout their first year, while the smoother-coated pups may not develop a good coat until late puppyhood (eight or nine months of age). At five or six weeks of age when the undercoat really starts coming in the sables and tricolors turn a mousy color. Check the hair at the back of the ears and top of the skull for an indication of their adult color. Mahogany sables begin to get long black guard hairs at this age, and golden sables will appear extremely washed out for a time.

SELLING THE PETS

By the time the litter is seven weeks old, time and space require that some of the puppies be sold to pet homes. You may want to let some show prospects go at seven or nine weeks also. The real problem now is not which puppy is pick of litter, but how good is the pick, and further, where does show quality stop and pet quality begin.

At this age puppies should move fairly true coming and going. Have someone call the puppy away from you so that he moves freely at a trot. Loose movement is not serious at this age, but cow hocks, hocking out, and crooked fronts will be fairly obvious and are unlikely to correct. Any really poor mover at this age should be culled. Instead of improving, poor movement may deteriorate further as the legs lengthen.

Side gait is easier to evaluate. The puppy that naturally falls into a trot is usually built correctly. The more effortlessly he moves, the less bounce, and the longer the stride, the better. A puppy with a short, choppy gait or one that never trots because he can't keep up with the others is a poor choice. Puppies with extreme reach and drive at this age may seem uncoordinated and a bit wobbly, but this should tighten and improve with maturity.

Overall balance and bone are more apparent now. A long neck may be hidden in puppy fuzz, but you should be able to feel the nice arch if it is going to be there, and the puppy should be pulling its neck up and using it. Bodies should still appear somewhat cobby. The weedy, nicely proportioned, but my Sea Isle linebred puppies, if over the chart at this age, rarely stay in. Huge bone and large joints indicate a great deal of growth potential. Another good indicator is head size. Theoretically, a puppy will grow until he grows into his feet and head. If he looks out of proportion he may have a lot of growing to do. Size of the nose leather may also give a clue to adult size.

Bites should be correct. Male puppies, ideally, have their testicles, although some do not come down until quite a bit later. The head is beginning to lengthen—but the same principles apply—a good head still has parallel planes, is not excessively deep in backskull as viewed from the side, and the length of foreface and backskull should be approximately equal. From the front, the head should form a blunt wedge. Cheekbones should be smooth, and there should be no prominent bumps or holes under the eyes. A bump above the eyes or a domey topskull may flatten. Quite often the seven-week-old will have less fill of muzzle and less underjaw than he had earlier. This may fill, but the muzzle should still appear well-rounded and the underjaw should not recede too much. The really snipey puppies should go as pets. Those puppies that formerly had full, rounded muzzles should come back. You may want to grow them out a bit longer. Your judgement here will depend somewhat on what was there earlier.

Pet puppy at eight weeks. Not enough foreface; too tiny.

Courseness in a young pup. Wideset ears. A candidate for oversize.

Another sweet pet puppy at seven weeks. Note large ears, lack of foreface.

extreme or long-bodied pup will become rangey, and the dumpy eight-week-old rarely becomes more elegant.

All four feet should point forward, not out at an angle. Very young puppies and puppies raised on wire may temporarily have splayed toes, but these should tighten up by ten weeks of age. Pasterns should be correct. Short, straight or weak pasterns are evident at this age and rarely change. Angulation front and rear approximates the adult, but shoulder angles often change during the coming months. Angulation rarely improves over what it is at seven weeks, and may, instead, get straighter.

At seven weeks you can tell something about size. Refer to the size chart in chapter 6. I have found that the Banchory crosses can be as much as an inch over chart at this age and still stay in size if they are balanced and

A lovely 10-week-old bitch puppy, probably Banchory line. Sometimes this much puppy at 10 weeks is extreme and/or oversize as an adult. (Photo by Dear)

A bitch linebred on Peter, about the same age. This one ended up a petite 14½ inches.

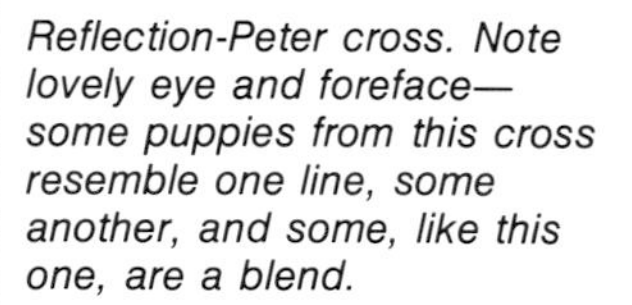

Reflection-Peter cross. Note lovely eye and foreface—some puppies from this cross resemble one line, some another, and some, like this one, are a blend.

Ch. Banchory A Blue Nun and Ch. Banchory Color My World as puppies. Compare with Sea Isle line pups (right) about the same age. (Photo by Krook)

Ch. Willow Wand All A Glow (left) and Ch. Willow Wand Touchdown (center) at 4 months. A leggy, awkward stage for these linebred Peter pups.

at 5 weeks.

Which puppy would you pick? Two puppies from Ch. Canden Kinni Charisma's litter by Banchory Reflection. Note the difference in type and early maturation achieved by outcrossing to the Banchory line.

Canden Count the Ways at 8 weeks. Note the elegant head carriage.

Color Guard of Kinni at 10 weeks. Note bone and substance.

Canden Count the Ways at eight months taking a five point Specialty win. (MikRon photo)

Ch. Color Guard of Kinni as a mature adult. He never "went off," but just consistently matured. He finished his championship at age 4. (Phogo by Jan)

Eyes tend to get rounder and larger, so the shape at this age should be excellent. Ears should be up on the head and tipping forward about half way. During the next few weeks they will go up further. Low ears will be evident and should be glued.

Light eye rims may be hereditary or the result of lack of vitamin A (from sunlight). Eye color is obvious. Light eyes will not darken.

NINE TO TWELVE WEEKS

The quality of a show puppy becomes more evident during these next few weeks. Movement will tighten. Personality, poise, and presence becomes more obvious and should certainly have some bearing on your selection of a show puppy. The most beautiful dog will never make it in the ring without that extra pizzaz and "look at me" attitude.

Except for the exceptional puppy that is always at the bottom or top of the size chart, size becomes easier to evaluate. The big puppy that begins to slow down and drop under the chart at ten to twelve weeks will probably stay in. The tiny puppy, if it is to make show size, should begin to grow at this age. A growth spurt between ten and fourteen weeks accompanied by large knuckles and a gangly look is a good clue that the pup will go over.

Structural and gait faults, except for looseness and playful prancing, will *not* improve. Bites that are off now, or forefaces that are too snipey, rarely get better. The best puppies remain balanced, sound, and elegant. Heads take on more the shape they will have as adults, and ear size and set, although still correctable, will be apparent. Problem ears should be "in training" at this age if you expect to have any permanent effect.

FOUR TO SIX MONTHS

Anything can happen now. Rarely does a Sheltie stay in balance and look really promising all through puppyhood. A few "ugly ducklings" become lovely specimens at six months, and many, many glamourous puppies go off during this age and some never regain their early promise. The safest bets for showing retain a certain amount of balance and poise through all the growth stages.

Study the photos throughout this chapter—they are worth a thousand words. And, if your really promising puppy goes off between four and six months, wait him out unless the fault is really severe. Even bites can come in a little crooked and later correct. Check to make sure the puppy canine teeth come out before the adult canines start to come in or the puppy teeth will force the new ones to grow at an angle.

Puppies this age need love and encouragement and plenty of room to romp and play. Their muscles are not ready for road work or jumping. Even jumping in kennel runs or against fences should be discouraged as it can cause elbows or hocks to go out. I like to see my show pups in good weight but not fat. Overweight puppies are also prone to bone and muscle malformation, sloppy movement, and broken down pasterns.

Coats need only to be kept clean, brushed, and occasionally misted with water. Coat texture and volume at this age is still soft and may be either sparse or very fluffy. If you have a beautifully coated puppy, enjoy the luxury. But if your prize baby is still sparsely coated, don't despair, it may still come at seven to nine months.

Lovely pup at 10 weeks— but there's too much of her. Note large knuckles. She went oversize.

THE TEENAGER

At six months the body proportions are nearing the adult outline, although the puppy is still undeveloped in chest and immature in gait. Between six months and one year topskulls flatten, holes fill, and underjaw and muzzle fill. Stops should become clean and distinct if they are ever going to be. Teething creates some bumpiness, but after the molars come in the muzzle fills and smooths, although this process continues in some lines up through the second year. Ears may be erratic all through the first year.

Some puppies, especially bitches, stop growing at six or seven months. A few grow until a year or even fifteen months of age. Most males stop or at least grow only minutely after nine months.

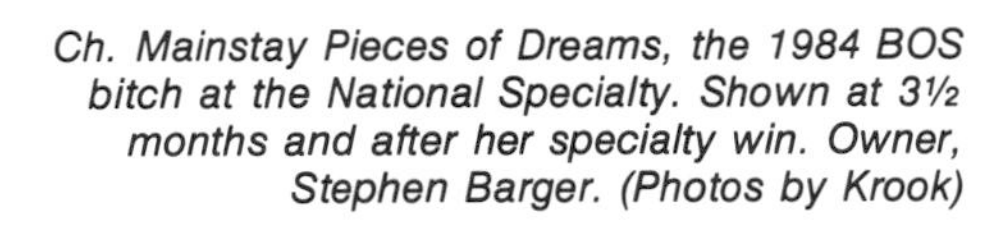

Ch. Mainstay Pieces of Dreams, the 1984 BOS bitch at the National Specialty. Shown at 3½ months and after her specialty win. Owner, Stephen Barger. (Photos by Krook)

Ch. Marwal Joshua of Jericho, a Ch. Calcurt Luke son, at 8 weeks old and after winning the Veteran Dog class at the National Specialty in 1983. Owner, Margaret Huening, Marwal. (Adult photo by Krook)

Ch. Ilemist the Iconoclast, a son of Banchory Reflection, at 10 weeks, 7 months, and 3 years. Note how this dog simply grew up and filled out...a rarity in Shelties. Owner, Julie Desi Maust and Pam Kitchin. (Carillon photos)

Rosmoor Once again at 4 months and at 10 months after winning second in the puppy herding group at a large match. Owner, Rose and Jennie Tomlin. (Photos by Krook and Gilbert)

Ch. Rockwoods Gold Strike, by Ch. Rorralore Sportin' Chance, at 3½ months, and as a mature adult. Note the elegant outline, bone, and underjaw as a youngster. Owner, Barbara Kenealy, Rockwod.

Ch. Ashford Promises Promises C.D. at 3 months, and 3 years of age. Owners, Ray and Dorothy Christiansen, Lynnlea.

Happy Glen's Flaming Fantasy, dam of BIS Ch. Happy Glen Royal Dream, at 11 weeks, 4 months, and taking a BOS win at 5 years of age. Owners, Barbara and Marvin Ross. (Adult photo by Lindemaier)

WHEN TO GIVE UP

Most Shelties go through at least one growth stage that makes you wonder why in the world you kept them. They may be thin, shelly, and gawky. Always base your decision to keep or discard a show prospect on what you know about the line, how the parents developed, and what the puppy was like at a previous stage. If a puppy showed exceptional early promise there is a good chance it will come back. If, on the other hand, you have kept a puppy that was mediocre as a baby, always hoping he will "come on" but at six months you are still hoping—forget him.

A Thunder Blue Daughter at nine weeks. Note lovely eye, full round muzzle, head proportion.

Banchory Private Lessons at three months. Heads become very fuzzy. Note eye, muzzle, bone and outline.

DEVELOPMENT IN THE VARIOUS LINES.

Not all Shelties develop in the same way. What you would pick in a Banchory puppy at eight weeks does not necessarily apply to what you would pick in another line. We asked some breeders to share with us how they make their selections.

Banchory

Donna Harden

Although type within a litter of Banchory pups does not vary that much, two categories of puppies are seen, differing primarily in size and onset of maturity. Some puppies are large, heavy-boned youngsters that hold type and balance all through puppyhood. Others are smaller pups, slower to come on, and less substantial. These small pups must have excellent finish of underjaw. If it isn't there in the first place, it won't come later. They should also be balanced. If these qualities are present in the young pups, the smaller pups may end up the pick of litter at six months.

Most Banchory puppies "fall apart" between four and six months of age. Shoulders may flatten, elbows are loose, rears high, and backs long. Balance may be off. But at six or seven months of age the top show pups should at least start pulling it together.

Banchory heads look unusually mature and even young pups have full rounded muzzles and deep, well-finished underjaws. The skull should be a clean, smooth wedge tapering slightly from ears to nose. The heads hold and the puppies grow up around their heads and into them. Skulls rarely widen with age. Those with wide, pie-shaped skulls should be weeded out early.

Fronts go through drastic stages. If a pup has a decent length and angle of upper arm, the shoulder blade usually lays back to match eventually. But shoulder blades "float" causing measurements to vary considerably and dogs to go through stages where the shoulder may appear very straight.

The old Sea Isle size chart is accurate for Banchory pups and those that are over it at three or four months of age usually go oversize. The rapidly growing pup that always stays in balance will usually stop growing in size at six to eight months. The eight or ten week old that is huge, with massive underjaw, is headed for oversize.

A typical four month old. Some Banchory pups get leggy, long, and very smooth coated at this age. Bumps may appear on the cheeks due to teething, but if the head was smooth before it will smooth out again later.

Can. Ch. Akirene's Command Performance, a male, at three months. Excellent outline, angulation, and balance are evident at this age. Owned by Akirene.

Banchory Brown Sugar at 6½ months. This is a pretty age for Banchory pups. Coat is good, neck and balance evident, and they are beginning to come together.

Can. Ch. Banchory Backstreet Blues, typical 8-month old blue bitch, now owned by Akirene.

Ch. Banchory Strike Me Silver, a Formal Notice son, at 5½ months.

Ch. Banchory Strike Me Silver as an adult.

Barwood

Barbara Thompson

My present line of dogs is basic Sea Isle—namely Peter—with an introduction from Banchory through the Formal Notice son Barwoods Formal Attire. When line-breeding or inbreeding, type varies very little within our litters. Outcrossing finds my bitches to be very strong for the family look.

Most Barwood puppies go through the ganglies at three to six months. Rears should remain fairly stable, but a full, round foreface at eight weeks and three months. Skulls are flat but often they don't completely finish development until the dogs are three years of age. However, you can get a fairly good idea of what you have at about one year. After that it is very slow to fill.

Eye set can usually be seen at three weeks; then the eyes can become very round again. At three-and-a-half months when the head has lengthened we want to see the almond eye and proper set in the head as large, round eyes at this age never develop the soft, sweet expression desired.

Ch. Barwoods Rhapsody at 3½ months.

Rhapsody at 5½ months. Note nice eye, angulation, straight legs.

Ch. Barwoods Rhapsody, dam of several champions, as an adult. (Photo by Booth)

fronts really do awful things sometimes. By eight months the basic dog is there and if I don't like the way they stand or they are not balanced, they won't ever be suitable. By eight months they are usually past their problems.

The underjaw and the balance of the head—muzzle to backskull—should be there at three weeks. After this the foreface tends to "fall away" and doesn't fully appear again until maturity. However, it is always desirable to have

Along with the growth charts, I also use the size of feet and knuckles at eight weeks and three months to monitor size. The tiny puppy that catches up quickly should be considered carefully; he is a candidate for oversize. Females are usually fully grown at eight to nine months. Males grow slightly after this. They are deep in chest and heavy in coat by eight months. At 1½ years, movement has improved tremendously.

Barwoods Formal Attire at 4 and 5½ months. Compare with Rhapsody and you can see the effect Formal Notice had on both outline and earlier maturation.

Buffy at 4½ weeks. Note bone, substance, straight forelegs.

Ch. Barwood Magic Moment at 8 wks. shows nice eye, head balance, and full foreface.

At 7 months she has elegance, outline, balance, and nice profile.

Kismet

Guy and Thelma Mauldin

Expect to see at birth pretty much the same type head as what we expect as an adult—full muzzle, flat topskull, decent stop. Our pups usually have nice arch of neck at birth, also. The head should be rectangular.

At eight weeks we start looking at how the pups move, particularly how they handle their rears. We also watch for good tail carriage as that has been somewhat of a problem.

At three months heads may become a little domey—something we don't worry about. It is also permissible for the foreface to diminish, but it should have filled in again by a year to a year-and-a-half. We generally grow out all puppies until at least three months of age, and the more promising ones are held until four or five months. Most pups can be judged on size according to the size chart in *Sheltie Talk,* but some pups that were bigger at a given age did not go oversize.

The "fall apart" stage for Kismet puppies occurs around five or six months of age and those pups usually

Ch. Kismet's Conquistador, a High Born son, at 7 months and as a mature adult. Note that the head simply filled out and matured with very little change.

Ch. Kismets Status Quo winning a puppy class at six months. (MikRon photo)

Ch. Kismets Status Quo going BOB at the 1981 ASSA Specialty at age 5.

don't come back together until they are a year old. Some stay balanced and just slowly mature. Front and rear angulation improve with age, but length of hock never improves. Kismet dogs are normally ready for the show ring between eighteen months and two years of age, although there have been exceptions.

Macdega

Tom Coen

The Peter-Luke sables usually develop more slowly than those in combination with Reflection. The "knockout" puppies in this family are rarely the most pleasing adults, and often become overdone and out of balance. The Reflection crosses can be more finished in head at an early age.

Other than this small difference, a good puppy is a good puppy and the selection for head, structure, angulation and outline, expression and temperament is the same no matter what the breeding. The Piano Man and Proof Positive puppies often show a remarkable maturity compared to the sables and yet they also hold their quality (or even seem to be less dog) with age, a definite must in this breeding program.

Peter-Luke puppies usually look least attractive between three and six months. Muzzle can disappear, ears can go haywire, coats flat, and in the tight Peter breedings front legs can seem impossible to set up correctly. With time, exercise, and proper nutrition, these problems correct themselves. Rears should never appear cowhocked or spraddle hocked. Spring of rib comes late in this line—after a litter or as late as three years in males.

Yearlings from the Peter line may appear shelly and males particularly need depth of chest and spring of rib. They are only approaching maturity at three, and continue to change subtly throughout their lifetime, but hold their quality well into old age. Frontal bones flatten, skulls fill in, and muzzles become rounder with maturity.

Ch. Philidove Kismet Heir Borne ("Mario") at 7 months.

Betty Whelen and Designed by Pocono, by Ch. Karelane Royal Flush. Note full muzzle and earset on this puppy.

Pocono

Betty Whelen

I do not pay much attention to new puppies except to be sure they are doing well. Around five weeks I like to see a square wedge shaped head with a definite stop right between the eyes. From a side view I want a slight, straight rise to the skull, which should be flat. I like to see ears small at the base and set high on the skull. I do not keep puppies as show quality with long, sliding stops or large heavy ears. I want to see a definite wedge with full, round muzzle and underjaw (not overdone).

I do not look for angulation until the puppy is two or three months old. I like medium body length, not too long or too short, and I like to see plenty of neck and good bone according to the size of the puppy.

I follow the size chart in *Sheltie Talk* religiously and get rid of the large ones as pets. Size to me has gotten out of control—too many champions today are well over the size limit and are used for breeding indiscriminately. If you have size back of your dogs, you are going to keep getting it. Use a good small Sheltie with your larger one, then line-breed and you will have more consistency in your litters as time goes on.

I like to see a good puppy develop all in one piece. Then when the puppy is old enough to show, it is ready to win. Training on a table and on a lead is very necessary, so that the dog puts out a perfect performance in that respect. Competition is very strong, and the better a puppy is trained the more chance it has.

Ch. Sandmere Starina at 4½ months, 9 months, and 2 years when she finished her championship. She is a daughter of Ch. Peter Pumpkin. Owner, Louella Ericksen. (Photos by Bushman and Klein)

Ch. Knightwood Timber, inbred Peter son, at 3½ months, 14 months, and as a mature adult. Owner, Nancy Lee Marshall.

At ten weeks.

At three months

About five months, out of balance

At eight months...a bit of fluff but not much bone or body substance.

At 20 months...sparse coat, still immature.

At three years old, just after winning a Specialty BOS and all-breed BOB.

Ch. Canden Kinni Charisma grows up. A Ch. Gerthstone's Jon Christopher daughter, she is linebred on Peter, and now dam of two champions. Owner, Betty Jo McKinney

Carmylie
Jean Simmonds

Ch. Philidove Carmylie In A Mist, by Ch. Philidove Heir Presumptive, at 2 years and, (below) at 3 or 4 months.

Can. Ch. Carmylie Foremost All's Fair, by Banchory Reflection ex Carmylie Kaher K-Sarah, at ten weeks; at four months (note the nice forface, eye, and outline); in the six-month uglies; and back together again though still immature at 15 months.

SEPTEMBER
Barbara Linden

Ch. September the Provider at 4 months old.

Ch. September the Provider at 6 months. At nine months he went RWD at the National.

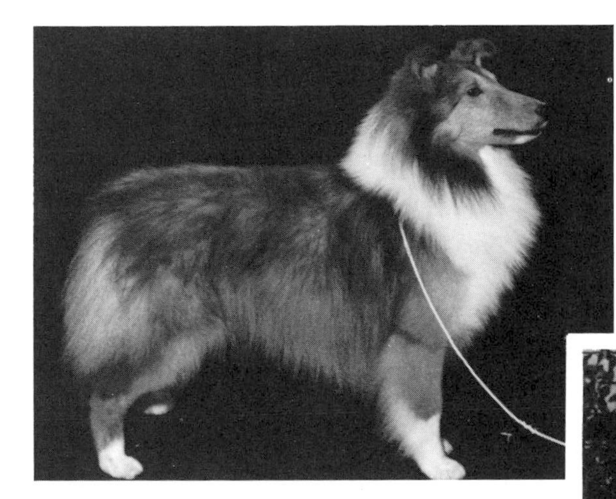

Ch. September Satin Slippers at 10 months of age, and as a lovely 14½ inch adult, age four.

A typical litter of September puppies. These seven week olds are by Ch. September the Convincer out of Satin Slippers. On the right is future Ch. Provider.

SHELTIE EVALUATION FORM*

A critique form such as this will assist you in evaluating puppies at different ages. Rate and score the pups yourself, then have another breeder rate them. Scoring puppies according to the standard at 8 weeks, three months, six months, and one year will help you to see the changes they make during maturation and also keep you objective.
(Note: I recommend that you evaluate the *untrimmed* dog. Somehow we have lost sight of the idea that we are supposed to breed for *naturally* good ears, head, stop, etc., not for the dog that can be sculptured into the correct outline with a scissors.)

Dog's Name:____________________________________ **Sex:**________ **Birthdate:**__________

Date of Rating:____________ **Scored by:** ____________________ **Age:**________ **Height at withers:**__________

Rate dog from one to five by checking each category, using the Standard as your guide.

	5 Outstanding	4 Very Good	3 Good	2 Fair	1 Poor
HEAD					
Scull					
Stop					
Planes					
Muzzle					
Underjaw					
Leanness					
Smoothness					
Bite					
Side Depth					
EYES					
Shape					
Set					
Color					
Size					
Haws					
EARS					
Size					
Set					
Break					
EXPRESSION					
NECK					
Length					
Set					
Arch					

	5 Outstanding	4 Very Good	3 Good	2 Fair	1 Poor
BODY					
Back Length					
Chest					
Topline					
Rib					
Substance					
FOREQUARTERS					
Shoulder Angle					
Upperarm Length					
Upperarm Position					
Straight Legs					
Pastern					
Soundness					
HINDQUARTERS					
Croup					
Angle					
Hock Length					
Soundness					
TAIL					
Length					
Set					
Carriage					
FEET					
Shape					
Strength					
Stance					

	5 Outstanding	4 Very Good	3 Good	2 Fair	1 Poor
BONE					
COAT					
Length					
Texture					
Undercoat					
Fit					
Color					
BALANCE					
ELEGANCE					
TEMPERAMENT					
SHOWMANSHIP					
GAIT					
Single Track					
Rear					
Front					
Side					
Rear Drive					
Front Reach					
Action					

Photo taken at time of rating.

OVERALL IMPRESSION (Please Comment)

____

____

____

Total Score ____________

**Modified from a tournament judging form designed by Lynn Broussard.*

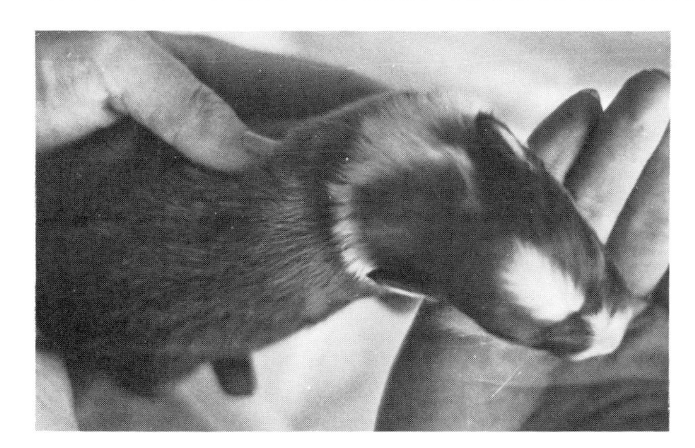

Four days

Four months.

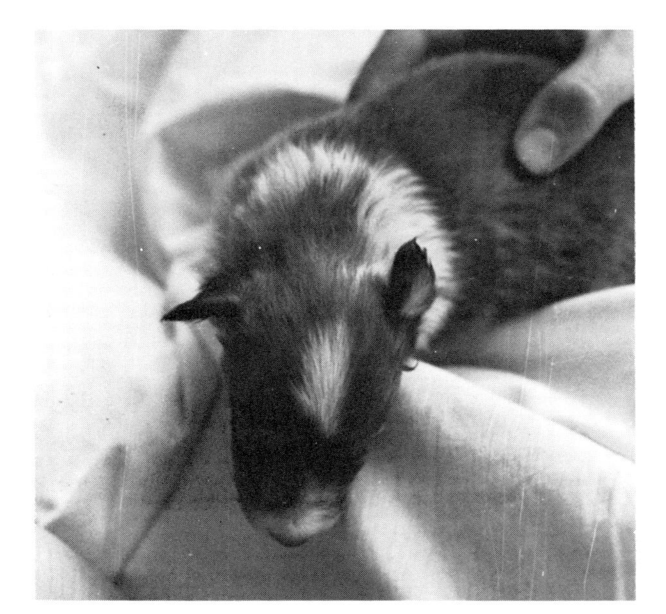

Three weeks

Seven months

Seven weeks.

Twelve months.

Sagebrush Jennifer Lee C.D.X., at various ages. Owned by Alicia Syler. (Photos by Syler)

Helping out the photographer! (Photo by Obermiller)

Creative Marketing 25

Your puppies have reached the adorable age of eight weeks; they are healthy, happy, well adjusted, and loveable. You hate to see them go, but you are sure they will be swept off by excited buyers with no trouble whatsoever. But alas, puppy sales don't come automatically. There may be little demand for Sheltie puppies in your area. Some people are not even aware such a breed exists. In addition, there are sure to be other more established breeders, and of course pet shops, in the area. Your puppy sales are only insured by proper planning, preparation, advertising, and artful presentation to the public. Otherwise your sweet, adorable balls of fur may grow into gangly, awkward teenagers eating their way into your pocketbook and right out of your heart as they require more and more care and become less personable sitting in your kennel.

Selling dogs can be both fun and rewarding, especially when customers come back years later with stories of loving companionship, exciting show wins, or adorable Sheltie puppies of their own. Many long time friendships evolve in this manner. The art of matching the right puppy with the right buyer will challenge you for years to come. If you look at your dogs as personalities capable of bringing happiness and companionship to their owners rather than as business commodities, your sales program is bound for success and your kennel on its way to building a reputation for satisfied buyers.

Before a litter is sold, they should have been weaned and eating solid food for at least a week. They should have their first DHL inoculation at least three days prior to leaving the kennel, and the litter papers should be back from AKC. Many breeders prepare a packet for each puppy containing the blue registration application; a pedigree; health, immunization, and worming record; and a leaflet or mimeographed sheet containing information on the care and training of a new puppy. Booklets of this nature may be obtained from dog food companies, dog publishers, or you can make up your own. "Are You a Responsible Dog Owner," put out by AKC, is also an excellent enclosure.

THE REGISTRATION PAPERS

When your litter is a few days old, you must fill out an application for registration giving the date of birth, number of male and female puppies, and the sire and dam of the litter. The application must be signed by the breeder (owner or lessee of the bitch) and the owner of the sire. It is filed with AKC and in about a month the "blue slips" will be received.

There is one "blue slip" (application for individual registration) for each puppy. As each puppy is sold, the breeder must fill in the sex, indicate the color (refer to the chapter on color inheritance if in doubt), give the name and address of the buyer and the date of transfer. If the breeder wishes the dog to carry his or her kennel name, he may write the name in the blanks provided for first and second choice of names. If the breeder wishes to name the dog before it is sold, he may do so either by filling in the choice of name on the application or by registering the dog individually in his own name and transferring ownership with the permanent registration papers. If the breeder's kennel name has been registered with the AKC (and *only* if it is registered) he must grant permission in writing by signing that portion of the application form. Otherwise, leave that portion of the form blank.

Kennel names are used to identify the produce of a particular breeder. They generally preface the name, or are used at the end of a name with the prefix "of" or "O'." If two breeders co-breed a litter or one breeder buys from another breeder, it is not uncommon for the puppy to be registered with both kennel names. As the seller, you have the right to request or demand that a puppy be registered with your kennel name, or, alternately, to request that the buyer not use your kennel name. If you are proud of the puppies you produce, having them bear your kennel name is an excellent, inexpensive way to advertise.

The new owner should be instructed to fill in his choice of name (if not already done) as well as the bottom portion of the application and mail it to the AKC with a $5.00 fee. In about thirty days he will receive a certificate of registration showing the permanent name and number assigned.

If you sell a dog without papers for any reason, or withhold registration papers until the dog has been neutered, you must have a written contract specifying that the papers have been withheld, that the buyer understands and agrees to these terms, and stating under what conditions, if any, the papers will be supplied. The contract should be filled out and signed in triplicate—one copy for the buyer, one for the seller, and one for AKC in case the buyer attempts to register the puppy on his own or in case of a dispute. The breeder keeps two copies in his files. If he should be contacted by AKC regarding registration of the dog, mailing a copy of the contract should settle the issue.

ADVERTISING

If you have or are forming a kennel and consistently show and breed dogs, advertising will be an on-going and long term project far in advance of any puppies you offer for sale. The primary purpose should be to introduce yourself to the fancy, establish your permanency, and build a favorable image of your kennel. Don't expect immediate results; breeders want to know that you have been around for a while and that you will consistently show and breed quality Shelties. Advertise in those national magazines which will reach the largest number of breeders and expect little or no response at first. After five or six consecutive advertisements during a year's period you should begin to reap the rewards of a planned advertising program.

Most of your show dog sales will come from advertisements in national breed magazines. These ads will reap little in the way of pet sales, which generally come from local advertisements or from advertisements in farm or all-breed dog magazines.

Advertising Show or Breeding Quality Shelties

Your better puppies will rarely go to local buyers. For one thing, there may not be enough market for show Shelties in the area. For another, it seems to be more fashionable (also sometimes more questionable) to buy a puppy from across the country than to buy from a local breeder.

Banchory A Blue Nun, left, and littermate. (Photo by Krook)

Reputations are made by repetition. Use small space ads run often to drive home a point. Emphasize your kennel's strengths and the goals you are working toward, time after time. Repeat and repeat and repeat. Look for the long term, not one time, results from your national advertisements.

Effective advertisements are short and to the point. They use headlines and photos effectively to catch attention and lead the reader into the copy. They talk about only one idea at a time, and they are not cluttered with extra photos or art. However, don't underestimate the value of a sharp, clear, attractive photograph.

Screening Buyers

Of course you won't want to sell your puppies to just anyone. Some people simply do not make good dog owners, or are not the type of person who would be happy with a Sheltie's sensitive personality. After a while you will begin to recognize these people and be able to deal with them.

You especially will want to avoid having one of your puppies go to a puppy mill breeder, pet shop supplier, or a pet owner who would breed irresponsibly. How do you recognize such buyers? Your common sense and intuition is sometimes your best guide. You can screen your buyer somewhat by rather extensive questioning. Do they own other dogs? What breed or breeds? Do they breed these dogs? Will they breed the puppy they buy from you? Do they plan to show? Where do they plan to keep the puppy—house, kennel, yard, etc.? Do they have a securely fenced area in which the animal can run? Will they agree to neuter a non-breeding quality pet? Are they aware of the expense of proper care and feeding? Will they sign a contract which says they will not sell puppies from this dog to pet shops?

In all cases of time payment, breeder's terms, etc., the registration papers are customarily held by the breeder until all the terms of the contract have been fulfilled. The contract must be dated and signed by both buyer and seller. The buyer receives the original, the seller keeps a copy for his files.

Terms for time payment should be specified carefully, with provisions for repossession of the puppy if terms are not met. Provisions for the neutering of pet Shelties may be spelled out. Usually this includes a provision that the papers will be held by the breeder until the written confirmation of neutering is received from the buyer's veterinarian. Or it may involve a refund of some portion of the purchase price when confirmation of neutering is received.

By the time puppies are ready to leave the nest the dam has become a hairless wonder with ears flying. It will take her four to six months to coat up again.

SALES CONTRACT FOR PET PUPPIES

On ______________ (date), ______________ (name) kennels agrees to sell the following ______________ (breed) to ______________ (name) of ______________ (address) for the sum of $ ______________

Color: ______________ Sire: ______________

Sex: ______________ Dam: ______________

Whelped: ______________ Reg.#: ______________

Registration papers will either be given with the puppy or will be transferred to the buyer immediately upon their receipt from AKC if they are still being processed.

It is understood that at the time of sale this dog is *not* considered to be of show or breeding quality, but is representative of its breed and is structurally and temperamentally suited as a companion and/or obedience dog. Beginning training classes are highly recommended for any family dog to insure a happy relationship with the animal. This dog is guaranteed for 48 hrs. against any health or temperament irregularities, and it is recommended the buyer have the puppy examined by a reputable veterinarian during this period. (NOTE: any puppy going to a new home may be a bit unsure of himself until he becomes completely familiar with his surroundings.) A full refund will be given for any pup found unsatisfactory during the first 48 hrs.

No other guarantee is given except in the case of an *hereditary* defect which develops to the extent it renders the dog unsuitable as a pet. In this instance a replacement will be given when one becomes available.

The buyer agrees not to use this animal for breeding except by the express permission of the breeders at a later date. Neutering of the animal is recommended.

Special provisions:

Signed: ______________ (buyer)

Signed: ______________ (seller)

Address: ______________

SALES CONTRACT FOR SHOW OR BREEDING QUALITY DOGS

On ______________ (date), ______________ (name) kennels agrees to sell to ______________ (name) of ______________ (address) the following ______________ (breed) for the sum of $ ______________

Name: ______________ Whelped ______________

Sire: ______________ Color: ______________

Dam: ______________ Sex: ______________

Reg. #: ______________

This animal is guaranteed to be free from all hereditary defects affecting its suitability for breeding, and is guaranteed to be free of disqualifying and serious faults of a structural or temperamental nature. Health is guaranteed for 48 hrs. and it is recommended that the buyer have the animal examined by a reputable veterinarian during that time.

A replacement or credit for the amount of purchase will be given for any animal sold for $ ______________ or more if the dog matures at less than the represented quality at 18 mos. of age, unless it is mutually agreed to determine this at another date.

Special Provisions of sale:

Signed: ______________ (buyer)

Signed: ______________ (seller)

Address: ______________

Sales Contract and Guarantee

A written sales contract should accompany each and every puppy sold. It should spell out exact price and terms of payment, sex, age, parentage of the puppy, health and other guarantees, exact terms of adjustment, replacement, and the time limit for same.

Receipts should be issued for all payments. If there is any doubt about the validity of a personal check the seller should ask for identification and hold the dog's registration papers and the contract until the check clears. Many breeders ask for cash or certified check payments.

DIRECT SELLING

The sale is half made when the buyer comes to your home to look. At this point he is definitely interested, he knows the price and probably feels it is within his range, and he has put some effort into the buying procedure.

A good dog salesman talks and demonstrates qualities. Talk about eyes, ears, stop, muzzle, coat, expression, angulation, temperament. Tell about satisfied customers, shows won, champions bred. Teach him about the breed as you demonstrate the puppy. Make sure he knows what is desirable in a Sheltie. Show him how your Sheltie will benefit him or fit his needs. Never belittle the competition or be negative in your approach.

Show some of your adult Shelties, especially those in peak condition and coat. Sheltie bitches go completely naked of coat soon after their litter is weaned and are a sorry sight to show. You may want to decline to show the bitch when she is at her worst because some pet buyers cannot believe such a bare animal ever looked like a Sheltie. If the buyer insists on seeing the dam, also show good photos of her when in coat. A flashy, coated Sheltie with a pleasing personality around the house will do wonders in selling pets.

Never reserve a puppy without a non-refundable cash deposit. You may miss other sales while holding a puppy for a buyer who later changes his mind and doesn't come back.

Holiday puppes? Advise buyers to take the pup home early or wait until the holiday bustle has calmed down. A new home, new faces, and the confusion of holiday activity is too much for a new pet.

Shelties and kids...a natural combination if they grow up together.

Orienting the Buyer

The new buyer will need to know about the puppy's diet, care, immunizations, grooming, and training. Since most of your puppies will be sold at the beginning of a long stage of teething and ear flying, it is a good idea to go over ear correcting and teething.

I like to include a kit with a few days' supply of feed, feeding instructions, a rawhide chew stick, dog care leaflet, sales contract, guarantee, pedigree, registration form, brief instructions on training a Sheltie, ear care and grooming, and my address and phone number. And of course I always like to recommend or give a good book on the subject.

FOLLOW UP

Your records will never be complete unless you follow up on most of your puppy sales for at least a year after the sale was made. This assures the buyer of your interest, makes friends, and insures that he is happy with the puppy. It also enables you to keep accurate records of height, temperament, and photos of mature littermates. You will find this invaluable in planning future breedings. Some ugly ducklings turn into beautiful show quality dogs and some lovely show prospects "go off" and become nothing more than pets. Your buyers will be happier and your breeding program more successful if you know about such cases.

ADVERTISING PHOTOGRAPHY

Good photographs are essential in advertising—one picture truly is worth a thousand words. A look at any current Sheltie magazine will convince you of the necessity for good photographs, emphasized even more by the frequent appearance of professional photos by Gulie Krook, Jan Haderlie, Dick Carter, Marna Obermiller and others who specialize in photographing our breed. A bad photo, on the other hand, can create a very unfavorable image.

Keep in mind the purpose for your ad—to promote your kennel, to advertise a stud dog, to sell puppies, or to have a professional come to a kennel or other convenient location for a day of shooting. Some local portrait studios will do animals. Since they may not be familiar with the breed, take several professional ad photos with you as an example. Attractive photos can also be obained inexpensively by having your child photographed with a Sheltie at one of the many promotional offers held by department stores.

With a good camera, plenty of patience, a few guidelines, and the assistance of a helper, anyone can learn to take acceptable advertising photos.

Shooting from a low angle improves background and emphasizes underjaw and foreface. (Photo by Larry Obermiller)

Cute puppy pictures sell. Post them on bulletin boards or use in ads to create appeal.

to promote a special dog. A kennel is promoted by picturing top bitches and dogs or promoting photos of show wins. Stud dogs are promoted by publishing outstanding portraits, pedigree, and photos or show win credits of their offspring. Charming puppy pictures are hard to resist. When promoting a special make sure the published photo not only flatters the dog, but the judge and handler as well.

Photo sessions with professional dog photographers may be arranged at major shows, especially specialties. If this is not convenient, a group of breeders might arrange

Equipment

I prefer either a 35mm camera with an 85 to 105mm lens (preferably zoom), or a 2¼ roll film camera with a 175mm lens and fast film such as Kodacolor 400 or Tri-X black and white. The faster film allows a higher shutter speed which will prevent blurring if the dog moves, and the moderate telephoto keeps you far enough from the dog so as not to distract or frighten him.

You will need several squeeky toys or other noisemakers. Food doesn't work because the dog will try to move toward the bait. A flash or silver reflector of some type is helpful in controlling shadows, and if you plan to take action or gait shots, a motor drive is almost essential. For black and white photos, a green filter will lighten green grass for a more contrasting background. A yellow filter may be used with blue merle dogs to provide more detail or to darken blue sky backgrounds. For color photography, an 81A warming filter will give sables a richer color.

Grooming

The most essential item for your photo session is an impecably groomed dog. He must be brushed thoroughly from the skin out or the coat will appear clumpy and unfitted. Ungroomed coats also appear wavy. White areas should be sparkling clean and heavily chalked. Other touchups normally made can be slightly exaggerated for black and white photos.

Pay special attention to head detail. Whiskers must be neatly trimmed, eyes and nostrils clear of mucous, hairs smoothed and face framing carefully combed and sprayed in position with hair spray. Super-hold human hair spray will keep the neck hair standing out, the topline correct, or the wind from blowing the coat too much on a breezy day. (Be sure to bathe out the spray later.) Frequent misting with water will add that full, healthy lift to the coat.

Backgrounds

Choose a background which is attractive, uniform in color and lighting, and which contrasts with the color of the dog—dark for a merle or golden sable; light for a tricolor or mahogany. If tree limbs or splotchy lighting distracts, using a larger f/stop will blur the background out of focus.

Techniques

Ideally, you will have two assistants—one to hold the dog and the other to toss the squeeky toy, advise on positioning, hold brushes and do touch-up grooming.

The camera should be at a level even with the dog's shoulder or eye. Never shoot down on a Sheltie—it will give him a dumpy, short-necked appearance. A short-legged dog or a male that you want to appear very masculine and elegant will look better if photographed from ground level. A leggy dog will appear more balanced if the camera is slightly above his eye-level.

For full body shots, position your camera directly in front of the withers or mid-section. However, to emphasize a good front, pretty frontal view of the head, or to foreshorten a long body, turn the dog's front about five inches toward you for a three-quarter view. Your point of focus should be the dog's shoulder, but be sure you have enough depth of field so the grass is in focus a few inches in front of the dog.

For head shots, shooting slightly upward, your camera lens at a level just below the dog's chin, may enable you to use the sky as a background and also emphasize a good underjaw or finish of muzzle. Heads are best photographed in profile, in a three-quarter front view, or directly in front with the camera at eye level. Watch for distortion if you come in too close with your camera. Better results are obtained by using a longer telephoto lens and standing farther away from the dog. Always focus on the eyes, using an f/stop small enough so the entire head will be in focus.

To get good structure shots of puppies you must hold the camera at their body level. A shallow zone of focus achieved by using a larger lens opening, throws the somewhat cluttered background out of focus. (Photo by Obermiller)

Selection

Examine each photo objectively before placing your ad. Is it a realistic picture of your dog? Are any faults emphasized? Do head planes appear correct or did the photographer's angle make the stop indistinct or the face appear dished? Are the legs placed correctly? Bad positioning can make a sound dog appear faulty or a well-angulated dog appear straight. Look at the underjaw—again, positioning can either emphasize or subtract.

Puppies are more difficult. They stand still momentarily, making focusing difficult, are like quicksilver to follow, and tire easily. For family record shots or photos to attract the pet buyer you may be able to contain the puppy by giving it a toy fastened to a string to keep it in a small area or by putting him in a box, basket, or chair. Better yet, give the puppy to a child and let the two entertain each other for some really charming shots.

If you want full body poses, you must have several helpers. Lightweight fishing line makes an unobtrusive collar and leash, and you will find a motor drive extremely helpful—when the pup finally stands you can click away several frames before he's gone again. Patience is essential. Many Shelties have become camera shy for life because of impatient amateurs losing their temper during a photo session. If you can't get cooperation for a body shot, try another time or settle for a cute head shot instead. Shadows cause heads to appear bumpy or full of holes, even if they are not. You may be so accustomed to seeing the dog in the flesh that you look right over a created fault in a photograph. Have another breeder look at the proofs also and see if you choose the same pose. Then have your choice blown up to the size you plan to use in the ad so you can re-evaluate it before sending it to the magazine.

Susan Ashbridge wisely chose a contrasting outfit to provide a nice background for Ch. Happy Glen Starting Stone. (Cott/Francis photo)

Natural backgrounds are often attractive. Ch. Kinni's Caprice. (Photo by Sadwith)

A blanket, sheet, or photographer's screen creates a nice continuous tone background for indoor shots. (Photo by Price) Keynote Kilts 'n' Kapers.

Barbara Linden frequently uses an evergreen hedge as a background for her dogs. This is September Kentucky Rain.

Ch. Montage Siasconset Sophia, age three months, by Ch. Northcountry Westering Son ex Ch. Berridale Alnphyll Brigette. Owner, Wendy Louring. (Photo by Krook)

The Civilized Sheltie 26

WHY TRAIN YOUR DOG?

The advantages of a trained dog are infinite, and Shelties are among the easiest breeds to train. The obedience-trained Sheltie performs well in nearly every situation because he has learned to relate a spoken command to an action. Once this is established, it is simple to add more commands and responses. At the very least, household obedience (sit, stay, down, and come) and lead training should be taught every dog. This training could save his life, or even yours, in a panic situation. A trained dog is welcome where other dogs are not; he is a pleasure to live with and a credit to his owner and his breed. But the greatest benefit is the communication and mutual respect established between dog and handler.

HOW YOUR SHELTIE THINKS

Understanding your Sheltie is a prerequisite to any attempt to train him. You have to remember that you are training an animal mind (not an immature human one) capable of giving specific responses to a limited number of commands. The dog cannot reason, he can only react to a familiar stimulus. Therefore, your commands must be consistent and you must demand instant obedience every time.

"Intelligence" as referred to animals is the ability to respond to many situations that take place in the animal's environment. In obedience training, however, the response of the dog does not depend on intelligence, but rather on his need to obey. Reward and punishment in one form or another is almost inevitably associated with the learning process in animals, both in training and in the wild. Shelties, even more than most breeds, respond best to praise following correction of an incorrect action. Food will bring much less enthusiastic results. Discipline should never be too harsh, and if the dog is punished so that he becomes confused, he may "come unglued" for some time. Patience is required for the best results.

In all training, you must present lessons in a manner that will not cause the dog to feel that obedience is punishment. Yet he must learn that failure to obey will bring correction. A dog must never be punished for poor, sloppy work, or for improper response to a command or signal. Help him understand and perform the act correctly the first time. *As long as he is trying, even if he makes mistakes, he must be praised.* The dog is the animal most easily discouraged in learning situations, and only firm, kind, persistent training will achieve successful results. Do not expect your dog to understand what you mean just because you or your neighbor's dog understands. He cannot read your mind; he understands but a limited few of your spoken words. He does understand and respond to praise, so use it freely to reinforce correct behavior.

One great concern to beginning trainers is the fact that most dogs will cower away from the trainer at the start of formal obedience training. This is natural; once the dog has built up confidence in his ability to please, cowering will stop. A good trainer encourages confidence in his dog.

GUIDELINES FOR ALL TRAINING

For best results, work your Sheltie a few minutes every day. This is much better than working an hour or two once a week. Keep lessons short, and as free of distractions as possible. Always wear soft-soled shoes during training. It is quite possible to break a Sheltie's foot if you step on it with hard soled shoes. Rubber soles also provide you better footing. Tailored slacks or casual clothing make the best training apparel. Full skirts or flare-legged pants can interfere with leash action and may cause the dog to work too wide. Standardizing your training procedure will give your Sheltie a better chance to learn and understand your words and cues.

1. When working your Sheltie on leash, at first keep him always on your left side. Be consistent in this from the beginning and he will never be underfoot.
2. Be consistent! This is the single most important aspect of training. If you ask a dog to do something, be sure he does it promply with only one command, and praise him immediately upon completion. If you correct him, be firm but reassuring, and praise lavishly once the correction has been made.
3. Use simple commands in an authoritative tone of voice, "Suzy, HEEL!" is a lot easier for your dog to understand than "Come on Suzy, Don't you think you would like to heel like a good girl?" The dog can't be expected to be more businesslike than you are, and he must learn to relate to a word command. This must be the same command, given the same way, and demanding the same response each time.
4. Corrections must be given instantly or not at all. Three minutes after the deed, the dog will not connect the correction with his action. Never, repeat NEVER, call a dog to you and punish him. He will think he was punished for coming and may decide not to make the same mistake again.
5. A Sheltie responds to correction and praise but not to unreasonable punishment. Correction is constructive and reinforced with praise. Shelties want to please and do not need rough treatment. They do need constant reassurance that they are pleasing you.
6. End each training session on a happy note. Have the dog complete an exercise he does well and praise him for it. Take a few minutes to play with the dog after each session. This relaxes both of you and allows you to part on friendly terms. Work as a team and try to understand your dog's viewpoint. You are doing things with him, not to him.

CORRECTING BAD HABITS

The best way to correct a bad habit is to avoid it in the first place. Your Sheltie must understand that you are the boss. While he does not need *strong* discipline, he does need control. From the beginning he should learn the meaning of "No." If necessary, the verbal correction may be accompanied with scruff shaking. You may have noticed a bitch pick a puppy up by the loose skin on his neck and shake him gently. We can copy this natural form of discipline by taking the puppy by the scruff and giving two or three shakes strong enough to make the legs move. Rough, vigorous shaking is not necessary and should be avoided. Never strike a Sheltie with your hand. A verbal correction and occasional use of a scruff shaking are the only disciplinary measures you need.

Repetition and consistency are important. You cannot allow the dog to jump on you or the furniture one time and scream at him for doing it the next time. Praise is important, also. Make absolutely sure your dog knows what you expect and is praised lavishly when he does it.

Jumping Up

This annoying habit is totally unnecessary. There are several methods. One of the best is simply to take the Sheltie's front paws as he jumps and make him run backwards, pushing him down. Use a firm word of correction such as "Off." Do not step on his toes—you may injure him and he can dance faster than you can. Another, less recommended method is to bump the dog in the chest with a knee. Puppies may be taught not to jump by meeting every attempt with a strong "No, Off!"

Dogs that jump on other people may be corrected by having the visitor apply one of the above methods or by using a "throw can" (a pop can filled with pennies or washers). The can is tossed in the direction of the dog, but never hits him. Give the command "No, Off' as you throw the can.

Chewing

All puppies chew during the teething stage, and even adult dogs need bones or chew toys for entertainment. Teach your puppy what is acceptable for him to chew by providing rawhide chewies, rubber toys, or other items. When he picks up an article of clothing, or shoes, or chews the furniture or carpeting, correct him with a sharp "No," or "Stop That." If he refuses to relinquish the article, pinch his lips against the biting surface of his teeth until he opens his mouth. Remove the article and give the puppy a "Sit" command for a few minutes. Praise him for good behavior and give him an acceptable item to chew.

Barking

Barking must be prevented before it becomes a habit if you want the training to stick even when you are not around to enforce it. Correct the puppy every time he barks for the wrong reason or for an extended period. You can train a puppy to bark two or three warning barks if you start young and are consistent with your discipline.

If a sharp "No bark!" is not sufficient, use the throw cans as mentioned above. Barking in the yard can be corrected with the use of a water hose in lieu of a throw can. Pea shooters can be used to aim rocks at a kennel wall as a noisemaking disciplinary measure. Always give the command "No bark" simultaneously with the noise. Throw chains and various sound devices sold by dog trainers are also effective. Electronic collars should be used sparingly, if at all.

The mother dog disciplines her puppy by scruff shaking.

Biting

Biting in any form is forbidden. Play biting and mouthing your hands, as well as tug of war games, should be discouraged. More serous attempts may be corrected by scruff shaking or by quickly running your hand down the dog's throat, pressing down on the back of his tongue and saying "No." Repeat the correction each time the dog attempts to bite or mouth you or your clothing. A Sheltie should not be allowed to growl or snap when being examined by another person such as your veterinarian. A firm correction and scruff shaking should be given at any sign of aggression.

CONFORMATION TRAINING

Conformation showing demands that a dog trot freely at your left side on a loose lead. This is not a "heel" and the heel command should not be used. The dog must learn to stand while being examined by a stranger, and he should "bait" or pull his ears up for a bite of liver of his favorite toy. Conformation training classes provide experience with some of the confusion that will be encountered in the show ring, and such classes are available in most cities. If you are training without the aid of a class, try to take the dog everywhere you can to accustom him to strange noises and places. Have strangers go over him in the same manner as a judge in the ring.

Correct a Sheltie for biting by running your hand down his throat.

Obedience training will only enhance a conformation dog if proper teachniques are used. In both areas, the idea is to have a dog who is both predictable and happy.

A puppy or an adult dog cannot be trained for the ring overnight, or even in a week. Some dogs take longer than others, however almost any dog who has a sound temperament and the proper training and conditioning can behave well in the show ring.

Do not have any other puppies present at this time, and not more than one or two older dogs, if any. The older dogs should be well trained and easy going, not the type which will snap at the puppy for food. They can be helpful if they serve as a model for the puppy to emulate.

Encourage the puppy to stand on all four feet by gently pushing him back with your hand or knee if he jumps up. Do not be concerned at this time with how he is standing. Most puppies, when they are excited about food, manage to stand in seemingly impossible positions, and always appear to have a crooked leg whenever you try to show them off. Don't worry, they'll outgrow this if they are basically sound. This part of the training is only meant to teach the puppy to stand on all fours, use his ears, and wait his turn for the food. It encourages attentiveness yet restraint. As an added bonus, the puppy will learn a variety of tastes and come to expect that whatever you are holding in your hand is a special treat.

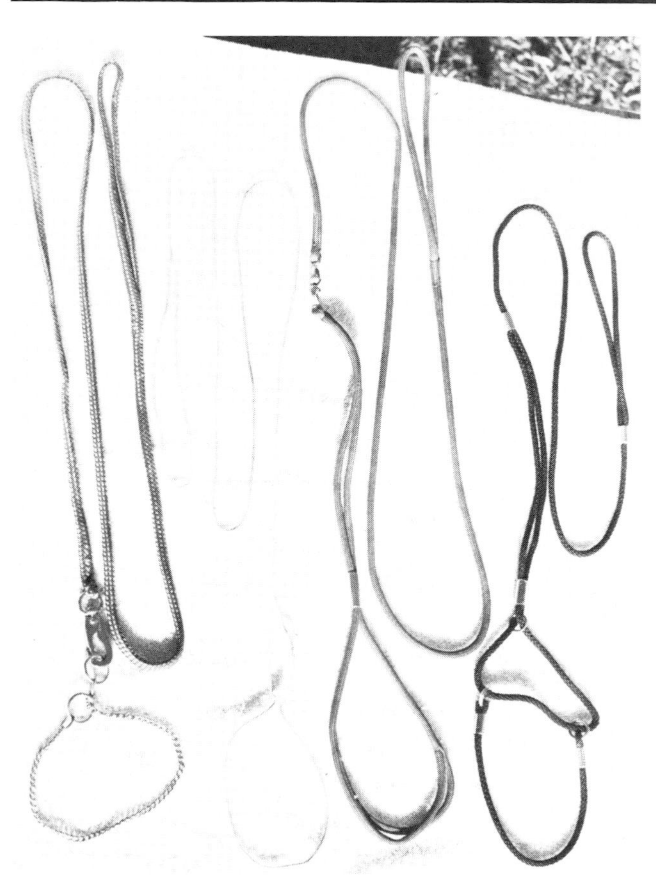

Various styles of show leads.

Teaching a puppy to bait on a table

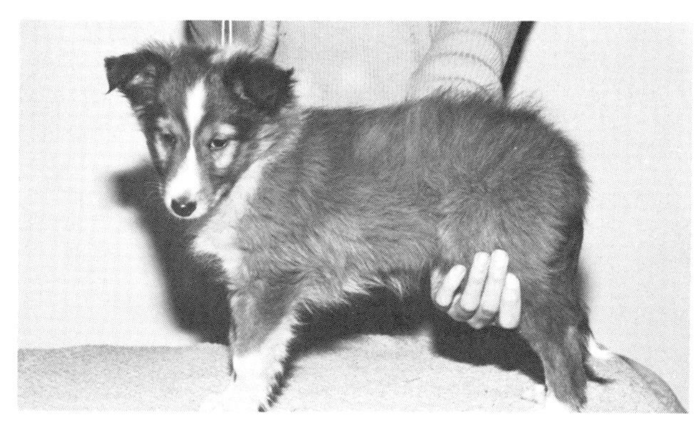

Even very young puppies can be taught to stack. Reach underneath the dog to move a rear leg.

Second Phase

The second important phase of show training begins when the puppy is about twelve weeks of age. It occurs separately from bait training and is part of the lead work.

Begin combining walks on leash with short sessions of stacking and baiting. Build confidence and make the sessions fun for the puppy. Vary the routine and the places where you work.

Whenever possible, have strangers pet your puppy or have friends go over him away from home. Remember that you are striving for a dog who is confident on lead, who comes to you willingly, and who is tolerant of strange places and people.

Third Phase

Begin to get it all together. I usually begin this when the puppy is about 4½ to five months old. There is no particular advantage to pressing the puppy at a younger age, and this often leads to shortcutting the critical period of confidence building in the puppy.

Switch to using an English martingale show lead (modified choke collar) on the pup, grab some bait and take him somewhere quiet to start practicing gaiting, stopping, and turning.

He must learn to respond to the bait exactly as he will be expected to do in the ring. He should stand squarely and show attentiveness and expression. I find it helpful to pivot and face the dog as I'm stopping. Many handlers hold out an open plan to signal a halt and alert the dog that baiting has begun. This gives him time to come to a smooth stop and set himself up. Practice gaiting in the show ring patterns until the puppy can perform any of them smoothly. Put special emphasis on teaching him to trot straight ahead without crabbing, pulling, or prancing.

One way to hand stack a dog's front—placing the feet individually

Another method of stacking is to lift the dog's front and drop him.

Lift the dog in this manner if both rear legs need to be positioned.

Most Shelties can be trained to stop on signal and stand squarely and free themselves. Note handler giving hand signal as she steps in front of dog.

Kneeling beside Sheltie affords more control.

Take a few minutes each session now to stack your Sheltie squarely and have him remain in that position for a few minutes. If he does not walk into a square stance, correct the placement of his legs in the following manner. If a back leg is out of position but the front is correctly placed, put one hand on his shoulders to anchor the front and with your other hand go down the out-of-position back leg to the hock. Grasping the hock firmly, move the leg into position. Always reach *under* the dog to reach a leg on the opposite side from you. If both back legs are poorly placed, run your hand down the back and up under the tail between the hind legs. Spread your fingers and lift the Sheltie slightly off the ground, resetting his legs in correct, position.

Since most judges now prefer to examine Shelties on a table, your puppy must also be trained to stack and bait on a grooming table. Short daily sessions of baiting on the table will increase his confidence. As he gets older, he may be taught to stay on the table without you holding him. He should learn to accept food from your hand and to be examined on the table without moving or pulling back. A dog that tries to pull back may be corrected by stacking him with his back feet at the very edge of the table. If he leans back, encourage him to pull forward by acting as if you are going to pull him off the table backwards by his tail, or by lifting him quickly backward off the table and dropping him slightly in the air before resetting him. A few such sessions and he will stand squarely for examination.

Most Sheltie dislike having their front legs moved. Rather than pick up a foot, place one hand under the chin and lift until the dog's feet barely clear the ground. Gently set him down and the front should fall into place. A better method on a grown dog is to grasp a handful of ruff on each side of the shoulder and lift. You can gauge exactly where you want each foot to fall, as well as the width between the feet, before you let the dog down.

When he is doing this well, take him back to the shopping center or wherever there is confusion. Have someone go over him gently as the judge will do in the ring. The puppy should now have confidence in you and in what he is doing so that he accepts this naturally. Be ready to get down on a knee to steady him at his own level if he starts to pull back from the "judge."

This has formed the foundation for any future training. You may want to attend a few matches or conformation classes to smooth out your handling under more ring-like conditions. This is as much for you as it is for the dog. Continue practicing until you and the puppy are working together as a real team. Never pressure a puppy—showing at this stage must be fun. Let him play in the ring and don't expect perfection. Your goal is a happy, relaxed showman. Later, when he's a year of age, you can concentrate on dependable performance and control.

Ch. Shamont Ruby Slippers, owned by Macdega, winner of three all-breed Best in Show and six Specialty BOB awards, and owner/handler Tom Coen proudly accept the honors. (Photo by Ashbey)

Off to the Dog Show! 27

Dog showing, along with horse racing and other activities developed for animal lovers, originated in England. The sport brings together exhibitors from all over the country to show the cream of their breeding programs under formal conditions as they compete for championships, Best of Breed, Best of Group, and Best in Show wins.

For the breeder the shows serve several important purposes. First, they provide a proving ground to test the results of his breeding program. Second, they enable him to weigh his dogs against the other entries, thus overcoming the kennel blindness that occurs when one never looks beyond his own back yard. Third, they enable him to see Shelties from other kennels which may have potential to improve his breeding program. Shows get his stud dogs out before the public where they may be noticed and used. Finally, as breeders meet and visit before and after classes much valuable discussion, evaluation, planning, and exchanging of viewpoints takes place. It is here, perhaps more than anywhere else, that the sincere and eager novice can learn. Here, too, he may find an old pro who is willing to teach him about showing, winning and losing, and how to be a good sport.

SHOWS AND MATCHES

Every licensed show or match is sponsored by an AKC licensed all-breed or specialty club. All-breed shows can be held only by all-breed clubs; and specialty clubs (such as Shetland Sheepdog clubs) can sponsor only shows for their particular breed.

Before a club is licensed to hold a "point" show it must earn the privilege by holding several "matches." These, organized much like a show, are strictly for fun and practice. Matches are an excellent place for the beginner to gain experience and finesse in showing his dog. Puppies as young as two months may be entered. There is no pre-entry in many cases; matches can be a spur of the moment fun outing for the family. No one cares if your puppy is only partially leash trained or if you make all kinds of handler errors in your presentation. No championship points are awarded and no champion dogs can be entered—every participant is there for the fun and experience, not for the win. Even the judges are usually novices who are gaining practice, possibly in preparation for future licensing to judge point shows.

There are several classifications of matches. "Fun" matches do not meet any AKC requirements. They are strictly for pleasure and may include team obedience events, classes for tiny puppies, and other non-regular classes. "B" matches are the first kind of match a club is required to hold to gain AKC recognition. No pre-entry is required but the show is organized in the same manner as a licensed show. A three to six month puppy class may be allowed. "A" matches publish premium lists and require pre-entry. A catalog is then published to give the club practice in handling this aspect of producing a show. Only standard regular and non-regular classes are allowed.

After several matches have been successfully sponsored, a club may apply to AKC for permission to hold a licensed show. If permission is granted the club receives notification that it has been licensed to hold a show at the specified date and location.

While members of the club select and notify judges, arrange for the ring stewards and announcers, and perform various other duties, the actual running of the show is usually handled by a superintendent who makes his living by organizing and promoting dog shows. This individual prints and distributes the premium list (entry blank), accepts entries, sets up the rings, prints the catalog, and is in charge of the operation of the show.

JUDGES

Judges are licensed by AKC to judge one breed, several breeds, or all breeds. Many are former breeders or handlers. It is not uncommon to find a Sheltie judge who is a former breeder-handler of some other herding breed such as Collies, German Shepherds, or Corgis. Some judges are very familiar with our particular breed; others are not. While the guideline for all judging is the breed Standard, you will encounter judges who go strictly by the Standard, judges who put undue emphasis on one certain factor (gait, head, expression, coat, showmanship), as well as those who judge only on overall type and balance, often because they are not that well-versed on the breed.

THE CLASSES

Classes are split by sex and progress from puppy to open classes for males, then back through the sequence from puppy to open bitches. Five regular classes are generally scheduled for each breed: puppy, novice, bred-by-exhibitor, American bred, and open.

Puppy Classes

Puppies must be at least six months old to enter a point show. Sometimes the class is split into two sections, six to nine months and nine to 12 months. In matches classes may be divided even further to allow for younger puppies. A puppy may be entered in any of the adult classes if the owner wishes—this is often done with a large or particularly mature puppy. An immature puppy should always be shown in the puppy class. A judge may hesitate to award the points to an overly mature puppy, assuming such pups will coarsen too much as adults.

Novice

Novice class is provided for dogs who have won less than three blue ribbons in licensed shows. This is a good class for a new handler or an unshown dog. Entries are usually small and the dogs, as well as most of the handlers, are inexperienced.

American-bred

This class is open to any dog of showable age bred in the United States. Competition is generally not as tough as in open class, and a young dog or one not in peak condition may look better here. An amateur handler may also prefer this class, and a handler showing a blue merle or tricolor Sheltie in predominantly sable competition may have a better chance at the points from the American-bred class; likewise for a sable being exhibited in "blue country."

Bred-by-exhibitor

This class should be a favorite of any breeder proud of his accomplishment, for only dogs owned or co-owned by their breeder can be entered. Competition is often stiff but numbers are smaller since many dogs are not eligible.

Open

Open class is for mature dogs and bitches in peak condition. It is also the only class in which an imported dog (even a puppy) can be shown. From this class come about 80% of the winners because the top dogs and handlers are usually entered here.

Best of Breed Competition

Only Champions of Record may be entered in the "Specials" or "Best of Breed" competition where they compete with other champions and with the winning non-champion dog and bitch of their breed.

Non-Regular Classes

Non-regular classes may be offered at any licensed show; they most often are seen at specialties. If offered, they will be listed separately in the premium list and will generally have special fees and requirements. Some common ones follow.

Brace classes. Two dogs exhibited as a team and judged on their overall quality, how well they show together, and on matching markings, size, color, etc. Brace obedience classes are also held.

Team classes. Four dogs exhibited together in either conformation or obedience teams.

Local classes. For dogs from a particular state, club or area.

Veterans class. For dogs over a certain age, usually seven years. This is the only non-regular class from which the winner may compete for Best of Breed. By all means show your older dog here if possible instead of competing against those in the bloom of youth. A good veteran is always a sentimental favorite with the ringside and often goes on to beat the youngsters.

Brood bitch class. A bitch exhibited with two to four of her offspring. Generally the bitch is not required to be entered in the regular class but the offspring must be entered there.

Stud dog class. A male with two to four of his offspring. Requirements generally the same as for the brood bitch class.

Futurities. For puppies under one year of age which have been nominated before birth, with nominations renewed at several stages of their growth. These are generally held in conjunction with specialty shows and a portion of the entry fees are split among the four winners.

HOW A SHOW PROGRESSES

Judging starts with the male puppies of each breed and progresses through all the males to open class. Then all first place males from these classes compete against one another for "Winners" dog. This is the *only male* at this show *to take points towards a championship.* A second place male is also chosen as Reserve Winners Dog.

Judging of the bitches proceeds in similar fashion. When the Winners bitch has been chosen, the two Winners (male and female) go into the Best of Breed class along with any champions, or "specials," that are entered. From these the judge must select his top Sheltie of the day—the Best of Breed.

He will also select a Best of Opposite Sex to the Best of Breed. In other words, if Best of Breed goes to a male, then either a bitch champion or the Winners bitch will be chosen for Best of Opposite. After these two places are awarded, the judge must also pick his Best of Winners from the two "Winners" formerly chosen.

Judging of all the other breeds takes place in similar fashion. The AKC breeds are divided into seven groups: Sporting, Hound, Working, Herding, Terrier, Toy, and Non-Sporting. The Shetland Sheepdog is a member of the Herding Group along with Australian Cattle Dogs, Bearded Collies, Belgian Malinois, Belgian Sheepdogs, Belgian Tervuren, Bovier Des Flanders, Briards, Collies, Old English Sheepdogs, Puli, and Cardigan and Pembroke Welsh Corgis. After the breed judging, the Best of Breed winners from each breed compete with the other winners in their group. Prizes one through four are awarded for each group. The seven Group One winners then compete for the top honor of the show, the Best in Show award.

"Best of Breed" from all the different breeds go into the ring once more at the end of the day to compete for group placements. As you can see, Shetland Sheepdogs and Corgis are the only small breeds in a ring of giants. What madness this! And what a joy and honor when a little Sheltie manages to take first place!

There are, then, seven group winners. These seven enter the ring a final time to compete for the coveted "Best in Show."

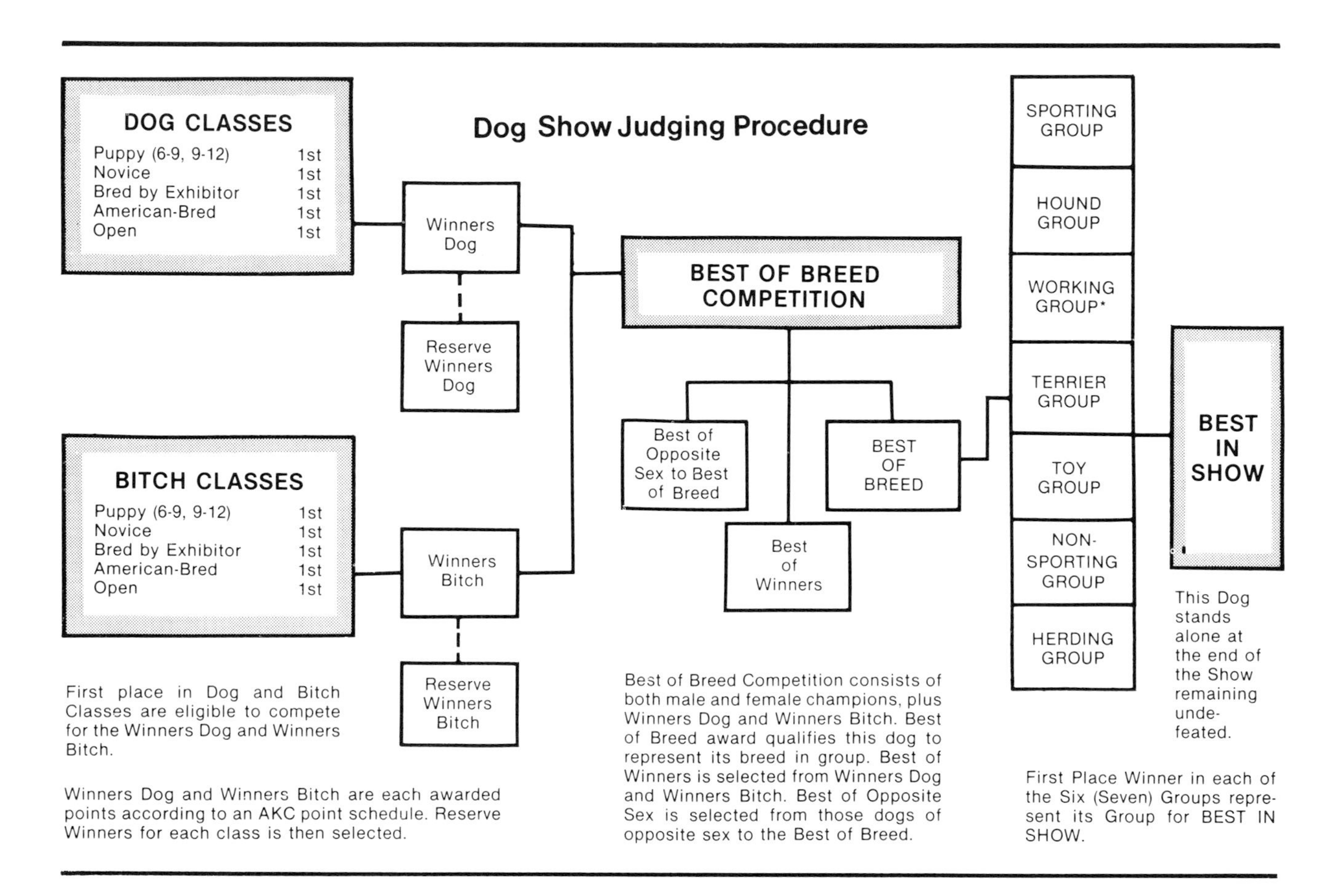

HOW A CHAMPIONSHIP IS ACQUIRED

Only the Winner's Dog and Winner's Bitch in each breed receive championship points. The number of points awarded depends on the number of dogs or bitches they defeat and will vary from zero to five points per show and from region to region. A scale of points appears in the front of each show catalog.

Points are tabulated on the basis of the number of dogs defeated. If there are more Shetland Sheepdog bitches entered than there are dogs, the points will be higher in bitches. Let's say there is a three-point major in bitches, and only one point in dogs. However, if the Winner's Dog also takes Best of Winners, he also is awarded three points. If he takes Best of Breed and then goes on to win a Group 1 over breeds that have had a five-point major that day, he will be awarded five points also.

Obedience trials may be held separate from or in conjunction with conformation shows. Any dog registered with AKC or possessing an ILP number is eligible to compete. Out of a possible 200 points, a dog must score at least 170 points and at least 50 percent of the points for each exercise in order to "qualify." Each qualifying score is called a "leg," and it takes three legs won under three different judges to earn a degree. (Nobody has ever explained to me why a four-legged dog only has to earn three legs to get a degree!)

Ch. Benayr Chimera Colloquy, BOB at 1976 Northern California Specialty. Owner, Susan Bentley. (MikRon photo)

To become a champion a dog must accumulate 15 points. Two of the wins must be "majors" (three or more points won at a single show) and these must be won under two different judges. A dog can accumulate 15 points and not become a champion if he does not have major wins. Winning a non-major show after a dog has 12 or 13 points and still needs a major to finish will accomplish nothing and a considerate exhibitor will withdraw his dog in such a case.

OBEDIENCE TRIALS

Obedience showing is always great fun! Here the dog wins strictly on how well he performs and not on how well he is groomed or how many handlers are in the ring. Shelties excel in obedience training and you will consistently find them among the top scoring dogs. It is a joy to show one; even more exhilarating is the thrill of having a conformation champion take High Score in Trial. These dogs prove beyond all doubt that beauty and brains go together!

There are three obedience titles varying in degree of difficulty: C.D. (Companion Dog) for dogs competing in the Novice class; the C.D.X. (Companion Dog Excellent) for those qualifying three times in Open class; and the U.D. (Utility Dog) for dogs shown in the Utility class.

Novice Class

Novice class is divided into section "A" for dogs whose owners have never completed an obedience degree, and "B" for professional handlers or anyone who has previously shown in obedience. The Novice exercise and scores awarded for correct completion are:

Heel on Leash	40 points
Stand for Examination	30 points
Heel Free	40 points
Recall	30 points
Long Sit	30 points
Long Down	30 points
	200 points

When a dog has completed the requirements for a C.D. degree he can no longer compete in Novice obedience classes.

Open Class

Open classes are also divided into sections "A" and "B," but this time "A" division is for all dogs who are owner handled and who have their C.D. but not their C.D.X. degree. Those dogs who have three qualifying scores in the class may continue to compete in section "B" along with dogs handled by professional trainers or handlers. Exercises are as follows:

Heel Free (off leash)	40 points
Drop on Recall	30 points
Retrieve on Flat	20 points
Retrieve over High Jump	30 points
Broad Jump	20 points
Long Sit	30 points
Long Down	30 points
	200 points

Utility

This most advanced class is open to any dog that has a C.D.X. degree. Exercises include a signal exercise where the dog performs a series of heeling maneuvers and other exercises in response to hand signals with no verbal commands used; a scent discrimination exercise in which the dog selects his handler's article from among many identical articles by scent alone; a directed retrieve in which the dog is signaled to pick up one of three gloves; a directed jumping exercise; and a group stand for examination. Utility dogs may continue to compete in both Open and Utility classes after they have qualified for the U.D. degree.

The ultimate achievement for the obedience dog is earning the title of Obedience Trial Champion (O.T.Ch.). Points are awarded for Open B and Utility competition based on the number of dogs competing in obedience at the trial. To become an obedience champion, the dog must have already received his U.D. title and must then accumulate 100 points, including at least three first place wins of which one is in Utility and one is in Open B.

For more complete information on rules and regulations, write to AKC for rule books which are available at no charge.

HOW TO ENTER

You can find out about upcoming shows from your local kennel club, training class, or by checking the national dog magazines. The American Kennel Club publishes a list of licensed shows in its official magazine, *Purebred Dogs, The AKC Gazette*. You will also find shows listed in *Dog World*, *The Kennel Review*, and others. Some of these are available on the newstand. Once you have entered a few shows you will be placed on the superintendent's mailing list, or you can write and request premium lists for shows in your area. This is usually a free service, but since printing and mailing costs are high, don't write unless you are seriously planning to enter several shows. A few superintendents have recently started charging a fee for these mailings. If this becomes the practice, I recommend spending the money on a subscription to "The AKC Gazette" which lists all pertinent information necessary for entering any show and includes a wealth of interesting and educational information as well.

Can. Ch. Rogene's My Golly Blue Holly, owned by Linda Lovejoy, attained her U.D. in three straight trials.

Premium lists give all the information pertinent to a show, including date, place, date entries close, judges, superintendent, non-regular classes offered, prizes, and entry blanks.

In order to enter an AKC licensed show you must fill out an official entry form. *Copies are not acceptable unless they also have the rules copied on the back of the form.* It is acceptable to scratch out the name and date of the show printed on the form and substitute the name and date of another show if you cannot obtain the correct form. Blank forms may be used for any show, and can be obtained from any superintendent or by writing AKC.

Entries close two to three weeks in advance of the show. This date is printed on the front of the premium list, and entries, correctly filled out and including the fee, must be in the hands of the superintendent by this date. No exceptions will be made. Incorrect forms may be returned unaccepted or the wins may be disallowed later by AKC. You must supply information regarding breed, sex, class entered, owner, breeder, dog's name and AKC number, date and country of birth, and name of sire and dam. If the show is a large one be sure to indicate dog's color; classes are often split by color .

The Judging Schedule

Four or five days before the show you will receive confirmation of your entry with your exhibitor's number indicated. This may be a photostat of your entry form with a number added, or a typewritten slip. You will also receive a judging schedule giving a list of breeds and the ring in which they will show. After the name of the breed will be three numbers representing the number of dogs, bitches, and champions (in that order) entered in that breed. The list also gives the approximate time of judging. Judging may occasionally run a little late, but will not start before the scheduled time. If the show is benched, the entry or premium list will tell you what time your dog is expected to be in his assigned place and how long he will be expected to remain at the show. Most shows are unbenched, and dogs need only be present for their own breed judging unless they take Best of Breed, in which case they will be expected to stay for group judging later.

A match, or practice show, may be as formal or informal as the sponsoring club wishes. Sanctioned matches are generally more formal than "fun" matches, and may require pre-entry just as a licensed show. Most matches allow registration the day of the match and classes are often designated solely by age: for example, three to six months, six to nine months, nine to 12 months, and adult.

Exact time for Sheltie judging is almost impossible to predict, but the waiting time can be well spent watching other breeds in competition. Much can be learned from watching the dogs gait and observing the ring procedure of judges and the handling methods of the various exhibitors.

PREPARING FOR THE SHOW

Exhibitors are as varied as people anywhere. Some arrive shortly before ring time, their last minute grooming done at home, carrying only a spray bottle and brush. Some bring everything, including the kitchen sink, moving in well equipped motor homes the night before the show with elaborate set-ups of exercise pens, canopys, lounge chairs, and grooming tables. In short, whatever you have the time for and can afford, do it.

For most, however, show-going means loading the necessities and our potential champion into the station wagon or van and taking off with the family for a day of fun and competition. Plan to arrive at least one hour before Shelties are scheduled (three hours if you plan to do most of your grooming at the show). Grooming equipment will vary with each individual and will depend on the amount of preparation you have done at home. You can get by with just your dog, a spray bottle filled with water, brush,

Junior handling is offered for boys and girls ten to seventeen years of age. Sondra Mauzy and Sharokee Woodstock. Sondra accumulated numerous Best Junior Handler awards and qualifed to compete in junior handling at Westminster KC while still in a body cast following back surgery. (Kohler photo)

Ch. Banchory Thousands Cheered, a Ch. Banchory Formal Notice daughter. "Cheerio" was owner/handled by Noel Bosse to become top winning bitch in breed history with six all-breed BIS at just three years of age. (Cott/Francis photo)

show lead, and bait. The person exhibiting several dogs will, of course, need crates and grooming tables to accommodate a larger number of dogs. Don't forget an extra show lead and drinking water from home. Changing his drinking water may give your Sheltie upset stomach or diarrhea.

A crate or exercise pen will come in handy. If you are a frequent exhibitor you may want to invest in shade cloths, an awning or canopy for hot weather shows. But, if you are showing only the dog, buy a dolly on which to roll your crate and do your grooming inside the building or tent provided. Newspapers or a piece of washable indoor-outdoor carpet makes a clean, sanitary floorcovering for the "x-pen." Shade can be created by covering the top of the pen with net screen or plastic tarps. Fasten the sides with snaps or clothes pins.

Clothes

Appropriate dress is important. In the past, shows were a major social event. In the East and in England, some of them resembled a fashion show with the ladies outdoing one another with original hats and costumes. Today we are much more casual. Slacks and sport shirts, preferably with a tie, are acceptable for male handlers. Dresses, skirts and blouses, culottes or pantsuits are worn by women exhibitors. Select clothing that allows you to move freely, skirts that don't hobble you, cling or ride up, and material that sheds dog hair easily. Light colors are less problem to keep clean; chalk and white hairs show on dark colored fabric. Look for clean, basic lines: straight or A-line skirts, pants that don't flare. Ruffles, full gathers, or bell bottom pants interfere with your dog.

Choose colors that frame and compliment your dog. If you are handling a sable Sheltie, light beige, red, blue, or green are good choices. Avoid clothing the same color as your dog. Bright blue, very light grey or black looks good with a merle; but if you will also be showing a triclor avoid black outfits and choose a contrasting color like white or red instead. Pockets large enough to hold a brush and liver are helpful. Fad styles are not generally recommended. although a few professionals adopt a certain style as their trademark. The primary objective is to look as neat and tastefully groomed as your Sheltie and to avoid distracting the judge's eye from your dog.

Shoes are vitally important. Choose comfortable footwear that provides good support for running. Jogging shoes, sneakers, and soft rubber-soled walking shoes are frequent choices. Women need shoes that don't appear cloddy with dresses, but high heels must be avoided. Soles

CHECKLIST OF SHOW EQUIPMENT

For Me	For My Sheltie
ESSENTIALS	
Judging schedule	Drinking water and bowl
Clothes brush	Grooming table
Jacket with pockets	Grooming box with tools
Wet-wipes or hand cleaner	Crate with pad or rug in it
Paper towels	Newspaper or carpet to lie on
Trash bag	Food (if overnight trip)
Pooper scooper	Liver or other bait
Grooming smock or apron	Two show leads
	Several terrycloth towels
	First aid and medical supplies
OPTIONAL	
Folding chairs	Exercise pen
Cooler with lunch and drinks	Shade cloth or canopy
Extra pair of shoes	Chew chips or toys
Raincoat	Blow dryer
	Grooming table cover
	Small throw rug for ringside

should be soft to avoid injury if you should accidently step on a paw.

LAST-MINUTE PREPARATIONS

When you have set up the grooming area, let the dog relax for a bit while you locate your ring, pick up your armband, and observe the judge you will be showing under. Most judges use the same pattern with every breed they judge that day, so determine his or her ring procedure, gaiting pattern, and preference for examining small dogs on the table. Watch for obvious personal preferences or dislikes.

Before your class, exercise your Sheltie one last time so he can eliminate. A human infant rectal suppository may be used if necessary. A constipated dog will not move out freely, and a nervous dog that was not allowed to exercise may provide some embarrasing moments in the ring.

About an hour prior to your class, rechalk the Shelties feet, legs, and underjaw. Don't dampen the hair too much or the chalk won't brush out. Using a blower or a brisk brushing should remove all traces of chalk. An exhibitor may be excused from the ring by a judge who finds grooming chalk or excess hair spray in a dog's coat.

Dampen your Sheltie from head to tail with a very light, fine mist of water. Brush and lift the hair, pulling the neck hair up to frame the face and create an elegant neckline. Smooth back and topline. If your Sheltie is long, brush the "pants" downward. To create length, brush this area back to give an illusion of better balance. Brush the legs so that every hair is standing straight out, giving the appearance of heavier bone.

A touch of vaseline will add shine to the nostrils, and setting gel or hairspray is used to smooth the checkbones and topskull and to set the ruff so it frames the head. Blazes may be whitened with a light touch of a chalk block.

Experiment with various products to see what works on your dog. Any product applied to build coat texture or body should be brushed out until no stiffness or stickiness is left. Some dogs will need more work than others, and it is up to you to decide how far you want to go in the creation of the "cosmetic Sheltie" that is often seen at the shows. The less you can do to your dog and still have him presentable, the better.

Ch. Chenterra Thunderation, the breed's all-time top winner. Owned by Stephen Barger. Shown 228 times, Thunder won 220 BOB, 78 Working Group 1sts, and 21 all breed BIS. He is currently sire of 21 champions. (Photo by Krook)

The Art of Showing 28

One final check of the dog and your own grooming and your're off to the ring. Carry a small pin brush, spray bottle of water, and some liver. The water bottle, of course, stays at ringside. (Liver is best prepared by boiling in salted water for twenty minutes, then baking ten minutes per side in a 300° oven. Once dried, liver prepared in this manner will keep for some time without spoiling and is not messy to carry.) Keep calm—your nerves transmit right down the lead to your dog. So concentrate on doing your best regardless of the placements and encourage your Sheltie. Showing, after all, should be fun!

At ringside, you will pick up your armband and place it on your left arm with the number facing forward so the judge can easily see it. Many judges request that exhibitors enter the ring in numerical order. If not so requested, it's your choice where you are in the lineup. If your Sheltie has good reach and drive he may be able to exhibit this better at the front of the line. If he moves better at a slow gait, he will look better at the end of the line where he is not being crowded. You should determine your dog's best speed by having a friend watch him gait before you go into the ring. If the dog ahead is too slow and prevents your dog from moving at full extension, slow down to allow space when you are behind the judge and move out when you cross in front of him. Some dogs should be moved fast going away from the judge, bringing the legs into a single track, but slower coming in to avoid emphasis on loose front movement. Be aware of your dog's strengths and weaknesses and move him accordingly, keeping your speed adjustments as subtle as possible.

You will enter the ring to the right, circling counter-clockwise. Most judges prefer that the dogs enter at a trot and continue around the ring until asked to halt. If you watch a few classes before yours you will be somewhat familiar with the judge's procedure. You must pay attention to both the judge and your dog at all time. Some judges are rather vague in their directions for gaiting or changing places in line; if you don't pay attention you may not get a second chance to move up for a placement. Most judges use arm signals to indicate "move forward" or "stop." Again, watching before your class goes in the ring will help you to understand your particular judge's pattern.

Your Sheltie should be trained to stand quietly while being examined by the judge, and should bring his ears up to show expression when requested to do so (using bait). If the dog uses his ears when he is being evaluated individually and in the final lineup for comparison to others, he should be allowed to relax at other times. Most Shelties become bored and quit baiting if you demand that they show continuously for half an hour. This is needlessly exhausting for both handler and dog and inconsiderate of the few judges who demand constant, non-stop showmanship in a Sheltie.

Most judges prefer a Sheltie be shown as naturally as possible, gaiting on a loose lead and walking naturally into a square stance. If your dog is unsure or stands incorrectly, you may need to kneel beside him and steady him with a hand on his collar and side. Don't be obvious about holding your dog up; it makes him appear shy.

THE SHOW LEAD

The show collar should be set high on your Sheltie's neck and worked into the skin so that it does not show. Make a part, first on one side of the neck and then the other, working the leash in as you go. Brush every hair out from under the lead and be sure that the hairs at the top of the neck are not matted down under the collar. Some handlers prefer to use a choke chain or a very narrow webb or leather collar instead of the martigale show lead. Be consistent so that when the collar is on, the dog knows he is going to be shown.

The leash should be a thin nylon cord that blends with the color of the dog. Fold loops of excess lead in the palm of your hand, shortening the lead until it is taut when your arm is extended straight out from your body. If you need to shorten the lead, take it up in folds which are concealed in your palm. Do not let the end dangle.

BAITING

I have seen just about everything edible used for baiting a dog, plus all types of small squeeky toys. Be considerate—noisemakers should not be loud enough to distract the dogs around you, and bait, if tossed, must be picked up. Some Shelties can be taught to catch bait. This is an effective attention-getter, but again, do not toss bait if it is likely to be dropped about the ring.

Your Sheltie should be trained to accept food from your hand while in the ring, and he should not be allowed to pick any food off the floor. If a piece of liver drops, he must be trained to ignore it and continue focusing on his handler.

Dont expect your Sheltie to keep his ears up and stare at a piece of liver continually. In a large class, he can be allowed to relax while the dogs ahead and behind you are being examined. As the judge is examining the Sheltie in front of you, begin to stack and bait your dog. Also, be quick to have your dog set up and baiting after the last dog in the class has been examined, and during the judge's first rundown of the class after you come in the ring.

A show dog must "bait" in the ring.

The dog is expected to stand while the judge examines him.

GAITING PATTERNS

One of four standard patterns is used for individual gaiting: straight down and back; an "L" pattern; a triangle; or a "T." Your Sheltie should be familiar with all four patterns so he will gait smoothly in a straight line regardless of which pattern the judge requests. Keeping the dog between yourself and the judge at all times makes a good appearance, but don't ask your dog to switch sides unless you have trained him to work smoothly on either side of you.

1. Do not crowd the dog ahead of you.
2. Do not block the judge's view of another dog.
3. Do not distract the other entries by tossing food or toys near them or making loud noises as you bait your own dog.
4. Be polite to the judge and other exhibitors.
5. Do not make excuses to the judge. He must rate your dog on appearance in the ring; he is not interested in why your dog is not in condition.

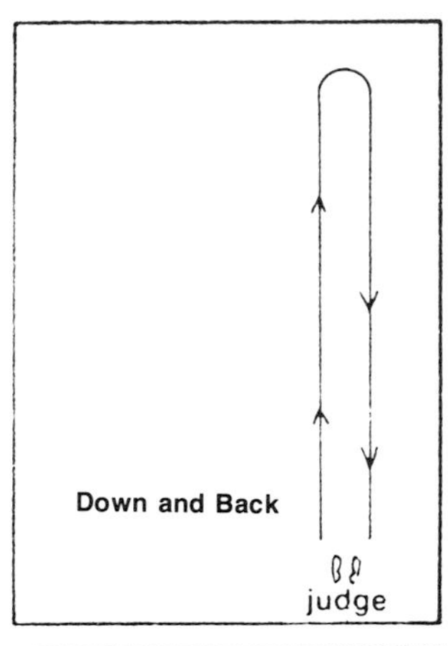

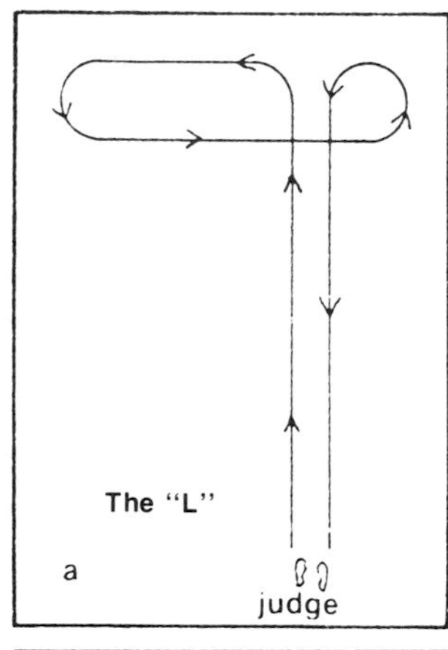

Most judges use one of these standard gaiting patterns when evaluating individual dogs.

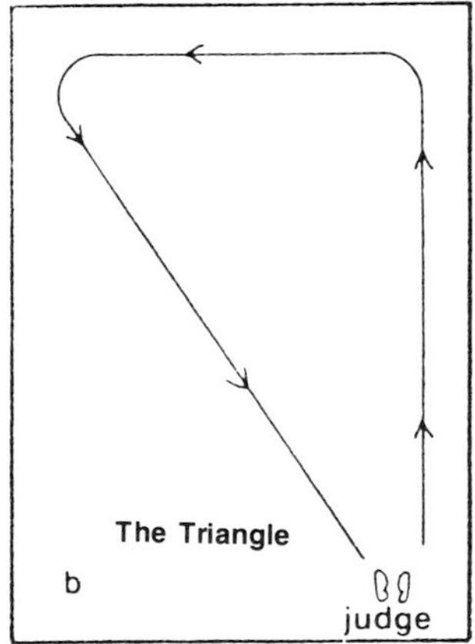

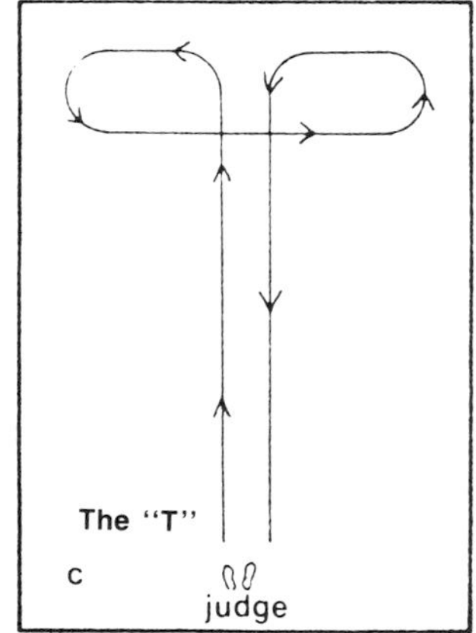

Shelties gaiting during an outdoor show.

If your dog breaks stride or begins playing, stop and start out smoothly again. Unless the judge can see the way the feet and legs move he will not be likely to place your dog. Any of the four patterns will bring you directly back to the judge. *Be sure the dog, not you, is lined up directly in front of the judge.* Slow the dog gradually as you approach, bringing him to a stop about six feet in front of the judge. A well trained Sheltie will stop squarely and bait on cue to show expression.

COURTESY IN THE RING

Certain courtesies are observed by all exhibitors:

6. Answer any questions politely and treat the judge with respect.

If another handler crowds you or blocks your dog from the judge, be courteous but firm in requesting him to move back. If a handler deliberately crowds you several times, summon the steward and file a complaint. Never make complaints to the judge; handling such problems is the function of the ring steward. You may ask a judge to clarify his directions if you do not understand them, but make every effort to pay attention so this is not necessary.

Judges

A judge generally uses the same gaiting pattern with all of his entries, so handlers at the end of a class are expected to know this pattern. It is tiresome and annoying if the judge must repeat instructions to every exhibitor. It is also disheartening to a judge to be treated discourteously. Most judges volunteer because they love dogs and hope their opinion will help improve the breed. Many pay some of their own expenses, and they rarely receive a salary for their work. They are on their feet all day, often enduring uncomfortable temperature, precipitation, or inadequate ventilation. The loud speaker may be aimed directly at their ears. Many judges are not young. A considerate exhibitor recognizes these things and gives the judge his respect whether or not he agrees with the judge's decisions. A few judges "play politics" with favorite handlers; some are rough with dogs, discourteous to exhibitors, or unqualified for judging Shelties. These few should not be allowed to spoil the entire sport. As an exhibitor you need to accept judges as people with shortcomings as well as strengths.

Am. Can. Ch. Robrovin Johnny Appleseed, A BIS winner, finished his championship before he was a year old and was a prominent winner in the Northwest for several years. Owners, Lorraine Still.

Ch. Valdawn's Talk of the Town, winner of 100 Best of Breeds and three times BOB at Westminster. Owned by Kay and Herb Searle. (Gilbert photo)

Any one placement is relative and may be reversed the following day by another judge. It is trite indeed to feel that you must win every time. At one time or another every exhibitor is defeated by a Sheltie he would not want to own, but whose quality cannot be denied. Different judges look for different qualities. A flashy dog who is reasonably sound may do well under an "all-rounder" (person who judges all breeds, usually not a Sheltie breeder) since this judge will look for fundamental traits such as structure, gait, substance, showmanship, coat, and balance. The "specialty" judge (usually a Sheltie breeder) may put emphasis on breed type, especially expression and head. A big coat, pretty color, or terrier showmanship will not compensate for "commonness" under the specialty judge. Different types of judges balance each other. Neither type of judge should be so blind as to totally ignore the other's viewpoint. Specialty winning dogs should not be beautiful cripples (lovely in type but lacking sadly in body qualities), nor Best in Show winners be flashy mutts who bear little resemblance to typey Shelties. You may notice that group winning Shelties aren't always the best representatives of the breed—they are too often simply the big, showy dogs that stand out easily. Once a breeder could safely assume a group winner would move well even if he lacked in type or refinement. But this isn't necessarily true now, so be aware that a show record is only as impressive as the dog to which it belongs.

If you don't agree with a particular judge it is your option not to show under him. But remember, a judge may put up a poor quality dog because everything else in the ring is even worse. Observe a judge's placements at several different shows before you form a definite opinion. Placements may be reversed tomorrow. If you can take pride in how well your dog showed and also take a few minutes to congratulate the winner, this is the essence of sportsmanship.

When your dog becomes a champion and is entered in the Specials class, stakes are even higher and competition tougher. The judge must consider very small details of perfection. If your Sheltie is overlooked, remember, there are numerous "off-duty authorities" at ringside who may have been far more impressed with your dog than was the judge. This is the ultimate victory.

Am. Can. Ch. Banchory in Dress Blues was the first show dog owned by Steve Klein and Debbie Baughman. They owner/handled him into the top twenty with a BIS and numerous group placements during their first two years of exhibiting.

Ch. Lynnlea Forever Amber C.D., took Best of Breed at the 1983 ASSA Specialty at eight years of age. Owner, Ray and Dorothy Christiansen.

SPORTSMANSHIP

Dog showing is a *sport*, and is supposed to be fun for both dogs and handlers. Whenever an exhibitor feels pressured to win, some of the fun is lost. No dog can be expected to win *every* time.

Good sportsmanship, ethics, modesty in victory, and honor in defeat are the considerations which enable you to enjoy showing. How you accept the win in relation to those who lose may well be the dividing line between making friends or enemies; between enjoying the show or having the day spoiled. Remember, placements may be re-

A relaxed, efficient, enthusiastic exhibitor will do more winning and develop fewer ulcers. A Sheltie is sensitive to and influenced by his handler's moods. He will look his best only when you both are relaxed and happy.

AMATEUR VS. PROFESSIONAL HANDLER

Any person who shows a dog in competition is called a handler. He can be the owner, a member of the owner's family, a friend, or a professional who earns a living showing dogs for others. In conformation showing, the term "handler" usually refers to the professional, a person who shows one or many breeds of dogs for a fee.

The fee varies with the handler and breed of dog. At this time, the average handling fee for a Sheltie is $25 to $35, including grooming and travel expenses. Board may be extra, and entry fees are not included.

Hiring a handler looks expensive on the surface, but in actuality may cost less than traveling to shows yourself. Time off from work, gas, motels, food, babysitters, and kennel help while you're gone all add up. A handler may "finish" a dog sooner (win enough points for a championship), but handling your own dog is more fun and there's a certain pride in finishing your own Shelties. Each owner must decide for himself which way is best. Many breeders exhibit at local shows and hire a handler for out of town circuits (several shows held consecutively in a short period of time). Others put the dog with a handler only at major point shows.

A handler is an expert in the ring. He tries hard to get every legitimate edge he can to win. Most handlers are courteous, efficient, and careful with the dogs. Any concerned owner would avoid hiring a handler who is impatient or rough with the dogs or who would not show and promote a dog to best advantage. A handler does not always win, but odds of his being considered are high. He will dress, groom, and handle better than the average owner, and is expert at conditioning and training. Good handlers are selective in the dogs they accept and show only dogs in peak condition.

A handler becomes familiar to judges, but most judges will not put up a handler just because they know and respect him. However, if a handler's reputation for handling fine dogs precedes him, the very fact that he has contracted to show a dog is in that dog's favor. The judges may look twice to determine just what the handler sees in the dog. This can be a distinct advantage for a plainly marked dog.

Am. Can. Mex. Ch. Benayr Grelore Fleetwood Mac CDX, owned by Mrs. Gene Dickinson.

Ch. Astolate Gold Award C.D., owned by Connie Hubbard.

Ch. Kismet Bi Surprise of Pocono, owned by Rhea Butler.

All these things make handlers tough competition. Don't complain if you are beaten by handlers unless you put as much effort into your presentation as they do. Many owner-handlers have established equal recognition. Anyone who looks or acts professional has a good chance in the ring. Repetitive showing gets your face known, and a trademark (particular dress, beard on a man, a certain distinctive ring manner, etc.) helps a judge remember you. Make sure the recollection is favorable.

Selecting a Handler

If you decide to hire a handler, select one with experience in the breed. Watch him handle as many dogs as possible. Do the dogs like him and respond well to him? Is he gentle yet firm? Is the dog shown to advantage or is the handler flaunting himself to the judge? Are both dog and handler well groomed? Is the handler taking all his dogs into the ring or is he sending some in with the groomer or assistant? Would you trust this handler to care for your dog properly and to handle public relations for you? Beware of the handler who carries 15 or 20 dogs per show or who exercises Shelties with St. Bernards. This person may be a fine handler but will simply not have the time to devote the individual attention a Sheltie needs.

You can find names and addresses of handlers in show catalogs, or magazines such as "Kennel Review."

Ch. September the Convincer, owned by Barbara Linden.

Jennie Tomlin, Best Junior Handler at the 1981 ASSA Specialty with Rosmoor Silver Sprite. (Rockwell photo)

Ch. Vanity Fair of Carmylie, C.D., owned by Jean Simmonds.

Ch. Wildoak Moon Reflection, owned by Pat Character.

However, I cannot recommend hiring a handler you have never watched unless he comes highly recommended by another Sheltie owner. Shelties need a special kind of handler and winning is useless if your dog freaks out as a result of pressure of improper treatment.

For your first contact with a handler, set up an appointment at home or after a show and take the dog under consideration along. No handler will do a good job with a dog he doesn't like, and the dog must like the handler, too. Openly discuss all terms of payment, responsibility, who is to show the dog, whether the handler will be showing another Sheltie at the same time, and any other questions you may have. Draw up a written contract to avoid future misunderstanding, and determine who is responsible for sending in entries.

FINISHING A CHAMPION

Perseverance is the single most important element in successful showing. You must believe in your dog and continue to show him against the odds if you expect to

Swedish and Norwegian Ch. Baronets Merle Snowflake, by Int. Ch. Shelgate Double Diamond, bred and owned by Monica Holmqvist.

1982 Swedish "Sheltie of the Year, Swedish and Finnish Ch. Shelgate Tom Tiddler, by Int, and Nord. Ch. Deloraine Dog Star, bred and owned by Anna Uthorn.

Ch. Macdega Oh Mi On Key, group winning son of Ch. Macdega the Piano Man. Owned by Macdega. (Ashbey photo)

Australian Ch. Tymawr Tapestry, sired by Imp. Ch. Merry Robin of Rodhill., owned by Sylvia Hayes, Merrylands, S.W. Australia.

make him a champion. He will often lose when you think he should win, but, if he is good eventually he will have his turn. There aren't many "cheap" champions in Shelties (dogs who finish quickly by default because there is little worthy competition). Even in remote areas Shelties entries are becoming fierce in number and quality, and it is no longer true that any Sheltie can finish if shown long enough under the right judges. It takes quality to win. On the other hand, even superb Shelties are seldom "fliers." A few finish in a minimum number of shows, but most take 20 or more shows to complete a championship.

Note appropriate dress of handler and that the Sheltie is stacked on a loose lead.

Some Shelties do better with their owner and some show up more with a handler. If your dog doesn't win in a reasonable number of shows, try putting him with a handler, or showing in a different region. Some dogs that lose in their home area will finish quickly in another part of the country against different competition.

It is not uncommon to spend will over $2000 to finish a dog. Show expenses are high and can only be rationalized as advertising and recreation. Just be glad the entire bill does not come due at once! Don't expect to make back your show expenses in stud fees—it may be possible but not likely.

SPECIALING A CHAMPION

The real challenge comes in the group and Best in Show ring. It takes a special type of Sheltie to do well here—not only an exceptional dog but a real showman and a dog that enjoys showing and traveling. To put a dog in the top twenty will require entering a large number of shows. Be selective of your judges, but keep the dog out as continually as possible while campaigning. Judges will begin to recognize and look for a top winning dog.

Advertising is important here. Most top winners are heavily promoted in publications read by the judges such as *The Chronicle* and *Kennel Review.* Whether we like to admit it or not, politics do play a part at this level.

While many breeders prefer to have a well-known professional handle their champion in the specials ring, owner handlers also are doing quite well with Shelties. If your dog has the quality to be a group winner, go for it!

The judge evaluates overall balance and outline.

WHEN TO STOP SHOWING

When the money involved outweights the dog's value, you must make a decision as to whether to continue. Don't give up without giving your dog a fair chance. Sometimes you need to wait for a young dog to mature. Other times, age begins to affect a dog's winning ability, clueing you it is time to stop. A top winner should no longer be campaigned when his percentage of show wins begins to slip noticeable.

In my experience, most novice exhibitors give up too easily. A Sheltie can lose ten shows in a row and then go on to finish quickly at another season, or in another area, or with another handler. Evaluate the alternatives carefully. Look at your dog as your competitors would, without making excuses, and being as objective as possible. Expect to spend money. If you can't afford it, don't buy a really top show dog. Breeders will not sell a good dog to someone they feel will not give every effort to finishing it, and if, by mistake, they do sell a dog to a novice who is not willing to make the investment, they will try to avoid making the same mistake again. Really exceptional Shelties are not easy to breed. If you have such a dog, give it every opportunity you can!

1982 Obedience Trial Champion Oh Mi Bodacious Thunder owned by Paulette Swartzendruber. Note the extreme alertness that made this dog a consistent top winner.

The Educated Sheltie 29

FORMAL OBEDIENCE

Shelties that are started in obedience too young may work well initially, but "sour" for advanced work. Let the youngster enjoy his puppyhood. Do not take a Sheltie to training class and demand perfection until he is at least six months old. Slower maturing Shelties may not be ready until a year of age.

Train your dog yourself. You will probably learn more than the dog, and besides, a professionally-trained dog is useless to you if you don't know how to control him. The dog's affection usually transfers to the person who trains him, so bear this in mind when deciding who will handle him. At least in the early stages, have only one person train the dog. Everyone gives commands a little differently, and the dog can easily become confused.

Many mistakes are due to handler errors, so if at all possible go to a class. An experienced instructor can stop problems in the early stages. Many dogs have been successfully trained at home, but it is a bit more difficult. If you intend to train without the aid of a class, try to work the dog in shopping centers or confusing surroundings occasionally. The dog unaccustomed to distraction may be unreliable in a show situation. Work on lead only until the dog knows the exercises completely. *Removing the leash too soon is the most common mistake made by the new trainer.*

A Sheltie who can do all the exercises covered in this chapter will be ready to compete for his C.D. (companion dog) degree, the first level available. More advanced work such as jumping, retrieving, and scent discrimination is highly individualized and so you should seek expert help (See Ch. 28 for a list of Open and Utility exercises). Training classes are available in most areas.

The following lessons are adapted from training aids written by Lewis V. "Vic" Cross, long-time training director for the Centennial Shetland Sheepdog Club of Greater Denver. Mr. Cross was an animal behaviorist and trainer with a devoted following and unequaled reputation. The lessons are divided into phases, each corresponding to one exercise. Most are intended to take *one week per phase;* a few may require a second week for perfection. Devote 15 minutes to half an hour once or twice a day to training each dog. Don't progress beyond the prescribed exercises in a week, and include a review of those already covered. If necessary, spend an extra week on a problem exercise. Vary the routine each day to prevent boredom, and to make sure the dog will work in any sequence.

Training Equipment

A properly fitting choke collar and a leather leash six feet long are all that are necessary for beginning training. Leather collars and chain leads are not suitable and do more harm than good. They are clumsy to handle and may injure or frighten the dog. A dog may be switched to a show lead for conformation showing after he is well lead-broken and knows "stand" and "stay."

The collar should be lightweight and just large enough to pass over the dog's head. It should never be over two inches longer than the dog's neck, unless he has an unusually large head. The collar may be made of chain or nylon. Nylon is lighter, but the sound and instant releasing action of chain is sometimes more effective. I buy the finest, lightest chain collars I can find, as the heavier ones are awkward on a Sheltie. Some trainers, however, prefer a slightly heavier collar because it does not become tangled in the hair and releases more easily. Whichever type you decide to use, buy the best quality choke collar available—one with smooth, strong links. Cheaper collars may have rough spots on the chain that will catch, preventing quick correction; or they may break easily.

A choke collar works on the principle of instant pressure when a correction is given, and instant release when the dog is where you want him. Therefore, the collar must be applied in the proper manner. Make it work correctly by holding one ring of the collar and dropping the chain through it to form a loop. Hold the loop in front of you with the loose end of the chain hanging down to form a "P." Face your Sheltie, placing the collar over his head with the loose ring hanging down on *his right side.* When the leash is attached and jerked upward, the collar should tighten. When the leash is released, the collar should automatically loosen.

Correct way to put on a choke collar. The "live" end to which the leash attaches comes over the dog's head on the right side.

Handler with dog sitting at heel position.

ACTUAL TRAINING LESSONS FOR NOVICE OBEDIENCE

In each of the exercises, it is important that the dog act instantly on command. Move with confidence and urgency, yet remain calm and in control of the situation. Always work the dog on your left side. The leash is held in the left hand, with the surplus ribboned up in the right hand rather than being wrapped around the hand or allowed to dangle. Use quick jerks, not constant pressure on the collar. A constantly taut lead causes constant "punishment" or pressure on the dog's neck and he will only fight the lead. When the leash is jerked sharply and released the choke collar becomes an effective correction. The dog will attempt to avoid the pull and soon learns to pay attention to your commands. He should learn to work with the leash slack except when corrections are given.

When you expect your dog to follow you, step off with your *left* leg. If you expect him to stay, leave on the *right* foot. The dog will learn to take his cues from your left leg. Speak commands firmly and clearly; do not shout.

Phase One—The Sit-Stay

In this exercise the dog is required to remain in a sitting postion, without so much as shifting a paw, until the owner has relieved him from his exercise by use of another command. He cannot whine, bark, or sniff around, even though the owner might be a hundred yards away. This is the most important exercise the dog will be taught in this course and *all* his future lessons will depend on your ability to enforce this command. There are some exercises that cannot be taught until your dog reliably "stays."

Do not become complacent if the dog does this exercise perfectly from the start. It is better if he challenges it at some time so that he can become aware that a correction will be made. This is the only way he will learn that he must stay under *any* circumstances, not just when he wants to. When he seems to be learning the exercise well, throw in some distractions to try to get him to break. These are more effective if done by someone other than yourself. You are *demanding* that the dog stay, you are not asking him to stay.

Correct heel position at a walk.

Giving the hand signal for "Stay."

Training the sit-stay. With your dog standing at your left, hold the lead in the left hand near the collar and the surplus lead in your right hand. Without using the dog's name, and with no forewarning, give a sharp command—"SIT!" Use only the one word and do not repeat it. Immediately reach down and grasp the collar with the right hand and let go of the lead that is in your left hand. Snap the lead upwards and backwards, throwing the dog off balance, and in a simultaneous move, with the *left* hand, tap him on the rump near the base of the tail.

The moment the dog is in a proper sitting position, praise him as though he had done it on his own. If he jumps up, repeat, with a quiet command of "STAY," but do *not* repeat the word "Sit."

With the right hand still holding the lead, give the command and signal to "STAY." The signal is given by bringing the open right hand, with palm down in front of the dog's muzzle. Stand close by your dog for a few moments until he has settled down a bit, then start walking away from him, making a circle to the right or left. Leave on the *right* foot.

Start and end each exercise in the same position. Walk around your dog's left side and stop at the point where you began, with him sitting at your left. Step forward and give him the command "FREE" or "OK." Get him to move right away and praise him well. By the end of the week you should be able to leave your dog on a sit and walk about 6 feet away. Face the dog for about a minute, neither of you moving, then return and walk around him to the heel position. Only after you have returned and given him a release command should he move.

If your dog should move from a stay, go to him quickly and with a firm reprimand, replace him. Get tougher with each succeeding correction. *Never correct him from a distance.* When sitting the dog, be certain that his front feet are well under him for support. Make him as secure and comfortable as possible. Dogs that are unwilling to stay can sometimes be aided by lopping the lead several times around the dog's neck with the balance of the lead dangling to the floor in front of him.

Right from the beginning, do not permit your dog to whine or bark while on a sit-stay. Correct him instantly the moment he tries. Grasp the muzzle and press his upper lips against the back teeth. Use enough pressure that he knows you mean it, combined with the verbal command "NO BARK." Just before leaving your dog again after you have corrected him, use praise. Don't leave him sitting there feeling that you are upset with him. Don't tug forward on the lead when he is first learning the sit, as this indicates that you are calling him toward you. Also, try not to lean over him.

When leaving the dog, walk at your normal pace, or the dog will become suspicious of your movements and try to follow you. Do not look back at your dog until you turn to face him.

Ring commands for the sit-stay exercise. All the dogs will be in the ring at the same time lined up against one side. The judge will give the command "Sit your dog." Each handler will sit his dog squarely as instructed and await the next command. The judge will then say "Leave your dog." Each handler will give his dog a command and signal to "stay" and leave immediately, starting on the right foot. Walk across the ring to the designated place and turn to face your dog. You will remain in this position with your arms hanging at your sides until given further instructions. You are not allowed to give verbal or non-verbal cues to your dog.

On the command "Return to your dog," you will walk back to the dog, and around behind him to the heel position. Keep him sitting until the final command, "Exercise finished," at which time you may release your dog. This is the only time praise is allowed in the ring.

Phase Two—Heel on Lead

In this exercise, the dog is taught to walk at your left side on a loose lead without pulling, lagging behind, or wandering in front of you. He must learn to walk at your pace, be it normal, slow, or a run, and he must be able to change directions quickly without tripping you. When you stop, he must sit at once at your left side without a command. While in the heeling postion he must not break pace or place, regardless of distractions.

The most important thing you must learn in this exercise is how to work with and maintain a loose lead at all times. The lead and collar must hang down under the dog's chin to form a loop of about four inches of slack. It is quite important that this slack be retained at all times because it permits the use of the "snap" or jerk of the lead which is much like "cracking the whip" in its effectiveness.

Touch the dog on the flank to encourage him to Stand Stay.

In the heeling exercises, walk energetically, with short strides. Be quick in all your actions, and demand quick sits of your dog. Make certain he sits straight; it is easier to train him to sit straight from the beginning than to correct a bad habit later. If his attention wanders, give him a quiet, yet excitable, command to "HEEL."

Training the heel on lead. With the dog sitting squarely at your left and his legs lined up alongside yours, hold the ribboned lead in your right hand and hold the lead near the collar (allowing the loop of slack) with the left hand. Give your dog's name, and the command "Rover, HEEL." Pause a second, then step off briskly with your left foot, giving a simultaneous jerk on the lead to get the dog into quick action. (In the ring, the judge will use the command "Forward" to begin the exercise.)

For the first few days, take only four steps and then bring the dog into a quick sit. The steps will end with the right foot so that the left leg is stationary when the dog is supposed to sit. (In the ring you will be given the command "HALT.") On the third step, reach down with the right hand and grasp the collar (not the leash) and let the left hand fall free. Sit the dog in the same manner you learned for the sit-stay. The stay command is not given, but the dog is expected to remain in position until given further orders. For the first four or five days you may give your dog a verbal command to "SIT" whenever you stop. After the fifth day delete this command so he doesn't learn to wait for your voice. Just snap him into the sit position each time you stop, and then praise him.

The dog should stay close while doing an about turn.

If the dog fails to remain in the proper heeling position, give a quick snap of the lead accompanied by a command "HEEL." Make it sound like a command, not a question. Make all corrections with your left hand, because a tug with the right hand will pull the dog into your path. Do not allow him to lag or forge ahead, even if it means a jerk with each stop at first. Keep the dog close enough that there is just room for your hand to pass between his body and your legs.

The right turn is made by pivoting off the right foot in a clockwise direction. Keep your left foot out of the dog's path, and give three or four quick jerks so the dog maintains the heel position as he follows the turn. Be gentle but insistent, with lots of verbal encouragement ("Good boy," "That's the way").

The left turn is again made by pivoting on the right foot, leading off in the new direction with your left foot. Bump the dog's shoulder to start him off in the right direction. Turn only 90 degrees. Make it look like an accident when you bump the dog, and praise him when he jumps the right way.

The about turn is always made to the right and is done with a series of small steps accompanied by several short jerks and praise. Do not pivot as this is harder for the dog to follow. Give the dog encouragement to stay close to you, and give him an instant's notice that you are changing direction.

The figure 8 is performed around two people acting as "posts." No command is given except "HEEL" and you will be asked to halt at irregular intervals. This exercise encourages the dog to make smooth turns at uneven speeds, and determines if he is gauging his speed to you.

Phase Three—Stand for Examination

In this exercise the dog is required to stand perfectly despite all sorts of distractions, including having strangers run their hands over him. He may look around or wag his tail, but he is not allowed to move a single paw, and he must not show signs of fear or resentment. Young puppies may be inclined to wiggle about. Be firm but gentle with them. Don't ever let them think the stand exercise is punishment.

Training the Stand. There are two ways to train the stand. The first method starts with the dog sitting at heel postion. With the lead in your right hand, give the command "STAND." Step forward with your left foot, bringing the dog into standing position. Take only a single step, pivoting to face your dog. Quickly touch his loin with your left hand to keep him from sitting. Hold for a minute. If he is in an awkward position, move his feet so that he is comfortable and standing squarely. Then give the command and hand signal to "STAY." Let go of his loin and stand facing him. When he understands the command to stand, gradually increase your distance from him and require him to stand as you circle behind him to the heel postion.

An alternative method is to walk your dog into the stand postion. As you are heeling, give the verbal command "STAND" accompanied by the hand signal to stay. As you do so, step in front of the dog. If he attempts to sit, check his motion with your fingers under his flank. Stand him squarely as before if necessary and gradually move further away from him.

If your dog moves, hold him in the loin to lift him up or prevent his forward motion. Do not jerk the lead. Repeat the command "STAY." Avoid staring at your dog or pulling him off balance with the lead as you walk away. On the return, step close to his right side so he is not tempted to close the gap, since you have taught him to heel close by your leg.

When the dog is steady for a minute or two with you standing at the end of the lead, introduce him to permitting another person to examine him and walk around him. Then teach him to stand for examination while the lead is dropped, and finally while the lead is removed entirely. Do not progress too fast. Be sure your Sheltie is perfectly steady at one stage before progressing to the next one.

In the ring, the stand for examination will be performed off lead, with the handler standing approximately six feet in front of the dog while the judge examines him.

Phase Four—The Come-Fore

This is a transition from heeling to the recall and is designed to aid in straight recalls and straight sits. It is a practice exercise only and will not be performed in the ring. The dog will begin in a heel position and end sitting in front facing you. You will not change the direction you are facing, but the dog will. You just start walking backwards.

Training the come-fore. While heeling forward, suddenly give the command "COME—FORE" with emphasis on the come. At this point, release your left hand from the lead, and when your right foot is forward, start running backward. Use the right hand to bring the dog directly in front of you. Stop after four or five steps. As you stop, the dog should be lined up straight, facing you, so that you can give the command "SIT." The dog will stop with his toes about three inches from yours. Next, give the order "HEEL" and step briskly forward, bumping the dog's right side so that he turns into the heel position and follows. Move quickly.

This is an easy lesson for both you and the dog.

Phase Five—The Finish

Now, the dog will learn to move to the heel position from the recall or come-fore. This exercise is difficult and will take repeated effort. Start in slow motion but speed up as time progresses. If you rush the dog, he will learn quicker.

Training the finish. Have the dog sit facing you, close enough so you can easily reach his collar. Take the lead in your left hand, and hold the ring of the collar. Give the command "HEEL" (sometimes differentiated from the previous command as "Hee-L"). Pause a second, then move the left hand back as far as you can reach, pulling the dog along, stepping back simultaneously with your left foot. Bring your foot back to standing position and the dog into the heel position and a quick sit. Eventually the dog should leap both directions.

Some dogs may have to be taught a variation of this exercise, where the dog goes around the handler in a clockwise direction to reach the heel position. In training this method the left foot remains planted, the right foot steps back and then returns as the dog is pulled around the handler. You must change hands on the leash twice as the dog is pulled around. Either method of finishing is

Training the Stand Stay. Walk to the end of the lead, wait, then return around the dog.

Training the Come Fore.

acceptable. Choose one and stick with it so the dog doesn't become confused.

Phase Six—The Recall

The recall will be carried out in three stages. The first stage is designed to help prevent crooked recalls and sloppy sits, at the same time affording maximum control over the dog's movements. The second stage encourages instant response from the dog. In the third stage the dog comes to you off lead. When he approaches, he will sit facing you as in the come-fore exercise and will remain there until given the command to finish.

Training this exercise requires a jerk which you may feel is too severe. Nevertheless, your dog must learn that when you say "COME," he must obey *instantly.* He will come to you because he has to, not because he wants to. *Never* give a second command in this exercise. After a few lessons the dog will come to you quickly, willingly, and happily. If you allow him to be hesitant from the beginning he will not be as confident.

Training the recall (part one). Place the dog in the heel position and give him a "STAY" command. Leave on the right foot and turn to face your dog from about 18

Training the Finish.

Training the Recall. A sharp jerk is given simultaneously with the command "Come."

inches away. Hold all of the lead and the ring of the collar in the right hand. Using the dog's name, give the command "Rover, COME." Pause a second, then with a quick, hard snap of the collar, start running backwards, encouraging the dog as you go. At first, limit your run to five or six steps.

Just before you stop, take one slow step, then freeze in your tracks. Simultaneously snap the dog into a straight sit in front of you as in the come-fore. You may use the left hand to put him into a sitting position. The moment he sits, give the command "STAY" and *praise him lavishly.*

No matter how well your dog performs, do not progress beyond this stage of training for the first few days. You can create extra problems by rushing too fast over the initial stages. Since you have absolute control with the collar, there is never a need for scolding or punishment.

Part two. This stage of training is the same as part one except you are now working the dog at the end of the lead. Be sure to *jerk* rather than pull the dog toward you. (The jerk is something the dog will want to avoid; a steady pull is not.) Alternate this exercise with some sit-stays so the dog does not begin to anticipate your command and come before he is told to do so.

Place the dog in a sit-stay and go to the end of the lead. Step far enough away that you have to stretch your arm forward to hold the leash. Holding the lead in the right hand, command "Rover, COME" and give one sharp jerk on the lead, bringing your hand to the opposite shoulder (fig. 10). As the dog leaps to his feet, run backward and call encouragingly to him in hopes of exciting him to come at a run. Reel the lead in hand over hand so the dog does not become entangled. Bring him into a fast, straight sit, give the command "STAY" and praise him. After about 12 days, attach a 10- or 15-foot cord to his collar and work at that distance. Once you have the dog coming to you, merely drop the line and begin running backwards. Eventually you can remove the lead completely.

Remember never to scold the dog from a distance. If he needs correction, *go to him.* No matter what he does, praise if he comes to you. Even if he bites your mother-in-law and runs to you for help, don't correct him if he comes to you. Go after him to punish him; never call him to you for punishment.

When the dog approaches on a recall, help him to sit straight. Don't jerk him around or he may sit out of reach. Voice is very important in this exercise. The dog's name is spoken in a normal tone, but the "Come" is higher pitched and louder. Make the command happy so he is not afraid to approach you. Teach your dog to come happily and quickly.

At this point do not combine the finish with the recall and do not hesitate to return to part one if your dog becomes confused or defiant.

Part three. You are now ready for the recall without a lead. Be sure the dog is ready for this stage; starting too soon means certain failure. Start the first off-lead session with three or four recalls from the end of the lead. Unsnap the leash and place the snap between the dog's feet, well behind his field of vision. Hold the end of the lead and allow the rest to lay along the ground. Reach down and adjust the collar so the dog will forget you have removed the lead. You may have to tug lightly on the ring which tightens the collar so the dog knows you are still in control.

Command "STAY" and step to the end of the lead, carrying the end just as you did in part two. Give the dog his command "COME" and jerk the lead as though it were still attached. Back up about two steps and encourage the dog to hurry. If the dog fails to obey your command, go quickly to him, scolding all the way. Snap on the lead and give three or four sharp recalls as in part one of this exercise. Then remove the lead and try again at a distance of about six or seven feet.

Gradually increase your distance until the dog will come to you from a distance of about 20 feet. If you have problems, cut the distance down for a few times. The dog must obey *every* time. Correct him without a second command. He should receive *enthusiastic praise* each time he comes. Limit your distance to about 20 feet, and perfect the recall before you combine it with the finish. Even after you have combined the two exercises do not ask the dog to finish every time or he may begin to anticipate.

Phase Seven—The Down-Stay

In this exercise you must train the dog to lie down on command and stay until you release him. Never repeat the command "DOWN." If a second command is needed, force the dog into position with the lead instead of repeating the verbal command.

Training the down-stay. At first your Sheltie will have to be placed into position. Start with him sitting at heel. Kneel beside him. Grasping his forelegs in your right hand, push gently on his shoulder with your left hand, pressing simultaneously away from you and downward. This should throw him slightly off balance. Pull his forelegs foreward, forcing him into the down position as you reassuringly, but firmly, command "DOWN." Give the command "STAY," and continue holding him down for several seconds. Then release him with an "OKAY" and praise. Repeat this exercise several times until your Sheltie seems confident and relaxed on the down.

After a few days, place the dog on a sit-stay and give the command "DOWN" while at the same time pulling down on his collar with your right hand. If he hesitates, down him with a sharp downward jerk on the lead near the collar. When he stays reliably with you standing in front, gradually increase your distance and return by circling behind him to the heel position. Eventually the dog should stay down while you walk twenty feet away and remain facing him for a period of five minutes. Add distractions to your training sessions at this point.

Phase Eight—Working Off-Lead

How can you control your dog off lead? By signals and commands used in a manner that remind him that the lead may be off but it is not far away. This will work, of course, only if you have maintained the loose lead while training, and if the dog knows his on-lead work *thoroughly.* Many trainers suggest going back to on-lead heeling if the dog fails to respond correctly off lead, but this only teaches the dog to work better on lead.

Training off-lead. While the dog is heeling on lead, switch all the lead to your left hand. Give one quick jerk and the command "HEEL," then quietly drop the lead. It is best to speed up slightly to keep the dog's attention. Take a few steps and halt. This should bring the dog to a quick, straight sit beside you. Pick up the end of the lead and repeat the procedure until he works as smoothly with the lead dragging as when you are holding it. If he heels wide, drop the lead on his left side. If he crowds, drop it between you. Don't forget to give praise and encouragement.

After a few weeks your Sheltie should down on the command without the pull on the leash. If he does not begin to do this on his own, place the lead under your foot, command "DOWN" and snap the lead down with your foot. Force him down without the use of your hand. Eventually he should learn to down on voice command alone without you moving a muscle.

Ring commands for the down-stay. All dogs are lined up as in the "sit" exercise. The judge will say "Down your dogs," and handlers, in unison, give the command "DOWN." You may use verbal or a hand signal command, but not the dog's name. The judge will next command "Leave your dogs," and each handler will say "STAY" and walk across the ring. The handlers then turn and face their dog. Stand with arms at your sides and await further instruction. Do not look directly at your dog either from a distance or after you return. Just peek once in a while to make sure he is behaving. After three minutes have elapsed, the judge will command "Return to your dogs," at which point you will return and circle the dog to the starting postition. When you hear "Exercise finished," release your dog with "FREE" or "OK." Don't heel forward before praising him or he will think the approval is for heeling.

Badgerton Red Riot O' Carmylie C.D.X. performs the Open exercise Retrieve Over The High Jump.

Sea Isle Skyhawk owned by Alison Miller, makes a flying leap over the broad jump, an open obedience class exercise. Pipsqueak and Alison competed for over a decade, during which time he won numerous High in Trial and High Combined awards. (Photo by Noel)

Off-lead heeling should come naturally at this point if you have done your homework thoroughly. Vary your patterns as time progresses, adding curves, right and left turns, about turns, and variable speed. Remove the lead entirely after a few days, and jerk the ring of the collar if you need to give correction.

This completes the novice exercises. Be sure your Sheltie is reliable in these exercises before beginning any advanced training. He has learned many exercises in a short time. If he becomes confused and "blows" an exercise, don't be too harsh unless he fails the same exercise repeatedly. Keep your lessons short (15 to 30 minutes) and try to train every day. A long session will not make up for a week's negligence and may only confuse and exhaust your Sheltie.

Ch. Mainstay Once Upon A Time, a Thunderation son owned by Jeannie Sardo and Steve Barger. (Photo by Krook)

The Career Dog 30

WHY HERD?

Herding is a challenge and a credit to any dog who has retained his herding instinct despite generations of non-use. Not all Shelties inherit the herding instinct, but those who do carry a sacred part of the breed heritage. Since it is virtually impossible to assess herding instinct without testing the dog on stock, I hope that more people will take an interest in herding as a *sport*. This explores the very essence of the Shetland SHEEPDOG and will help in preserving the unique, endearing Sheltie character. Dual purpose show dogs who can still do a useful day's work are the ultimate accomplishment. Such dogs will be able to excel in any field of practical or competitive endeavor and will be a joy to live with.

ANYONE CAN ENJOY HERDING

Herding, the natural occupation for which our Shelties were developed, can be one of the most exciting and rewarding sports. One need not live on a ranch to enjoy herding. In the Denver area we are fortunate to have a group of interested persons who have formed the Stock Dog Fanciers of Colorado Club. Members represent several breeds of stock dogs. The club owns a small herd of sheep and cattle plus numerous ducks, all of which are available to members. Ducks react much like sheep and are a cheap, efficient way to start a Sheltie herding. Three or four ducks kept in a backyard can be used to train a sheepdog in the middle of a city. We find it advisable to periodically trade ducks with other enthusiasts as they become "dog-wise" and learn the routine. If you trade or use different ducks every few days they never quite know what to expect and are better subjects.

Herding Instinct

A good stock dog must have herding instinct. Herding can be taught, but a Sheltie uninterested in livestock will never be a *good* herder. Testing for instinct is difficult in a puppy, as a dog may not "start to run" (show interest in herding) until seven or eight months of age, and sometimes not until 18 months. Most show some signs earlier, however, and their success as a herder can be determined by the owner's reaction at this time. City dogs show herding instinct by circling the yard on patrol, keeping children supervised, "herding" a large ball around the yard with their noses and feet, chasing strange people and animals from the yard, chasing cars or birds, and being a "mother hen" with other dogs or small children. Scolding a puppy so he feels he must never do these things can ruin him for herding. Instead, he should be encouraged in those which are acceptable.

His reaction when introduced to livestock is most important, and as long as the dog does no real damage, any positive action should be encouraged. An older dog who has never seen sheep may take repeated exposure to show interest. Try a timid dog on ducks first. Familiarity with livestock may hasten the reaction, and many dogs who totally ignore stock initially may show interest in herding once they feel comfortable in the unfamiliar surroundings.

There are two types of interest. One is purely chasing, often accompanied by "gripping" or biting the livestock. This is normal in young, inexperienced dogs but should be corrected. The best dogs show a natural inclination to keep the sheep (or ducks) bunched together and will tend to move them into a corner and hold them there without charging. Encourage the dog to bring the stock toward you or else drive them forward. Excessive barking is not necessary. A Sheltie, however, because of his size, may use his voice to command the same respect as a silent dog of a larger breed.

Seraphim's Prince Indigo Blue C.D., Seraphim Shelties, demonstrates the quick reflexes necessary in a herding dog.

Why Dogs Herd[1]

Herding is believed to be a perversion of the hunting instinct natural to the wild ancestor of the dog. In any pack there were faster dogs which ran ahead of the game and turned it back toward the pack, and slower ones who followed and completed the kill. The slow type evolved into the hunting and trailing dogs (particularly some of the hound breeds) and the forerunners of the pack were later trained by man to become the herding dogs. Puppies still show this hunting instinct by their willingness to attack stock. This is modified as the dog gets older, and becomes acceptable herding behavior.

Strong "eye" (staring at the stock with frozen posture) is likely an offshoot of pointing, and indeed, it has been proven that herding dogs actually do use their noses as much as relying on eyesight. Blind dogs can still effectively herd on familiar ground. "Eye," the pride of Border Collie fans, is one manner of showing interest, but does not have to be present for a dog to herd. Too much "eye" is a disadvantage as the dog may stare mesmerized at the stock and be oblivious to his frustrated handler who has become hoarse from shouting at the dog. Shelties usually show only moderate "eye" or none at all, yet they tend to be extremely responsive to their handlers.

What Makes a Good Herding Dog

Besides herding instinct, certain characteristics are important in a prospective herding dog. The best combina-

[1]Much of this section is based on information from: John Holmes. *The Farmer's Dog*. London: Popular Dogs Publishing Co. Ltd., 1973.

tion is submissiveness and herding desire in equal amounts. Submissiveness is essential, for without it the dog is uncontrollable. This is perhaps the greatest argument against the overly aggressive, terrier-type Sheltie who would rather bite a sheep than herd it. John Holmes, an expert in all aspects of herding dogs and long time breeder of Border Collies and Welsh Corgis (both of whom are supposed to be more aggressive than Shelties) says, "In the working of sheep, implicit obedience is essential and, in the evolution of the herding breeds, it is unlikely that the occasional 'pack-leader type' would be bred from.

Banchory Blue Bonnet, Seraphim Shelties, on a "down" to keep sheep in the corner.

Ducks are a cheap and convenient substitute for sheep.

It is, therefore, very rare to find a dog with a strong leading instinct in the breeds to which I shall be referring, but that does not rule out the possibility of your being unlucky enough to get one."[2] Obviously, he feels that such a dog is a definite liability in any of the shepherd breeds.

The dog you select should also be of normal intelligence, but intelligence is not the most important thing. The troublemaker who is "too smart for his own good" is not always the best bet, but he may use herding as an outlet for his frustrations. Often a quiet dog will excel when exposed to sheep.

If a dog is left to herd without direction, his instinct will become stronger with age while his submissiveness decreases. It is important for the trainer to establish authority as the "pack leader" to whom the dog will remain submissive in direct proportion to increased aggressiveness with sheep. A city-bred Sheltie may be so overly conscious of the handler's dominance that he doesn't dare become distracted by the sheep. This is even more true if he has just completed beginning obedience training or has been punished for chasing in the past. If the dog is given encouragement which reassures his urge to herd, instinct will take over in time.

I find it best to cultivate the herding instinct before obedience training. The dog who has been obedience trained before he works stock will watch the handler rather than the sheep, while the reverse is preferable. However, formal training will only enhance a dog who is already secure in his ability to herd. First the dog should get control of the stock, then the handler gets control of the dog.

The overly aggressive dog is easily distracted from his work and does not exhibit the intense loyalty necessary to make him a trustworthy guardian of his flock. Suspicion of unfamiliar people and things is desirable in a herding dog and may save his life and the life of his flock, but unreasonable fear is bad. A frightened dog will not be any more dependable in an emergency than the one which greets the enemy like part of the family or is oblivious to its presence.

Training A Young Dog With An Older One

An "old wives' tale" has led people to believe that a puppy must be started herding by working with an older, well-trained dog. While this method can give a dog an idea of what herding is all about, it should not be used beyond the introductory stages. A dog started alone may take longer to "start to run" but will generally work better in the long run. The dog who becomes dependent on another dog may refuse to work alone or with any dog but his "teacher."

Control of a herding dog depends on dominance of the trainer. If two dogs work together, the inexperienced one will accept the trained dog as the "pack leader" and the handler is even less in control. It is harder to correct the bad habits of a dog trained this way than to train him from scratch. Working herding dogs in pairs encourages a natural hunting desire rather than the modified herding actions, and the dogs may become rough. Only after they are thoroughly trained, with the trainer firmly established as the dominant personality, should two or more dogs be worked together as a team.

How to Begin

There are as many ways to train a herding dog as there are trainers. Trial and error will determine your best

[2] *The Farmer's Dog,* p. 210.

results, but here are a few tips which have helped us get started.

1. If the dog can be controlled verbally, he may be worked off-lead. Otherwise start him on a long lead, 30 to 50 feet in length. This is attached to his choke collar and kept on all the time until he is reliable about going "down" on command in spite of the distraction of the sheep. Much of the time he can work free but dragging the lead. The lead may hinder the enthusiasm of an unsure dog.

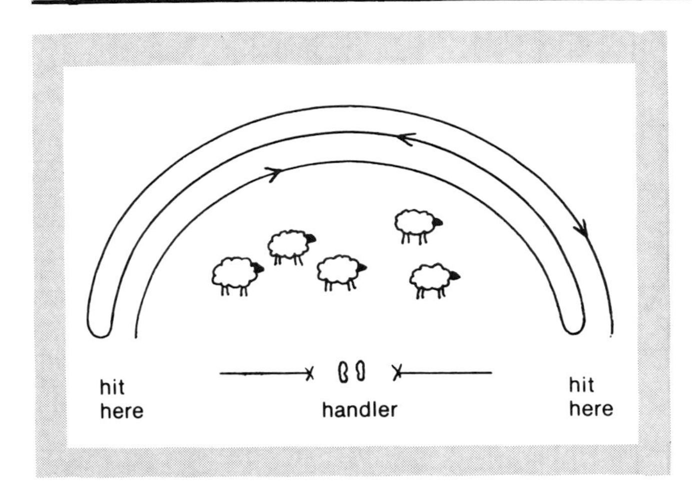

Train the dog to work behind the sheep and bring them toward you.

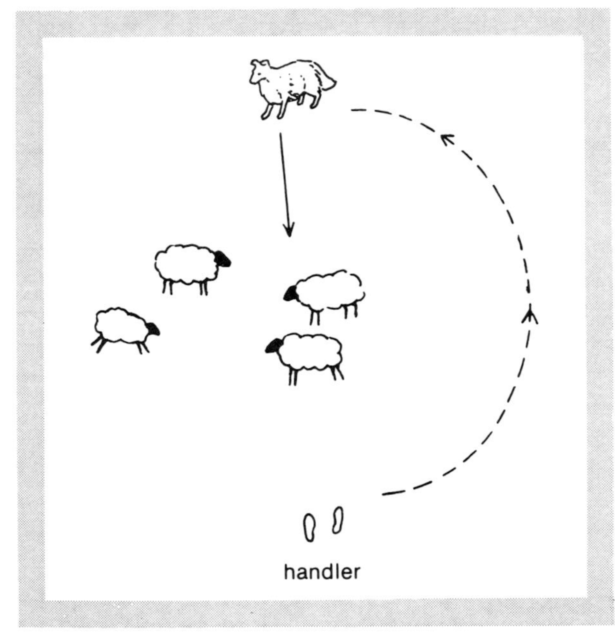

The "walk on" requires the dog to approach the sheep in a straight line. He may be asked to do an outrun to reach the proper position.

2. Commands vary with each handler. Some use voice commands; others a whistle. The dog must know the command "DOWN" and obey it instantly. "Down" is used to stop a charging dog, to allow the stock to become calm, and to get the dog's attention for further instructions. Some trainers substitute "haw" and require only that the dog stop in his tracks. Other trainers use both commands, saving the "down" for emergencies when the dog's bobbing up and down will startle the sheep into awareness of the dog. "Easy" usually means to slow down or hesitate.
3. Some communication as to which way the flock is to be moved must be established. One way is to down the dog opposite the desired direction of movement and give the command "WALK ON" meaning drive the flock directly ahead. Commands meaning "left," "right," "go out around the flock," "come," and "go around behind the handler" are also fundamental. I enjoy the traditional "way to me" (right) and "go by" (left) for directional herding. You may prefer to improvise your own commands.
4. Portable panels are easily constructed to form "gates" through which the dog must move the stock.
5. Since many trials include a water obstacle, it may be helpful to train the dog to retrieve ducks from a pond by herding around them. Some Shelties do not like getting their feet wet, so increasing familiarity with water is necessary.
6. The shepherd's crook or stick, used as an extension of the trainer's arm, is a valuable training aid. It is easily seen at a distance, and is used during early training to teach the dog directions and to encourage a wider outrun. If the dog resists commands he can be pushed gently in the direction you wish him to go

with the crook. Don't frighten him or he may be discouraged from coming close when necessary.

Actual Training Pointers

Initially you should let the dog sniff and test the sheep without interference. Once interested, most Shelties will circle around the stock to bunch them together. Your dog will show a definite preference to circle one direction, and after he has confidence with the stock you must concentrate on training him to go the other direction.

As the dog is circling the flock, start running backward and encourage him to bring the sheep toward you. You will probably have to make turns to slow the sheep enough to be easily handled. If the sheep run past you, make an about turn and the dog will naturally circle to the opposite side to continue bringing them toward you. Work at first with about three sheep, preferably the type which stick together rather than scattering.

As the dog encircles the stock toward you, hit the ground with your stick as he approaches and command him back in the other direction. This keeps him on the opposite side of the stock from you (fig. 5). As he returns from the other direction, send him back behind the sheep again, thus creating the zigzag herding pattern. The dog will constantly bunch the sheep but will also accomplish moving the flock toward you at all times. If he tries to circle around you, continually move in front of him, forcing him to reverse and go back around the stock.

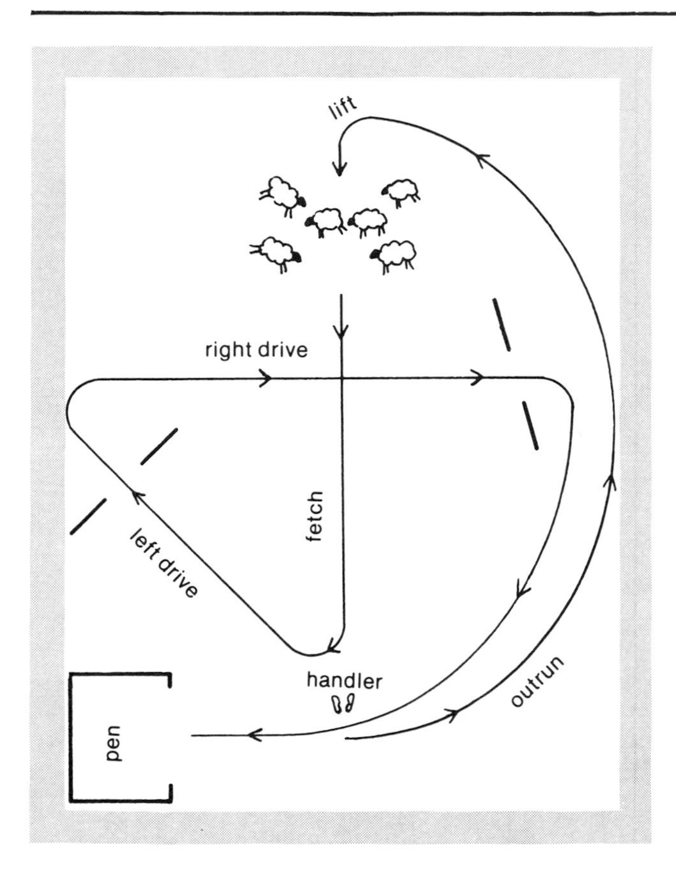

A standard herding pattern used at trials.

Young Shelties are introduced to a ewe.

The "outrun" involves the dog's circling the flock away from the trainer to a point opposite the direction in which the sheep are to be moved. This action is natural for most Shelties as they fall into the category of *herding* dogs. (Some breeds or individuals are naturally heelers or drivers instead of herders. Herders were developed for sheep; drivers for cattle. All stock dogs tend to do one or the other and must be taught the unnatural maneuver.) The Sheltie's natural outrun may be too near the sheep and should be widened with training. With the dog on lead, send him toward the flock but with the crook direct him so he must swing wide. Encourage him to keep going.

Once this routine becomes familiar, lead the dog between the sheep and the fence to teach him to move them out of a corner. The commands to move the sheep are to the *dog's* left or right.

Commands are most effective if spoken in a low tone. Decide which commands you want to use and be consistent. Give lots of encouragement and give the dog time to build his confidence at each step.

Initially work only on the outrun and directions. Eventually your dog should drop anywhere in his circle, change direction, or change speed on command, come when called, and generally be a usable farm dog.

You will then be ready to teach the "walk on" or drive, which goes against the dog's instinct. Put your Sheltie back on lead. Teach him to move the sheep straight ahead, driving either toward or away from you. This will complete everything your dog needs to do an honest day's work. With experience he will be able to work at greater distances with less help from the trainer.

Herding Trials

At this time AKC does not award herding degrees or sanction herding trials. The North American Sheepdog Society is probably the most standardized organization holding trials in this country. There are also numerous local organizations, each of which has its own rules and awards. The Denver Stockdog Fanciers have devised three progressive degrees which give encouragement to beginners as well as experts. The first degree, Stockdog I, is awarded when the dog will dependably "down" on and off stock, making him safe to work off lead. The Stockdog II degree is based on directional control and herding interest, and the Stockdog III tests the dog for proficiency in either herding or driving, whichever is not natural to the dog. Local groups can be formed which emulate this procedure.

Although most competitive sheep trials are dominated by Border Collies, the few Shelties competing have performed admirably. Notable is *American and Canadian Champion Markrisdo's B.A. Pat'Chez,* a small tricolor who achieved top herding recognition four consecutive years, proving that conformation Shelties can indeed still be functional. Many other Shelties have achieved success, both as trial dogs and as actual working farm dogs.

Formal trials usually are conducted in a set "run" or pattern. Each part of the run counts a certain number of points, but a great deal of interpretation is allowed in the judging. The judge is the final authority and can stop a run he feels either does not meet his standards or endangers the stock.

The rules and definitions are:

Outrun—10 points. In starting each run the contestant and his dog shall take position at any point in the handler's circle—this same position to be the "fixed" position for all work during the "gather and drive." With the sheep in place, and upon signal from the course director, the run for each dog begins. On the outrun the dog may be directed to go either "right" or "left," and each dog shall carry along on this given line until beyond the sheep. Cross-over shall cause deduction of points according to the judge's decision. The dog shall go "wide" and "beyond" the sheep before circling in so as to come upon the sheep from the "far side" in preparation for the "lift."

Lift—5 points. The lift should be cautious, the dog well balanced on the flock, the sheep not unduly startled, held quietly and firmly, and moved off steadily with the dog in full control.

Fetch—10 points. The "fetch" should be on a near straight line from point of contact and lift to the handler; swerving, zig-zagging, or other deviation from the near-straight line to involve loss of points. The nature of the work, and the condition and handling of the sheep to be the foremost consideration. The fetch ends when the sheep enter the designated area.

Driving—15 points (7½ each). From the handler's position in the back half of the handler's circle the dog is required to drive the sheep away on a diagonal to the left, towards and through "gate No. 1;" thence horizontally across the field to and through "gate No. 2," each drive to be a near straight line. If either gate is not negotiated on first try, no re-try will be allowed. Failure to negotiate either gate will involve a loss of points or not, according to the decision of the judges under each circumstance. The drive ends when the sheep are through or past gate No. 2.

Penning—15 points. The "penning" begins immediately after the second drive through gate No. 2. The sheep are to be brought in a near straight line from the gate to the pen. The contestant shall open the gate of the pen, either to the right or to the left, so that it continues in a straight line to the side of the pen to which it is fastened, and this opening shall not be changed until the sheep are confined. When the gate is opened, the contestant shall grasp the end of a rope six feet long, tied to the open end of the gate, and shall confine his movements to the limit fixed by this rope. Each dog shall work its assigned sheep into the open pen unassisted in any way by the handler, other than directions given by spoken, whistled, or otherwise imparted command. *Any dog that fails to pen the assigned sheep shall not be rewarded more than two-thirds the total points for the work he has accomplished.*

(*Note:* failure to pen will actually cost the dog 30 points, so the handler may elect to skip an earlier section if time runs short.)

CAN YOUR DOG TRACK?

Since prehistoric times, man has depended on dogs for hunting, protection, sounding an alert in times of danger, and detecting the presence of an outsider before he becomes visible. All of these functions require use of the dog's unique ability to identify and follow a scent. Much has been written on the subject of tracking, but nothing as simple and complete as the recent book *Go Find!* by L. Wilson Davis.[3] Anyone interested in more information on tracking is referred to this source.

The ability to track and the natural inclination to do so are inherent in every dog to some degree. Mr. Davis stresses that following a track is accomplished by more than just a highly developed sense of smell. Since even strong camouflaging odors such as gasoline and skunk spray do not confuse an experienced dog, it is obvious that dogs have the unique ability to follow a track by relying on something other than smell as we know it.

Tracking is based on three assumptions:

1. That the dog can identify a track as being different from all others. This is presumed to be due to the presence of a chemical substance, "sebum," which is slightly different in each person.
2. That the dog can follow a track on the ground, realizing that some substances record a track better than others.

[3]L. Wilson Davis, *Go Find! Training Your Dog to Track.* New York: Howell Book House, Inc., 1974.

Handler encourages dog to pick of track. Ch. Sea Isle Clancey of Sagebrush C.D.X., Sagebrush Shelties.

The dog should pull into the harness as he finds the track.

Dogs sometimes rely on air scenting. (Syler photos)

The way in which the handler holds the lead is important.

3. That the dog can follow an airborne track. This can carry a dog through difficult terrain where the ground track may be faint or intermittent.

A dog often uses the air track to double check when following a ground track and vice versa. These tracks may be separated by quite a distance on a windy day and airborne tracks tend to "settle" on higher places, such as bushes, or in ditches.

From intricate tests given to trained dogs, it has been learned that a dog can follow tracks which were thought to be impossible. He can isolate a unique track and follow it through unbelievable distractions, interference, difficult terrain, and unfavorable weather conditions. In one of the trials, the tracklayer got into a car and resumed the track at a distant point. In another he changed to sterile shoes in the middle of the course, and in still another he swam underwater for quite a distance with a snorkle and emerged on the opposite bank of the river. Although we do not know how he does it, we must accept the dog's ability to follow even these tracks. One very hard test involved deep plowing a field after the track was laid, and dousing a field with gasoline and burning it before the dog followed the track. I have the utmost respect for dogs who can follow tracks through these conditions!

The handler reads his dog through tension on the lead.

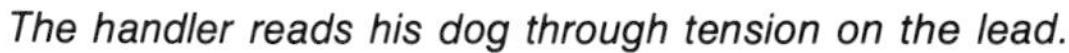

Finding the article at the end of the track.

The most common mistake discovered during these tests involved handler errors. When the handler tried to outguess the tracklayer, the dog usually became confused and lost the track. Handlers tend to underestimate their dog's potential and do more harm than good by interfering.

Practical Applications of Tracking

Most people who train a tracking dog do so with the idea of obtaining the "T" title awarded by AKC for successful completion of tracking requirements. This serves as a foundation for any form of advanced tracking activity.

Tracking is an invaluable aid in police and military work. Tracking dogs have been successfully used for locating lost persons, sniffing out illegal drugs and contraband items, locating mines and explosives, and retrieving missile parts.

Most challenging to the average person is participation in search and rescue work. This can be frustrating because dogs are often used as a last resort after a track is old and thoroughly trampled by searchers. But imagine the thrill of finding even one lost child who might not have survived another night in the elements. This is not a pipe dream, but a feasible reality for anyone willing to take the time for adequate training and participation.

Less dramatic but more frequently needed, are the services of a tracking dog in everyday life. He can recover a lost glove or set of keys which might leave you stranded away from home. There are a thousand small instances in which a Sheltie trained in tracking could be useful.

Equipment Used in Tracking

A tracking dog is worked on a harness, rather than a collar, because most dogs are trained not to pull against a collar. The harness allows maximum comfort and freedom, and encourages the dog to pull. In tracking a handler "reads" his dog's actions through the taut lead as the dog works.

The finished tracking dog works at the end of a long lead. Forty feet is the maximum length and many handlers prefer 20 feet. A lead approximately 30 feet long is adequate for any condition, although during early training the lead will be held much closer to the dog. The lead is usually made of nylon webbing or light cord. Handling a dog on a track is much like reining a fine horse, except that the dog is in control. In both cases the person maintains proper tension on the lead for communication with the animal. Development of light, flexible hands enhances this communication.

Stakes with flags attached for easy visibility are used to identify the training course for the handler. During trailing periods he learns to recognize whether or not the dog is actually on the track and how to interpret the responses of any particular dog. Stakes are placed at the start and completion of a track, plus one is used to mark each turn. During an actual test only the start is marked.

An article is dropped at the end of the track to signify completion. Most people use a glove or wallet since these are used in official tests, however any small item bearing the scent of the tracklayer will do.

Prerequisites for Tracking

A prospective tracking dog should be mature and controllable. The exercises required for a C.D. obedience degree are highly desirable as a foundation before training in tracking is begun. These exercises are needed for proper control and communication, and a dog trained in basic obedience has a much greater chance of succeeding as a tracking dog (refer to chapter 30). These same exercises enhance a herding dog or any other form of advanced training.

The Course

During initial training, the course will be fairly straight. It can be a field or an area as small as a large back yard. Fifty yards is adequate for beginning tracks, and these can be retraced several times during a training session. The track is intensified each time it is covered as long as the same path is used each time. As training progresses, the track is lengthened and turns are added. Commands are informal and determined by the individual handler. "Go find it" is often used, with phrases of encouragement interspersed throughout the exercise.

Requirements for the Tracking Degree

The first step in passing the tracking test is obtaining "certification" from a licensed tracking judge. This involves an informal test given to assure that the dog is qualified to compete in a test. It helps avoid unnecessary expense and time required to set up a test for dogs who are not ready. The certification test is usually somewhat easier than the actual tracking test, but this is determined by each individual judge.

After receiving certification your dog has six months in which to compete in a tracking test. Successful completion of one test is required to earn the "TD," Tracking Dog degree. If you do not qualify within the six month period your dog will need to be re-certified.

An advanced tracking degree "TDX," is also available, and Shelties are also eligible for Shutzhund FH titles—no protection work is required.

Complete rules and regulations for tracking competition are available from the AKC.

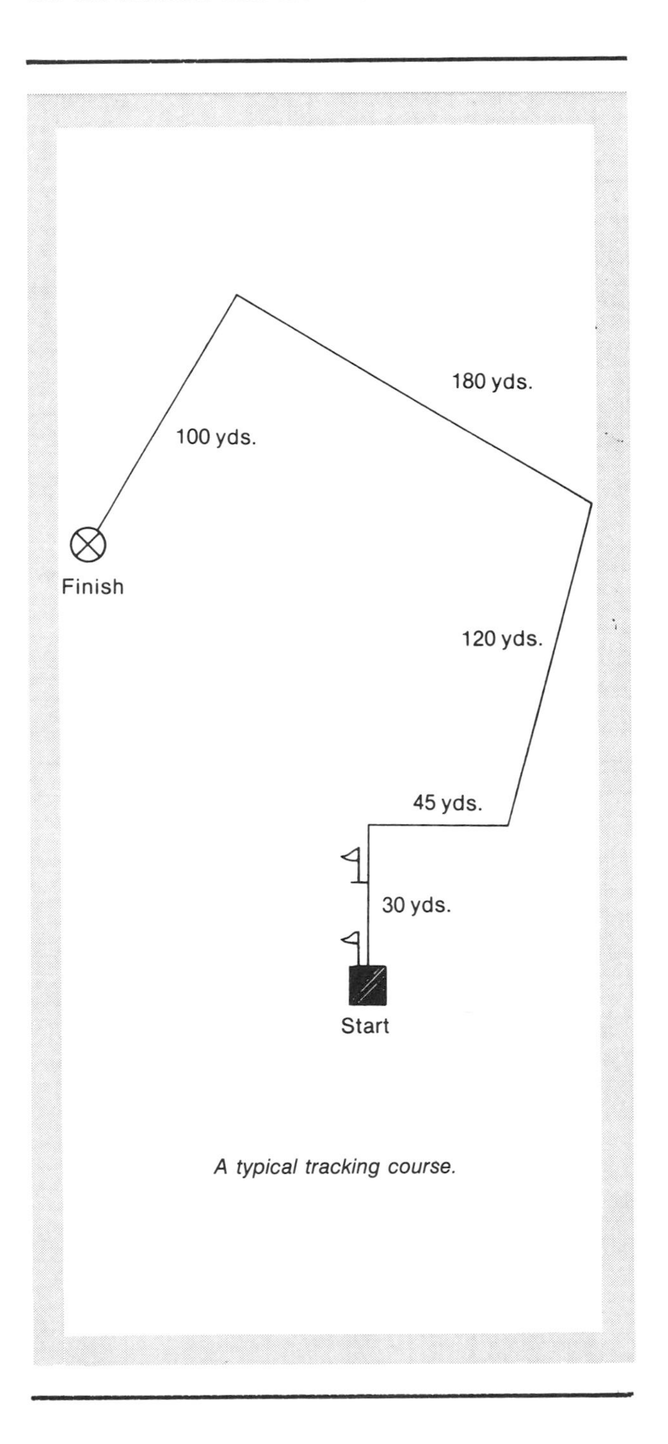

A typical tracking course.

WHAT AM I TO YOU?

M. Kummer

As a pup I dreamed and wondered
What life would hold in store:
For ME, I thought, there's something GREAT
Beyond that kennel door.

Out there are needy people
And I have much to give:
Love, and wit, and gentleness,
To help them learn to live.

I'd be someone's protector,
Keep little ones from harm,
Or guide an old man's weary steps,
Or help to run a farm.

I'd run and bark and jump and play
With friends along a sandy shore.
I'd roll in meadows thick and green
That lie beyond that kennel door.

I lay here waiting—longing,
As the days and years went by;
My owner kept me fed and brushed,
But inside, let me die.

I do not think of greatness now,
I'm old and filled with pain.
My owner has some ribbons,
But I have lived in vain.

I cannot think what could have been,
My dreams are filled with hope no more,
Just floor and walls and broken heart
For me behind this kennel door.

CCofA "Bulletin"
Feb. 1984

Appendices

BOOKS ABOUT SHETLAND SHEEPDOGS

The ASSA Handbooks

Published Biannually by American Shetland Sheepdog Association. Yearbook editor: Dorothy Christensen, Rt. 1, Box 177H, Lockport, IL 60441

Davis, Mary. *Shetland Sheepdogs.* London: Arthur Barker Ltd., 1973.

An interesting English book including information on care, breeding, and raising Shelties, with a good chapter on great English dogs of the past, many of whom are in the background of American Shelties.

Herbert, B. M. and J. M. *The Shetland Sheepdog.* London: W. and G. Foyle Ltd., 1961.

A small booklet containing some interesting facts about major modern kennels in Great Britain.

Moore, Catherine Coleman. *The Complete Shetland Sheepdog.* Middleburg, Virginia: Denlinger's, 1960.

An excellent book by one of America's first and foremost Sheltie breeders. Covers the background and early history of the breed as well as general information about Shelties. Now out of print.

Osborne, Margaret. *The Shetland Sheepdog.* New York: Arco Publishing Co., Inc., Revised 1962.

Written by a noted English breeder and judge, this book is a delight to read. Covers the early origin of Shelties, English lineage, English show Standard, and general information on breeding and showing.

Riddle, Maxwell. *The New Shetland Sheepdog.* New York: Howell Book House, Inc., 1974.

Shelties from a judge's viewpoint. Includes information on Shelties in Canada, the Shetland Islands, current winning and producing Shelties, and general background of the breed. Lavishly illustrated with many of the breed's greats.

Simmonds, Jean Daniels. *The Illustrated Shetland Sheepdog Standard.*

A must for every breeder or exhibitor of Shelties. Handsomely illustrated to explain and clarify the points of the Standard.

OTHER RECOMMENDED READING

Brucker, Jeff and Betty. *Preparation and Presentation of the Show Dog.* Atlanta: Brucker Enterprises, 1978.

Burnham, Patricia Gail. *Playtraining Your Dog.* New York: St. Martins Press, 1980.

Burns, Marca, and Fraser, Margaret N. *Genetics of the Dog.* London: Oliver and Boyd, 1966.

Campbell, William E. *Behavior Problems in Dogs.* Santa Barbara: American Veterinary Publications, 1975.

Carlson, Delbert G., D.V.M., and Griffin, James, M.D. *Dog Owners Home Veterinary Handbook.* New York: Howell Book House, 1981.

Collins, Donald, D.V.M. *The Collins Guide to Dog Nutrition.* New York: Howell Book House, Inc., 1972.

Elliott, Rachel Page. *The New Dogsteps.* New York: Howell Book House, 1983.

Holmes, John. *The Farmers Dog.* London: Popular Dogs Publishing Co. Ltd., 1970.

Holst, Phyllis A., D.V.M. *Canine Reproduction: A Breeder's Guide.* Loveland: Alpine Publications, 1985.

Hutt, Frederic B. *Genetics for Dog Breeders.* San Francisco: W. H. Freeman & Co., 1979.

Lyon, McDowell. *The Dog In Action.* New York: Howell Book House, 1971.

Onstott, Kyle. Revised by Phillip Onstott. *The New Art of Breeding Better Dogs.* New York: Howell Book House, Inc., 1970.

Pfaffenberger, Clarence J. *The New Knowledge of Dog Behavior.* New York: Howell Book House, 1970.

Rutherford, Clarice, and Neil, David H. MRCVS. *How To Raise A Puppy You Can Live With.* Loveland: Alpine Publications, 1981.

Sabella, Frank. *The Art of Handling Show Dogs.* Hollywood: B & E Publications, 1980.

Spira, Harold, *Canine Terminology.* New York: Howell Book House, 1982.

DOG MAGAZINES

Sheltie Pacesetter, P. O. Box 3230, Palos Verdes, CA 90274 (bi-monthly)

Sheltie International, P. O. Box 6369, Los Osos, CA 93412 (bi-monthly)

Dog World, 29 N. Wacker Dr., Chicago, IL 60606-3298 (monthly all-breed)

AKC Gazette, The Official Journal for the Sport of Purebred Dogs, 51 Madison Avenue, New York, NY 10010 (monthly)

Front & Finish: The Dog Trainers News, H & F Publications, R. R. 1, Box 57, Wataga, IL 61488

ORGANIZATIONS

Shelti-Data, pedigrees, statistics, pedigree books, career records, etc. Ann Hedge, 1880 E. Andromeda Pl., Tucson, AZ 85737-3412

Am. Shetland Sheepdog Assoc. Handbooks, annual records of winners and producers. Also *Sheltie Rescue,* Dorothy Christiansen, 13520 Bruce Rd., Lockport, IL 60441

The Shetland Sheepdog Library, Karen D. Hostetter, 4206 Dolphin Rd., Louisville, KY 40220

The American Kennel Club, registers all breeds. For information on breeds or breed clubs, club secretaries, educational videos, etc., write: American Kennel Club, 5580 Centerview Dr., Raleigh, NC 27606-3390

Regional Shetland Sheepdog Clubs. (Obtain address of current secretary from the ASSA). If you don't find a club listed for your area, write AKC or ASSA as new clubs are forming all the time.

Alamo Area SSC
Albuquerque SSC
Centennial SSC of Gr. Denver
Central Indiana SSC
Central New York SSC
Chicagoland SSC
Cleveland SSC
Colonial SSC
Dallas SSC
Des Moines SSC
El Paso SSC
Evergreen State SSC
Gr. Milwaukee SSC
Gr. St. Louis SSC
Harrisburg SSC
Interlocking SSC of Monee
Interstate SSC
Lochland SSC
Maumee Valley SSC
Miami Valley SSC
Mid-Arizona SSC
Mid-Florida SSC
Midlands SSC
Pacific Northwest SSC
Potomac Valley SSC
Santiago SSC
Scioto SSC
Shoreline SSC of Baytown
SSC of Tidewater
Western Massachusetts SSC
Western Michigan SSC
SSC of Austin
SSC of Georgia
SSC of Gr. Baltimore
SSC of Gr. Birmingham
SSC of Greater Detroit
SSC of Greater Miami
SSC of Gr. New Orleans
SSC of Gr. San Diego
SSC of Greater Tucson
SSC of Hawaii
SSC of Houston
SSC of Memphis
SSC of No. California
SSC of Northern New Jersey
SSC of So. California
Carolina SSC
Central California SSC
Central Illinois SSC
Central Oklahoma SSC
Downeast SSC of Gr. Portland
Eastern Iowa SSC
Gr. Spokane SSC
Gr. Jacksonville SSC
Tampa Bay Area SSC
Trinity Valley SSC
Gr. Kansas City SSC
Green Bay SSC
Kentuckiana SSC
Long Island SS Fanciers
Nashville SSC
No. Nevada SS Fanciers
Rock River Valley SSC
Tri-State SSC
West Texas SSC
Sacramento Valley SSC
SSC of Anchorage
SSC of So. Nevada

Talk Like a Breeder

AKC — American Kennel Club.
Almond eye — Almond shaped rims.
Angulation — The angles formed by the meeting of bones; shoulder and upper arm; stifle and hock.
Balance — Symmetry; each part being in proper perspective to the whole.
Best In Show (BIS) — The dog judged best of all animals competing in a given dog show.
Bitch — A female dog.
Bite — The manner in which the teeth meet when the mouth is closed.
Blaze — White markings running up the face of a Sheltie.
Blue merle — Marbled, a varigated grey and black pattern, frosted with definite black patches.
Board — To care for a dog owned by others for a fee.
Bone — Substance, the size of a dog's bone in proportion to his height.
Breed — A specific unique type of dog selected and maintained by man. In our case the Shetland Sheepdog. To mate two animals.
Breeder — A person who owns the dam of a litter. One who selectively breeds dogs.
Brood bitch — A breeding female dog.
Butterfly nose — A nose which remains partially pink. Faulty in an adult Sheltie, normal in young puppies.
Canines — Dogs and their wild cousins. The fang teeth.
Castrate — Surgical removal of the testicles of a male dog.
Cat-foot — A round, compact foot; faulty in a Sheltie.
Coloboma — A congenital abnormality of the eye resulting from failure of some portion of the fetal fissure to close. May affect several portions of the inner eye.
Companion Dog (C.D.) — The novice obedience degree awarded by AKC.
Companion Dog Excellent (C.D.X.) — The intermediate obedience degree awarded by AKC.
Champion (Ch.) — A prefix denoting that the dog has defeated a certain number of dogs at several shows to earn this title from AKC.
Character — Temperament, individuality, worthiness, and expression distinctive of the breed.
Cheeky — Bumpy or sharp areas over the cheekbones. Faulty.
Chest — The trunk part of the body including between the elbows and along the ribs.
China eye — A light blue eye with no merling.
Chiseled — A clean, precise head.
Choke collar — A training collar which tightens when one loop is pulled.
Coat — The dog's hair; the quantity, quality, or color of the coat.
Cobby — Short bodied, compact in build.
Collar — White markings around the neck.
Condition — The health, weight, and coat of a Sheltie. To accustom a dog to a particular stimulus and response.
Conformation — The structure and appearance of the dog. The quality as compared to the breed Standard.
Cow-hocked — The hocks turn inward viewed from the rear.
Crossbreed — A dog whose parents are purebred but different breeds.
Croup — The part of the topline from the loin to tail.
Cryptorchid — A male dog whose testicles have not descended to the normal position in the scrotum. Correctly used either as unilateral or bilateral chryptorchidism. Commonly used to mean both testicles withheld or missing (bilateral).
Dam — The mother dog.
Dewclaw — The extra toe on the inside of the leg; should be removed at least on rear legs on a Sheltie.
Distichiasis — The presence of two separate rows of lashes on one eyelid. The aberrent row usually grows inward and can cause eye irritation.
Disqualification — A fault specified by the breed Standard which prevents the dog from competing in the conformation ring.
Dog — A male dog, sometimes used for animals of both sexes.
Dog show — A competitive sport where dogs are judged on their comparative merits according to the breed Standard.
Domey — Rounded in topskull rather than flat. Faulty but often seen during developmental stages of puppies.
Double coat — The guard hairs, harsh and weather resistant; the under coat, soft and insulating.

Elbow — The joint between the forearm and the upper arm.

Elbowing out — Elbows swinging away from the body rather than flat along the ribs.

Expression — The look of the face dependent upon eyes, ears, head shape, and temperament.

Faking — Artificial alteration of the dog's natural appearance beyond accepted grooming measures.

Fancier — A person interested in a particular breed or aspect of dogs.

Feathering — The long hair on the legs, pants, and belly of a Sheltie; fringe.

Fiddle front — Crooked front legs.

Flying ears — Ears which tend to prick.

Foreface — The head from nose to stop including the muzzle and underjaw.

Front — The forelegs and shoulder assembly plus ribs.

Fundus — The back layers of the eye which can be seen with an ophthalmascope.

Gait — The way a Sheltie moves at a trot.

Gay tail — Tail carried forward over the back.

Groom — To brush, trim, bathe, or otherwise neaten a dog's appearance.

Guard hairs — The stiffer hairs comprising the outer coat.

Hackney — Lifting the front feet too high. Prancing (faulty in a Sheltie).

Handler — A person who handles a dog in the show or obedience ring or at herding or tracking trials. Sometimes refers to a professional handler.

Harefoot — A long, usually flat foot. Faulty.

Haw — The third eyelid which vertically crosses the eye on the inside corner.

Heat — The female's breeding season.

Heel — To stay close to the handler's left side.

Height — The measurement from ground to withers.

Hock — The joint between stifle and metatarsus. Incorrectly used to mean the metatarsal bones from hock to foot.

Inbreeding — The mating of two closely related dogs.

Kennel — A building, run, crate, or enclosure used to house dogs. An establishment involved in keeping or breeding dogs.

Knuckling over — The front legs bow forward at the pasterns; double jointed. Faulty.

Layback — The angle of the shoulder blade to vertical.

Lead — A leash or rope attached to the collar to restrain a dog.

Leather — The flexible part of the ear.

Level bite — Teeth meet evenly at their edges. Faulty in a Sheltie.

Linebreeding — The breeding of dogs within a general bloodline.

Litter — All the siblings from one whelping; may consist of one or more puppies.

Loin — The portion of the body from ribs to croup.

Mask — The darker shading above the eyes and on the skull on a sable.

Match — An informal practice show.

Monorchid — A unilateral chryptorchid.

Muzzle — The upper part of the foreface. Also a strap used to prevent a dog from biting bv being tied around the muzzle.

Outcrossing — The mating of unrelated individuals of the same breed.

Overshot — The top teeth protrude beyond the lower teeth.

Pace — A gait with both legs on the same side moving together.

Paddling — Moving with the front legs thrown outward.

Pads — The soles of the feet.

Pastern — The lower portion of the front legs. The wrist.

Pedigree — The written ancestry of a dog.

Pigeon-breast — A chest with the breastbone protruding.

Points — The tan markings on a tricolor or blue merle. Also points won toward a championship for various wins.

Premium list — The advance entry information for a show obtained from the superintendent or show secretary.

Prick ear — Ear carried erect with no forward break.

Professional handler — A person licensed by AKC to handle dogs for a fee.

Put down — To be left unplaced at a show. Also means to euthanize a dog.

Puppy — A dog under 12 months of age.

Pure-bred — A dog whose sire and dam were uncrossed specimens of the same breed.

Quality — Refinement, virtue as determined by the breed Standard.

Racy — Tall, rangey, light build.

Register — To record with AKC.

Roach back — A convex curvature of the back toward the loin.

Sable — The brown coat color from golden to mahogany.

Scissors bite — The top teeth overlap the bottom teeth and touch on the inside edges.

Self color — A blue or other color with no contrast. Usually the nose and eyerims blend with the coat.

Semi-erect ears — Ears carried erect with the tips breaking forward.

Sire — The father dog.

Soundness — Health and correctness of build. Especially correct gait.

Spay — To surgically remove reproductive organs from a bitch.

Spring of ribs — Curvature of the ribs over the chest area.

Stack — To position a dog's feet squarely in a show stance.

Stance — Manner of standing.

Standard — The written description of the ideal Sheltie against which all dogs are judged.

Standoff coat — A full coat which stands away from the body.

Stern — The tail.

Stifle — The knee; the bone from the stifle joint to the hock.

Stop — The break from muzzle to topskull between the eyes as viewed from the side.

Straight shoulders — Insufficiently laid back.
Stud book — The recording of producing dogs by AKC.
Stud dog — A male used for breeding.
Substance — Bone or heaviness of an animal.
Swayback — A weak or drooping back.
Tracking dog (T.D.) — A degree given to a dog who passes the AKC tracking test.
Throatiness — Excess skin under the throat.
Ticked — Freckled; usually dark spots on the legs or collar.
Tricolor — Black with tan and white markings.
Tuck-up — Concave line of the belly under the loin.
Type — The sum total of traits which make a Shetland Sheepdog unique as a breed.
Utility dog (U.D.) — The most advanced obedience degree awarded by AKC.
Undershot — The teeth on the lower jaw protrude beyond the top teeth. Faulty.
Upper arm — The humerus bone in the foreleg. The area from shoulder blade to forearm.
Weaving — A serpentine motion when gaiting.
Weedy — A dog lacking substance and bone.
Whelping — The birth of a litter.
Whelps — Newborn puppies.
Whisker — Long hair on the muzzle.
Winners — The dog or bitch which takes points towards its championship at a show.
Withers — The point of the shoulder blade on the top-line.
Wry mouth — Crooked or misaligned teeth.

Alena Gomez, one year, with a seven-week-old bitch puppy. (Photo courtesy Alane Gomez)

Index

A family of Rockwoods champions. Bottom left, Mom, Shylove Rockwood Show-Off C.D., dam of 5 champions, right, Dad, Ch. Rockwoods Bac Talk (by Peter Pumpkin). Center, left, Ch. Rockwoods Sylvan Seafarin Man; right, Ch. Alician's Rockwood Talk Bac. Top, Ch. Rockwoods Nite Enchantment C.D.; Ch. Rockwoods Repeat Performance, Rockwoods Senstive Prince. Breeder, Barbara Kenealy.

A DOG LOVER'S PRAYER

Lord, you knew that there would be times when man would need another kind of friend—one who would not criticize, nor blame, nor make demands, nor question. One who would only listen and love.

And so you gave us the dog. Not just one dog, but a dog to suit every temperament and personality.

Lord, we thank you for man's best friend. Help us to remember that he also belongs to you.

Therefore, while we are to enjoy him, we are not to mistreat him, nor alter his health and ability to function by breeding to suit our foolish whims. We are not to thwart his purpose by keeping him isolated where he cannot learn to function in our world.

Teach us, Lord, not to inflict pain and suffering to gain our selfish ends—sometimes as frivolous as a purple ribbon, and not to breed so many of his kind that homes cannot be found and he is left homeless and starving, or sentenced to death in a shelter.

Help us, Lord, to love our friend, the dog, in such a way that it reflects your love and compassion for mankind, whom you have called your friend.